Computer Concepts

SIXTH EDITION – ILLUSTRATED

INTRODUCTORY

Computer Concepts

SIXTH EDITION – ILLUSTRATED

INTRODUCTORY

June Jamrich Parsons / Dan Oja

THOMSON
COURSE TECHNOLOGY

Australia • Canada • Mexico • Singapore • Spain • United Kingdom • United States

Computer Concepts—Illustrated Introductory, Sixth Edition
Parsons/Oja

Executive Editor:
Rachel Goldberg

Senior Acquisitions Editor:
Marjorie Hunt

Senior Product Manager:
Christina Kling Garrett

Associate Product Manager:
Shana Rosenthal

Editorial Assistant:
Janine Tangney

Senior Marketing Manager:
Joy Stark

Marketing Coordinator:
Melissa Marcoux

Adapting Author:
Rachel Biheller Bunin

Developmental Editor:
Pamela Conrad

Production Editor:
Cecile Kaufman

Copy Editor:
Gary Spahl

Media Developers:
Donna Mulder, Fatima Lockhart,
Keefe Crowley, Tensi Parsons

CD Development:
MediaTechnics Corporation

Interior Designer:
Stephanie Fall

Cover Designer:
Steve Deschene

Photo Researcher:
Christina Micek

Composition:
GEX Publishing Services

Photographers:
Greg Manis, Joe Bush, David S. Bunin,
Emily C. Bunin, Rachel B. Bunin

Illustrator:
Eric Murphy

About This Book

Teaching and writing about computer concepts can be extremely challenging. How do we engage students of all levels and keep their interest? How do we teach them concepts to help them succeed in their jobs and to help them be knowledgeable consumers of technology? As we set out to create this Sixth Edition of Computer Concepts—Illustrated Introductory, our goals were to develop a computer concepts text book that:

- Speaks to the needs of both the beginning student, as well as the student who has some experience with computers

- Engages students of all levels by presenting concepts in a clear and attractive new design, using large graphics and friendly, easy-to-understand language

- Excites students by engaging them in a wide variety of learning and reinforcement activities on our revamped Online Companion Web site, which features interactive labs, online games, video clips, Podcasts of the Issue articles from the book, and much more

- Provides varied, flexible, and meaningful exercises and projects to help students understand complex concepts quickly and easily

If you've used previous editions of this book, you'll notice this edition has a new design. As in previous editions, each concept is presented on a two-page spread so that students can learn all they need to know about a topic without turning the page. However, the new design integrates the pictures more closely with the text so that text and pictures appear together on both the left and right pages. This tight integration of text and pictures makes it even easier for students to understand and process the presented concepts.

As we set out to create this Sixth Edition, we spoke with many instructors who have used previous editions of the book to understand their needs. We thank the following instructors for generously sharing their valuable insights:

Ann Bonner, Community College of Baltimore
Elma Cantu, St. Edwards University, New College
Michael Hanna, Colorado State University
Ted Janicki, Mount Olive College
Amie Mayhall, Olney Central College
Dr. Carlos Segami, Barry University
Gary Sparks, Metro Community College
Teresa Tegeler, Olney Central College

Preface

Welcome to *Computer Concepts — Illustrated Introductory, Sixth Edition*! If you are new to computers, this book and its accompanying Interactive CD and Online Companion Web site will provide a friendly, visual, and dynamic introduction to computer concepts and will help you become a knowledgeable user and consumer of technology. If you are already a computer user and have some familiarity with computer concepts, this book will help you expand your knowledge by becoming more proficient at using computers and understanding the technology behind computers.

Designed for All Users

The modular approach and the unique page layout of this book make it an appropriate learning tool for both the novice and the experienced user. Each lesson focuses on a relevant concept and is presented on two facing pages so that you don't have to turn the page to find an illustration or finish a paragraph. Also, because the text is organized in a modular fashion, you can choose to read all the lesson material or only those paragraphs where you need to "fill in the gaps."

Up-to-Date Information

Technology moves quickly, and we have made sure to include the most current information on computer topics in this book. You will learn about the latest issues in security and how to keep your computer protected from current threats. You will learn about Podcasting, blogging, and RSS feeds. You will learn about the different options available for connecting to the Internet, how to use a basic e-mail system, and how to protect your computer from unwanted spam. You will also learn about the latest trends in storage devices including USB drives and storage media such as HD-DVDs and Blu-ray DVDs. The book will keep you up-to-date on Internet technology including information on the latest Internet browsers such as FireFox.

A single concept is presented in a two-page "information display" to help you absorb information quickly and easily

Easy-to-follow introductions to every lesson focus on a single concept to help you get the information quickly

Defining Internet basics

If you are looking for information, if you want to communicate with someone, or if you want to buy something, the Internet offers abundant resources. The Internet has changed society. E-mail and instant messaging have caused a major shift in the way people communicate. Online stores have changed our shopping habits. The ability to easily download music and video has changed the entertainment industry and stirred up controversy about intellectual property.

■ The **Internet backbone** defines the main routes of the Internet. See **Figure A-15**. The Internet backbone is constructed and maintained by major telecommunications companies. These telecommunications links can move huge amounts of data at incredible speeds.

Figure A-15: The Internet backbone

Personal computers are connected to regional and local communications links, which in turn connect to the Internet backbone; data transport works seamlessly between any two platforms—between PCs and Macs, and even between personal computers and mainframes.

■ Communication among all of the different devices on the Internet is made possible by **TCP/IP (Transmission Control Protocol/ Internet Protocol)**, which is a standard set of rules for electronically addressing and transmitting data.

■ Most of the information that is accessible on the Internet is stored on servers. These servers use special **server software** to locate and distribute data requested by Internet users.

■ Every device that's connected to the Internet is assigned a unique number, called an **IP address** that pinpoints its location on the Internet. To prepare data for transport, a computer divides the data into small chunks called **packets**. Each packet is labeled with the IP address of its destination and then transmitted. When a packet reaches an intersection in the Internet's communications links, a device called a **router** examines the packet's address. The router

checks the address in a routing table and then sends the packet along the appropriate link towards its destination. As packets arrive at their destinations, they are reassembled into the original file.

■ A **Web site** can provide information, collect information through forms, or provide access to other resources, such as search engines and e-mail.

■ The Internet revolutionized business by directly linking consumers with retailers, manufacturers, and distributors through electronic commerce, or **e-commerce**.

■ Electronic mail, known as **e-mail**, allows one person to send an electronic message to another person or to a group of people. A variation of e-mail uses a **mailing list server** to send messages to everyone on a **listserv**. A listserv is a public list of people who are interested in a particular topic. Messages sent to the mailing list server are automatically distributed to everyone on the mailing list.

■ **Usenet** is a worldwide bulletin board system that contains thousands of discussion forums on every imaginable topic called **newsgroups**. Newsgroup members post messages based on their interests to the bulletin board; these messages can be read and responded to by other group members.

■ The Internet allows real-time communication. For example, a **chat group** consists of several people who connect to the Internet and communicate in real time by typing comments to each other. A private version of a chat room, called **instant messaging (IM)**, allows people to send messages, images, and hyperlinks back and forth instantly. **Internet telephony** allows voice conversations to travel over the Internet. Internet telephony requires special software at both ends of the conversation and, instead of a telephone, it uses a headset connected to a computer.

■ Internet servers store a variety of files including documents, music, software, videos, animations, and photos. The process of transferring one of these files from a remote computer, such as a server, to a local computer, such as your personal computer, is called **downloading**. Sending a file from a local computer to a remote computer is called **uploading**. See **Figure A-16**.

14　　*Computer Concepts*

Modular text allows you to jump to sections to cover exactly what you need to learn

Large photos, screenshots, and drawings are integrated into the text to better illustrate the lesson concepts

FYIs provide pertinent user information or additional background information on the lesson concept

Colored icons indicate that technology element is featured for that lesson

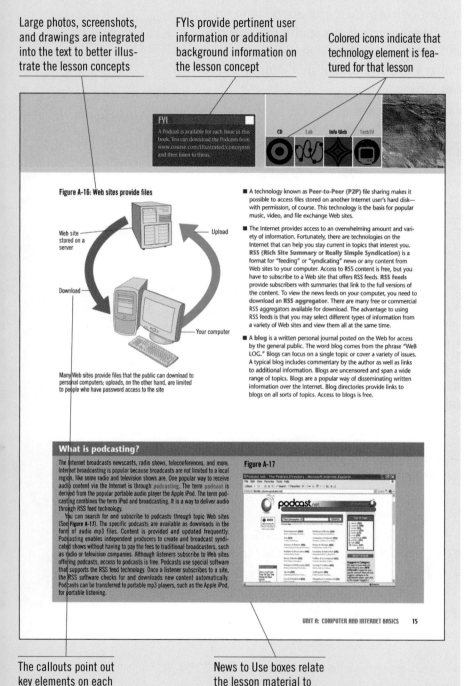

FYI

A Podcast is available for each Issue in this book. You can download the Podcasts from www.course.com/illustrated/concepts6 and then listen to them.

CD   Lab   Info Web   TechTV

Figure A-16: Web sites provide files

Web site stored on a server

Upload

Download

Your computer

Many Web sites provide files that the public can download to personal computers; uploads, on the other hand, are limited to people who have password access to the site

■ A technology known as **Peer-to-Peer (P2P)** file sharing makes it possible to access files stored on another Internet user's hard disk—with permission, of course. This technology is the basis for popular music, video, and file exchange Web sites.

■ The Internet provides access to an overwhelming amount and variety of information. Fortunately, there are technologies on the Internet that can help you stay current in topics that interest you. **RSS (Rich Site Summary** or **Really Simple Syndication)** is a format for "feeding" or "syndicating" news or any content from Web sites to your computer. Access to RSS content is free, but you have to subscribe to a Web site that offers RSS feeds. **RSS feeds** provide subscribers with summaries that link to the full versions of the content. To view the news feeds on your computer, you need to download an **RSS aggregator**. There are many free or commercial RSS aggregators available for download. The advantage to using RSS feeds is that you may select different types of information from a variety of Web sites and view them all at the same time.

■ A **blog** is a written personal journal posted on the Web for access by the general public. The word blog comes from the phrase "WeB LOG." Blogs can focus on a single topic or cover a variety of issues. A typical blog includes commentary by the author as well as links to additional information. Blogs are uncensored and span a wide range of topics. Blogs are a popular way of disseminating written information over the Internet. Blog directories provide links to blogs on all sorts of topics. Access to blogs is free.

What is podcasting?

The Internet broadcasts newscasts, radio shows, teleconferences, and more. Internet broadcasting is popular because broadcasts are not limited to a local region, like some radio and television shows are. One popular way to receive audio content via the Internet is through podcasting. The term podcast is derived from the popular portable audio player the Apple iPod. The term podcasting combines the term iPod and broadcasting. It is a way to deliver audio through RSS feed technology.

You can search for and subscribe to podcasts through topic Web sites (See **Figure A-17**). The specific podcasts are available as downloads in the form of audio mp3 files. Content is provided and updated frequently. Podcasting enables independent producers to create and broadcast syndicated shows without having to pay the fees to traditional broadcasters, such as radio or television companies. Although listeners subscribe to Web sites offering podcasts, access to podcasts is free. Podcasts use special software that supports the RSS feed technology. Once a listener subscribes to a site, the RSS software checks for and downloads new content automatically. Podcasts can be transferred to portable mp3 players, such as the Apple iPod, for portable listening.

Figure A-17

UNIT A: COMPUTER AND INTERNET BASICS   15

The callouts point out key elements on each illustration

News to Use boxes relate the lesson material to real-world situations to provide additional practical information

Relevant Topics

Learning about computer concepts can be overwhelming with so much information available. In writing this book, we have made sure to provide the most relevant topics that affect you in your everyday life. Each two-page lesson provides the most essential information that you need to know about that topic; it does not overwhelm you with technical details. Also, the Issue and Computers in Context features at the end of every unit focus in on topics that are important to our society. In these features you will read about the issues surrounding topics such as e-mail privacy, software piracy, recycling computers, online voting, and more.

Online Companion Web Site

Not all of us learn best by reading text. That's why we have created a dynamic Online Companion Web site that features a wide variety of activities and resources to help you learn and reinforce the concepts in the book. The Online Companion contains interactive **Student Edition Labs** that provide a dynamic way to learn concepts such as file management, e-mail, and virus protection. You can also play three different **online games** to test your knowledge of topics covered in the book to help you ace the test. If you are tired of reading, you can watch **TechTV video clips** on hot topics like protecting yourself from Internet identify spoofing and phishing, or you can download **Podcasts** of all the Issues featured in the book. The Online Companion provides links to the **InfoWebLinks** that provide up-to-date articles on topics covered in the book.

Interactive CD

One more way to step beyond just reading the text, is with the reengineered Interactive CD. Bring many of the figures in the book to life with a **ScreenTour** or **video** clip. **InfoWebLinks** will take you to articles on topics like ad blockers or web censorship. **Interactive end-of-unit exercises** include Fill in the Best Answer and Practice Tests. Use the **New Perspectives Labs** and lab assignments for hands-on practice and prove you've mastered a concept.

About the Technology

Online Companion

The Online Companion for *Computer Concepts, Sixth Edition* has been enhanced with a bold new design, tracking capabilities through CoursePort, Podcasts, and up-to-date games, labs, and TechTV video clips. Icons in the book direct you to the Online Companion for TechTV clips and InfoWebLinks.

We have reorganized the content into the following categories:

Boost Your Knowledge

- **Student Edition Labs**—allows you to master hundreds of computer concepts through observation, step-by-step practice, and review questions. Answers to review questions are now tracked through the Universal Gradebook in CoursePort.

- **TechTV Video Clips**—stay on top of emerging technologies and technology-related issues with this library of video clips.

- **InfoWebLinks**—the computer industry changes rapidly. Get up-to-date information by exploring the concept on the InfoWebLink site.

- **Buyer's Guide**—in the market for a new computer system? This Buyer's Guide will help you organize your purchasing decisions to get the best deal on a computer that meets your needs.

- *New* **Podcasts of Issue articles**—for each Issue article in the book, we have included an MP3 file that can be downloaded and listened to on your iPod, MP3 Player, computer, or other listening device.

Test Your Knowledge

- Online Games—our three online games, "Don't Tell Me," "Fake Out," and "Lightning," give you a fun, interactive way to strengthen your knowledge of concepts in each lesson. All three games offer remediation back to the book to help you study for tests. Your scores can be tracked through CoursePort.

Visit www.course.com/illustrated/concepts6 to check out all these great features!

About the Technology

Interactive CD

Colored icons next to a lesson objective and in the banner on the right page of the lesson tell you when to use the Interactive CD.

CD Videos and ScreenTours

Videos and ScreenTours enhance learning and retention of key concepts. A CD icon indicates you can view an interactive concept on the CD.

InfoWebLinks

InfoWebLinks connect you to Web links, film, video, TV, print, and electronic resources, keeping the book and URL's up-to-date. An InfoWeb icon indicates you can link to further information on the lesson topic by accessing the InfoWeb site, using your browser and an Internet connection.

Interactive Exercises

A CD icon indicates that you can complete activities on the Interactive CD. Interactive exercises include the Issues, Fill in the Best Answers, Practice Tests, and Labs.

New Perspectives Labs

Concepts come to life with the New Perspectives Labs—highly interactive tutorials that combine illustrations, animations, digital images, and simulations. Labs guide you step-by-step through a topic, and present you with QuickCheck questions to test your comprehension. You can track your QuickCheck results using a Tracking Disk. (See the Before You Begin section for more information.) Lab assignments are included at the end of each relevant unit. A Lab icon indicates a Lab is featured for the lesson concept. The following Labs are available with the Interactive CD:

Unit A
Making a Dial-Up Connection
Browsing and Searching
Using E-Mail

Unit B
Operating a Personal Computer

Unit C
Using the Windows Interface
Installing and Uninstalling Software

Unit D
Working with Binary Numbers
Benchmarking
Working with Windows Explorer

Unit E
Tracking Packets
Securing Your Connection

Unit F
Backing Up Your Computer

Unit G
Working with Cookies

Unit H
Working with Bitmap Graphics
Video Editing

About the Technology

Interactive CD

Studies show that the more you interact with the concepts, the faster you'll learn them. The CD that accompanies your book is designed to be an ineractive learning environment.

Will the Interactive CD work on my computer? The Interactive CD works on most computers that run Windows. Just follow the steps below to start the CD. If you have trouble, check with your instructor or technical support person. Technical support is available at **www.mediatechnics.net/np5cd/support.htm**.

How do I start the CD? Follow these simple steps to get started:

1. Make sure your computer is turned on.
2. Insert the CD in the CD drive.
3. Wait a few seconds until the Interactive CD has loaded. The main Computer Concepts screen appears, along with the Tracking Options dialog box.
4. The Interactive CD allows you to save your scores for practice tests, labs, and other activities. If you are sending scores to your instructor, Click the OK button. The Tracking Option dialog box closes and the Interactive CD is ready for using.
5. To disable tracking, make sure the box *Save tracking data* is empty. If the box contains a check mark, click the box to empty it.

Manual Start:

   a. Click the Start button on the Windows taskbar.

   b. When the Start menu appears, click Run.

   c. Type d:\start.exe in the Open text box of the Run dialog box, then click OK. If your CD-ROM drive is not "d" you should substitute the correct drive letter, for example, q:\start.exe.

How do I navigate through the CD? The Interactive CD menu and toolbar, near the top of the screen, contain tools you can use for navigation. The Next and Back buttons turn one page at a time.

What are the other menu and navigation options? The menu bar includes a Web links menu with options that open your browser and connect to InfoWebLinks, the Online Companion, and the Course Technology Web site. The menu bar also includes a Help menu where you can access instructions and troubleshooting FAQ's. The Glossary button provides access to definitions for key terms. The Annotation button appears when your instructor has posted comments or lecture notes. If your instructor has not posted annotations, the button will not appear.

How do I exit the Interactive CD? When you have completed a session and want to close the Interactive CD, you can click the button in the upper-right corner of the title bar, or you can click Edit on the menu bar, then click Exit. Figure 1 helps you locate the Close button and navigation tools.

Figure 1: Key features of the Interactive menu and toolbar

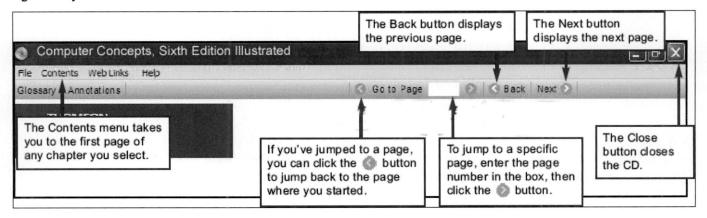

Instructor Resources

The Instructor Resources CD is Course Technology's way of putting the resources and information needed to teach and learn effectively into your instructor's hands. With an integrated array of teaching and learning tools that offer a broad range of technology-based instructional options, we believe this CD represents the highest quality and most cutting edge resources available to instructors today. Many of these resources are available at **www.course.com**.

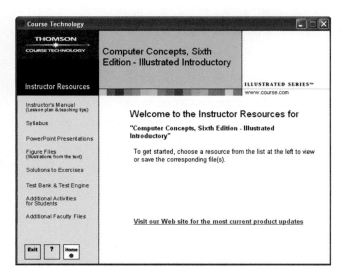

- Instructor's Manual—Available as an electronic file, the Instructor's Manual is quality-assurance tested and includes a lecture note for every lesson, Teaching Tips, Quick Quizzes, and Classroom Activities.

- Syllabus—Instructors can prepare and customize their course easily using this sample outline.

- PowerPoint Presentations—Each unit has a corresponding PowerPoint presentation that can be used in lecture, distributed to students, or customized.

- Figure Files—Includes every image from the book that can be used to create transparencies or a PowerPoint presentation.

- Solutions to Exercises—Solutions to Exercises contains examples of the work in the End-of-Unit material and Extra Independent Challenges.

- Test Bank & Test Engine—ExamView is a powerful testing software package that allows instructors to create and administer printed, computer (LAN-based), and Internet exams. ExamView includes hundreds of questions that correspond to the topics covered in this text, enabling students to generate detailed study guides that include page references for further review. The computer-based and Internet testing components allow students to take exams at their computers, and also saves you time by grading each exam automatically.

- Additional Activities for Students—Materials provided here are Extra Independent Challenge exercises, a first-time buyer's guide, a guide to the Interactive CD, and our Classic Labs.

- Additional Faculty Files—In this section, instructors will find a WebTrack Guide on using a WebTrack account, and other helpful documents.

Bring concepts and lessons to life with interactive **Student Edition Labs** and **SAM Computer Concepts**. For more information on Student Edition Labs visit **www.course.com/illustrated/concepts6**. And, for SAM Computer Concepts information visit **http://samcentral.course.com**.

Online Offerings We offer a full range of content for use with MyCourse 2.1, BlackBoard and WebCT to simplify the use of Computer Concepts in distance education settings, or to supplement your traditional class. For more information, visit **www.course.com**.

Author Acknowledgements

My thanks to Dan Oja and June Parsons for entrusting me and the Illustrated team to once again adapt the New Perspectives Computer Concepts book into the Illustrated format. Special thanks to Nicole Pinard for having the vision to let me create the first Illustrated Concepts book and then continue with the project through all the editions. Thanks to Marjorie Hunt, the Senior Acquisitions Editor, for her support and vision for this new design. I am eternally grateful to Pam Conrad, the Development Editor. Working with Pam is always a wonderful experience. Pam is an invaluable asset to the team, always seeing the big picture while managing to keep focus on all the important details. As a personal friend and colleague she contributes strength, vision, and intelligence to the project. I thank her for her partnership.

Christina Kling Garrett was a wonderful Project Manager, keeping all the components on track and providing good humor and guidance throughout. Thanks to Cecile Kaufman, the production editor, for working with the development team and the compositor on this bold new design, and seeing the pages come together all under a very tight schedule. Thanks to Gary Spahl, the copyedit pass was phenomenal; I appreciate all his contributions to perfect the manuscript. Thanks to GEX for all their hard work and creativity with the new design. A special thanks to Jennifer, Emily, Michael, and David.

On behalf of the entire Illustrated team, we hope you find this book a valuable resource for your students.
—Rachel Biheller Bunin, Adapting Author

We offer heartfelt thanks to all of the members of the Illustrated team for contributing their vision, talent, and skills to make this book a reality. Special thanks to Rachel Biheller Bunin for her fast and efficient work as the adapting author; Pamela Conrad for her insights as the developmental editor; Cecile Kaufman for her solid work as the production editor; and Christina Kling Garrett for tracking all the bits and pieces of this project. Whether you are a student or instructor, we thank you for using our book and hope that you find it to be a valuable guide to computers and software.
—June Parsons, Dan Oja, and MediaTechnics for the New Perspectives Series

CREDITS

Unit A:

Figure A-1: Courtesy of Acer Inc.; Courtesy of Microsoft Corporation; Courtesy of Apple Computer, Inc.

Figure A-5: Courtesy of Fujitsu Ltd. and Microsoft Corporation

Figure A-6: Courtesy of hp and PalmOne

Figure A-7: Courtesy of the IBM Corporation

Figure A-8: Courtesy of Microsoft Corporation

Figure A-9: a. Courtesy of Alienware
b. Courtesy of Apple Computer, Inc.
c. Courtesy of Media Technics
d. Courtesy of Sony Electronics, Inc.
e. Courtesy of Acer, Inc. and Microsoft Corporation
f. Courtesy of Apple Computer, Inc., Apple IMAC 17"

Figure A-10: a. Courtesy of Sony Electronics, Inc.
b. Courtesy of Intel Corporation

Figure A-17: Podcast Networks/Podcast.net

Figure A-19: Courtesy of Linksys

Figure A-24: www.Loc.gov

Figure A-30: Courtesy of Napster

Unit B:

Figure B-1: b. Courtesy of TDK Corporation
e. Courtesy of SanDisk Corporation

Figure B-2: Courtesy of Intel Corporation and Sematech, Inc.

Figure B-4: Courtesy of IBM Research

Figure B-5: Courtesy of Intel Corporation

Figure B-11: a. Courtesy of Sony Electronics, Inc.
b. Courtesy of Kingston Technology
c. Courtesy of SanDisk Corporation
d. Courtesy of SanDisk Corporation
e. Courtesy of Kingston Technology

Figure B-12: Courtesy of Intel

Figure B-13: a. Courtesy of Logitech, Inc.
b. Courtesy of Microsoft Corporation
c. Courtesy of Research In Motion
e. Courtesy of Think Outside, Inc. and Palm, Inc.

Figure B-15: a. Courtesy of IBM Corporation
c. Courtesy of Kensington Technology Group
d. Courtesy of XGAMING, INC.

Figure B-16: Courtesy of ATI Technologies, Inc.

Figure B-17: a. Courtesy of Sony Electronics, Inc.
b. Courtesy of Sony Electronics, Inc.
c. Courtesy of ViewSonic® Corporation

Figure B-19: Courtesy of Canon Inc.

Figure B-23: Courtesy of D-Link Corporation

Figure B-24: Courtesy of Dell, Inc.

Figure B-25: b. Courtesy of Epson America, Inc.
d. Courtesy of Olympus
e. Courtesy of Wacom Technology Corp.

Figure B-30: Computer History Museum

Figure B-31: Courtesy of Business Wire and Lages & Assoc.

Figure B-32: © Gabe Palmer/CORBIS

Figure B-33: Courtesy of inPhase Technologies

Unit C:

Figure C-16: Emily C. Bunin

Figure C-23: Courtesy of Microsoft Corporation

Figure C-27: Ashley Gilbertson/AURORA

Figure C-28: a. Courtesy of PalmOne, Inc.
b. Courtesy of Microsoft Corporation
c. Courtesy of Symbian
d. Courtesy of Microsoft Corporation

Unit D:

Figure D-5: PGA Courtesy of Intel Corporation

Unit E:

Figure E-2: Courtesy of Bob Metcalfe

Figure E-7: Courtesy of D-Link Systems

Figure E-8: Courtesy of Linksys

Figure E-9: Courtesy of Linksys

Figure E-16: a. Courtesy of Nokia
c. Courtesy of NETGEAR, Inc.

Figure E-17: Courtesy of Dell, Inc.

Figure E-27: Courtesy of Hewlett Packard.

Figure E-30: Photography courtesy of the University of Illinois at Urbana-Champaign Archives

Figure E-31: John Henley/CORBIS

Unit F:

Figure F-1: JAMES PATRICK COOPER/BLOOMBERG

Figure F-2: AP/Wide World Photos

Figure F-4: a. Courtesy of Iridian Technologies, Inc.
c. Courtesy of Gem Plus

Figure F-5: © F-Secure Corporation

Figure F-22: A. Ramey/PhotoEdit

Figure F-23: Peter Macdiarmid/Reuters/Corbis

Brief Contents

Contents

● = CD ෴ = Lab ◆ = Info Web ■ = TechTV

Defining computers

Whether you realize it or not, you already know a lot about computers. You've picked up information from advertisements and magazine articles, from books and movies, from conversations and correspondence, and perhaps even from using your own computer and trying to figure it out. This lesson provides an overview designed to help you start organizing what you know about computers, provide you with a basic understanding of how computers work, and help you become familiar with basic computer vocabulary.

- The word "computer" has been part of the English language since 1646, but if you look in a dictionary printed before 1940, you might be surprised to find "computer" defined as a person who performs calculations! Prior to 1940, machines that were designed to perform calculations were referred to as calculators and tabulators, not computers. The modern definition and use of the term "computer" emerged in the 1940s, when the first electronic computing devices were developed.

- Most people can formulate a mental picture of a computer, but computers do so many things and come in such a variety of shapes and sizes that it might seem difficult to distill their common characteristics into an all-purpose definition. At its core, a **computer** is a device that accepts input, processes data, stores data, and produces output, all according to a series of stored instructions.

- A **computer system** includes hardware, peripheral devices, and software. **Figure A-1** shows two examples of a basic computer system. **Hardware** includes the devices that process data. The term "hardware" refers to the computer as well as components called peripheral devices. **Peripheral devices** expand the computer's input, output, and storage capabilities.

- An **input device**, such as a keyboard or mouse, gathers input and transforms it into a series of electronic signals for the computer. An **output device** (such as a monitor, printer, or speakers) displays, prints, or transmits the results of processing from the computer memory.

- A computer requires instructions called **software**, which is a **computer program** that tells the computer how to perform particular tasks. You may have read or heard about the terms Windows software or Macintosh software. You will learn more about the different types of software in a later unit.

- A **computer network** consists of two or more computers and other devices that are connected for the purpose of sharing data and programs. For example, a **LAN (local area network)** is simply a computer network that is located within a limited geographical area, such as a school computer lab or a small business.

- The **Internet** is the largest network in the world. It is a collection of local, regional, national, and international computer networks that are linked together to exchange data and distribute processing tasks.

What's a peripheral device?

Today, the term "peripheral device" designates equipment that might be added to a computer system to enhance its functionality. A printer is a popular peripheral device, as is a digital camera, USB drive, scanner, joystick, or graphics tablet. Though a hard disk drive seems to be an integral part of a computer—after all, it's built right into the system unit—by the strictest technical definition, a hard disk drive is classified as a peripheral device. The same goes for other storage devices and the keyboard, monitor, sound card, speakers, and modem.

Computer and Internet Basics

Define computers

Explore computer functions

◆ Categorize computers

Examine personal computer systems

Explore data, information, and files

◆ Introduce application and system software

◎◆ Define Internet basics

◎〰 Connect to the Internet

◎◆ Understand World Wide Web basics

◎〰◆ Use Web browsers

◎〰◆◆ Understand e-mail basics

◆ **Tech Talk:** The Boot Process

◆ **Computers in Context:** Marketing

◎◆ **Issue:** E-mail Privacy—Who Is Reading Your E-mail?

Overview

Computer literacy is determined by a person's ability to use computer terms properly and computer programs proficiently. Unit A provides an overview of computer and Internet technologies that a person needs to be computer literate. The unit begins by defining the basic characteristics of a computer system and then provides a quick overview of data, information, and files. You will be introduced to application software, operating systems, and platform compatibility. You will get a basic overview of the Internet, the Web, and e-mail. The Tech Talk discusses the boot process, the sequence of events that happens when you turn on your computer. You will also have an opportunity to look at computers in the context of marketing. The Issue looks at the topic of e-mail privacy.

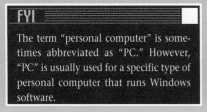
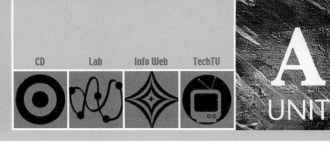
Figure A-1: Basic computer systems

Exploring computer functions

To really understand computers, you need to understand the functions they perform. The components of a computer system work together to accomplish the basic computer functions—accept input, process data, store data, and produce output.

■ Accept input. A computer accepts input. Computer **input** is whatever is put into a computer system. Input can be supplied by a person, by the environment, or by another computer. Examples of the kinds of input that a computer can accept include the words and symbols in a document, numbers for a calculation, pictures, temperatures from a thermostat, music or voice audio signals from a microphone, and instructions from a computer program.

■ Process data. A computer processes data. In the context of computing, **data** refers to the symbols that represent facts, objects, and ideas. Computers manipulate data in many ways, and this manipulation is called **processing**. Some of the ways that a computer can process data include performing calculations, sorting lists of words or numbers, modifying documents and pictures, drawing graphs, and keeping track of your score in a video or computer game. The instructions that tell a computer how to carry out the processing tasks are referred to as a computer program, or simply a "program." These programs are the software. In a computer, most processing takes place in a **processor** (also known as a microprocessor) called the **central processing unit (CPU)**, which is sometimes described as the "brain" of the computer.

■ Store data. A computer stores data so that it will be available for processing. Most computers have more than one location for storing data, depending on how the data is being used. **Memory** is an area of a computer that temporarily holds data waiting to be processed, stored, or output. **Storage** is the area of a computer that holds data on a permanent basis when it is not immediately needed for processing. For example, while you are working on it, a document is in memory; it is not in storage until you save it for the first time. After you save the document, it is still in memory until you close the document, exit the program, or turn off the computer. Documents in memory are lost when you turn off the power. Stored documents are not lost when the power is turned off.

■ Produce output. **Output** consists of the processing results produced by a computer. Some examples of computer output include reports, documents, music, graphs, and pictures. An output device displays, prints, or transmits the results of processing.

■ **Figure A-2** helps you visualize the input, processing, storage, and output activities of a computer.

Understanding the importance of stored programs

Early computers were really nothing more than calculating devices designed to carry out a specific mathematical task. To use one of these devices for another task, it was necessary to rewire or reset its circuits—a task best left to an engineer. Modern computers use stored programs, which means that instructions for a computing task can be loaded into a computer's memory. These instructions can easily be replaced by different instructions when it is time for the computer to perform a different task. The stored program concept allows you to use your computer for one task, such as word processing, and then easily switch to a different type of computing task, such as editing a photo or sending an e-mail message. The ability to use stored programs is the single most important characteristic that distinguishes a computer from other simpler and less versatile devices.

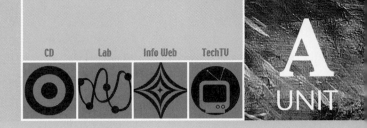
Figure A-2: Basic computer functions

A computer processes data. The CPU retrieves the input (such as images and text) and then processes the input (the text and images); the input (the text and images) is temporarily held in memory; from memory, the processed data (the text and images) can be output, usually to a monitor, printer, speakers, or storage medium

A computer produces output. You use an output device, such as a monitor, printer, or speakers to see or hear the results of processing, that is, the computer output

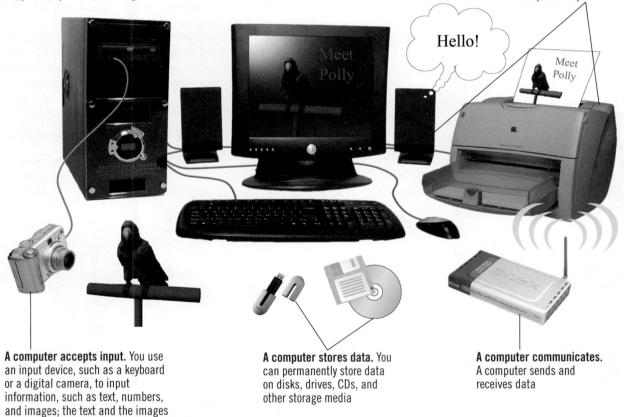

A computer accepts input. You use an input device, such as a keyboard or a digital camera, to input information, such as text, numbers, and images; the text and the images are temporarily held in memory

A computer stores data. You can permanently store data on disks, drives, CDs, and other storage media

A computer communicates. A computer sends and receives data

Categorizing computers

Computers are versatile machines, but some types of computers are better suited to certain tasks than others. Computers are categorized according to how they are used, what they cost, their physical size, and their processing capability. Categories help consumers purchase the computer most appropriate for the required tasks. To reflect the current computer technology, computers are categorized as follows: personal computers, handheld computers, videogame consoles, servers, workstations, mainframes, and supercomputers.

■ A **personal computer (PC)**, also called a **microcomputer**, is designed to meet the computing needs of an individual. It typically provides access to a wide variety of computing applications, such as word processing, photo editing, e-mail, and Internet access. Personal computers include **desktop computers**, as illustrated in **Figure A-3**, and **notebook computers** (sometimes called "laptop computers"), as illustrated in **Figure A-4**. **Tablet computers** are portable computing devices featuring a touch-sensitive screen that can be used as a writing or drawing pad, see **Figure A-5**.

■ A **handheld computer**, such as an iPAQ, a Palm, a Blackberry, or a PocketPC, features a small keyboard or touch-sensitive screen and is designed to fit into a pocket, run on batteries, and be used while you are holding it. See **Figure A-6**. A **PDA (Personal Digital Assistant)** is typically used as an electronic appointment book, address book, calculator, and notepad. Inexpensive add-ons make it possible to send and receive e-mail, use maps and global positioning to get directions, maintain an expense account, and make voice calls using cellular service. With its slow processing speed and small screen, a handheld computer is not powerful enough to handle many of the tasks that can be accomplished using desktop, notebook, or tablet personal computers.

Figure A-3: A desktop personal computer

Figure A-5: A tablet personal computer

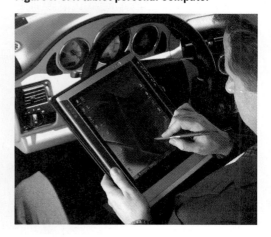

Figure A-4: A notebook personal computer

Figure A-6: A handheld personal computer

■ Computers that are advertised as **workstations** are usually power-ful desktop computers designed for specialized tasks. A workstation can tackle tasks that require a lot of processing speed, such as medical imaging and computer-aided design. Some workstations contain more than one processor. Most have circuitry specially designed for creating and displaying three-dimensional and animated graphics.

■ A **mainframe computer** is a large and expensive computer capable of simultaneously processing data for hundreds or thousands of users. Mainframes are generally used by businesses, universities, or governments to provide centralized storage, processing, and management of large amounts of data where reliability, data security, and centralized control are necessary. Its main processing circuitry is housed in a closet-sized cabinet. See **Figure A-7**.

■ A computer is a **supercomputer** if, at the time of construction, it is one of the fastest computers in the world. Because of their speed and complexity, supercomputers can tackle tasks that would not be practical for other computers. Typical uses for supercomputers include breaking codes and modeling worldwide weather systems. A supercomputer CPU is constructed from thousands of processors.

■ In the computer industry, a **server** can refer to computer hardware, to a specific type of software, or to a combination of hardware and software. In any case, the purpose of a server is to "serve" the computers on a network (such as the Internet or a LAN) by supplying them with data. A personal computer, workstation, or software that requests data from a server is referred to as a client.

■ Just about any personal computer, workstation, mainframe, or super-computer can be configured to perform the work of a server. Typically, servers do not include sound cards, DVD players, and other peripherals, that consumers expect on their desktop computers.

Figure A-7: A mainframe computer

How do personal computers, notebooks, and video consoles differ?

A desktop computer has separate components. A desktop computer fits on a desk and runs on power from an electrical wall outlet; the main unit can be housed in either a vertical case or a horizontal case.

A notebook computer is small and lightweight, giving it the advantage of portability. It has a keyboard, monitor, and system in one compact unit. It can run on power supplied by an electrical outlet, or it can run on battery power.

A "pure" tablet computer configuration lacks a keyboard (although one can be attached) and resembles a high-tech clipboard. A "convertible" tablet computer is constructed like a notebook computer, but the screen folds face up over the keyboard to provide a horizontal writing surface.

A **videogame console** (see **Figure A-8**), such as the Nintendo® GameCube™, the Sony PlayStation®, or the Microsoft XBox®, is also a computer. Videogame consoles contain processors that are equivalent to any found in a fast personal computer, and they are equipped to produce graphics that rival those on sophisticated workstations. Add-ons make it possible to use a videogame console to watch DVD movies, send and receive e-mail, and participate in online activities, such as multiplayer games.

Figure A-8

Examining personal computer systems

The term "computer system" usually refers to a computer and all of the input, output, and storage devices that are connected to it. Despite cosmetic differences among personal computers, see **Figure A-9**, a personal computer system usually includes standard equipment or devices. These devices may vary in color, size, and design for different personal computers. **Figure A-10** illustrates a typical desktop personal computer system; refer to it as you read through the list of devices below.

- **System unit**. The system unit is the case that holds the power supply, storage devices, and the circuit boards, including the main circuit board (also called the "motherboard"), which contains the processor. Notebook computers are a single unit that include the system unit, monitor, a built-in keyboard, and speakers.

- **Display device**. Most computers have a display device called a **monitor**. The monitor is the primary output device. The monitor for a desktop computer is a separate component, whereas the monitor for a notebook computer is a built-in, flat panel display.

- **Keyboard**. Most computers are equipped with a keyboard as the primary input device.

- **Mouse**. A mouse is a common input device designed to manipulate on-screen graphical objects and controls.

- **Storage devices**. A storage device is used to store data on a computer or to share data among computers. Storage devices are both input and output devices. Most personal computers have more than one type of storage device. Each storage device uses a different **storage medium**. The primary storage device is the **hard disk drive**. Almost all computers have a hard disk drive that is usually mounted inside the system unit. External and removable hard disk drives are available that can plug into the USB port on the system unit. A **floppy disk drive** is mounted inside the system unit and opens to accept floppy disks. A **CD drive** and a **DVD drive** are usually mounted inside the system unit and open to accept CDs or DVDs. A **USB flash drive** plugs directly into a USB port on the computer system unit. Data is "read from" a storage medium, and often can be "written to" a storage medium.

Figure A-9: Typical personal computer systems

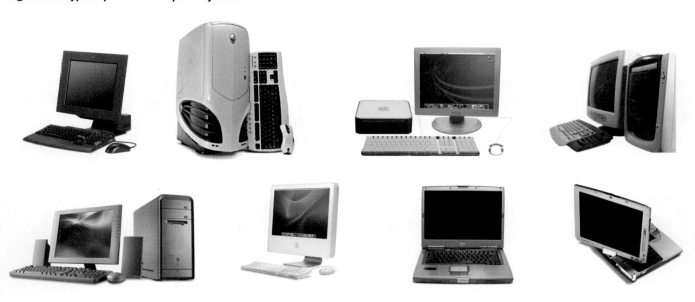

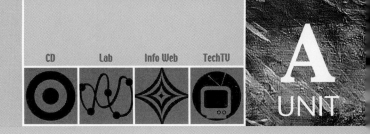

■ **Speakers** and **sound card**. Speakers and a small circuit board, called a sound card, are required for high-quality music, narration, and sound effects. A desktop computer's sound card sends signals to external speakers. A notebook's sound card sends signals to internal speakers. The sound card is an input and an output device, while speakers are output devices.

■ **Modem** and **network card**. Some personal computer systems include a built-in modem that can be used to establish an Internet connection. There are many ways to connect to the Internet, so there are many types of modems. A modem is both an input and an output device. Modems can be internal or external. In addition to a modem, a network card is used to connect a computer to a network or cable Internet connection.

■ **Printer**. A printer is an output device that produces computer-generated text or graphical images on paper.

Figure A-10: Components of a typical computer system

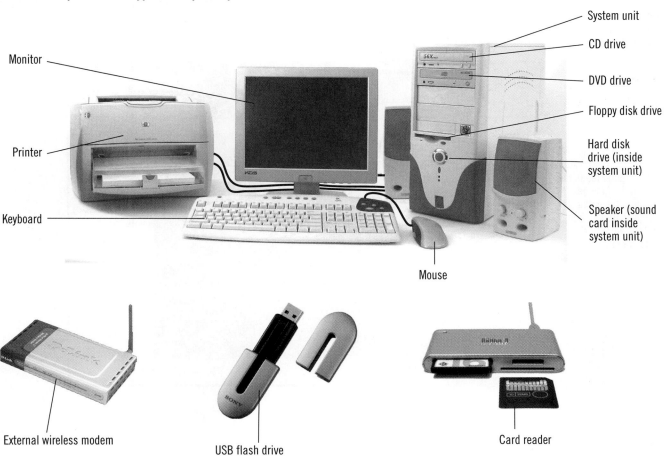

Exploring data, information, and files

In everyday conversation, people use the terms "data" and "information" interchangeably. Nevertheless, some computer professionals make a distinction between the two terms. They define **data** as the symbols that represent people, events, things, and ideas. Data becomes **information** when it is presented in a format that people can understand and use. As a rule of thumb, remember that data is used by computers; information is used by people. See **Figure A-11**.

■ Have you ever gotten a computer file you couldn't read? It could be because the data has not been converted to information. Computers process and store data using codes designed expressly for electronic data. One of these codes is the **binary number system**, which has only two digits: 1 and 0. Other codes, such as **ASCII** and **EBCDIC**, also use 0s and 1s to represent data.

■ Computers use these codes to store data in a digital format as a series of 1s and 0s. Each 1 or 0 is a **bit**, and 8 bits are called a **byte**. The bits and bytes that are processed and stored by a computer are data. The output results of processing data—the words, numbers, sounds, and graphics—are information.

■ A computer stores data in files. A **computer file**, usually referred to simply as a **file**, is a named collection of data that exists on a storage medium, such as a hard disk, a floppy disk, a USB flash drive, a CD, or a DVD. Although all files contain data, some files are classified as "data files," whereas other files are classified as "executable files."

■ A **data file** contains data. For example, it might contain the text for a document, the numbers for a calculation, the specifications for a graph, the frames of a video, or the notes of a musical passage.

Figure A-11: The difference between data and information

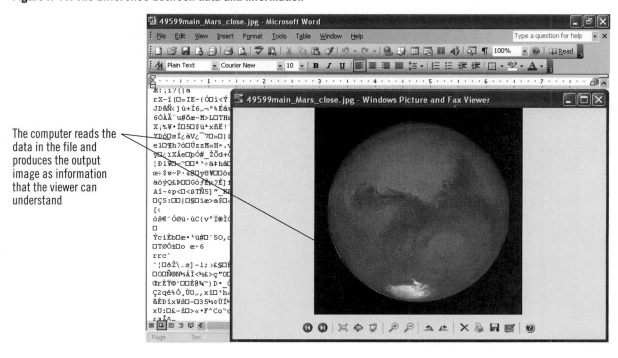

The computer reads the data in the file and produces the output image as information that the viewer can understand

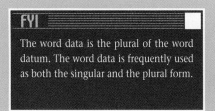

CD   Lab   Info Web   TechTU

A
UNIT

■ An **executable file** contains the programs or gives the instructions that tell a computer how to perform a specific task. For example, the word processing program that tells your computer how to display and print text is stored as an executable file.

■ You can think of data files as passive because the data does not instruct the computer to do anything. Executable files, on the other hand, are active because the instructions stored in the file cause the computer to carry out some action.

■ Every file has a name, the **filename**, which often provides a clue to its contents. A file also has a **filename extension** usually referred to simply as an "extension" that further describes a file's contents. For example, in Pbrush.exe, "Pbrush" is the filename and "exe" is

the extension. As you can see, the filename is separated from the extension by a period called a "dot." To tell someone the name of this file, you would say, "P brush dot e-x-e."

Executable files typically have .exe extensions. Data files have a variety of extensions, such as .jpg, .bmp or .tif for a graphic, .mid for synthesized music, .wav for recorded music, or .htm for a Web page. Each software program assigns a specific filename extension to the data files it creates. As a user, you do not decide the extension; rather, it is automatically included when files are created and saved, for example .xls for files created with Microsoft Excel or .doc for files created with Microsoft Word. Depending on your computer settings, you may or may not see the filename extension assigned to a file. **Figure A-12** shows a list of files, including the filename extensions.

Figure A-12: Filenames and filename extensions

Filename   Filename extension

Introducing application and system software

A computer's application software and operating system make a computer run. As a computer user, you are probably most familiar with application software. Different types of application software are installed on your computer. However, there is usually only one operating system on your computer; the operating system is not another type of application software. You can run many applications at one time, but only one operating system at one time.

■ **Application software** is a general term used to classify the computer programs that help a person carry out a variety of tasks. Word processing software, for example, helps people create, edit, and print documents. Personal finance software helps people keep track of their money and investments. Video editing software helps people create and edit home movies and even some professional, commercially released films.

■ An **operating system** is essentially the master controller for all of the activities that take place within a computer system. An operating system is classified as **system software** because its primary purpose is to help the computer system monitor itself in order to function efficiently. Most of the time people interact with the operating system without realizing it. However, people do interact with the operating system for certain operational and storage tasks, such as starting programs and locating data files.

■ Popular personal computer operating systems include Microsoft Windows and Mac OS. Microsoft Windows Mobile and Palm OS control most handheld computers. Linux and UNIX are popular operating systems for servers. Microsoft Windows (usually referred to simply as "Windows") is the most widely used operating system for personal computers. As shown in **Figure A-13**, the Windows operating system displays menus and simulated on-screen controls designed to be manipulated by a mouse.

The term "Windows software" refers to any application software designed to run on computers that run Microsoft Windows as their operating system. For example, a program called Microsoft Word for Windows is a word processing program that can be used on a computer running the Windows operating system. It is an application program that is referred to as "Windows software."

Figure A-13: The Windows OS interface

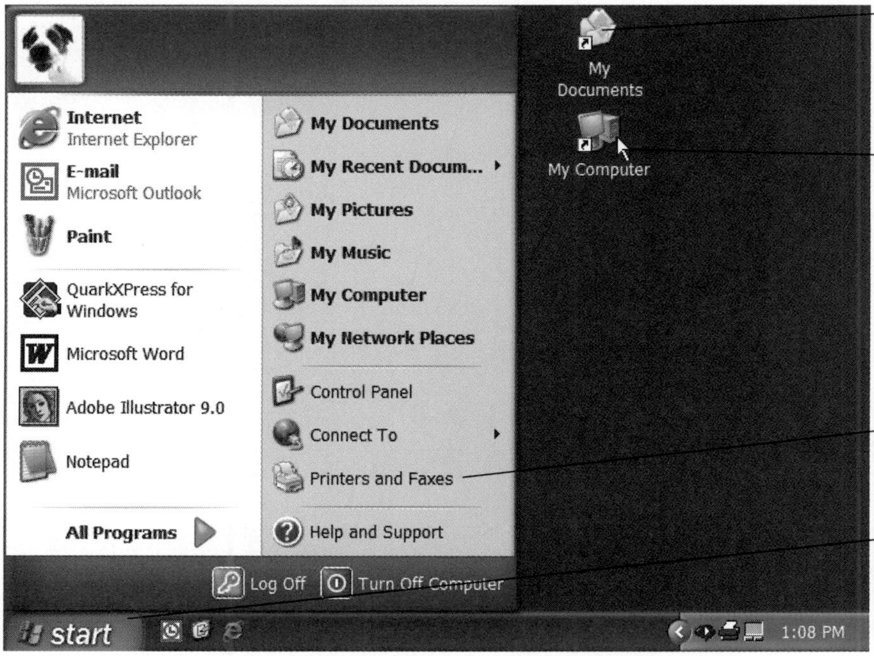

Small pictures called "icons" represent objects, such as disk drives and documents

An on-screen pointer can be positioned on an object by moving the mouse

A menu is a list of options; clicking an option selects it

The Start button provides access to a menu of program, document, and customization options

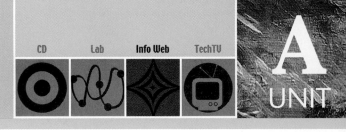
■ An operating system affects compatibility. Computers that operate in essentially the same way are said to be "compatible." Two of the most important factors that influence compatibility and define a computer's platform are the processor and the operating system. A **platform** consists of the underlying hardware and software of the computer system. Today, two of the most popular personal computer platforms are PCs and Macs.

PCs are based on the design for one of the first personal computers—the IBM PC. A huge selection of personal computer brands and models based on the original PC design and manufactured by companies such as IBM, Hewlett-Packard, Toshiba, Dell, and Gateway are on the shelves today. The Windows operating system was designed specifically for these personal computers. Because of this, the PC platform is sometimes called the "Windows platform." Most of the examples in this book pertain to PCs because they are so popular.

Macintosh computers are based on a proprietary design for a personal computer, manufactured almost exclusively by Apple Computer, Inc. The stylish iMac is one of Apple's most popular computers, and it uses Mac OS as its operating system. See **Figure A-14**.

■ The PC and Mac platforms are not compatible because their processors and operating systems differ. Consequently, application software designed for Macs does not typically work with PCs. However, different versions of some application software have also been created so that one version exists for the Windows platform and another version exists for the Macintosh platform. When shopping for new software, it is important to read the package to make sure that it is designed to work with your computer platform.

Different versions of some operating systems have been created to operate with more than one processor. For example, one version of the Linux operating system exists for the PC platform and another version exists for the Mac platform.

Figure A-14: The Mac OS interface

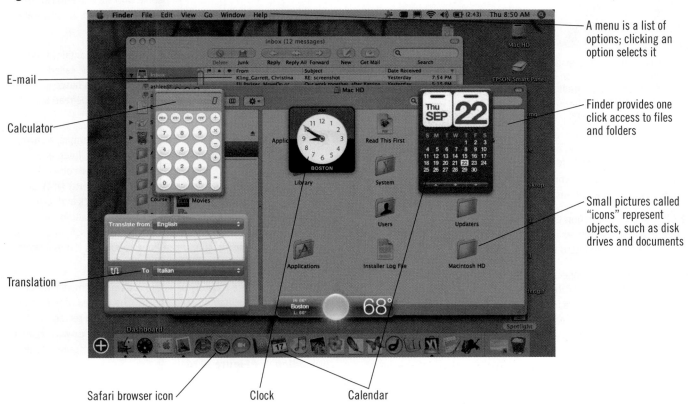

E-mail

Calculator

Translation

Safari browser icon

Clock

Calendar

A menu is a list of options; clicking an option selects it

Finder provides one click access to files and folders

Small pictures called "icons" represent objects, such as disk drives and documents

Defining Internet basics

If you are looking for information, if you want to communicate with someone, or if you want to buy something, the Internet offers abundant resources. The Internet has changed society. E-mail and instant messaging have caused a major shift in the way people communicate. Online stores have changed our shopping habits. The ability to easily download music and video has changed the entertainment industry and stirred up controversy about intellectual property.

- The **Internet backbone** defines the main routes of the Internet. See **Figure A-15**. The Internet backbone is constructed and maintained by major telecommunications companies. These telecommunications links can move huge amounts of data at incredible speeds.

Figure A-15: The Internet backbone

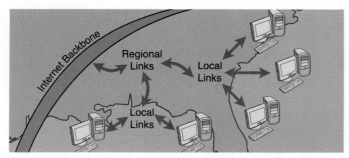

Personal computers are connected to regional and local communications links, which in turn connect to the Internet backbone; data transport works seamlessly between any two platforms—between PCs and Macs, and even between personal computers and mainframes

- Communication among all of the different devices on the Internet is made possible by **TCP/IP (Transmission Control Protocol/ Internet Protocol)**, which is a standard set of rules for electronically addressing and transmitting data.

- Most of the information that is accessible on the Internet is stored on servers. These servers use special **server software** to locate and distribute data requested by Internet users.

- Every device that's connected to the Internet is assigned a unique number, called an **IP address** that pinpoints its location on the Internet. To prepare data for transport, a computer divides the data into small chunks called **packets**. Each packet is labeled with the IP address of its destination and then transmitted. When a packet reaches an intersection in the Internet's communications links, a device called a **router** examines the packet's address. The router

checks the address in a routing table and then sends the packet along the appropriate link towards its destination. As packets arrive at their destinations, they are reassembled into the original file.

- A **Web site** can provide information, collect information through forms, or provide access to other resources, such as search engines and e-mail.

- The Internet revolutionized business by directly linking consumers with retailers, manufacturers, and distributors through electronic commerce, or **e-commerce**.

- Electronic mail, known as **e-mail**, allows one person to send an electronic message to another person or to a group of people. A variation of e-mail uses a **mailing list server** to send messages to everyone on a **listserv**. A listserv is a public list of people who are interested in a particular topic. Messages sent to the mailing list server are automatically distributed to everyone on the mailing list.

- **Usenet** is a worldwide bulletin board system that contains thousands of discussion forums on every imaginable topic called **newsgroups**. Newsgroup members post messages based on their interests to the bulletin board; these messages can be read and responded to by other group members.

- The Internet allows real-time communication. For example, a **chat group** consists of several people who connect to the Internet and communicate in real time by typing comments to each other. A private version of a chat room, called **instant messaging (IM)**, allows people to send messages, images, and hyperlinks back and forth instantly. **Internet telephony** allows voice conversations to travel over the Internet. Internet telephony requires special software at both ends of the conversation and, instead of a telephone, it uses a headset connected to a computer.

- Internet servers store a variety of files including documents, music, software, videos, animations, and photos. The process of transferring one of these files from a remote computer, such as a server, to a local computer, such as your personal computer, is called **downloading**. Sending a file from a local computer to a remote computer is called **uploading**. See **Figure A-16**.

FYI

A Podcast is available for each Issue in this book. You can download the Podcasts from www.course.com/illustrated/concepts6 and then listen to them.

CD   Lab   Info Web   TechTU

A UNIT

Figure A-16: Web sites provide files

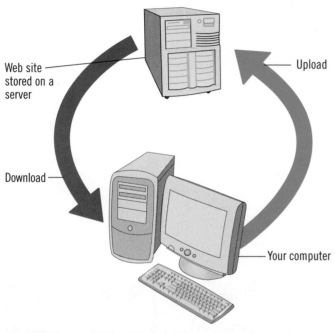

Web site stored on a server

Upload

Download

Your computer

Many Web sites provide files that the public can download to personal computers; uploads, on the other hand, are limited to people who have password access to the site

■ A technology known as **Peer-to-Peer (P2P)** file sharing makes it possible to access files stored on another Internet user's hard disk—with permission, of course. This technology is the basis for popular music, video, and file exchange Web sites.

■ The Internet provides access to an overwhelming amount and variety of information. Fortunately, there are technologies on the Internet that can help you stay current in topics that interest you. **RSS (Rich Site Summary** or **Really Simple Syndication)** is a format for "feeding" or "syndicating" news or any content from Web sites to your computer. Access to RSS content is free, but you have to subscribe to a Web site that offers RSS feeds. **RSS feeds** provide subscribers with summaries that link to the full versions of the content. To view the news feeds on your computer, you need to download an **RSS aggregator**. There are many free or commercial RSS aggregators available for download. The advantage to using RSS feeds is that you may select different types of information from a variety of Web sites and view them all at the same time.

■ A **blog** is a written personal journal posted on the Web for access by the general public. The word blog comes from the phrase "WeB LOG." Blogs can focus on a single topic or cover a variety of issues. A typical blog includes commentary by the author as well as links to additional information. Blogs are uncensored and span a wide range of topics. Blogs are a popular way of disseminating written information over the Internet. Blog directories provide links to blogs on all sorts of topics. Access to blogs is free.

What is podcasting?

The Internet broadcasts newscasts, radio shows, teleconferences, and more. Internet broadcasting is popular because broadcasts are not limited to a local region, like some radio and television shows are. One popular way to receive audio content via the Internet is through podcasting. The term podcast is derived from the popular portable audio player the Apple iPod. The term podcasting combines the term iPod and broadcasting. It is a way to deliver audio through RSS feed technology.

You can search for and subscribe to podcasts through topic Web sites (See **Figure A-17**). The specific podcasts are available as downloads in the form of audio mp3 files. Content is provided and updated frequently. Podcasting enables independent producers to create and broadcast syndicated shows without having to pay the fees to traditional broadcasters, such as radio or television companies. Although listeners subscribe to Web sites offering podcasts, access to podcasts is free. Podcasts use special software that supports the RSS feed technology. Once a listener subscribes to a site, the RSS software checks for and downloads new content automatically. Podcasts can be transferred to portable mp3 players, such as the Apple iPod, for portable listening.

Figure A-17

Connecting to the Internet

To take advantage of the Internet, you will have to establish a communications link between your computer and the Internet. Possibilities include using your existing telephone line, a cable television line, a personal satellite link, wireless or cell phone service, or special high-speed telephone services. Being on the Internet is often referred to as being **online**.

■ To connect to the Internet your computer needs a device called a **modem** which converts your computer's digital signals into a type of signal that can travel over telephone lines. **Figure A-18** shows various types of computer modems.

■ A **dial-up connection** requires a device called a **voiceband modem**. To establish a dial-up connection, your computer's modem dials a special access number, which is answered by an Internet modem. Once the connection is established, your computer is "on the Internet." When you complete an Internet session, you must "hang up" your modem. You can choose to disconnect automatically or manually; either way the connection is discontinued until the next time you dial in.

Figure A-18: Computer modems

A computer that has a modem will have a place to plug in a standard phone cable

An external modem connects to the computer with a cable

An internal modem is installed inside the computer's system unit

A PC card modem is typically used in a notebook computer

A modem card slides into a notebook computer's PC card slot

What services does an Internet Service Provider provide?

To access the Internet, you do not typically connect your computer directly to the backbone. Instead, you connect it to an Internet Service Provider (ISP) that in turn connects to the backbone. An ISP is a point of access to the Internet. An ISP typically provides a connection to the Internet and an e-mail account. Some ISPs offer proprietary services that are available only to subscribers. These services might include content channels with articles on health, hobbies, investing, and sports; activities specially designed for kids and teens; antispam and security software; a variety of voice and text messaging services; and free (and virus-free) software. ISP customers arrange for service, in this case for Internet access, for which they pay a monthly fee. In addition to a monthly fee, an ISP might also charge an installation fee. The ISP that you select should provide service in the places that you typically use your computer. If your work takes you on the road a lot, you'll want to consider a national ISP that provides local access numbers in the cities that you visit.

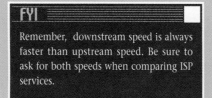

FYI

Remember, downstream speed is always faster than upstream speed. Be sure to ask for both speeds when comparing ISP services.

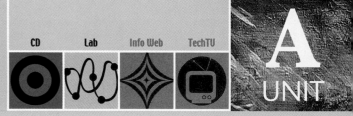

CD   Lab   Info Web   TechTU

A
UNIT

Theoretically, the top speed of a dial-up connection is 56 Kbps, meaning that 56,000 bits of data are transmitted per second. Actual speed is usually reduced by distance, interference, and other technical problems. This speed is useable for e-mail, e-commerce, and chatting. It is not, however, optimal for applications that require large amounts of data to be transferred quickly over the Internet.

■ **Cable modem service** is offered to cable company customers for an additional monthly charge and usually requires two pieces of equipment: a network card and a cable modem. A **network card** is a device that's designed to connect a personal computer to a local area network. A **cable modem** (see **Figure A-19**) changes a computer's signals into a form that can travel over cable TV links.

Figure A-19: A cable modem usually connects to your computer using one of the supplied Ethernet or USB cables

■ Cable modem access is referred to as an **always-on connection**, because your computer is, in effect, always connected to the Internet, unlike a dial-up connection that is established only when the dialing sequence is completed. A cable modem sends and receives data at a speed that is suitable for most Internet activities, including real-time video, interactive online gaming, and teleconferencing.

■ Many telephone and independent telecommunications companies offer high-speed, always-on connections. **DSL (Digital Subscriber Line)** is a generic name for a family of high-speed Internet links. Each type of DSL provides different maximum speeds but, like cable connections, they are all suitable for most Internet activities. DSL connections require proximity to a telephone switching station, which can be a problem for speed-hungry consumers who don't live near one. See **Figure A-20**.

■ Another Internet connection option is **DSS (Digital Satellite Service)**, which today offers two-way Internet access. Consumers are required to rent or purchase a satellite dish and pay for its installation. Downloads are generally faster than uploads.

■ An **ISP (Internet Service Provider)** is a company that maintains Internet computers and telecommunications equipment in order to provide Internet access to businesses, organizations, and individuals. Some parts of the Internet (such as military computers) are off limits to the general public. Other parts of the Internet limit access to paid members.

■ User IDs and passwords are designed to provide access to authorized users and to prevent unauthorized access. A **user ID** is a series of characters, letters, and possibly numbers that becomes a person's unique identifier, similar to a social security number. A **password** is a different series of characters that verifies the user ID, similar to the way a PIN (personal identification number) verifies a customer's identity at an ATM machine.

Figure A-20: Maximum speed of service depends on many factors, including your Internet Service Provider

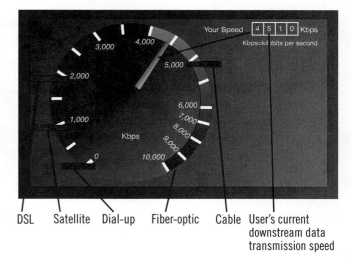

DSL   Satellite   Dial-up   Fiber-optic   Cable   User's current downstream data transmission speed

More about passwords

Typically, your ISP provides you with a user ID and password that you use to connect to the Internet. You will accumulate additional user IDs and passwords from other sources for specific Internet activities, such as reading New York Times articles or participating in an online auction. The process of entering a user ID and password is usually referred to as "logging in" or "logging on." Typically, when you log in and enter your password, a series of asterisks appears on the screen to prevent someone from looking over your shoulder and discovering your password. The rules for creating a user ID are not consistent throughout the Internet, so it is important to read all of the instructions carefully before finalizing your user ID.

Understanding World Wide Web basics

In the 1960s, long before personal computers or the Internet existed, a Harvard student named Ted Nelson wrote a term paper in which he described a set of documents, called **hypertext**, that would be stored on a computer. He envisioned that while reading a document in hypertext, a person could use a set of "links" to view related documents. A revolutionary idea for its time, today hypertext is the foundation for a part of the Internet that is often called "the Web" by the millions of people who use it every day.

■ The **Web** (short for "World Wide Web") is a collection of files that are interconnected through the use of hypertext. Many of these files are documents called **Web pages**. Other files are photos, videos, animations, and sounds that can be incorporated into specific Web pages. Most Web pages contain **links** (sometimes called "hyperlinks") to related documents and media files. See **Figure A-21**.

■ A series of Web pages can be grouped into a **Web site**—a sort of virtual "place" on the Internet. Every day, thousands of people shop at online department stores featuring clothing, shoes, and jewelry; visit research Web sites to look up information; and go to news Web sites, not only to read about the latest news, sports, and weather, but also to discuss current issues with other readers.

■ Web sites are hosted by corporations, government agencies, colleges, and private organizations all over the world. The computers and software that store and distribute Web pages are called **Web servers**.

■ Every Web page has a unique address called a **URL (uniform resource locator)**. For example, the URL for the Cable News Network Web site is http://www.cnn.com. Most URLs begin with http://. **HTTP (Hypertext Transfer Protocol)** is the communications standard that is instrumental in transporting Web documents over the Internet. When typing a URL, the http:// can usually be omitted, so www.cnn.com works just as well as http://www.cnn.com.

Figure A-21: A Web page

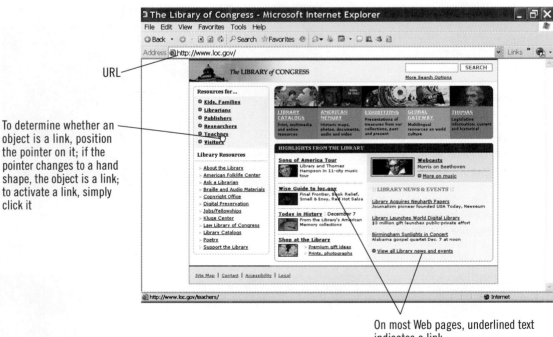

URL

To determine whether an object is a link, position the pointer on it; if the pointer changes to a hand shape, the object is a link; to activate a link, simply click it

On most Web pages, underlined text indicates a link

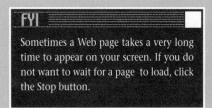

FYI
Sometimes a Web page takes a very long time to appear on your screen. If you do not want to wait for a page to load, click the Stop button.

CD   Lab   Info Web   TechTU

A
UNIT

■ Most Web sites have a main page that acts as a doorway to the rest of the pages at the site. This main page is sometimes referred to as a **home page**. The URL for a Web site's main page is typically short and to the point, like www.cnn.com.

■ The site might then be divided into topic areas that are reflected in the URL. For example, the CNN site might include a weather center www.cnn.com/weather/ and an entertainment page www.cnn.com/showbiz/. The filename of a specific Web page always appears last in the URL. Web page filenames usually have an .htm or .html extension, indicating that the page was created with **HTML (Hyptertext Markup Language)**, a standard format for Web documents. **Figure A-22** identifies the parts of a URL.

■ A URL never contains a space, even after a punctuation mark. An underline character is sometimes used to give the appearance of a space between words, as in the URL www.detroit.com/restaurants/best_restaurants.html. Be sure to use the correct type of slash— always a forward slash (/). Servers that run some Web sites are case sensitive, which means that an uppercase letter is not the same as a lowercase letter. On these servers, typing www.cmu.edu/Overview.html (with an uppercase "O") will not locate the page that's stored as www.cmu.edu/overview.html (with a lowercase "o").

Figure A-22: A URL

http://www.cnn.com/showbiz/movies.htm

Web protocol standard

Web server name

Folder name

Document name and filename extension

The URL for a Web page indicates the computer on which it is stored, its location on the Web server, a folder name, its filename, and its filename extension

Using search engines

The term **search engine** popularly refers to a Web site that provides a variety of tools to help you find information on the Web. A **keyword** is any word or phrase that you type to describe the information that you are trying to find. Based on your input, the search engine provides a list of pages.

Depending on the search engine that you use, you may be able to find information by entering a description, filling out a form, or clicking a series of links to review a list of topics and subtopics (Topic Directory). To use a topic directory, simply click a general topic. When a list of subtopics appears, click the one that's most relevant to the information you are trying to locate. If your selection results in another list of subtopics, continue to select the most relevant one until the search engine presents a list of Web pages that meet your criteria. See **Figure A-23**. If you use two different search engines to search for the same thing, you will probably get different results. Some search engines give the highest ranks to sites that are accessed most frequently, while others give top ranking to sites in which your key terms appear most frequently. Some search engines sell top billing and some maintain a separate area for paid links.

Figure A-23

Yahoo! - Microsoft Internet Explorer provided by Comcast

File   Edit   View   Favorites   Tools   Help

Back   Search   Favorites   Media

Address http://www.yahoo.com/

Business & Economy
B2B, Finance, Shopping, Jobs...

Computers & Intern
Internet, WWW, Software...

News & Media
Newspapers, TV, Radio...

Entertainment
Movies, Humor, Music...

Recreation & Sp
Sports, Travel, A...

Regional
Countries, Regions, US States...

• Save at 1-800 Contacts a
  shipping!

Yahoo! Recreation - Microsoft Internet Explorer provided by Comcast

File   Edit   View   Favorites   Tools   Help

Back   Search   Favorites   Media

Address http://dir.yahoo.com/Recreation/

Recreation Categories

• Amusement and Theme Parks@
• Automotive (6313) NEW!
• Aviation (849)
• Booksellers@
• Chats and Forums (6)
• Cooking@
• Dance@
• Employment (6)
• Events (10)

• Games (15843) NEW!
• Hobbies (2896) NEW!
• Home and Garden (868) NEW!
• Magazines (62)
• Motorcycles@
• Outdoors (27037) NEW!
• Pets@
• Sports (82430) NEW!
• Television@

Redefine

YOUR PASSION FOR PERFORMANCE

Using Web browsers

A Web browser, usually referred to simply as a **browser**, is a software program that runs on your computer and helps you view and navigate Web pages. See **Figure A-24**. A browser provides a window in which it displays a Web page. The borders of the window contain a set of menus and controls to help you navigate from one Web page to another. Current popular browsers are Microsoft Internet Explorer® (IE), Firefox™, Opera, and Netscape Navigator® (Navigator). Safari is a popular browser for the Mac.

■ Whether it's called a "URL box," an "Address box," or a "Location box," most browsers provide a space near the top of the window for entering URLs.

■ If you want to view the Web page www.dogs.com/boxer.html, you enter the URL into the Address box. When you press [Enter] on the keyboard, the browser contacts the Web server at www.dogs.com and requests the boxer.html page. The server sends your computer the data stored in boxer.html. This data includes the information that you want to view and embedded codes, called **HTML tags**, that tell your browser how to display the information. The tags specify details such as the color of the background, the text color and size, and the placement of graphics. **Figure A-25** shows that a browser assembles a document on your computer screen according to the specifications contained in the HTML tags.

■ Web browsers offer a remarkably similar set of features and capabilities. HTML tags make it possible for Web pages to appear similar from one browser to the next.

■ The browser's Back button lets you retrace your steps to view pages that you've seen previously. Most browsers also have a Forward but-

ton, which shows you the page that you were viewing before you clicked the Back button.

■ Your browser lets you select a **home page**, which is the Web page that appears every time you start your browser. Whenever you click the Home button, your browser displays your home page. This home page is different than the home page of a Web site.

■ Typically, a browser provides access to a print option from a button or a menu, allowing you to print the contents of a Web page. You should always preview before printing because a Web page on the screen may print out as several printed pages.

■ To help you revisit sites from previous sessions, your browser provides a **History list**. You can display this list by clicking a button or menu option provided by your browser. To revisit any site in the History list, click its URL. Many browsers allow you to specify how long a URL will remain in the History list.

■ If you find a great Web site and you want to revisit it sometime in the future, you can add the URL to a list, typically called **Favorites** or **Bookmarks** so you can simply click its URL to display it.

Figure A-24: Internet Explorer browser

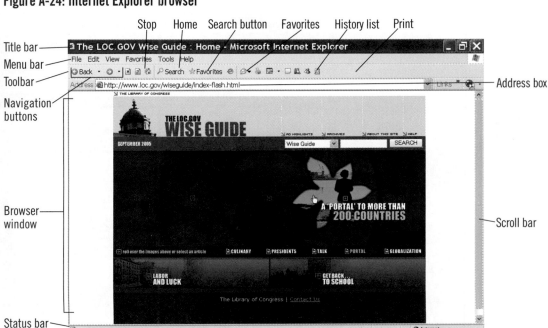

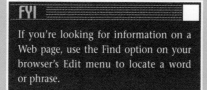

FYI

If you're looking for information on a Web page, use the Find option on your browser's Edit menu to locate a word or phrase.

Figure A-25: A Web page in Internet Explorer and the HTML code used to display it

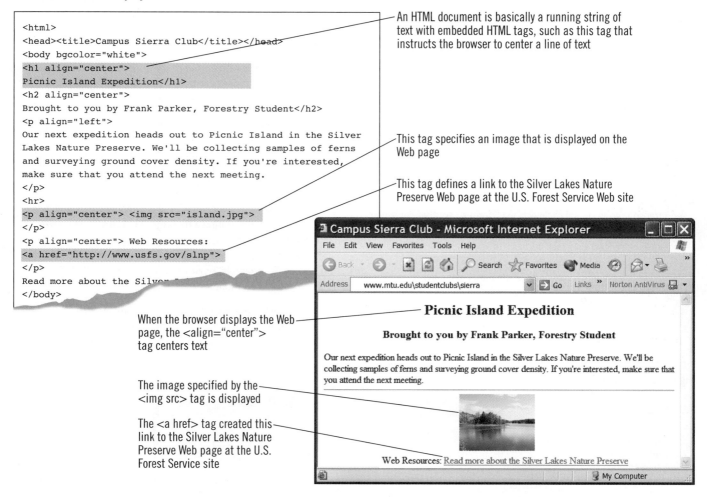

```
<html>
<head><title>Campus Sierra Club</title></head>
<body bgcolor="white">
<h1 align="center">
Picnic Island Expedition</h1>
<h2 align="center">
Brought to you by Frank Parker, Forestry Student</h2>
<p align="left">
Our next expedition heads out to Picnic Island in the Silver
Lakes Nature Preserve. We'll be collecting samples of ferns
and surveying ground cover density. If you're interested,
make sure that you attend the next meeting.
</p>
<hr>
<p align="center"> <img src="island.jpg">
</p>
<p align="center"> Web Resources:
<a href="http://www.usfs.gov/slnp">
</p>
Read more about the Silver...
</body>
```

An HTML document is basically a running string of text with embedded HTML tags, such as this tag that instructs the browser to center a line of text

This tag specifies an image that is displayed on the Web page

This tag defines a link to the Silver Lakes Nature Preserve Web page at the U.S. Forest Service Web site

When the browser displays the Web page, the <align="center"> tag centers text

The image specified by the <img src> tag is displayed

The <a href> tag created this link to the Silver Lakes Nature Preserve Web page at the U.S. Forest Service site

Copying text, sound, and images from a Web page

Most browsers let you save a copy of a Web page and place it at the storage location of your choice. Most allow you to save a copy of a graphic or sound that you find on a Web page. Most browsers also provide a Copy command that allows you to copy a section of text or an image from a Web page, which you can then paste into one of your own documents. You can right-click selected text or an image to see the Save menu options. You can also use the browser's menu bar. To copy a passage of text from a Web page, select the text (see **Figure A-26**), click Edit on the menu bar, then click Copy. Next, switch to your own document and use the Paste command. To keep track of the source for any copied sound, text, or images, you can also use the Copy command to copy the Web page's URL from the Address box, and then paste the URL into your document. In many programs, URLs paste as links. When you click or [Ctrl] click, the pasted URL from the Web page will open in a browser window.

Figure A-26

Understanding e-mail basics

Billions of e-mail messages speed over the Internet each year. Whether you are sending e-mail globally or to a friend next door, e-mail works in the same way because of the global system of computers and software that transmits, receives, and stores e-mail messages. Any person with an e-mail account can send and receive e-mail.

■ An **e-mail account** provides the rights to a storage area, or mailbox, supplied by an e-mail provider, such as an ISP. Each mailbox has a unique address that typically consists of a user ID, the @ symbol, and the name of the computer that maintains the mailbox. For example, suppose that a university student named Dee Greene has an electronic mailbox on a computer called rutgers.edu. If her user ID is "dee_greene," her **e-mail address** would be dee_greene@rutgers.edu.

■ An **e-mail message** is a document that is composed on a computer and transmitted in digital or "electronic" form to another computer. Every message includes a message header. The message header includes the recipient's e-mail address, the address of anyone who is receiving a copy of the message, the message subject, and the name of any file attachments. The body of the e-mail contains your message. The message header and body are usually displayed in a form, as shown in **Figure A-27**. Basic e-mail activities include writing, reading, replying to, and forwarding messages. Messages can be printed, kept for later reference, or deleted. See **Table A-1**.

■ Any file that travels with an e-mail message is called an **e-mail attachment**. In addition to text, you can send digital photos, video, and sounds, as e-mail attachments.

■ Today, most e-mail software allows you to create e-mail messages in HTML format. Why use HTML format for your e-mail? HTML messages can contain fancy formatting. The only limitation is that your e-mail recipients must have HTML-compliant e-mail software; otherwise, your message will be delivered as ASCII text.

■ Although e-mail is delivered quickly, it is important to use proper netiquette when composing a message. **Netiquette (Internet etiquette)** is a series of customs or guidelines for maintaining civilized and effective communications in online discussions and e-mail exchanges. For example, typing in all caps, such as "WHAT DID YOU DO?" is considered shouting and rude.

■ An **e-mail system** is the equipment and software that carries and manipulates e-mail messages. It includes computers and software called **e-mail servers** that sort, store, and route mail.

Figure A-27: Composing a message

1. When you compose an e-mail message, you begin by entering the address of one or more recipients and the subject of the message

2. You can also specify one or more files to attach to the message

3. The body of the e-mail message contains the message itself

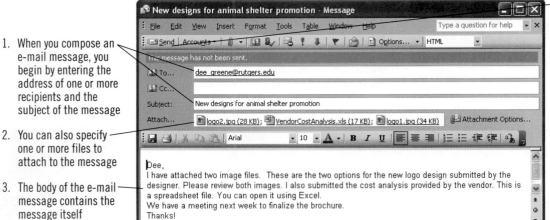

4. When you are done composing the message, click the Send button; when the message is sent, your e-mail software adds the date and your e-mail address to identify you as the sender

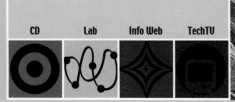

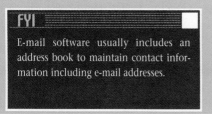

CD   Lab   Info Web   TechTV

A

UNIT

■ E-mail is based on **store-and-forward technology**, a communications method in which data that cannot be sent directly to its destination will be temporarily stored until transmission is possible. This technology allows e-mail messages to be routed to a server and held until they are forwarded to the next server or to a personal mailbox.

■ Three types of e-mail systems are widely used today: POP, IMAP, and Web-based mail. **POP (Post Office Protocol)** temporarily stores new messages in your mailbox on an e-mail server. See **Figure A-28**. Most people who use POP have obtained an e-mail account from an ISP. Such an account provides a mailbox on the ISP's **POP server**, which is a computer that stores your incoming messages until they can be transferred to your hard disk. Using POP requires e-mail client software. E-mail software called Outlook Express, is supplied with

Microsoft Windows. Other e-mail software is also available. This software, which is installed on your computer, provides an Inbox and an Outbox. When you ask the e-mail server to deliver your mail, all of the messages stored in your mailbox on the POP server are transferred to your computer, stored on your computer's disk drive, and listed as new mail in your Inbox. You can then disconnect from the Internet, if you like, and read the new mail at your leisure.

IMAP (Internet Messaging Access Protocol) is similar to POP, except that you have the option of downloading your mail or leaving it on the server. **Web-based e-mail**, the most commonly used, keeps your mail at a Web site rather than transferring it to your computer. Examples of Web-based e-mail are Yahoo! mail, GMail, and Hotmail. Before you can use Web-based e-mail, you'll need an e-mail account with a Web-based e-mail provider.

Figure A-28: Incoming and outgoing mail

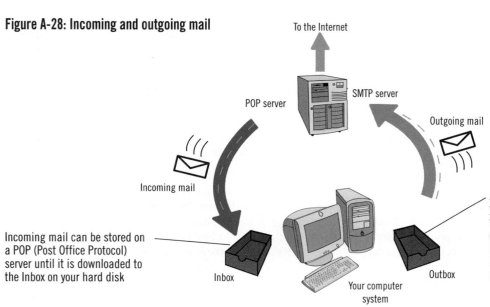

To the Internet

SMTP server

POP server

Outgoing mail

Incoming mail

An Outbox temporarily holds mesages that you have composed, but that have not been transmitted over the Internet; when you go online, you can send all the mail that is being held in your Outbox; outgoing mail is routed by an SMTP (Simple Mail Transfer Protocol) server, instead of by the POP server

Incoming mail can be stored on a POP (Post Office Protocol) server until it is downloaded to the Inbox on your hard disk

Inbox

Your computer system

Outbox

Table A-1: E-mail features

FEATURE	USE TO	FEATURE	USE TO
Reply	Send a reply to recipients of an e-mail; includes the original message	Priority Assign a priority level to your e-mail messages	Sort e-mail messages by date received, sender name, subject, or priority
Forward	Pass an e-mail on to other people	Automated away message	Reply to messages with a standard message when you will not be responding for a few days
Cc:	Send a "carbon copy" of a message to one or more recipients	Block	Refuse messages that arrive from a particular e-mail address
Bcc:	Send a "blind carbon copy" of a message to one or more recipients	Distribution list	Create an e-mail "group" that consists of several e-mail addresses so you can send the same message to a group of people at one time

Tech Talk **The Boot Process**

The sequence of events that occurs between the time that you turn on a computer and the time that it becomes ready to accept commands is referred to as the **boot process** or "booting" your computer. Your computer boots up by first loading a small program, called a "bootstrap" program, into memory, then it uses that small program to load a large operating system. Your computer's small bootstrap program is built into special ROM (read-only memory) circuitry housed in the computer's system unit. When you turn on a computer, the ROM circuitry receives power and it begins the boot process.

What is the purpose of the boot process? The boot process involves a lot of flashing lights, whirring noises, and beeping as your computer performs a set of diagnostic tests called the **power-on self-test (POST)**. The good news is that these tests can warn you if certain crucial components of your computer system are out of whack. The bad news is that these tests cannot warn you of impending failures. Also, problems identified during the boot process usually must be fixed before you can start a computing session.

The boot process serves an additional purpose—loading the operating system from the hard disk into memory so that it can help the computer carry out basic operations. Without the operating system, a computer's CPU is basically unable to communicate with any input, output, or storage devices. It cannot display information, accept commands, store data, or run any application software. Therefore, loading the operating system is a crucial step in the boot process.

Some of a computer's memory is "volatile" random access memory (RAM), which cannot hold any data when the power is off. Although a copy of the operating system is housed in RAM while the computer is in operation, this copy is erased as soon as the power is turned off. Given the volatility of RAM, computer designers decided to store the operating system on a computer's hard disk. During the boot process, a copy of the operating system is copied into RAM, where it can be accessed quickly whenever the computer needs to carry out an input, processing, output, or storage operation. The operating system remains in RAM until the computer is turned off.

Six major events happen during the boot process:

1. Power up. When you turn on the power switch, the power light is illuminated and power is distributed to the computer circuitry.

2. Start boot program. The processor begins to execute the bootstrap program that is stored in ROM.

3. Power-on self-test. The computer performs diagnostic tests of several crucial system components.

4. Identify peripheral devices. The operating system identifies the peripheral devices that are connected to the computer and checks their settings.

5. Load operating system. The operating system is copied from the hard disk to RAM.

6. Check configuration and customization. The processor reads configuration data and executes any customized startup routines specified by the user.

What if I turn on a computer and nothing happens? The first step in the boot process is the power-up stage. Power from a wall outlet or battery activates a small power light. If the power light does not come on when you flip the "on" switch, you should check all the power connections and be sure everything is plugged in properly.

What kinds of problems are likely to show up during the power-on self-test? The POST checks your computer's main circuitry, screen display, memory, and keyboard. It can identify when one of these devices has failed, but it cannot identify intermittent problems or impending failures. The POST notifies you of a hardware problem by displaying an error message on the screen or by emitting a series of beeps. A **beep code** provides your computer with a way to signal a problem, even if the screen is not functioning. You can check the documentation or Web site for your computer to find the specific meaning of numeric error codes. The printed or online reference manual for a computer usually explains the meaning of each beep code.

Should I try to fix these problems myself? If a computer displays error messages, emits beep codes, or seems to freeze up during the boot process, you can take some simple steps that might fix it. First, turn the computer off, check all the cables, wait five seconds, then try to start the computer again. Refer to **Figure A-29** for a power-up checklist. If you still encounter a boot error after trying to restart the computer several times, contact a technical support person.

What is the long list of stuff that appears on my screen during the boot process? After the POST, the bootstrap program tries to identify all of the devices that are connected to the computer. The settings for each device appear on the screen, creating a list of rather esoteric information.

On occasion, a device gets skipped or misidentified during the boot process. An error message is not produced, but the device does not seem to work properly. To resolve this problem, shut down the computer and reboot it. If a device is causing persistent problems, you may need to check the manufacturer's Web site to see if a new software patch will improve its operation.

Do computers have trouble loading the operating system or applying customization settings? Problems during the last stages of the boot process are rare, except when a disk has been inadvertently left in the floppy disk drive. Before computers were equipped with hard disk drives, floppy disks were used to store the operating system and application

software. As a legacy from these early machines, today's computers first check the floppy disk drive for a disk containing the operating system. If it does not find a disk in the drive, it proceeds to look for the operating system on the hard disk. However, if a floppy disk happens to be left in drive A, the computer will assume that you want to boot from it and will look for the operating system on that disk. The error message "Non-system disk or disk error" is the clue to this problem. Remove the floppy disk and press any key to resume the boot process.

How do I know when the boot process is finished? The boot process is complete when the computer is ready to accept your commands. Usually, the computer displays an operating system prompt or main screen. The Windows operating system, for example, displays the Windows desktop when the boot process is complete.

If Windows cannot complete the boot process, you are likely to see a menu that contains an option for Safe Mode. **Safe Mode** is a limited version of Windows that allows you to use your mouse, monitor, and keyboard, but not other peripheral devices. This mode is designed for troubleshooting, not for real computing tasks. If your computer enters Safe Mode at the end of the boot process, you should use the Shut Down command on the Start menu to shut down and turn off your computer properly. You can then turn on your computer again. It should complete the boot process in regular Windows mode. If your computer enters Safe Mode again, consult a technician.

Figure A-29: Power-up checklist

✓ Make sure that the power cable is plugged into the wall and into the back of the computer.

✓ Check batteries if you're using a notebook computer.

✓ Try to plug your notebook into a wall outlet.

✓ Make sure that the wall outlet is supplying power (plug a lamp into it and make sure that it goes on when you turn it on).

✓ If the computer is plugged into a surge strip, extension cord, or uninterruptible power supply, make sure that it is turned on and functioning correctly.

✓ Can you hear the fan in your desktop computer? If not, the computer's power supply mechanism might have failed.

Computers in Context Marketing

Computers have opened new vistas for communicating with consumers.

The American Marketing Association has changed its official defintion of marketing several times since 1935. The latest official definition of *marketing* is "Marketing is an organizational function and a set of processes for creating, communicating, and delivering value to customers and for managing customer relationships in ways that benefit the organization and its stakeholders." A person-in-the-street definition might simply be that marketing is an attempt to sell products.

Computers first played a role in marketing as research tools for quickly crunching numbers from consumer surveys, sales figures, and projections. Statistics derived from that data helped companies focus development efforts on the most promising products and market them effectively. Marketing research data made one fact very clear: even the most effective advertising could not convince everyone to buy a particular product. A costly prime-time television ad, for example, might be seen by millions of viewers, but many of them have no interest at all in the advertised product. To better target potential buyers, marketers turned to direct marketing.

"The Internet and the World Wide Web have become the most important new communication media since television, and ones that are fundamentally reshaping contemporary understanding of sales and marketing." Jim Sterne, author.

Direct marketing attempts to establish a one-to-one relationship with prospective customers rather than waiting for them to learn about a product from general, impersonal forms of advertising, such as billboards, radio spots, television commercials, and newspaper ads. The first direct marketing techniques included personalized letters, catalogs, and telemarketing. Customer names, addresses, and telephone numbers were mined from extensive computer databases maintained by mailing list brokers. Lists could be tailored in rudimentary ways to fit target markets. Selling snow tires? Get a list of consumers in northern states.

"Dear Carmen Smith, you might already have won…" Just about everyone in America has received a personalized sweepstakes mailing. Initially, personalized names were crudely inserted using dot matrix printers, but today high-speed laser printers dash off thousands of personalized letters per hour and use graphics capabilities to affix signatures and address envelopes that appear to have been handwritten in ink.

Telemarketing is a technique for telephone solicitation. Computerized autodialers make it possible for telemarketers to work efficiently. An autodialer is a device that can dial telephone numbers stored in a list. It can also generate and dial telephone numbers using a random or sequential number generator.

A "smart" autodialer, called a preemptive dialer, increases a telemarketer's efficiency even more by automatically calling several numbers at the same time and only passing a call to the marketer when a person answers. If you have picked up the telephone only to hear silence or a disconnect, it was likely an autodialer that connected to more than one person at the same time and dropped your call. Preemptive dialers eliminate telemarketing time that would be otherwise wasted with busy signals, answering machines, and so on.

The Internet opened up dramatic new horizons for in-direct marketing by providing an inexpensive conduit for collecting information about potential customers and distributing targeted direct marketing. According to Internet marketing guru and author Jim Sterne, "The Internet and the World Wide Web have become the most important new communication media since television, and ones that are fundamentally reshaping contemporary understanding of sales and marketing." Today, a vast amount of information flows over the Internet and marketers are trying to harness that information to most efficiently communicate their messages to prospective customers.

Market analysts are interested in consumer opinions about companies and products. Analysts for companies like Ford, Microsoft, and Sony track opinions on the Internet by monitoring message boards, discussion sites, and blogs. Google's BlogSearch, as well as software tools that use technology similar to Google's Web search technology, such as Intelliseek and Cymfony, are refined to sift through blogs for phrases or words to determine a blogger's feelings about a particular topic. For example, "Ford Ranger" and "love" and "dependable" would be interpreted that the blogger is happy with that particular vehicle.

E-commerce Web sites offer a global distribution channel for small entrepreneurs as well as multinational corporations. Consumers can locate e-commerce sites using a search engine. Some search engines allow paid advertising to appear on their sites. Clever marketers use search engine optimization techniques to get their Web sites to the top of search engine lists.

Another way to drive traffic to an e-commerce site is banner advertising that clutters up Web pages with inviting tag lines for free products. Clicking the ad, such as the one shown in **Figure A-30**, connects consumers to the site. The cost of placing a banner ad depends on the click-through rate—the number of consumers who click an ad. Sophisticated banner ad software displays the banner ad across an entire network and monitors click-through rates. Not only does this software keep track of click throughs for billing purposes, it can automatically adjust the sites that carry each ad to maximize click-through rates.

The word "marketing" combined with "Internet" is often associated with the tidal wave of spam that is currently crashing into everyone's Inbox. These mass spam e-mails, however bothersome, are a very crude form of direct marketing. Typically, spammers use

Figure A-30

"unscrubbed" mailing lists containing many expired, blocked, and invalid e-mail addresses. This hit-or-miss strategy is cheap. Ten million e-mail addresses can be rented for as low as $100 and server bandwidth provided by e-mail brokers costs about $300 per million messages sent.

Marketing professionals regard massive e-mail spamming with some degree of scorn because most lists do not narrow the focus to the most promising customers. Worse yet, consumers react by installing spam filters. Some spammers try to evade spam filters. More than one Web site offers marketers a free service that analyzes mass e-mail solicitations using a Spam filter simulator. If the solicitation cannot get through the filter, the service offers suggestions on what to change so the message slips through.

In contrast to gratuitous spammers, marketing professionals have learned that opt-in mailing lists have much higher success rates. Consumers who have asked for information more often appreciate receiving it and act on it. Opt-in consumers are also more willing to divulge information that develops an accurate profile of their lifestyle so marketers can offer them the most appropriate products.

Issue E-mail Privacy—Who Is Reading Your E-mail?

When you drop an envelope into the corner mailbox, you probably expect it to arrive at its destination unopened, with its contents kept safe from prying eyes. When you make a phone call, you might assume that your conversation will proceed unmonitored by wiretaps or other listening devices. Can you also expect an e-mail message to be read only by the person to whom it is addressed?

In the United States, the Electronic Communications Privacy Act of 2000 prohibits the use of intercepted e-mail as evidence unless a judge approved a search warrant. But, that does not mean the government is not reading your e-mail. Heightened security concerns after the September 11, 2001 terrorist attacks resulted in the rapid passage of the Patriot Act, which became law on October 26, 2001. In an effort to assist law enforcement officials, the Patriot Act relaxes the rules for obtaining and implementing search warrants and lowers the Fourth Amendment standard for obtaining a court order to compel an ISP to produce e-mail logs and addresses.

Think of your e-mail as a postcard, rather than a letter, and save your controversial comments for face-to-face conversations.

To eavesdrop on e-mail from suspected terrorists and other criminals, the FBI developed a technology that scans through e-mail messages entering and leaving an ISP's e-mail system to find e-mail associated with a person who is under investigation. Privacy advocates are concerned because this software scans all messages that pass through an ISP, not just those messages sent from or received by a particular individual.

Although law enforcement agencies are required to obtain a court order before intercepting e-mail, no such restriction exists for employers who want to monitor employee e-mail. Although many U.S. businesses monitor employee e-mail, intentional eavesdropping is only one way in which the contents of your e-mail messages might become public. The recipient of your e-mail can forward it to one or more persons—people you never intended for it to reach. Your e-mail messages could pop up on a technician's screen in the course of system maintenance, updates, or repairs. Also, keep in mind that e-mail messages—including those you delete

from your own computer—can be stored on backups of your ISP's e-mail server. You also need to be aware that some e-mail providers retain your e-mail and gather information about you in exchange for the e-mail service they provide. You need to know what information your e-mail provider collects via your e-mail and what the e-mail provider does with that collected information. For example, some Web-based e-mail providers—particularly those that make you look at ads in exchange for free accounts—collect information on how often you log in and they monitor your keystrokes to find out which links you click. E-mail providers claim they gather this information to use internally so they can deliver the best possible service, prevent fraud, and select the ads for products that you are most likely to buy. Before selecting an e-mail provider, find out what information the e-mail provider collects, and then decide if that is acceptable to you. You might wonder if such open access to your e-mail and your ad-viewing habits is legal. The answer in most cases is yes.

The United States Omnibus Crime Control and Safe Streets Act of 1968 and the Electronic Communications Privacy Act of 1986 prohibit public and private employers from engaging in surreptitious surveillance of employee activity through the use of electronic devices. However, two exceptions to these privacy statutes exist. The first exception permits an employer to monitor e-mail if one party to the communication consents to the monitoring. An employer must inform employees of this policy before undertaking any monitoring. The second exception permits employers to monitor employees' e-mail if a legitimate business need exists and the monitoring takes place within the business-owned e-mail system.

Employees generally have not been successful in defending their rights to e-mail privacy because courts have ruled that an employee's right to privacy does not outweigh a company's rights and interests. Courts seem to agree that because a company owns and maintains its e-mail system, it has the right to monitor the e-mail messages the system carries.

Like employees of a business, students who use a school's e-mail system cannot be assured of e-mail privacy. When a CalTech student was accused of sexually harassing a female student by sending lewd e-mail to her and her boyfriend, investigators retrieved all the student's e-mail from the archives of the e-mail server. The student was expelled from the university even though he claimed that the e-mail had been "spoofed" to make it look as though he had sent it, when it had actually been sent by someone else.

What is spam?

Spam is unwanted electronic junk mail that arrives in your Inbox. A majority of today's proliferation of spam is generated by marketing firms that harvest e-mail addresses from mailing lists, membership applications, and Web sites. Some spam messages advertise illegal products. Others are outright scams to try to get you to download a virus, divulge your bank account numbers, or send in money for products you will never receive. Beware of offers that seem just too good to be true —these offers are probably spam.

A **spam filter** automatically routes advertisements and other junk mail to the Deleted Items folder maintained by your e-mail client. Spam filters can be effective for blocking spam and other unwanted e-mails, however, they sometimes block e-mail messages you want. After activating spam filters, periodically examine your Deleted Items folder to make sure the filters are not blocking e-mails that you want.

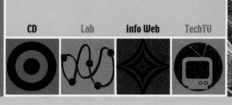
Why would an employer want to know the contents of employee e-mail? Why would a school be concerned with the correspondence of its students? It is probably true that some organizations simply snoop on the off chance that important information might be discovered. Other organizations have more legitimate reasons for monitoring e-mail. An organization that owns an e-mail system can be held responsible for the consequences of actions related to the contents of e-mail messages on that system. For example, a school has a responsibility to protect students from harrassment. If it fails to do so, it can be sued along with the author of the offending e-mail message. Organizations also recognize a need to protect themselves from false rumors and industrial espionage. For example, a business wants to know if an employee is supplying its competitor with information on product research and development.

Many schools and businesses have established e-mail privacy policies, which explain the conditions under which you can and cannot expect your e-mail to remain private. These policies are sometimes displayed when the computer boots or a new user logs in. Court decisions, however, seem to support the notion that because an organization owns and operates an e-mail system, the e-mail messages on that system are also the property of the organization. The individual who authors an e-mail message does not own all rights related to it. The company, school, or organization that supplies your e-mail account can, therefore, legally monitor your messages. You should use your e-mail account with the expectation that some of your e-mail will be read from time to time. Think of your e-mail as a postcard, rather than a letter, and save your controversial comments for face-to-face conversations.

Interactive Questions

❏ Yes   ❏ No   ❏ Not Sure   **1.** Do you think most people believe that their e-mail is private?

❏ Yes   ❏ No   ❏ Not Sure   **2.** Do you agree with CalTech's decision to expel the student who was accused of sending harassing e-mail to another student?

❏ Yes   ❏ No   ❏ Not Sure   **3.** Should the laws be changed to make it illegal for employers to monitor e-mail without court approval?

❏ Yes   ❏ No   ❏ Not Sure   **4.** Would you have different privacy expectations regarding an e-mail account at your place of work compared to an account you purchase from an e-mail service provider?

Expand the Ideas

1. Do you believe that your e-mail probably will not be read by anyone besides your intended recipient? Knowing that your e-mail is not private, will you be more careful in what you send via the e-mail system? Why or why not?

2. Should the laws be changed to make it illegal for employers to monitor e-mail without court approval? Why or why not?

3. Should the privacy laws governing an e-mail account at your place of work differ from an account you purchase from an e-mail service provider? Why or why not?

End of Unit Exercises

Key Terms

Always-on connection	E-mail account	LAN (local area network)	RSS
Application software	E-mail address	Link	RSS aggregator
ASCII	E-mail attachment	Listserv	Safe Mode
Beep code	E-mail message	Mailing list server	Search engine
Binary number system	E-mail servers	Mainframe computer	Server
Bit	E-mail system	Memory	Server software
Blog	Executable file	Microcomputer	Software
Bookmark	Favorites	Modem	Sound card
Boot process	File	Monitor	Spam
Browser	Filename	Mouse	Spam filter
Byte	Filename extension	Netiquette	Speakers
Cable modem	Floppy disk drive	Network card	Storage
Cable modem service	Handheld computer	Newsgroup	Storage device
CD drive	Hard disk drive	Notebook computer	Storage medium
Central processing unit (CPU)	Hardware	Online	Store-and-forward technology
Chat group	History list	Operating system	Stored program
Computer	Home page	Output	Supercomputer
Computer file	HTML	Output device	System software
Computer literacy	HTML tag	Packet	System unit
Computer network	HTTP	Password	Tablet computer
Computer program	Hypertext	Personal Digital Assistant (PDA)	TCP/IP
Computer system	IMAP	Peer-to-Peer (P2P)	Uploading
Data	Information	Peripheral device	URL
Data file	Input	Personal computer (PC)	USB flash drive
Desktop computer	Input device	Platform	Usenet
Dial-up connection	Instant messaging (IM)	Podcast	User ID
Display device	Internet	Podcasting	Videogame console
Downloading	Internet backbone	POP	Voiceband modem
DSL	Internet Service Provider (ISP)	POP server	Web
Digital Satellite Service (DSS)	Internet telephony	Power-on self-test (POST)	Web-based e-mail
DVD drive	IP address	Printer	Web page
EBCDIC	ISP	Processing	Web server
E-commerce	Keyboard	Processor	Web site
E-mail	Keyword	Router	Workstation

Unit Review

1. Make sure that you can define each of the key terms in this unit in your own words. Select 10 of the terms with which you are unfamiliar and write a sentence for each of them.

2. Explain the basic functions of a computer: input, processing, storing, and output. Explain why the stored program concept is important to all of this.

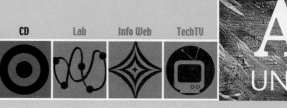

3. Identify and describe the purpose of each of the components of a basic personal computer system.

4. Describe the difference between an operating system and application software.

5. Define computer platform. Then discuss what makes two computer platforms compatible or incompatible.

6. List at least five resources that are provided by the Internet and describe each of the resources, exlpain how they are used, and indicate if you have used the resource and how.

7. Make a list of the ways to connect to the Internet presented in this unit and specify characteristics of each.

8. Describe the components of a URL and of an e-mail address.

9. Describe the rules that you should follow when copying text and images from the Internet.

10. Define "browser," then describe how a browser helps you navigate the Web.

Fill in the Best Answer

1. The basic functions of a computer are to accept input ~~data~~, process data, store data, and produce output.

2. A computer processes data in the central processing unit.

3. The idea of a(n) stored program means that instructions for a computing task can be loaded into a computer's memory.

4. The System unit unit is the case that holds the main circuit boards, processor, power supply, and storage devices for a personal computer system.

5. A device that is an integral part of a computer but that can be added to a computer is called a(n) peripheral device.

6. Executable files usually have a(n) _______ extension.

7. A(n) operating system is the software that acts as the master controller for all of the activities that take place within a computer system.

8. The main routes of the Internet are referred to as the Internet backbone.

9. Communication between all of the different devices on the Internet is made possible by TCP/~~IP~~ /IP.

10. Most of the data and information that's accessible on the Internet is stored on servers that are maintained by various businesses and organizations.

11. An Internet connection requires a device called a(n) Modem to convert signals so they can travel from the computer to the ISP.

12. A popular way to receive audio content via the Internet that you can listen to on a portable mp3 player is through POD casting.

13. A(n) blog is a written personal journal posted on the Web for access by the general public.

14. The process of entering a user ID and password is referred to as Logging on

15. Every Web page has a unique address called a(n) URL.

16. A browser assembles a Web page on your computer screen according to the specifications contained in the HTML tags.

17. Whenever you start your browser, it displays your HOme page.

18. A(n) browser fetches and displays Web pages.

19. Store-and-forward technology stores messages on an e-mail Server until they are forwarded to an individual's computer.

20. For many e-mail systems, a(n) POP server handles incoming mail, and a(n) SMTP server handles outgoing mail.

Practice Tests

When you use the Interactive CD, you can take Practice Tests that consist of 10 multiple-choice, true/false, and fill-in-the blank questions. The questions are selected at random from a large test bank, so each time you take a test, you will receive a different set of questions. Your tests are scored immediately, and you can print study guides to determine which questions you answered incorrectly. If you are using a Tracking Disk, save your test scores.

End of Unit Exercises

INDEPENDENT CHALLENGE 1

When discussing computers and computer concepts it is important to use proper terminology. Unit A presented you with many computer terms that describe computer equipment. If you would like to explore any of the terms in more detail, there are online dictionaries that can help you expand your understanding of these terms.

1. For this Independent Challenge, write a one-page paper that describes the computer that you use most frequently.

2. Refer to the Key Terms used in this unit and use terms from this unit to describe your computer components and the functions they perform.

3. In your final draft, underline each Key Term that you used in your paper. Follow your professor's instructions for submitting your paper either as an e-mail attachment or as a printed document.

INDEPENDENT CHALLENGE 2

Suppose that producers for a television game show ask you to help them create a set of computer-related questions for the next show. You will compose a set of 10 questions based on the information provided in Unit A. Each question should be in multiple-choice format with four possible answers.

1. Write 10 questions: two very simple questions, five questions of medium difficulty, and three difficult questions. Each question should be on an index card.

2. For each question, indicate the correct answer on the back of each card and the page in this book on which the answer can be found.

3. Gather in small groups and take turns asking each other the questions.

INDEPENDENT CHALLENGE 3

 The Computers in Context section of this unit focused on how computers have influenced and changed the scope and methods for marketing products and services. For this independent challenge, you will write a two- to five-page paper about how computers and technology have influenced and affected marketing based on information that you gather from the Internet.

1. To begin this Independent Challenge, log on to the Internet and use your favorite search engine to find information on current uses of technology in marketing to get an in-depth look at the topic. Are computers granting an unfair advantage to companies who use them to market their products?

2. Determine the viewpoint that you will present in your paper about computers in marketing. You might, for example, decide to present the viewpoint that it all comes down to the product (does it meet the needs of the consumer) and computers do not provide any unfair advantage. Whatever viewpoint you decide to present, make sure that you can back it up with facts and references to authoritative articles and Web pages.

3. Place citations to your research (include the author's name, article title, date of publication, and URL) at the end of your paper as endnotes, on each page as footnotes, or along with the appropriate paragraphs using parentheses. Follow your professor's instructions for submitting your paper via e-mail or as a printed document.

INDEPENDENT CHALLENGE 4

 A new ISP is getting ready to open in your area, and the president of the company asks you to design a print ad. Your ad must communicate all pertinent information about the ISP.

1. Before starting on the design, use your favorite search engine to find out more about ISPs in your area. Gather information to use in your ad, such as the type of services offered (dial-up, cable modem, etc.), the speed of service, the geographical coverage, price, and special or proprietary services.

2. Make up a name for your ISP. Design a print ad for the company using a computer or freehand tools. Submit your ad design along with a short written summary that describes how this ad reflects the ISP and the services it offers.

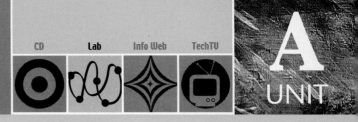
LAB: Making a Dial-Up Connection

1. Start the interactive part of the lab. Insert your Tracking Disk if you want to save your QuickCheck results. Perform each of the lab steps as directed and answer all of the lab QuickCheck questions. When you exit the lab, your answers are automatically graded and your results are displayed.

2. Make a list of at least five ISPs that are available in your area. If possible, include both local and national ISPs in your list.

3. Suppose that you intend to create manually a dial-up connection icon for AT&T WorldNet. What's missing from the following information?

- AT&T's dial-in telephone number and country
- AT&T's IP address
- Your password

4. Provide the following information about the Internet connection that you typically use: Name of ISP, type of Internet connection (dial-up, DSL, cable modem, DSS, school network, or business network), connection speed, and monthly fee. (If you don't currently have Internet access, describe the type of connection that you would like to use.)

LAB: Browsing and Searching

1. Start the interactive part of the lab. Insert your Tracking Disk if you want to save your QuickCheck results. Perform each of the lab steps as directed and answer all of the lab QuickCheck questions. When you exit the lab, your answers are automatically graded and your results are displayed.

2. Make a note of the brand and location of the computer that you're using to complete these lab assignments.

3. Examine the Favorites or Bookmarks list. How many pages are included in this list? Link to three of the pages, and provide their URLs and a brief description of their contents.

4. Suppose that you want to make your own trail mix, but you need a recipe. In three different search engines, enter the query: "trail mix" AND "recipe". (Refer to the Search Engines InfoWeb for a list of popular search engines.) Describe the similarities and differences in the results lists produced by each of the three search engines.

5. Conduct a second search to find the blue book price for a Taurus. Use the search engine of your choice to determine whether the query: "Blue book price" Taurus -"used car" provides the same results as the query: Blue book price Taurus -"used car".

Make sure that you enter each query exactly as specified, including the quotation marks and no space after the hyphen. Explain the similarities and differences in the query results.

LAB: Using E-Mail

1. Start the interactive part of the lab. Insert your Tracking Disk if you want to save your QuickCheck results. Perform each of the lab steps as directed and answer all of the lab QuickCheck questions. When you exit the lab, your answers are automatically graded and your results are displayed.

2. Using the e-mail software of your choice, send an e-mail message to kendra_hill@cciw.com. In the body of your message, ask for a copy of the "Most Influential Person Survey."

3. Wait a few minutes after sending the message to Kendra Hill, then check your mail. You should receive a survey from Kendra Hill. Reply to this message and Cc: your instructor. In your reply, answer each question in the survey, interspersing your answers with the original text. Send the reply, following the procedures required by your e-mail provider.

4. Examine the address book offered by your e-mail software. Describe how much information (name, home address, business address, birth date, telephone number, fax number, etc.) you can enter for each person. In your opinion, would this address book be suitable for a business person to use for storing contact information? Why or why not? Send the descriptions and answers to these questions to your instructor in an e-mail.

Student Edition Labs

Student Edition Labs

Reinforce the concepts you have learned in this unit through the **E-Mail** Student Edition Lab, available online at the Illustrated Computer Concepts Web site.

SAM Labs

If you have a SAM user profile, you have access to additional content, features, and functionality. Log in to your SAM account and go to your assignments page to see what your instructor has assigned for this unit.

End of Unit Exercises

Visual Workshop

The digital divide is defined as the difference in rates of access to computers and the Internet among different demographic groups. With the explosion of the Internet and the technology that drives the information age, forward-thinking social reformers recognized early on the potential for a divide between the "haves" and the "have nots." There have been global as well as local initiatives to connect the world. There have been global as well as local initiatives to connect the world. See **Figure A-31**. Government, private, and not-for-profit organizations, concerned with the impact of the digital divide, designed studies to help them analyze the causes and effects of this phenomenon. These studies have been conducted for the past few decades. Both private and government organizations have been working to bring technology to all regions of the world.

Figure A-31

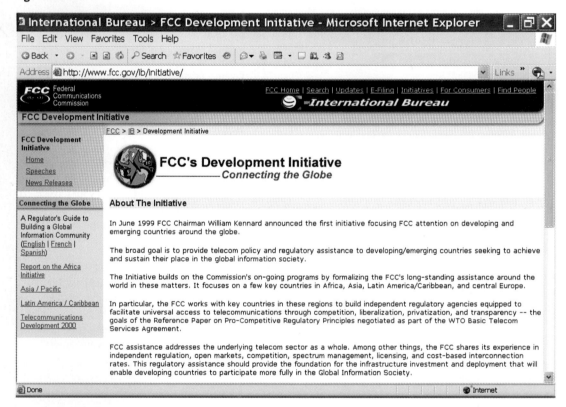

1. Is there a solution to the digital divide? Connect to the Internet and use your favorite search engine to search on the key phrase "digital divide." Find sites that include links to articles and research studies that address the digital divide. Review the findings for two studies or articles. Write a short paper summarizing these studies or articles. In your conclusion, comment on how you feel the digital divide affects our society and what we as a society should do about it, if anything.

2. Could you live without computers? Computers are ubiquitous; beyond the obvious applications, such as using your word processor to write a report, you come in contact with them during the course of your day in simple activities such as shopping in a supermarket or getting cash from your bank's ATM machine. Create a log to track your daily activities that involve computers. Keep the log for one week. At the end of the week, write a summary of any surprises or insights you have as to how computers affect your life.

3. Is there a digital divide in your community? Create a survey that will determine Internet access and computer ownership among people that you know. The survey should consist of 5–10 questions. You want to find out, within a chosen sector, who owns a computer, if they own more than one, what they use the computer(s) for, if they have Internet access, and if they access the Internet from their home or elsewhere. Be sure to survey at least 20 people. The survey should be anonymous but include demographic information. Compile the results of your survey into a chart and write a short summary explaining your findings.

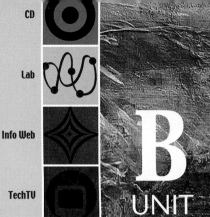

CD

Lab

Info Web

TechTV

Computer Hardware

B
UNIT

Introduce storage technology
Compare storage technologies
Compare storage media and devices
Explore hard disk technology
Explore CD/DVD technology
Explore solid state storage
Examine input devices
Compare display devices
Compare printers
Understand expansion slots, cards, and ports
Explore peripheral devices

Tech Talk: The Windows Registry
Computers in Context: The Military
Issue: Why Recycle Computers?

Overview

This unit provides an overview of computer hardware, with several lessons focusing on the various technologies that enable a computer to store and retrieve data and programs. You will learn the difference between magnetic storage, optical storage, and solid state storage. You will learn about input devices, such as keyboards and printers, and output devices, such as monitors and printers. You will learn about the components of a computer's expansion bus, including various types of expansion slots and cables, as well as a variety of peripheral devices that can enhance your computer use. In the Tech Talk, you will learn how the Windows Registry tracks software and devices that are installed. You will also have an opportunity to look at computers in the context of the military. The Issue discusses the effects of computers on the environment.

Introducing storage technology

The basic functions of a computer are to accept input, process data, store data, and produce output. When you want to store data permanently, you save the data using storage technology. The term **storage technology** refers to data storage systems that enable a computer to store and retrieve data and programs. Each data storage system has two main components: a storage medium and a storage device. A **storage medium** is the disk, hard drive, tape, memory card, CD, DVD, or other media that holds data. For some examples of storage media, see **Figure B-1**. A **storage device** is the mechanical apparatus that records and retrieves data from a storage medium. Storage devices include hard disk drives, card readers, tape drives, CD drives, DVD drives, flash drives, solid state drives, floppy disk drives, and Zip drives. For some examples of storage devices, see **Figure B-2**. Understanding the strengths and weaknesses of each storage technology will enable you to use each device appropriately and with maximum effectiveness.

- Computers can be configured with a variety of storage devices, such as a hard disk drive, CD drive or DVD drive, flash drive or solid state card reader, floppy disk drive, or Zip drive. Some storage technologies provide extremely fast access to data. Some storage technologies are more dependable than others. Some storage technologies are portable among computers (such as flash drives), others are fixed in one computer (such as hard drives).

- Data is copied from a storage device into RAM, where it waits to be processed. **RAM** (random access memory) is a temporary holding area for the operating system, the file you are working on (such as a word processing document), and application program instructions. RAM is not permanent storage. In fact, RAM is very **volatile**, which means data in RAM can be lost easily. That is why it is important to store data permanently.

RAM is important to the storage process. You can think of RAM as the connection between your computer's storage devices and its storage media. After data is processed in RAM, it is usually copied to a storage medium for more permanent safekeeping. Sometimes people confuse RAM and hard disk storage. To differentiate between RAM and hard disk storage, remember that RAM holds data in circuitry that is directly connected to the motherboard, whereas hard-disk storage places data on a storage medium. RAM is temporary storage; hard disk storage is more permanent. In addition, RAM usually has less storage capacity than hard disk storage.

- The process of recording or storing data is often referred to as "writing data" or "saving a file" because the storage device writes the data on the storage medium to save it for later use. The process of retrieving data is often referred to as "reading data," "loading data," or "opening a file."

Figure B-1: Examples of storage media

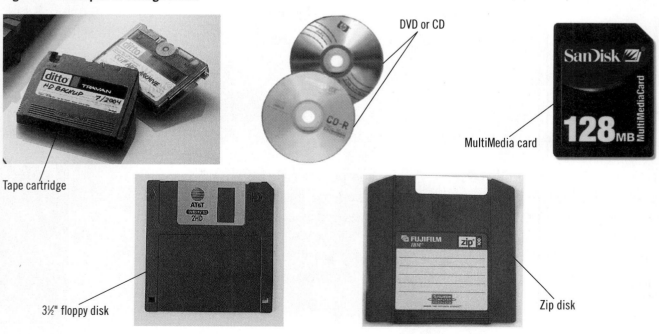

Tape cartridge

DVD or CD

MultiMedia card

3½" floppy disk

Zip disk

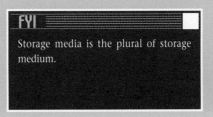
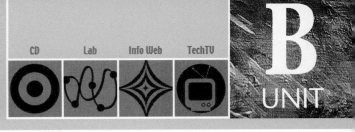
FYI

Storage media is the plural of storage medium.

Figure B-2: Examples of storage devices

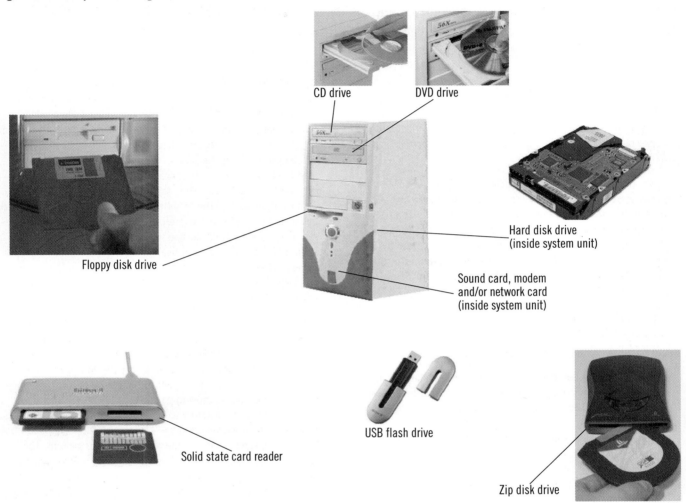

CD drive   DVD drive

Floppy disk drive

Hard disk drive (inside system unit)

Sound card, modem and/or network card (inside system unit)

Solid state card reader

USB flash drive

Zip disk drive

The science of data representation

Letters, numbers, musical notes, and pictures do not pass from the keyboard or other input device through the circuitry of a computer and then jump out onto the screen or printer. So how is it that a computer can work with documents, photos, videos, and sound recordings? The answer to that question is what data representation and digital electronics are all about. Data representation makes it possible to convert letters, sounds, and images into electrical signals. Digital electronics makes it possible for a computer to manipulate simple "on" and "off" signals, which are represented by 1s and 0s, to perform complex tasks.

Data representation is based on the binary number system, which uses two numbers, 1 and 0, to represent all data. When data is stored, these 1s and 0s must be converted into a signal or mark that is fairly permanent, but which can be changed when necessary. The data is not literally written as "1" or "0." Instead, the 1s and 0s must be transformed to change the surface of a storage medium. Exactly how this transformation happens depends on the storage technology. For example, floppy disks store data in a way that is different from the way CD-ROMs store data.

Comparing storage technologies

Three types of storage technologies commonly used for personal computers are magnetic, optical, and solid state. Each storage technology has advantages and disadvantages. To compare storage devices, you need to understand the fundamental distinctions between each technology.

■ **Magnetic storage** stores data by magnetizing microscopic particles on the disk or tape surface. The particles retain their magnetic orientation until that orientation is changed, thereby making disks and tape fairly permanent but modifiable storage media. Hard disk, floppy disk, Zip disk, and tape storage technologies can be classified as magnetic storage.

Before data is stored, the particles on the surface of the disk are scattered in random patterns. A **read-write head** mechanism in the disk drive reads and writes the magnetized particles that represent data. The disk drive's read-write head magnetizes the particles and orients them in either a positive or negative direction. See **Figure B-3**. These patterns of magnetized particles are interpreted as the 0s and 1s that represent data. Data stored magnetically can be changed or deleted simply by altering the magnetic orientation of the appropriate particles on the disk surface. This feature of magnetic storage provides flexibility for editing data and reusing areas of a storage medium containing data that is no longer needed.

Magnetic media is not very durable. Data stored on magnetic media such as floppy disks can be altered by magnetic fields, dust, mold, smoke particles, heat, and mechanical problems with a storage device. For example, a magnet should never be placed on or near a floppy disk because it will alter the magnetic particles on the disk, destroying the data. Magnetic media gradually lose their magnetic charge, which results in lost data. Some experts estimate that the reliable life span of data stored on magnetic media is about three years.

■ **Optical storage** stores data as microscopic light and dark spots on the disc surface. The dark spots are called **pits**, and it is possible to see the data stored on a CD or DVD storage medium using a high-powered microscope. See **Figure B-4**. The lighter, nonpitted surface areas of the disc are called **lands**. This type of storage is called optical storage because a low-power laser light is used to read the data stored on an optical disc. When the beam strikes a pit, no light is reflected. When the laser strikes a reflective surface, light bounces back to the read head. The patterns of light and dark between pits and lands are interpreted as the 1s and 0s that represent data. CD and DVD storage technologies make use of optical storage. Data recorded on optical media is generally considered to be less susceptible to environmental damage than data recorded on magnetic media. The useful life of a CD-ROM disc is estimated to exceed 200 years.

■ **Solid state storage** stores data in a nonvolatile, erasable, low-power chip. A solid state storage medium stores data in a microscopic grid of cells. See **Figure B-5**. A card reader transfers data between the card and a computer. Solid state storage provides faster access to data than magnetic or optical storage technology because it includes no moving parts. Very little power is required, which makes solid state storage ideal for battery-operated devices. Solid state storage is very durable—it is virtually impervious to vibration, magnetic fields, or extreme temperature fluctuations. The capacity of solid state storage does not currently match that of hard disks, CDs, or DVDs. The cost per megabyte of storage is higher than for magnetic or optical storage. A variety of compact storage cards, pens, and memory sticks are classified as solid state storage.

Figure B-3: Magnetic storage

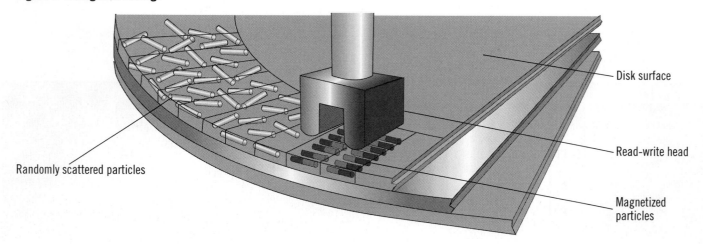

Disk surface

Read-write head

Randomly scattered particles

Magnetized particles

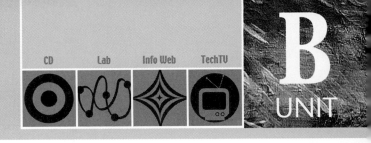

Figure B-4: Optical storage

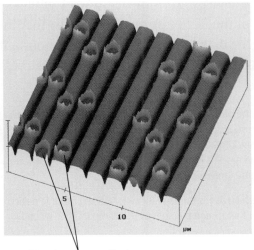

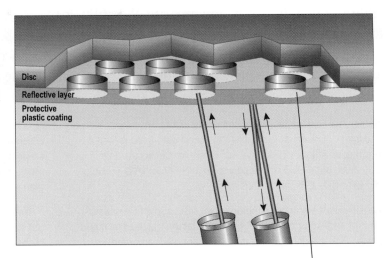

The pits on an optical storage disc as seen through an electron microscope; each pit is 1 micron in diameter

When a CD-ROM disc is manufactured, a laser burns pits into a reflective surface; these pits become dark non-reflective areas on the disc

Figure B-5: Solid state storage

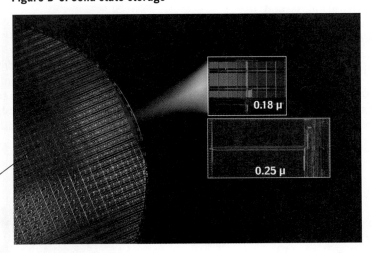

Microscopic grid

Exploring floppy disk technology

A floppy disk is a round piece of flexible Mylar plastic covered with a thin layer of magnetic oxide and sealed inside a protective casing. A standard floppy for personal computing is a 3½" disk with a capacity of 1.44 MB—low for today's storage needs. Floppy disk technology is also used for Zip disks.

A floppy disk features a write-protect window, which is a small square opening that can be covered by a moveable plastic tab on the disk. When you open the window, the disk is "write-protected," which means that a computer cannot write or save data on the disk. Floppies, which provide one type of inexpensive, removable storage for personal computer systems, are still used today. But in general, floppies have been replaced by more efficient portable media, such as solid state jump drives. In fact, because local computer networks and the Internet have made it easy to share data files without physically transporting them from one place to another, many of today's computers do not come with a floppy disk drive.

Comparing storage media and devices

When trying to determine the best storage technology systems for a job, it is useful to apply four criteria: versatility, durability, speed, and capacity. Versatility is the ability of a device and its media to work with more than one storage technology. Durability determines the ability of the device or media to last so that the data will be accessible. Speed is the time it takes to retrieve or access the data—a factor that is very important in determining how efficiently you work. Finally, capacity is the amount of data each technology can store.

- Versatility. Some storage devices can access data from only one type of medium. More versatile devices can access data from several different media. A floppy disk drive, for example, can access only floppy disks, but a DVD drive can access data DVDs, DVD movies, audio CDs, data CDs, and CD-Rs.

- Durability. Most storage technologies are susceptible to damage from mishandling or other environmental factors, such as heat and moisture. Some technologies are less susceptible than others. Optical and solid state technologies tend to be less susceptible than magnetic technologies to damage that could cause data loss.

- Speed. There are two factors to take into account when considering storage technology speed: access time and data transfer rate time. Not surprisingly, storage devices that can access data quickly are preferred over storage devices with slow data access. **Access time** is the average time it takes a computer to locate data on the storage medium and read it. Access time for a personal computer storage device, such as a disk drive, is measured in **milliseconds** (thousandths of a second, abbreviated as ms). Lower numbers indicate faster access times. For example, a drive with a 6-ms access time is faster than a drive with an access time of 11 ms. Random-access devices have the fastest access times.

  Random access (also called "direct access") is the ability of a device to "jump" directly to the requested data. Floppy disk, hard disk, solid state, CD, and DVD drives are random-access devices. A tape drive, on the other hand, must use slower **sequential access**, which reads through the data from the beginning of the tape. The advantage of random access becomes clear when you consider how much faster and easier it is to locate a song on a CD (random access) than on a cassette tape (sequential access).

  Data transfer rate is the amount of data that a storage device can move from the storage medium to the computer per second. Higher numbers indicate faster transfer rates.

- Capacity. **Storage capacity** is the maximum amount of data that can be stored on a storage medium, measured in kilobytes (KB), megabytes (MB), gigabytes (GB), or terabytes (TB). The amount of data that a disk stores—its capacity—depends on its density. **Disk density** refers to the closeness of the data on the disk surface. The higher the disk density, the more data it can store. Higher capacity is almost always preferred. **Table B-1** compares the capacity of various storage devices and media.

- The system unit case for a desktop computer contains several storage device "parking spaces" called **drive bays**. A notebook computer generally has one drive bay. See **Figure B-6**. Bays come in two widths—5¼" and 3½". Internal drive bays are located inside the system unit and are designed for hard disk drives, which do not use removable storage media. Any drive that uses removable media or has to be controlled manually by pushing a button or inserting the media into a slot must use an external drive bay.

Figure B-6: Drive bays

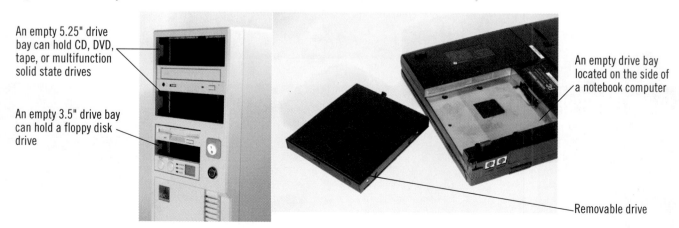

An empty 5.25" drive bay can hold CD, DVD, tape, or multifunction solid state drives

An empty 3.5" drive bay can hold a floppy disk drive

An empty drive bay located on the side of a notebook computer

Removable drive

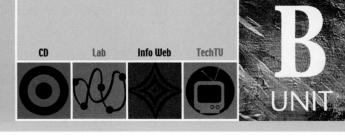
FYI

Tape storage access time is measured in seconds, not in milliseconds, which is one reason why tape is simply too slow to be practical as your computer's main storage device.

Table B-1: Capacities of commonly used storage

	STORAGE TECHNOLOGY	CAPACITY	COMMENTS
MAGNETIC	SuperDisk™	120 MB or 240 MB	Offers portability, simplicity, speed, and security; each requires its own proprietary drive; much slower access than a hard disk drive
	Zip disk™	100 MB, 250 MB, and 750 MB	Same as above
	Jaz™ disk	1 GB, 2 GB	Same as above
	Fixed hard disk	40–200 GB	High storage capacity, fast and convenient, economical storage-cost/megabyte, is susceptible to damage or theft of your computer
	External hard drive	160 GB (average)	Fast, but transfer rate depends on computer system; drive can be removed and locked in a secure location
	Removable hard disk	160 GB (average)	Fast, limited capacity, disks can be removed and locked in a secure location
	Miniature hard disk	20–80 GB	Used for portable music and video players, such as iPods
OPTICAL	CD	700 MB	Limited capacity, cannot be reused, long shelf life, CDs and DVDs can be removed and locked in a secure location
	CD-RW	700 MB	Limited capacity, reusable, long shelf life
	Writable DVD	4.7 GB	High capacity, long shelf life
	Double layer DVD	8.5 GB	Two recordable layers on the same side and can store a large amount of data
	HD-DVD	15 GB	High capacity, long shelf life
	Blu-ray DVD	25 GB	High capacity, used to record, rewrite, and play back HD video; can store large amounts of data; dual-layer versions available that store 50 GB
SOLID STATE	USB flash drive	32 MB–8 GB	Portable, durable, high capacity, used to transfer files
	Memory card	32 MB–4 GB	Portable, durable, high capacity, used to transfer digital camera images
TAPE	Tape	30 GB (average)	Good capacity, reasonable media cost, convenient backups can be run overnight but slow, they can take 15–20 minutes to back up 1 GB of data

Exploring hard disk technology

Hard disk technology is the preferred type of main storage for most computer systems. Hard disks provide more than enough storage capacity for most users and provide faster access to files than other storage technologies. Hard disks can be fixed or removable.

- The terms "hard disk" and "hard disk drive" are often used interchangeably. Hard disks can be internal or external. The term "fixed disk" is also used to refer to hard disks. Miniature hard drives refer to the drives used in mobile devices, such as the 1.8" drive featured on Apple's iPod digital music player.

- A **hard disk** is one or more platters and their associated read-write heads. A **hard disk platter** is a flat, rigid disk made of aluminum or glass and coated with magnetic iron oxide particles. Personal computer hard disk platters are typically 3½" in diameter.

- Hard disk drive speed is sometimes measured in **revolutions per minute (rpm)**. The faster a drive spins, the more rapidly it can position the read-write head over specific data. For example, a 7,200 rpm drive is able to access data faster than a 5,400 rpm drive.

- Hard disk platters are divided into tracks and sectors into which data is written. A vertical stack of tracks is called a **cylinder**, which is the basic storage bin for a hard disk drive. Data is stored at the same track and sector location on all platters in the cylinder before moving the read-write head to a new sector. **Figure B-7** provides more information on how a hard disk drive works.

Figure B-7: How a hard disk works

The drive spindle supports one or more hard disk platters; both sides of the platter are used for data storage; more platters mean more data storage capacity; hard disk platters rotate as a unit on the spindle to position read-write heads over specific data; the platters spin continuously, making thousands of rotations per minute

Each data storage surface has its own read-write head, which moves in and out from the center of the disk to locate data; the head hovers only a few microinches above the disk surface, so the magnetic field is much more compact than on a floppy disk; as a result, more data is packed into a smaller area on a hard disk platter

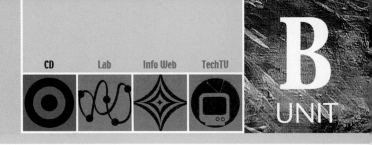

B UNIT

■ Computer ads typically specify the capacity, access time, and speed of a hard disk drive. So "160 GB 8 ms 7200 RPM HD" means a hard disk drive with 160 gigabyte capacity, access time of 8 milliseconds, and speed of 7,200 revolutions per minute.

■ A hard drive storage device includes a circuit board, called a **controller**, which positions the disk and read-write heads to locate data. Disk drives are classified according to the type of controller they use, such as Ultra ATA, EIDE, and SCSI.

■ The storage technology used on many PCs transfers data from a disk, through the controller, to the processor, and finally to RAM before it is actually processed. **DMA (direct memory access)** technology allows a computer to transfer data directly from a drive into RAM, without intervention from the processor. This architecture relieves the processor of data-transfer duties and frees up processing cycles for other tasks. **UDMA (ultra DMA)** is a faster version of DMA technology. DMA and Ultra ATA are companion technologies.

A common storage configuration for PCs pairs an Ultra ATA drive with UDMA data transfer.

■ Hard disks are not as durable as many other storage technologies. The read-write heads in a hard disk hover a microscopic distance above the disk surface. If a read-write head runs into a dust particle or some other contaminant on the disk, or if the hard disk is jarred while it is in use, it might cause a **head crash**. A head crash damages some of the data on the disk. To help prevent contaminants from contacting the platters and causing head crashes, a hard disk is sealed in its case.

Removable hard disks or hard disk cartridges can be inserted and removed from the drive. Removable hard disks increase the storage capacity of your computer system, although the data is available on only one disk at a time. Removable hard disks also provide security for data by allowing you to remove the hard disk cartridge and store it separately from the computer.

Understanding tape storage

Tape storage technology consists of a tape drive for the storage device and a tape for the storage medium. Tape drives are available in either internal or external models. An internal tape drive fits into a standard drive bay. An external model is a stand-alone device that you can connect to your computer with a cable.

Tape is a sequential, rather than a random access, storage medium. Data is arranged as a long sequence of bits that begins at one end of the tape and stretches to the other end. As a result, tape access is much slower than hard drive access. In fact, access times for a tape are measured in seconds rather than in milliseconds. A tape may contain hundreds, or in the case of a mainframe, thousands of feet of tape.

The most popular types of tape drives for personal computers use tape cartridges for the storage medium. A **tape cartridge** is a removable magnetic tape module similar to a cassette tape. **Figure B-8** shows several different kinds of tape used with personal computer tape drives.

Figure B-8

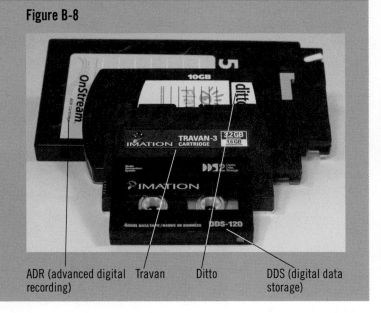

ADR (advanced digital recording)　Travan　　Ditto　　DDS (digital data storage)

Exploring CD/DVD technology

Optical storage media use one of three technologies: read-only (ROM), recordable, or rewritable. Both **CDs (compact discs)** and **DVDs ("digital video disc"** or **"digital versatile disc")** use optical storage technologies. The suffix associated with a CD or DVD helps you recognize the type of technology used to create the CD or DVD. CD-ROM specifies "read-only" technology, CD-R specifies "CD recordable" technology, and CD-RW specifies "CD rewritable" technology. DVDs have two types of recordable and two types of rewritable formats. The recordable formats are designated as DVD-R and DVD+R. The rewritable formats are designated as DVD-RW and DVD+RW. There are so many different formats because one standard has not emerged as the industry leader.

■ **CD drives** and **DVD drives** are storage devices that use optical storage technology to read data on computer or audio CDs or DVDs respectively. **Figure B-9** illustrates how a CD or DVD drive uses laser technology to read data. CD and DVD drives contain a spindle that rotates the disc over a laser lens. The laser directs a beam of light toward the underside of the disc. Dark "pits" and light "lands" on the disc surface reflect the light differently. As the drive reads the disc, these differences are translated into the 0s and 1s that represent data.

   Table B-2 summarizes types of drives as well as their capabilities. Storing computer data and creating music CDs requires a recordable or rewritable drive.

■ **Read-only (ROM) technology**. A computer CD-ROM or DVD disc contains data that was stamped on the disc surface when it was manufactured, such as commercial software, music, and movies.

■ Examples of CDs and DVDs using read-only optical technology follow. For all of these examples, data cannot be added, changed, or deleted from these discs.

   CD-DA (compact disc digital audio) is the format for commercial music CDs. Music is typically recorded on audio CDs by the manufacturer.

   DVD-Video (digital versatile disc video) is the format for commercial DVDs that contain feature-length films.

   CD-ROM (compact disc read-only memory) was the original format for storing computer data. Data is stamped on the disc at the time it is manufactured.

   DVD-ROM (digital versatile disc read-only memory) contains data stamped onto the disc surface at the time of manufacture.

Figure B-9: How a CD drive works

Laser lens directs a beam of light to the underside of the CD disc

Drive spindle spins the disc

Laser pickup assembly senses the reflectivity of pits and lands

Tracking mechanism positions a disc track over the laser lens

CD   Lab   Info Web   TechTU

Table B-2: CD and DVD drive capabilities

DRIVE	PLAYS AUDIO CDs	PLAYS DVD MOVIES	READS CD DATA	READS DVD DATA	CREATES MUSIC CDs	STORES DATA ON CDs	STORES DATA ON DVDs
CD-ROM drive	X		X				
CD-R drive	X		X		X	X	
CD-RW drive	X		X		X	X	
DVD/CD-RW drive	X	X	X	X	X	X	
DVD+R/+RW/CD-RW drive	X	X	X	X	X	X	X

■ **Recordable (R) technology** uses a laser to change the color in a dye layer sandwiched beneath the clear plastic disc surface. The laser creates dark spots in the dye that are read as pits. The change in the dye is permanent, so data cannot be changed once it has been recorded. Usually, you can record your data in multiple sessions, that is, you can add two files to your CD-R disc today and then add more files to the same disc tomorrow.

CD-R (compact disc recordable) discs store data using recordable technology.

DVD+R or **DVD-R (digital versatile disc recordable)** discs store data using recordable technology similar to a CD-R, but with DVD storage capacity.

■ **Rewritable (RW) technology** uses "phase change" technology to alter a crystal structure on the disc surface. Altering the crystal structure creates patterns of light and dark spots similar to the pits and lands on a CD. The crystal structure can be changed from light to dark and back again many times, making it possible to record and modify data much like on a magnetic storage disk.

CD-RW (compact disc rewritable) discs store data using rewritable technology. Stored data can be recorded and erased multiple times.

DVD+RW or **DVD-RW (digital versatile disc rewritable)** discs store data using rewritable technology similar to CD-RW, but with DVD storage capacity. **Figure B-10** shows how to place a CD or DVD in a drive.

Figure B-10: Inserting a disc

CD drive

DVD drive

What is Blu-ray?

Blu-ray DVDs are the latest trend in optical storage technology. Blu-ray technology is positioned to become the new DVD standard. The format was developed to enable recording, rewriting, and playback of HD video, as well as storing large amounts of computer data including photographs and audio files. A single-layer Blu-ray Disc can be used to record over 2 hours of HDTV or more than 13 hours of standard-definition TV. The dual-layer versions of the discs can hold 50 GB. Blu-ray gets its name from the shorter "blue" laser wavelength that allows it to store substantially more data than a DVD, which has the same physical dimensions but uses red laser technology.

Exploring solid state storage

Solid state storage is portable, provides fast access to data, and uses very little power. It is an ideal solution for storing data on mobile devices and transporting data from one device to another. Solid state storage is widely used in consumer devices such as digital cameras, MP3 music players, notebook computers, PDAs, and cell phones.

■ Solid state storage uses a technology that stores data in a non-volatile, erasable, low-power chip. The chip's circuitry is arranged as a grid, and each cell in the grid contains two transistors that act as gates. When the gates are open, current can flow and the cell has a value that represents a "1" bit. When the gates are closed, the cell has a value that represents a "0" bit. Very little power is required to open or close the gates, which makes solid state storage ideal for battery-operated devices, such as digital cameras. Once the data is stored, it is nonvolatile—the chip retains the data without the need for an external power source.

■ Some solid state storage requires a device called a **card reader** to transfer data to or from a computer; others plug directly into a computer's system unit. Consumers today can select from a variety of solid state storage media, as seen in **Figure B-11**.

■ A **USB flash drive** is a portable storage device featuring a built-in connector that plugs directly into a computer's USB port. A USB flash drive requires no card reader, making it easily transportable from one computer to another. Nicknamed "pen drives" or "key-chain drives," USB flash drives are about the size of a large paperclip and so durable that you can literally carry them on your key ring. When connected to your computer's USB port, you can open, edit, delete, and run files stored on a USB flash drive just as though those files were stored on your computer's hard disk.

■ **CompactFlash (CF) cards** are about the size of a matchbook and provide high storage capacities and access speeds. CompactFlash cards include a built-in controller that reads data from and writes data to the card. CompactFlash cards use a card reader to transfer data from the card to your computer; the built-in controller tells the card reader what to do. With their high storage capacities and access speeds, CompactFlash cards are ideal for use on high-end digital cameras that require megabytes of storage for each photo.

Figure B-11: Popular solid state storage options

USB flash drive:
32 MB–8 GB storage

CompactFlash card:
8 MB–8 GB storage

MultiMedia card:
32 MB–2 GB storage

SecureDigital card:
32 MB–4 GB storage

SmartMedia card:
32 MB–128 GB storage

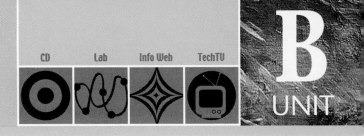
■ **MultiMedia cards (MMC)** offer solid state storage in a package about the size of a postage stamp. Initially used in mobile phones and pagers, use of MultiMedia cards has spread to digital cameras and MP3 players. Like CompactFlash cards, MultiMedia cards include a built-in controller, so MMC readers are electronically simple and very inexpensive.

■ **SecureDigital (SD) cards** are based on MultiMedia card technology, but they feature significantly faster data transfer rates and include cryptographic security protection for copyrighted data and music. SecureDigital cards are popular for digital images and MP3 storage. They use a card reader to copy data from the card to a computer.

■ **SmartMedia cards** were originally called "solid state floppy disk cards" because they look much like a miniature floppy disk. Unlike other popular solid state storage, SmartMedia cards do not include a built-in controller, which means that the SmartMedia card reader manages the read/write process. These cards are the least durable of the solid state storage media and should be handled with care.

■ Many solid state card readers have several slots for different types of solid state storage media. See **Figure B-12**.

Figure B-12: Solid state card reader

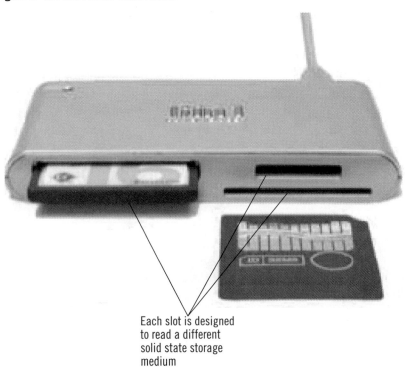

Each slot is designed
to read a different
solid state storage
medium

Why use solid state storage?

Solid state storage systems provide high-capacity, durability, and speed, which make them suitable for many storage needs. A solid state memory card in a digital camera can hold data for hundreds of snapshots. You can remove the card from the camera and insert it into a card reader that is connected to a computer. Once the card is connected to your computer, you can transfer the files to your hard drive so the photos can be edited using the computer's graphics software and transmitted via the computer's Internet connection. Or, moving data the other way, you can download MP3 music files and store them on a solid state memory card. Then, you can insert the card into a portable MP3 player so you can hear your favorite tunes while you are on the go. Solid state storage is also ideal for portable computing, that is, transporting data from one computer to another. For example, you can transfer data from your home computer to a solid state storage medium and then bring that storage medium to a computer in your school lab or your workplace. Whether you are using the solid state memory card with a camera, an MP3 player, or for some other portable computing needs, the data on the memory card can be erased so the card can be reused.

Examining input devices

Most computer systems include a keyboard and pointing device as the primary input devices for basic data input. Although you do not have to be a great typist to use a computer effectively, you should be familiar with the computer keyboard and its special keys. The most popular pointing devices for personal computers include mice, trackballs, pointing sticks, trackpads, and joysticks.

■ Most computers are equipped with a keyboard. You can even find keyboards on handheld devices—entering text and numbers is an important part of most computing tasks. A computer keyboard includes the basic **typing keypad** with keys or buttons with letters and numbers as well as several keys with characters and special words to control computer-specific tasks. You use the keys to input commands, respond to prompts, and type the text of documents. **Figure B-13** illustrates a variety of keyboards you might encounter on various computing devices. Virtually every computer user interface requires you to use a keyboard.

In addition to the basic typing keypad, desktop and notebook computer keyboards include a **navigation keypad** with keys such as the Home, End, and arrow keys, which you can use to efficiently move the screen-based insertion point or cursor. An **insertion point** or **cursor** indicates where the characters you type will appear. The insertion point appears on the screen as a flashing vertical bar. The cursor appears on the screen as a flashing underline. You can change the location of the insertion point or cursor using the arrow keys or the pointing device.

Function keys at the top of many keyboards are designed for computer-specific tasks. For example, [F1] often opens a Help window. Most desktop computer keyboards also include a calculator-style **numeric keypad**.

Modifier keys (the [Ctrl], [Alt], and [Shift] keys) are located at the periphery of the typing keypad. You can use the [Ctrl], [Alt], and [Shift] keys in conjunction with the other keys on the keyboard to expand the repertoire of available commands or to access menu options. Such combinations are called **keyboard shortcuts**.

Figure B-13: Computer keyboards

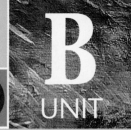

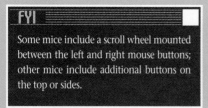

CD   Lab   Info Web   TechTU

■ A **pointing device** allows you to manipulate an on-screen pointer and other screen-based graphical controls. A standard desktop computer uses a mouse as its primary pointing device. It is possible to add a mouse to many notebook computers. A **mouse** includes one or more buttons that can be "clicked" to input commands. To track its position, a mouse uses one of two technologies: mechanical or optical. See **Figure B-14**. A mechanical mouse reads its position based on the movement of a ball that rolls over a mouse pad placed on a desk; an optical mouse uses an onboard chip to track a light beam as it bounces off a surface, such as a desk, clipboard, or mouse pad. Most computer owners prefer the performance of an optical mouse because it provides more precise tracking, greater durability, less maintenance, and more flexibility to use the mouse on a wide variety of surfaces without a mouse pad.

Pointing sticks, trackpads, and trackballs are typically used with notebook computers as an alternative to a mouse. See **Figure B-15**. A **pointing stick**, or **TrackPoint**, looks like the tip of an eraser embedded in the keyboard of a notebook computer. It is a space-saving device that you can push up, down, or sideways to move the on-screen pointer. A **touchpad**, also called a **trackpad,** is a touch-sensitive surface on which you can slide your fingers to move the on-screen pointer. A **trackball** looks like a mechanical mouse turned upside down. You use your fingers or palm to roll the ball and move the pointer.

■ A **joystick** looks like a small version of a car's stick shift. Moving the stick provides input to on-screen objects, such as a pointer or a character in a computer game. Joysticks can include several sticks and buttons for arcade-like control when playing computer games.

■ Additional input devices such as scanners, digital cameras, and graphics tablets are handy for working with graphical input. Microphones and electronic instruments provide input capabilities for sound and music.

Figure B-14: Mechanical and optical mice

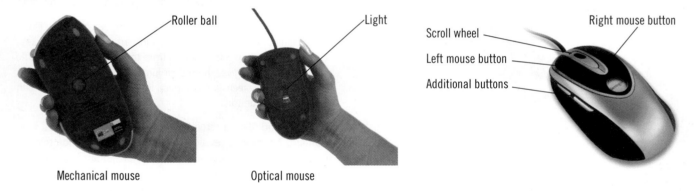

Roller ball   Light   Right mouse button

Scroll wheel

Left mouse button

Additional buttons

Mechanical mouse   Optical mouse

Figure B-15: Other pointing devices

Pointing stick   Trackpad   Trackball   Joystick

Comparing display devices

A computer display system is the main output device for a computer. Two key components of a computer display system are a graphics card and a display device, such as a monitor or screen.

- A **graphics card** (also called a "graphics board" or a "video card") contains circuitry that generates the signals for displaying an image on the screen. It also contains special video memory, which stores screen images as they are processed. The amount of video memory is the key to how fast a screen updates the information being displayed. Speed is an important factor for fast action games, 3-D modeling, and graphics-intensive desktop publishing. In addition to video memory, most graphics cards contain special graphics accelerator technology to further boost performance. Graphics circuitry can be built into a computer's motherboard or supplied as a small circuit board, like the one in **Figure B-16**, that plugs into the motherboard. Typically, the graphics card circuitry is built into the motherboard of a notebook computer.

Figure B-16: PC graphics card

- Display devices use one of three technologies: CRT, LCD, and plasma. See **Figure B-17**.

- For many years, CRT monitors were the only display devices available for desktop computers. **CRT (cathode ray tube)** technology uses gun-like mechanisms to direct beams of electrons toward the screen and activate individual dots of color that form an image—much like a color TV. A CRT's **refresh rate** (also referred to as "vertical scan rate") is the speed at which the screen is repainted. The faster the refresh rate, the less the screen flickers. Refresh rate is measured in cycles per second, or Hertz. CRT monitors offer an inexpensive and dependable computer display.

- **LCD (liquid crystal display)** technology produces an image by manipulating light within a layer of liquid crystal cells. LCDs are standard equipment on notebook computers. The advantages of an LCD monitor include display clarity, low radiation emission, portability, and compactness. Stand-alone LCDs, referred to as "LCD monitors" or "flat panel displays," are available for desktop computers as a replacement for CRT monitors. They are, however, more expensive than CRT monitors.

- **Plasma screen technology** creates an on-screen image by illuminating miniature colored fluorescent lights arrayed in a panel-like screen. The name "plasma" comes from the type of gas that fills fluorescent lights and gives them their luminescence. Like LCD screens, plasma screens are compact, lightweight, and more expensive than CRT monitors.

- CRT, LCD, and plasma screens can be equipped with NTSC (standard American television) or HDTV (high-definition television) circuitry so they can accept television signals from an antenna or cable. This technology lets you simultaneously view computer data and television on the same display device using split-screen or picture-in-picture format.

Figure B-17: Display device technology options

CRT

LCD

Gas Plasma

- The computer's graphics card sends an image to the monitor at a specific **resolution**, defined as the maximum number of horizontal and vertical pixels that are displayed on the screen. Standard resolutions include 800 x 600 and 1024 x 768. Higher resolutions are possible given enough memory on the graphics card and a monitor capable of displaying that resolution. At higher resolutions, the computer displays a larger work area with text and other objects appearing smaller. The two screen shots in **Figure B-18** help you compare a display at different resolutions.

- Image quality is determined by screen size, dot pitch, resolution, and color depth. **Screen size** is the measurement in inches from one corner of the screen diagonally across to the opposite corner. Typical monitor screen sizes range from 13" to 21". On most monitors, the viewable image does not stretch to the edge of the screen. Instead, a black border makes the viewing area smaller than the screen size. Many computer ads include a measurement of the **viewable image size (vis)**. For example, a 15" monitor might have a 13.9" vis.

- A monitor's **viewing angle width** indicates how far to the side you can still clearly see the screen image. A wide viewing angle indicates that you can view the screen from various positions without compromising image quality. CRT and plasma screens offer the widest viewing angles. Graphics artists tend to prefer CRT screens, which display uniform color from any angle.

- **Dot pitch (dp)** is a measure of image clarity. A smaller dot pitch means a crisper image. Technically, dot pitch is the distance in millimeters between like-colored pixels, the small dots of light that form an image. A dot pitch between .26 and .23 is typical for today's monitors.

- The number of colors that a monitor and graphics card can display is referred to as **color depth** or "**bit depth**." Most PCs have the capability to display millions of colors. When you set the resolution at 24-bit color depth (sometimes called "True Color"), your PC can display more than 16 million colors and produce what are considered photographic-quality images. Windows allows you to select resolution and color depth.

Figure B-18: Comparing screen resolutions

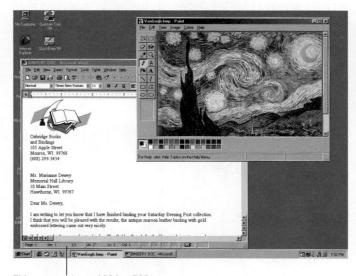

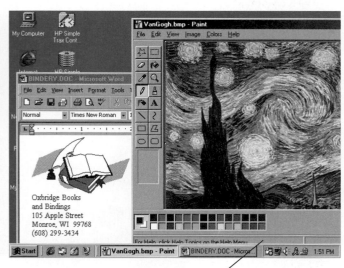

This screen shows 1024 × 768 resolution; notice the size of text and other screen-based objects

This screen shows 800 × 600 resolution; text and other objects appear larger on the low-resolution screen, but you see a smaller portion of the text and other objects

Comparing printers

Printers are one of the most popular output devices available for personal computers. Printers differ in resolution and speed, both of which affect the print quality and price. With rapidly advancing technology, it is important to understand the different types of printers and features and what the specifications mean. Today's best-selling printers typically use ink jet or laser technology. Printer technologies for specialized applications include dot matrix, solid ink, thermal transfer, and dye sublimation.

- Printer resolution—the density of the grid of dots that create an image—determines the quality or sharpness of printed images and text. Resolution is measured by the number of dots printed per linear inch, abbreviated as **dpi**. At normal reading distance, a resolution of about 900 dots per inch appears solid to the human eye, but a close examination of color sections will reveal a dot pattern. Good quality printers are rated from 2400 to 4800 dpi. More expensive high quality printers have resolutions of 9600 dpi.

- Printer speed is measured by the number of pages per minute (ppm) output. Color printouts typically take longer than black-and-white printouts. Pages that contain mostly text tend to print more rapidly than pages that contain graphics. Most printers for personal or small business use are rated from 15 to 30 ppm. Laser and thermal printers can rate over 40 ppm.

- **Duty cycle** determines how many pages a printer is able to churn out. Printer duty cycle is usually measured in pages per month. For example, on average, a personal laser printer has a duty cycle of about 3,000 pages per month—that means roughly 100 pages per day.

- Memory capacity is required to print color images and graphics-intensive documents. For example, a laser printer might have between 64 MB and 120 MB of memory.

- A computer sends data for output to the printer along with a set of instructions on how to print that data. **Printer Control Language (PCL)** is the most widely used language for communication between computers and printers, but **PostScript** is an alternative printer language that many publishing professionals prefer.

- A printer connects to your computer using one of the following connection options: USB port, serial port, parallel port, or network port.

- An **ink jet printer** has a nozzle-like print head that sprays ink onto paper to form characters and graphics. Ink jet printers use two cartridges: a black ink cartridge and a color cartridge that holds colored inks. Most ink jet printers are small, lightweight, and inexpensive, yet produce very good quality color output. See **Figure B-19**.

- **Photo printers** often use thermal dye technology to produce photographic quality images. These printers have slower output speeds that produce professional quality images on specialized papers.

Figure B-19: Ink jet printer

Most ink jet printers use **CMYK color**, which requires only cyan (blue), magenta (pink), yellow, and black inks to create a printout that appears to have thousands of colors

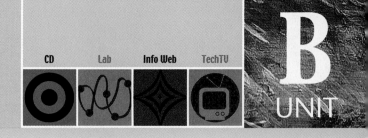
■ A **laser printer** (see **Figure B-20**) uses a technology that produces dots of light on a light-sensitive drum. Laser printers are a popular technology for situations that require high-volume output or good-quality printouts.

Figure B-20: Laser printer

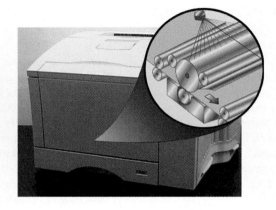

Electrostatically charged ink is applied to the drum, then transferred to paper

■ A **dot matrix printer** (see **Figure B-21**) produces characters and graphics by using a grid of fine wires. Dot matrix speeds are measured in characters per second (cps). These printers are slower than inkjet or laser printers. A fast dot matrix device can print at speeds up to 455 cps, or about five pages per minute. Unlike laser and ink-jet technologies, a dot matrix printer actually strikes the paper and, therefore, can print multipart carbon forms. Today, dot matrix printers are used primarily for "back-office" applications that demand low operating cost and dependability but not high print quality.

■ Other types of printer technologies include **solid ink** and **thermal wax transfer**. These are used mainly in business settings because the specialized purpose of these printers and the high per-page cost makes these printers too costly for the average consumer.

Figure B- 21: Dot matrix printer

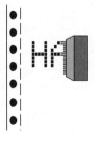

Dot matrix printers can print text and graphics; some even print in color using a multicolored ribbon; with a resolution of 140 dpi, a dot matrix printer produces low-quality output with clearly discernible dots forming letters and graphics

Print head contains a matrix of thin wires

As the print head moves across the paper, the wires strike the ribbon and paper in a pattern prescribed by your PC

Understanding expansion slots, cards, and ports

Within a computer, data travels from one component to another over circuits called a **data bus**. One part of the data bus runs between RAM and the processor; the other part runs between RAM and various peripheral devices. The segment of the data bus between RAM and peripheral devices is called the **expansion bus**. As data moves along the expansion bus, it may travel through expansion slots, cards, ports, and cables. This lesson takes a closer look at slots, cards, and ports; the next lesson looks at cables.

■ An **expansion slot** is a long, narrow socket on the motherboard into which you can plug an expansion card. The motherboard is the main circuit board in the computer that holds the components that control the processing functions. An **expansion card** is a small circuit board that provides a computer the ability to control a storage device, an input device, or an output device. Expansion cards are also called "expansion boards," "controller cards," or "adapters." To insert an expansion card, you slide it into an expansion slot, where it can be secured with a small screw. See **Figure B-22**.

Figure B-22: Inserting an expansion card

Most desktop computers have four to eight expansion slots, but some of the slots usually contain factory-installed expansion cards, such as the following: **graphics card** (sometimes called a "video card"), which provides a path for data traveling to the monitor; **modem card**, which provides a way to transmit data over phone lines or cable television lines; **sound card**, which carries data out to speakers and headphones, or back from a microphone; **network card**, which allows you to connect your computer to a local area network.

A desktop computer may have up to three types of expansion slots. Each expansion card is built for only one type of slot. ISA, PCI, and AGP slots are different lengths, so you can easily identify them by opening your computer's system unit and looking at the motherboard. **ISA (industry standard architecture)** slots are an old technology, used today only for some modems and other relatively slow devices. **PCI (peripheral component interconnect)** slots offer fast transfer speeds and typically house a graphics card, sound card, video capture card, modem, or network interface card. Newer versions of PCI include **PCI-X** and **PCI-Express**. **AGP (accelerated graphics port)** slots provide a high-speed data pathway that is primarily used for graphics cards.

■ Most notebook computers are equipped with an external slot called a **PCMCIA (personal computer memory card international association) slot**. Typically, a notebook computer has only one of these slots, but the slot can hold more than one PC card (also called "PCMCIA expansion cards"). **Figure B-23** shows a PC card in a notebook computer that has high-speed data and fax modem capabilities so users can connect to a variety of data-communications devices and services.

Figure B-23: PC card for a notebook computer

■ An **expansion port** is any connector that passes data in and out of a computer or peripheral device. See **Figure B-24**. Both personal computers and notebook computers have ports. Ports are sometimes called "jacks" or "connectors." An expansion port is often housed on an expansion card so that it is accessible through an opening in the back of the computer's system unit. Ports that have been added with expansion cards usually protrude through rectangular cutouts in the back of the case. The built-in ports on a computer usually include a mouse port, keyboard port, serial port, and USB port.

■ **USB (universal serial bus) ports** are probably the most popular ports for connecting peripheral devices. Most computers feature several USB ports, which provide connectivity for lots of USB devices. On many computer models, USB ports are conveniently located on the front of the system unit so that peripherals can be easily connected and disconnected. Many kinds of peripheral devices—including mice, scanners, printers, and joysticks—are available with USB connections. Several types of storage devices, such as USB Flash drives, also use USB connections. The Windows OS automatically recognizes most USB devices as soon as they are plugged into the USB port.

Figure B-24: Expansion ports on a typical desktop computer

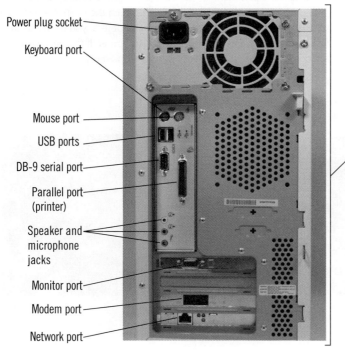

Power plug socket

Keyboard port

Mouse port

USB ports

DB-9 serial port

Parallel port (printer)

Speaker and microphone jacks

Monitor port

Modem port

Network port

Typical rear ports

Card readers

USB ports

Exploring peripheral devices

All computers use peripheral devices to input, output, and store data. **Peripheral devices** connect to a computer to enhance its functionality. Today, USB currently is the most popular technology for connecting peripheral devices. Installing high-end graphics and sound cards for a multimedia or serious gaming computer typically requires you to open the system unit.

■ Peripheral devices expand and modify your system. Although the keyboard, printer, monitor, storage devices, and mouse can be considered peripheral devices, most people do not consider them to be peripheral devices because they are necessary to perform basic computer functions. **Figure B-25** shows examples of several peripheral devices. A **computer projection device** is an output device that produces a large display of the information shown on the computer screen. A **scanner** is an input device that converts a page of text or images into a digital format. A **multifunction device** works both as an input and an output device to combine the functions of a printer, scanner, copier, fax, and answering machine. A **digital camera** is an

input device that records an image in digital format. A **graphics tablet** is an input device that accepts input from a pressure-sensitive stylus and converts strokes into images on the screen. A **Web cam** is an input device used to capture live video and transmit it over the Internet.

■ In order for a peripheral device to work, a connection must be made between it and the motherboard; often the connection is made using a cable. To install a peripheral device, you must match the peripheral device to a port on the computer. If the right type of port is not available, you might have to add an expansion card.

Figure B-25: Examples of peripheral devices

Computer projection device

Scanner

Multifunction device

Digital camera

Graphics tablet

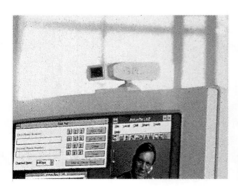
Web cam

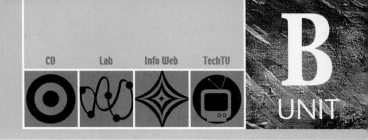
■ **Figure B-26** describes the cable connectors you might need in order to connect a peripheral device to your PC. If you need to purchase a cable, be sure the cable connectors match the ports on both the peripheral device and the computer.

Remember, when you install a peripheral device, you are basically creating a connection for data to flow between the device and the computer. The installation might simply require connecting a cable, or it might require installing an expansion card. If you own a desktop computer, you might have to open the system unit. Before doing so, make sure you unplug the computer and ground yourself—that means that you are releasing static electricity by using a special grounding wristband or by touching both hands to a metal object before opening the system unit.

■ PCs include a feature called **Plug and Play** (also known as **PnP**) that automatically takes care of technical details for installing just

about every popular peripheral device. Once the peripheral device is connected to the motherboard, PnP should recognize the new device. If not, you will probably have to install device driver software.

■ Each peripheral device requires software called a **device driver**, which sets up communication between your computer and the device. The directions supplied with your new peripheral device will include instructions on how to install the device driver if it does not happen automatically when you start the computer. Typically, you will use the device driver supplied on a CD once to get everything set up, then you can put the CD away. If you ever need to restore your computer or reinstall the device, you may need to install the driver again. If the peripheral device still does not work, check the manufacturer's Web site for a device driver update, or call the manufacturer's technical support department.

Figure B-26: PC cables and connectors

	CONNECTOR	DESCRIPTION	DEVICES
	Serial DB-9	Connects to serial port, which sends data over a single data line one bit at a time at speeds of 56 Kbps	Mouse or modem
	Parallel DB-25M	Connects to parallel port, which sends data simultaneously over 8 data lines at speeds of 12 Mbps	Printer, external CD drive, Zip drive, external hard disk drive, or tape backup device
	USB	Connects to universal serial bus (USB), which sends data over a single data line and can support up to 127 devices. USB-1 carries data at speeds up to 12 Mbps; USB-2, at 480 Mbps	Modem, keyboard, joystick, scanner, mouse, external hard disk drive, MP3 player
	SCSI C-50F	Connects to SCSI port, which sends data simultaneously over 8 or 16 data lines at speeds between 40 Mbps and 640 Mbps; supports up to 16 devices	Internal or external hard disk drive, scanner, CD drive, tape backup device
	IEEE 1394	Connects to the FireWire port, which sends data at 400 Mbps	Video camera, DVD player
	VGA HDB-15	Connects to the video port	Monitor

Tech Talk The Windows Registry

To many computer owners, the Windows Registry is simply a mysterious "black box" that is mentioned occasionally in articles about computer troubleshooting. It is certainly possible to use a computer without intimate knowledge of the Registry, but it is useful to understand that the Registry is the "glue" that binds together many of the most important components of a PC: the computer hardware, peripheral devices, application software, and system software. See **Figure B-27**. After reading this Tech Talk section, you should have a basic understanding of the Registry and its role in the operation of a computer system.

Figure B-27: Items tracked by the Windows Registry

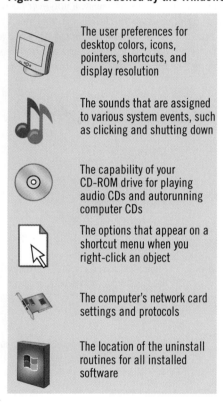

The user preferences for desktop colors, icons, pointers, shortcuts, and display resolution

The sounds that are assigned to various system events, such as clicking and shutting down

The capability of your CD-ROM drive for playing audio CDs and autorunning computer CDs

The options that appear on a shortcut menu when you right-click an object

The computer's network card settings and protocols

The location of the uninstall routines for all installed software

Why does a PC need the Registry? You know that you use application software to direct the operations that a computer carries out. For some operations, particularly those that involve hardware, the application software communicates with the operating system. The operating system might communicate with device drivers or, in some cases, it can communicate directly with a peripheral device.

To act as an intermediary between software and peripheral devices, your operating system needs information about these components: where they are located, what has been installed, how they are configured,

and how you want to use them. A special type of memory called **CMOS memory** holds the most essential data about your computer's processing and storage hardware, but the **Windows Registry** keeps track of your computer's peripheral devices and software so that the operating system can access the information it needs to coordinate the activities of the entire computer system. Some examples of specific data that the Registry tracks include your preferences for desktop colors, icons, pointers, shortcuts, and display resolution; the sounds that are assigned to various system events, such as clicking and shutting down; the capability of your CD-ROM drive for playing audio CDs and autorunning computer CDs; the options that appear on a shortcut menu when you right-click an object; your computer's network card settings and protocols; and the location of the uninstall routines for all installed hardware and software.

The contents of the Registry are stored in multiple files in the Windows/System folder of your computer's hard drive and are combined into a single database when Windows starts. Although each version of Windows uses a slightly different storage scheme, the basic organization and function of the Registry is similar in all versions.

Windows stores the entire contents of the Registry in two files: System.dat and User.dat. System.dat includes configuration data for all the hardware and software installed on a computer. User.dat contains user-specific information, sometimes called a "user profile," which includes software settings and desktop settings.

The Registry has a logical structure that appears as a hierarchy of folders, as shown in **Figure B-28**. There are six main folders in the Registry, and their names begin with HKEY. Each folder contains data that pertains to a particular part of a computer system.

Your actions update the Registry whenever you install or remove hardware or software. Device drivers and the Windows Plug and Play feature automatically update the Registry with essential information about the hardware's location and configuration. The setup program for your software provides similar update services for newly installed software.

You also make changes to the Windows Registry by using the dialog boxes for various configuration routines provided by the operating system and application software. For example, if you want to change the desktop colors for your user profile, you do so by selecting the Settings option from the Start menu, clicking Control Panel, and then selecting the Display option. Any changes that you make to the settings in the Display Properties dialog box (**Figure B-29**) will be recorded in the Windows Registry. The Windows Help System provides the following warning, "Registry editors are available that enable you to inspect and modify the registry. However, you should not need to do so. Instead, allow Windows programs to modify the system registry as needed. It is strongly recommended that you do not edit registry settings yourself."

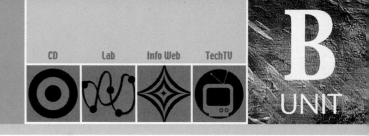
Figure B-28: The Windows Registry is organized as a hierarchy of folders and files

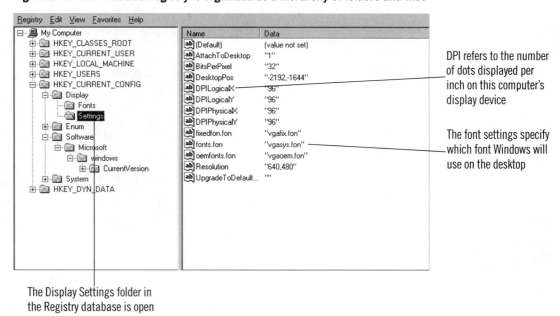

DPI refers to the number of dots displayed per inch on this computer's display device

The font settings specify which font Windows will use on the desktop

The Display Settings folder in the Registry database is open

Figure B-29: The Display Properties dialog box

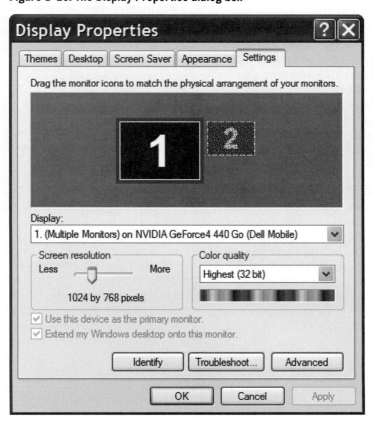

Changes that you make when using the Display Properties dialog box automatically update the corresponding entries in the HKEY_CURRENT_CONFIG folder of the Registry

Computers in Context The Military

The military, an early pioneer in computer and communications technologies (see **Figure B-30**), continues to be the driving force behind technologies that have revolutionized everyday life. During World War II, the U.S. military initiated a classified research program, called Project PX, to develop an electronic device to calculate artillery firing tables; each table required weeks of grueling manual calculations. Project PX produced ENIAC (Electrical Numerical Integrator And Calculator), one of the first general-purpose electronic computers. When ENIAC was completed in 1946, the war was over, but ENIAC's versatile architecture could be used for other calculations, such as designing hydrogen bombs, predicting weather, and engineering wind tunnels. ENIAC's technology evolved into the computers used today.

> Computers and communications technology have become an integral part of high-tech military operations.

After Project PX, the military continued to support computer research. Like most large corporations, the military used mainframe computers to maintain personnel, inventory, supply, and facilities records, and then distribute this data to terminals at other locations via rudimentary networks. Because all data communication flowed through the mainframe, a single point of failure for the entire system was a possible risk. A malfunction or an enemy "hit" could disrupt command and control, sending the military into chaos. To eliminate this risk, the armed forces created the Advanced Research Projects Agency (ARPA) to design a distributed communications system that could continue operating without a centralized computer. The result was ARPANET, which paved the way for the data communications system we know today as the Internet. ARPANET was activated in 1967, but the .mil domain that designates U.S. military Web sites was not implemented until 1984. Today, computers and communications technology have become an integral part of high-tech military operations.

The U.S. Department of Defense (DoD) currently maintains two data communications networks: SIPRNet, which is a classified (secret-level) network and NIPRNet, which provides unclassified services. The DoD's public Web site, called DefenseLINK, provides official information about defense policies, organizations, budgets, and operations. "The mission of DefenseLINK is to support the overall mission of the Department of Defense by providing official, timely and accurate information about defense policies, organizations, functions and operations. Also, DefenseLINK is the single, unified starting point for finding military information on-line." *source: http://www.defenselink.mil/admin/about.html*

Figure B-30

U.S. Apache helicopters, for example, are equipped with computer-based Target Acquisition Designation Sights, laser range finder/designators, and Pilot Night Vision Sensors. These arcade-style controls are also used by tank drivers in the U.S. Army's 4th Infantry Division. Each vehicle in this "Digitized Division" is equipped with a Force 21 Battle Command Brigade and Below/Blue Force Tracking system, a satellite-based situational awareness system, which works like a battlefield Internet to transmit data about the location of friendly and enemy forces from one vehicle to another using wireless communication.

The Force 21 touch screen shows friendly troops in blue, and a global positioning satellite (GPS) system updates their positions automatically. Enemy troops spotted by helicopters are shown as red icons. To get information on any friendly or enemy vehicle, a soldier can simply touch one of the blue or red icons. To send text messages—much like cell phone and computer instant messaging—a soldier touches the Message button.

The built-in GPS system provides location and route information. Force 21 computers are installed in shock-resistant cases and equipped with a cooling system that eliminates the need for a fan, which might pull in dust, dirt, or water. The computers run Sun Microsystem's Solaris operating system because it is less vulnerable to viruses and intrusion attacks than Microsoft Windows. To prevent enemy capture and use, Force 21 computers have a self-destruct mechanism that can be triggered remotely.

In addition to pilots and tank drivers, battlefield soldiers will soon be equipped with "wearable" computer and communications equipment. The $2 billion Land Warrior program will provide high-tech weaponry, such as the Integrated Helmet Assembly Subsystem (IHAS) for soldiers.

IHAS is a helmet-mounted device that displays graphical data, digital maps, thermal images, intelligence information, and troop locations. It also includes a weapon-mounted video camera so that soldiers can view and fire around corners and acquire targets in darkness (see **Figure B-31**).

The military has also conducted research in computer simulations that are similar to civilian computer games. "Live" military training is dangerous and equipment costs millions of dollars. With computer simulations, however, troops can train in a true-to-life environment without physical harm or equipment damage. Flying an F-16 fighter, for example, costs about $5,000 an hour, but flying an F-16 simulator costs only $500 per hour. The military uses simulators to teach Air Force pilots to fly fighter jets, Navy submarine officers to navigate in harbors, and Marine infantry squads to handle urban combat.

Military trainers agree that widespread use of computer games helps prepare troops to adapt quickly to real situations. A 24-year-old preflight student at Pensacola Naval Air Station modified the Microsoft Flight Simulator game to re-create a T-34C Turbo Mentor plane's controls. After logging 50 hours on the simulator, the student performed so well on a real plane that the Navy used his simulation to train other pilots. Today, a growing cadre of computer and communications specialists is needed to create and maintain increasingly complex military systems.

Figure B-31

An army once depended on its infantry, but today's high-tech army depends equally on its database designers, computer programmers, and network specialists. Even previously low-tech military jobs, such as mechanics and dietitians, require some computer expertise. New recruits are finding military computer systems easy to learn, based on their knowledge of civilian technologies such as the Internet and computer games.

Although most citizens agree that an adequate national defense is necessary, the cost of defense-related equipment, personnel, and research remains controversial. In 1961, President Dwight Eisenhower warned "We must guard against the acquisition of unwarranted influence, whether sought or unsought, by the military-industrial complex." Many socially motivated citizens and pacifists protested diverting tax dollars from social and economic programs to the military-industrial complex that Eisenhower cautioned against. In retrospect, however, military funding contributed to many technologies we depend on today. For example, detractors tried to convince the government that Project PX was doomed to failure, but ENIAC research contributed significantly to computers as we know them today. Skeptics saw no future for the fruits of ARPANET research, but it led to the Internet, which has changed our lives significantly.

Issue Why Recycle Computers?

Keeping up with technology means replacing your computer every few years, but what should you do with your old, outdated computer? According to the National Safety Council, an estimated 300 million computers will be obsolete by the year 2007. A recycling company called Back Thru the Future Micro Computer, Inc., estimates that 63 million computers will be retired in 2005 alone, compared with 20 million that became obsolete in 1998. Back Thru the Future Micro Computer, Inc., estimates that printer ink cartridges are discarded at the rate of almost eight cartridges every second in the United States alone. A recycling company called GreenDisk estimates that about 1 billion floppy disks, CDs, and DVDs end up in landfills every year.

U.S. landfills already hold more than 2 million tons of computer parts, which contain toxic substances such as lead, phosphorus, and mercury. A computer monitor can contain up to six pounds of lead. See **Figure B-32**.

"In this world of rapidly changing technology, disposal of computers and other electronic equipment has created a new and growing waste stream."

Environmental Protection Agency (EPA) report.

Many computers end up in landfills because their owners were unaware of potential environmental hazards and simply tossed them in the garbage. In addition, PC owners typically are not provided with information concerning the options for disposing of their old machines. Instead of throwing away your old computer, you might be able to sell it; donate it to a local school, church, or community program; have it hauled away by a professional recycling firm; or send it back to the manufacturer.

Figure B-32

With the growing popularity of Internet auctions and dedicated computer reclamation sites, you might be able to get some cash for your old computer. At Web sites, such as the Computer Recycle Center (www.recycles.com), you can post an ad for your "old stuff." On the Web, you can find several businesses, such as Computer Renaissance, that refurbish old computers and sell them in retail stores.

Donating your old computer to a local organization does not actually eliminate the disposal problem, but it does delay it. Unfortunately, finding a new home for an old computer is not always easy. Most schools and community organizations have few resources for repairing broken equipment, so if your old computer is not in good working order, it could be more of a burden than a gift. In addition, your computer might be too old to be compatible with the other computers that are used in an organization. It helps if you can donate software along with your old computer. To provide a legal transfer, include the software distribution disks, manuals, and license agreement. And remember, once you donate the software, you cannot legally use it on your new computer unless it is freeware or shareware. If you cannot find an organization to accept your computer donation, look in your local Yellow Pages or on the Internet for an electronics recycling firm that will haul away your computer and recycle any usable materials.

In recent years, about half the states in the U.S. have taken some legislative action to curtail the rampant disposal of obsolete computer equipment. A few years ago, Californians were faced with the prospect of tax hikes to deal with alarming increases in electronic waste, but activists questioned if tax increases were fair to individual taxpayers who generate very little electronic waste. Now, consumers buying computers in California have to pay a recycling fee at the time of purchase. Other lawmakers propose to make manufacturers responsible for recycling costs and logistics. "Extended producer responsibility" refers to the idea of holding manufacturers responsible for the environmental effects of their products through the entire product life cycle, which includes taking them back, recycling them, or disposing of them. Some manufacturers currently participate in voluntary producer responsibility programs. IBM recently implemented its PC Recycling Service program, which allows you to ship any make of computer, including system units, monitors, printers, and optional attachments, to a recycling center for a nominal fee. Consumers who buy toner cartridges for laser printers, such as from Hewlett-Packard, are provided with a postage-paid shipping box so they can return the cartridges for recycling. These programs and others are important steps in the effort to keep our planet green.

As stated in an Environmental Protection Agency (EPA) report, "In this world of rapidly changing technology, disposal of computers and other electronic equipment has created a new and growing waste stream." Proposed legislation in the European Union, Great Britain, Australia, China, and Japan are also addressing ways to manage the electronic waste stream and keep our planet green. The economics of a mandatory take-back program are likely to increase product costs because manufacturers would typically pass on recycling costs to consumers. Basic to the issue is the question of "Who pays?" Should it be the taxpayer, the individual, or the computer manufacturer?

B UNIT

Interactive Questions

☐ Yes   ☐ No   ☐ Not sure   **1.** Have you ever thrown away an old computer or other electronic device?

☐ Yes   ☐ No   ☐ Not sure   **2.** Are you aware of any options for recycling electronic equipment in your local area?

☐ Yes   ☐ No   ☐ Not sure   **3.** Would it be fair for consumers to pay a recycling tax on any electronic equipment that they purchase?

Expand the Ideas

1. Have you ever thrown away an old computer or other electronic device? If so, how did you dispose of it? Did you donate it, pass it along, or just throw it in the garbage? Write a short essay explaining what your options were at the time, any thoughts about recycling or donating you might have had, and exactly how you got rid of the old computer.

2. Research options for recycling electronic equipment in your local area. Create a chart showing ways to get rid of an old computer, include the positive and negative aspects of each option. Include specific details for recycling or donating the computers, such as names or addresses.

3. Would it be fair for consumers to pay a recycling tax on any electronic equipment that they purchase? Research the current trends. Include any important legislation or pending legislation in your area or around the world that you feel is relevant. Compile your findings in a short report. Include your opinion in the conclusion.

End of Unit Exercises

Key Terms

Access time	DVD	Mouse	Screen size
AGP	DVD drive	Multifunction device	SecureDigital (SD) card
Bit depth	DVD+R	MultiMedia card (MMC)	Sequential access
Card reader	DVD-R	Navigation keypad	SmartMedia card
CD	DVD-ROM	Network card	Solid ink printer
CD-DA	DVD+RW	Numeric keypad	Solid state storage
CD drive	DVD-RW	Optical storage	Sound card
CD-R	DVD-Video	PCI	Storage capacity
CD-ROM	Expansion bus	PCI-Express	Storage device
CD-RW	Expansion card	PCI-X	Storage medium
CMOS memory	Expansion port	PCMCIA slot	Storage technology
CMYK color	Expansion slot	Peripheral device	Tape
Color depth	Function key	Photo printer	Tape cartridge
CompactFlash (CF) card	Graphics card	Pits	Thermal wax transfer printer
Computer projection device	Graphics tablet	Plasma screen technology	Touchpad
Controller	Hard disk	Plug and Play (PnP)	Trackball
CRT	Hard disk platter	Pointing device	Trackpad
Cursor	Head crash	Pointing stick	TrackPoint
Cylinder	Ink jet printer	PostScript	Typing keypad
Data bus	Insertion point	Printer control language (PCL)	UDMA
Data transfer rate	ISA	RAM	USB flash drive
Device driver	Joystick	Random access	USB port
Digital camera	Keyboard shortcut	Read-write head	Viewable image size (vis)
Disk density	Lands	Recordable technology	Viewing angle width
DMA	Laser printer	Refresh rate	Volatile
Dot matrix printer	LCD	Resolution	Web cam
Dot pitch	Magnetic storage	Revolutions per minute (rpm)	Windows Registry
Dpi	Millisecond	Rewritable technology	
Drive bay	Modem card	ROM technology	
Duty cycle	Modifier key	Scanner	

Unit Review

1. Make sure that you can use your own words to define the bold terms that appear throughout the unit.

2. Describe the advantages and disadvantages of magnetic storage, optical storage, and solid state storage.

3. Create a grid with each type of storage device written across the top. Make a list of the corresponding media down the left side of the grid. Working down each column, place an X in the cells for each of the media that can be read by the device listed at the top of the column.

4. Summarize important uses for each type of storage technology.

5. Summarize the different technologies available for display devices. Be sure to include advantages and disadvantages.

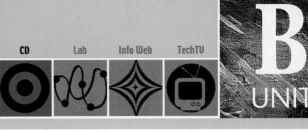

6. Create a table to summarize what you know about the different printer technologies that were discussed in this unit.

7. List any peripheral devices that are attached to your computer. Describe what each one does. Be sure to identify each one as input, output, or storage. Identify how it is connected to your system unit.

8. If possible, identify USB ports on your computer and list any devices you have connected through USB ports. Are the ports on the front or back of the system unit? Explain how you were able to use those devices.

9. Look at the front of your computer and identify the devices that are in the drive bays. List each device and explain what it does.

10. Count the number of cables coming out of the back of your computer. Using Figure B-26, identify each type of cable and what it connects.

Fill in the Best Answer

1. Data on an optical storage medium is stored as _____ and lands.

2. _access time_ time is the average time that it takes a computer to locate data on a storage medium and read it.

3. A computer can move directly to any file on a(n) _____ access device, but must start at the beginning and read through all of the data on a(n) _____ access device.

4. Higher disk _controller_ provides increased storage capacity.

5. Printer _____ Language is the most widely used language for communication between computers and printers.

6. Ultra ATA refers to a type of _____ used by a hard disk drive.

7. Printer output is measured by _page_ _per_ _min_ (ppm).

8. A variety of compact storage cards, pens, and sticks can be classified as _Solid State_ storage, which stores data in a nonvolatile, erasable, low-power chip.

9. The _expansion_ bus carries data from RAM to peripheral devices.

10. AGP and PCI are types of expansion _____, which are part of a personal computer's motherboard.

11. Many peripheral devices come packaged with device _____ software.

12. Color printouts typically take _longer_ to print than black-and-white printouts.

13. Most people set their monitors to a(n) _resolution_ of 800 x 600 or 1024 x 768.

14. The number of colors that a monitor can display is referred to as bit _depth_ .

15. The advantages of an LCD _monitor_ include display clarity, low radiation emission, and portability.

16. The most popular printers for personal computers are _ink jet_ , which are inexpensive and produce good-quality color printouts.

17. Today's PCs include a feature called Plug and _play_ that automatically takes care of technical details for installing peripheral devices.

18. A _modifier_ key, such as the [Ctrl] key, is used in conjunction with other keys to expand the functionality of each key.

19. TrackPoints and touchpads are alternative _input_ devices often found on notebook computers.

20. A read-write _head._ is a mechanism in the disk drive that reads and writes the magnetized particles that represent data.

Practice Tests

When you use the Interactive CD, you can take Practice Tests that consist of 10 multiple-choice, true/false, and fill-in-the blank questions. The questions are selected at random from a large test bank, so each time you take a test, you will receive a different set of questions. Your tests are scored immediately, and you can print study guides to determine which questions you answered incorrectly. If you are using a Tracking Disk, save your test scores.

End of Unit Exercises

INDEPENDENT CHALLENGE 1

You know that you are really a tech wizard when you can decipher every term and acronym in a computer ad. But even the most knowledgeable computer gurus sometimes need a dictionary for new terms.

1. For this independent challenge, photocopy a full page from a current computer magazine that contains an ad for a computer system. On the copy of the ad, use a colored pen to circle each descriptive term and acronym.

2. On a separate sheet of paper, or using a word processor, list all of the terms that you circled and write a definition for each term. If you encounter a term that was not defined in the unit, use a computer dictionary, such as the Webopedia Web site (www.webopedia.com) or the Internet Encyclopedia Wikipedia Web site (http://en.wikipedia.org/wiki), to locate the correct definition.

3. Prepare your list to submit to your instructor. Add a summary paragraph indicating why you would or would not purchase the computer in the ad and list any additional information that you need before making a decision.

INDEPENDENT CHALLENGE 2

Storage technology has a fascinating history. Mankind has developed many ways to retain and store data. From the ancient days when Egyptians were writing on papyrus to modern day holographic technologies, societies have found ways to retain more and more information in permanent and safe ways.

1. To complete this independent challenge, you will research the history of storage technologies and create a timeline that shows the developments. Be sure to include such items as 78-rpm records and 8-track tapes. Your research should yield some interesting technologies and systems.

2. For each technology, list the media, the device used to retrieve the information, two significant facts about the technology, the era in which it was used or popular, and what lead to its demise or obsolescence, or why it is still popular.

3. You can create the timeline using images or just words. This is a creative project. Your best research, artistic, and communication skills come together to create this timeline.

INDEPENDENT CHALLENGE 3

It is important that you are familiar with the type of computer you use daily. You may need to consult your technical resource person to help you complete this independent challenge.

1. Identify the components on your computer. What type of computer are you using? What kind of system unit do you have?

2. What peripheral devices are attached to your computer? List the name, manufacturer, and model number of each device, if available. How are these devices attached or connected to your system unit?

3. Draw a sketch of your computer. Label each component and identify what it does.

INDEPENDENT CHALLENGE 4

 The Issue section of this unit focused on the potential for discarded computers and other electronic devices to become a significant environmental problem. For this independent challenge, you will write a short paper about recycling computers based on information that you gather from the Internet.

1. To begin this independent challenge, consult the Internet and use your favorite search engine to search for and find Web pages to get an in-depth overview of the issue.

2. Determine the specific aspect of the issue that you will present in your paper. You might, for example, decide to focus on the toxic materials contained in computers that end up in landfills. Or you might tackle the barriers that discourage the shipment of old computers across national borders. Whatever aspect of the issue you decide to present, make sure that you can back up your discussion with facts and references to authoritative articles and Web pages.

3. You can place citations to these pages (include the author's name, article title, date of publication, and URL) at the end of your paper as endnotes, on each page as footnotes, or in parentheses following with the appropriate paragraphs. Follow your professor's instructions for submitting your paper via e-mail or as a printed document.

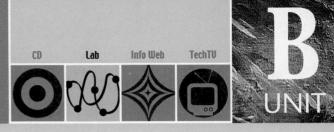
LAB: Operating a Personal Computer

1. Start the interactive part of the lab. Insert your Tracking Disk if you want to save your QuickCheck results. Perform each of the lab steps as directed and answer all of the lab QuickCheck questions. When you exit the lab, your answers are automatically graded and your results are displayed.

2. Make a note of the brand and location of the computer that you are using to complete these lab assignments.

3. Use the Start button to access your computer's Control Panel folder. Describe the status of your computer's power saver settings.

4. Preview the screen savers that are available on the computer that you use most frequently. Select the screen saver that you like the best and describe it in a few sentences.

5. What is the purpose of an Fn key? Does your computer keyboard include an Fn key? Explain why or why not.

6. In your own words, describe what happens when you (a) click the Close button, (b) hold down the Ctrl, Alt, and Del keys, (c) press the reset button, and (d) select the Shut Down option.

Student Edition Labs

Student Edition Labs

Reinforce the concepts you have learned in this unit through the **Using Input Devices**, **Peripheral Devices**, and **Maintaining a Hard Drive** Student Edition Labs, available online at the Illustrated Computer Concepts Web site.

Sam Labs

If you have a SAM user profile, you have access to additional content, features, and functionality. Log in to your SAM account and go to your assignments page to see what your instructor has assigned for this unit.

End of Unit Exercises

Visual Workshop

If you thought a holograph was just the image of Princess Leia saying "Obi-Wan Kenobi, you are my only hope," think again. Holographic storage devices are in development as a means to respond to the growing need for large-volume data storage. Holographic technologies promise data retrieval speeds far exceeding magnetic, optical, or solid state storage, and capacities far beyond anything currently available. According to a Web page from InPhase Technologies, a company specializing in holographic technologies, "Holographic storage is an optical technology that allows 1 million bits of data to be written and read out in single flashes of light. Thousands of holograms can be stored in the same location throughout the entire depth of the medium." Researchers are working to make this technology an affordable reality. **Figure B-33** shows the InPhase Technologies Web site.

Figure B-33

1. Use your favorite search engine to find and read two articles about advances in holographic storage. Write a brief summary of each article and, based on what you read, explain the basics of how holographic memory works. Be sure to cite your sources.

2. Research the current trends in holographic development. Are there any existing applications? How far has the technology come? What companies are working to develop these technologies? How far are we from using holocubes for data storage?

3. Write a scenario that includes the requirements and applications for holographic storage. Consider how game developers might stand to gain from this technology. Under what circumstances do you think such technologies would be useful, and what types of data do you think would best take advantage of this new technology?

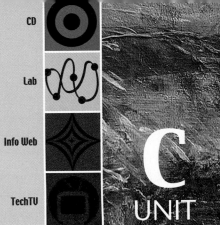

Computer Software

Overview

A computer can be a drafting station, typesetting machine, flight simulator, music remixing machine, filing system, video editing system, or simply a calculator—all because of software. Software is a set of instructions that tell a computer how to perform a specific task. You will learn the fundamental process that drives how computers interpret software. You will learn about a computer's most important system software, its operating system. You will get an overview of software applications, including office productivity software. You will learn about the types of software available for creating and editing graphics, video, and music. You will also read about the software used for education and reference, entertainment, and business. Finally, the unit wraps up with important practical information on software copyrights and licenses. The Tech Talk reviews how to install software using distribution media and downloaded software. You will also have an opportunity to look at computers in the context of journalism. The Issue discusses software piracy.

Introducing computer software

Software consists of computer programs, support programs, and data files that work together to provide a computer with the instructions and data necessary for carrying out a specific type of task, such as document production or Web browsing. In common practice, the term "software" is used to describe a commercial product that can be distributed on storage media, such as CDs and DVDs, or made available as a download via the Internet. You will learn about the components of computer software and how they work together to help you complete tasks.

■ Software is categorized as either application software or system software. **Application software** helps you carry out tasks such as creating documents, crunching numbers, and editing photographs by using a computer. **System software**—your computer's operating system, device drivers, and utilities—helps your computer carry out its basic operating functions. **Figure C-1** shows some software types in each category.

■ Software typically includes files that contain computer programs. A **computer program**, or "program," is a set of self-contained instructions that tell a computer how to solve a problem or carry out a task. A key characteristic of a computer program is that it can be started or "run" by a computer user.

■ At least one of the files included in a software package contains an executable program designed to be launched, or started, by users. On PCs, these programs are stored in files that typically have .exe filename extensions and are sometimes referred to as **executable files**. When using a Windows PC, you can start an executable file by

clicking its icon, selecting it from the Start menu, or entering its name in the Run dialog box.

■ Other files supplied with a software package contain programs that are not designed to be run by users. These **support programs** contain instructions for the computer to use with the main executable file. A support program is "called," or activated, by the main program as needed. For example, the word processing program calls on support programs to run the spelling checker when you use the spelling checker in a word processing program. Windows software support programs often have filename extensions, such as .dll and .ocx.

■ A **program data file** contains any data that is necessary for a task, but that is not supplied by the user. For example, when a word processing program checks spelling by comparing the words in a document with the words in a dictionary file, the dictionary file is a program data file that is supplied by the software, not by the user. Program data files supplied with a software package have filename extensions such as .txt, .bmp, and .hlp.

Figure C-1: Software categories

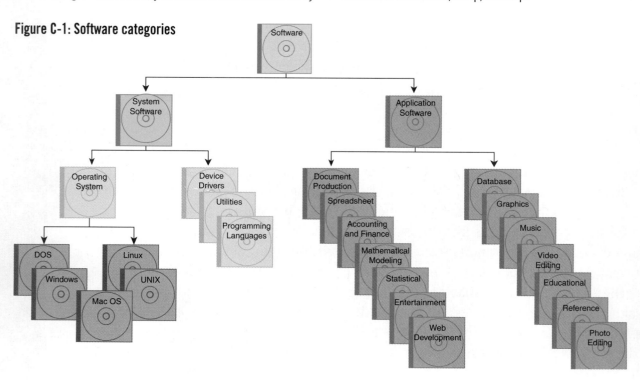

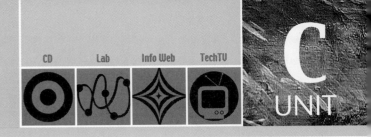

■ A software program usually consists of an executable file plus several support programs and program data files. See **Figure C-2**. Support programs and program data files can usually be modified without changing the main executable file, which offers a great deal of flexibility and efficiency for software developers. This modular approach can significantly reduce the time required to create and test the main executable file, which usually contains a long and fairly complex program. The modular approach also allows software developers to reuse their support programs and adapt preprogrammed support programs for use in their software.

■ Most software is designed to provide a task-related environment, which includes a screen display, a means of collecting commands and data from the user, the specifications for processing data, and a method for displaying or outputting data. **Figure C-3** is a simple computer program that converts a Fahrenheit temperature to Celsius and displays the result.

Figure C-2: Installed files for a software program

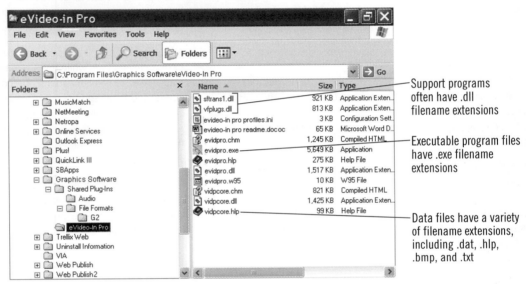

Figure C-3: A simple computer program

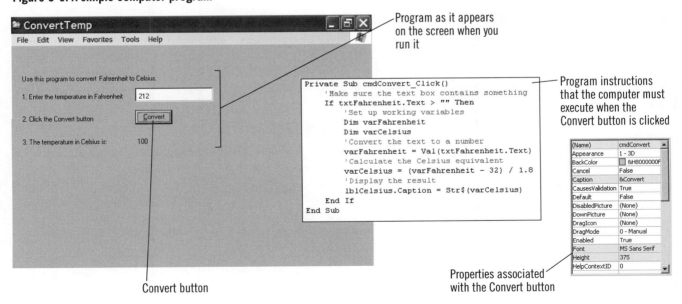

Convert button

Explaining how computers interpret software

Computer programmers write the instructions for the main programs and support programs that become the components of a computer software product. The finished software product is then distributed by the programmers themselves or by software publishers, which are companies that specialize in packaging, marketing, and selling commercial software. Most businesses, organizations, and individuals purchase commercial software to avoid the time and expense of writing their own. Learning how programmers write the instructions and how a processor translates these instructions will help you understand how software works.

■ A **programming** or **computer language** provides the tools that a programmer uses to create software. These languages help the programmer produce a lengthy list of instructions called **source code**. Most programmers today prefer to use **high-level languages**, such as C++, Java, COBOL, and Visual Basic, which have some similarities to human languages and produce programs that are fairly easy to test and modify.

■ A processor interprets the programmer's instructions, but the processor can only understand **machine language**—the instruction set that is "hard wired" within the processor's circuits. Instructions written in a high-level language must be translated into machine language before a computer can use them.

■ Translating instructions from a high-level language into machine language can be accomplished by two special types of programs: compilers and interpreters. **Figure C-4** gives you an idea of what happens to high-level language instructions when they are converted into machine language instructions. A simple instruction to add two numbers becomes a long series of 0s and 1s in machine language.

■ A **compiler** converts high-level instructions into a compiled program, which is a new file containing machine language instructions. A compiler translates all of the instructions in a program as a single batch, and the resulting machine language instructions, called **object code**, are placed in a new file.

■ As an alternative to a compiler, an **interpreter** converts one instruction at a time while the program is running. An interpreter reads the first instruction in a script, converts it into machine language, and then sends it to the processor. The interpreter continues in this way to convert instructions until all instructions are interpreted. See **Figure C-5**. An interpreted program runs more slowly than a compiled program because the translation process happens while the program is running.

Figure C-6 illustrates how a video editing program works when installed on a computer that is running Windows. The files included in this software package interact with the hardware when you select commands to edit videos.

Figure C-4: Converting a high-level language instruction to a machine language instruction

High-level Language Instruction	Machine Language Equivalent	Description of Machine Language Instructions
Answer = FirstNumber + SecondNumber	10001000 00011000 010000000	Load FirstNumber into Register 1
	10001000 00010000 00100000	Load SecondNumber into Register 2
	00000000 00011000 00010000	Perform ADD operation
	10100010 00111000	Move the number from the accumulator to the RAM location called Answer

Figure C-5: What an interpreter does

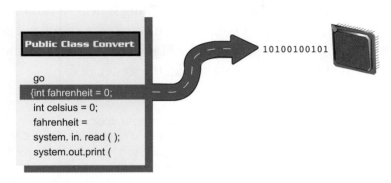

The interpreter converts instructions one instruction at a time

Public Class Convert

```
    go
   {int fahrenheit = 0;
    int celsius = 0;
    fahrenheit =
    system. in. read ( );
    system.out.print (
```

10100100101

Figure C-6: How software works

1. When you start the eVideo-In Pro software, the instructions in the file eVidpro.exe are loaded from disk into RAM and then sent to the processor

2. eVidpro.exe is a compiled program, so its instructions are immediately executed by the processor

3. As processing begins, the eVideo-In Pro window opens and the graphical controls for video editing tasks appear; the program waits for you to select a control by clicking it with the mouse

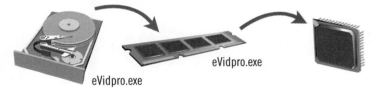

eVidpro.exe

eVidpro.exe

4. Based on your selection, eVidpro.exe follows its instructions and performs the actions you specify; many of the instructions for these actions are included in the main executable file; if not, eVidpro.exe calls a support program, such as Sftrans.dll

5. If you access eVideo-In Pro Help, eVidpro.exe loads the data file eVidpro.hlp

6. eVidpro.exe continues to respond to the controls you select until you click the Close button, which halts execution of the program instructions, closes the program window, and releases the space the program occupied in RAM for use by other programs or data

Sftrans.dll

eVidpro.hlp

Exploring operating systems

An **operating system (OS)** is system software that is the master controller for all of the activities that take place within a computer system. If you understand how an operating system works, you will understand how your computer performs its many functions. For example, when you issue a command using application software, the software tells the operating system what to do. See **Figure C-7**. While you interact with application software, your computer's operating system is working behind the scenes.

- The operating system manages a computer's resources by interacting with application software, device drivers, and hardware. The term **resource** refers to any computer component that is required to perform work. For example, the processor is a resource. RAM, storage space, and peripherals are also resources.

- **Figure C-8** illustrates some common operating system tasks. Your operating system stores and retrieves files from storage media, such as disks and CDs. It remembers the names and locations of all your files and keeps track of empty spaces where new files can be stored. It communicates with device driver software so that data can travel smoothly between the computer and the peripheral resources. If a peripheral device or driver is not performing correctly, the operating system usually displays an on-screen warning about the problem so you can take corrective action.

- Many activities called "processes" compete for the attention of your computer's processor. To manage these competing processes, your computer's operating system helps the processor switch tasks. When you want to run more than one program at a time, the operating

system has to allocate specific areas of memory for each program that is open and running. See **Figure C-9**. The operating system is also a program, so it requires memory too. If the operating system fails to protect each program's memory area, data can get corrupted, programs can "crash," and your computer will display error messages.

- Your computer's operating system ensures that input and output proceed in an orderly manner, and it provides buffers to hold data while the computer is busy with other tasks. By using a keyboard buffer, for example, your computer never misses one of your keystrokes, regardless of how fast you type.

- Many operating systems also influence the "look and feel" of your software by determining the kinds of menus, toolbars, and controls that are displayed on the screen, and how these objects react to your input. Most operating systems today support a **graphical user interface**, which provides a way to point and click using a mouse to select menu options and move graphical objects that are on the screen. The term graphical user interface is sometimes abbreviated "GUI" and referred to as a "gooey."

Figure C-7: How the operating system interacts with application software

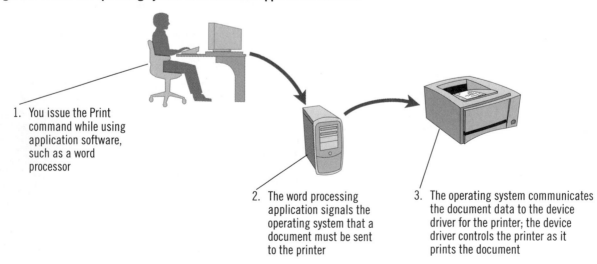

1. You issue the Print command while using application software, such as a word processor

2. The word processing application signals the operating system that a document must be sent to the printer

3. The operating system communicates the document data to the device driver for the printer; the device driver controls the printer as it prints the document

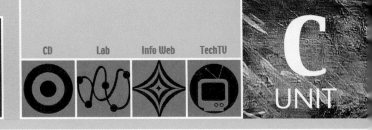
Figure C-8: Operating system tasks

Manage processor resources

Manage memory

Keep track of storage resources

Ensure that input and output proceed in an orderly manner

Establish basic elements of the user interface

■ In general, the operating system program is quite large and so it is stored on a hard disk, except for the operating system's small **bootstrap program**, which is stored in ROM. Handheld computers and videogame consoles are the exception because, typically, their entire operating systems are small enough to be stored in ROM. The bootstrap program supplies the instructions needed to load the operating system's core into memory when the system boots. The core part of the operating system, called the **kernel**, provides the most essential operating system services, such as memory management and file access. The kernel stays in memory all the time your computer is on. Other parts of the operating system, such as customization utilities, are loaded into memory as they are needed. **Utilities** are tools you can use to customize your computer environment.

Figure C-9: The operating system and RAM

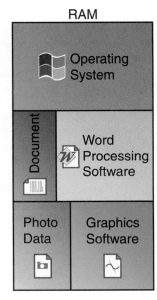

How does the operating system manage processor resources?

A computer can take advantage of performance-enhancing technologies, such as multitasking, multithreading, and dual-core or multiple processors, if its operating system support these technologies. **Multitasking** provides processor and memory management services that allow two or more tasks, jobs, or programs to run simultaneously. Most of today's operating systems, including the OS on your personal computer, offer multitasking services. Within a single program, **multithreading** allows multiple parts, or threads, to run simultaneously. For example, one thread for a spreadsheet program might be waiting for input from the user while other threads perform a long calculation. Multithreading can speed up performance on single- or multiple-processor computers. Many new computers include dual-core processors or multiple processors, which means the operating system supports a division of labor among all the processing units.

Comparing operating systems

The operating system determines the user interface, the way in which you interact with your computer, and it controls the hardware and the software so your computer can perform tasks. This lesson discusses categories of operating systems and compares the main features of the Windows, Mac OS, Unix, Linux, and mobile operating systems.

- A **single-user operating system** handles input, output, and processing requests from one user at a time. Operating systems for handheld computers and many personal computers fit into the single-user category.

- A **desktop operating system** is one that is designed for a desktop, notebook, or tablet personal computer. The computer that you typically use at home, at school, or at work is most likely configured with a desktop operating system. Typically, these operating systems are designed to accommodate a single user, but they may also provide networking capability.

- A **multiuser operating system** is designed to deal with input, output, and processing requests from many users at the same time. One of this system's most complex activities is scheduling all of the processing requests that must be performed by a centralized computer, often a mainframe.

- A **network operating system**, or **server operating system**, provides communications and routing services that allow computers to share data, programs, and peripheral devices. While multiuser and network operating systems may sound as though they are the same, a multiuser operating system schedules requests for processing on one centralized computer; a network operating system simply routes data and programs to each user's local computer, where the actual processing takes place.

- **DOS** (Disk Operating System), developed by Microsoft, was introduced on the original IBM PC in 1982. Although IBM called this operating system PC-DOS, Microsoft marketed it under the name MS-DOS. DOS can still be accessed from every version of Microsoft Windows by clicking the Start button on the Taskbar, clicking Run, and then typing "command" or "CMD". DOS offers utilities—such as Ping, Tracert, Copy *, msconfig, and netstat—which are used by tech-savvy computer users to troubleshoot problems.

- **Microsoft Windows** is installed on the vast majority of the world's personal computers. Since its introduction in 1985, Windows has evolved through several versions. The latest version is Windows Vista. Microsoft currently offers several types of Windows operating systems. Home, Professional, and Workstation editions are designed for personal computers. Server editions are designed for LAN, Internet, and Web servers. The Media Center edition is specially designed for media computers. Embedded editions are designed for handheld devices such as PDAs and mobile phones. The Windows logo in the lower-left corner of the taskbar indicates that the computer is running some version of Windows.

- **Mac OS**, for the Apple Macintosh computer, has been through a number of versions. The current version is OS X (version 10). The Apple logo at the top of the screen is an indicator that a computer is running Mac OS.

- Both Mac OS and Windows base their user interfaces on the graphical interface model that was pioneered at Xerox. The interface requires a mouse to point and click icons and menus. A quick comparison of **Figure C-10** and **Figure C-11** shows that both Windows and Mac interfaces feature rectangular work areas for multitasking services and provide various icons and menus for easy access to commands. Both also provide basic networking services.

Figure C-10: Microsoft Windows

Icons represent computer hardware and software

Your Name

The Windows operating system gets its name from the rectangular work areas that appear on the screen-based desktop; each work area can display a different document or program, providing a visual model of the operating system's multitasking capabilities

Two different programs can run in two separate windows

The Start button provides access to a menu of programs, documents, and utilities

The taskbar indicates which programs are running

Figure C-11: Mac OS

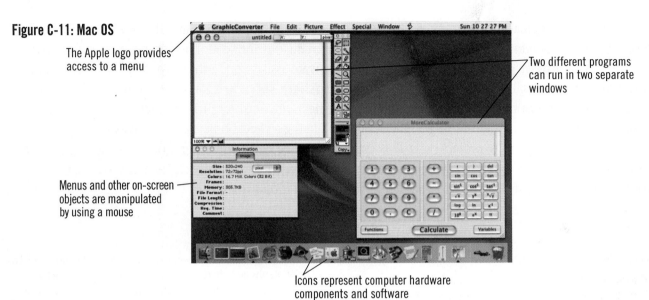

The Apple logo provides access to a menu

Two different programs can run in two separate windows

Menus and other on-screen objects are manipulated by using a mouse

Icons represent computer hardware components and software

Because programs that run on a Windows PC generally will not run on a Macintosh computer and vice versa, many of the most prolific software publishers produce one version of their software for Windows and another version for Mac OS.

- The **UNIX** operating system was developed in 1969 at AT&T's Bell Labs. It gained a good reputation for its dependability in multiuser environments. UNIX has also evolved through many versions. It is mainly used for mainframes and microcomputers.

- The **Linux** operating system (see **Figure C-12**), which is based on a version of UNIX, was developed by Linus Torvalds in 1991. Linux is unique because it is distributed under the terms of a General Public License (GPL), which allows everyone to make copies for his or her own use, to give it to others, or to sell it. This licensing policy has encouraged programmers to develop Linux utilities, software, and enhancements. Linux is primarily distributed over the Web. Although Linux is designed for microcomputers, it shares several technical

features with UNIX, such as multitasking and multiuser capabilities. These features make Linux a popular operating system for e-mail and Web servers as well as for local area networks. Although a comparatively limited number of programs run under Linux, and it requires more technical savvy than Windows and Mac OS, Linux has been gaining popularity as a desktop operating system. Some new personal computers now come configured with Linux.

- **Palm OS**, **Windows Mobile OS**, and **Symbian OS** are popular PDA and smartphone operating systems. These simpler and smaller operating systems can be stored in ROM, are ready almost instantly when the unit is turned on, and provide built-in support for touch screens, wireless networking, and cellular communications.

- **Windows XP Tablet Edition** is the operating system supplied with just about every tablet computer. Its main feature is handwriting recognition, which accepts printed input from the touch-sensitive screen.

Figure C-12: Linux

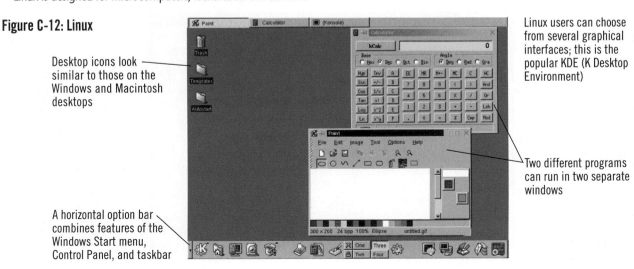

Desktop icons look similar to those on the Windows and Macintosh desktops

Linux users can choose from several graphical interfaces; this is the popular KDE (K Desktop Environment)

Two different programs can run in two separate windows

A horizontal option bar combines features of the Windows Start menu, Control Panel, and taskbar

Defining office productivity software

Most office work involves creating documents, managing numbers, and organizing data. If you are writing a paper, designing a brochure for your new startup company, or laying out the school newspaper, you will probably use some form of **document production software**. This software assists you with composing, editing, designing, printing, and electronically publishing documents. **Spreadsheet software** is used for numerical calculations based on simple equations or more complex formulas. Spreadsheets are ideal for projects that require repetitive calculations, such as budgeting, maintaining a grade book, balancing a checkbook, tracking investments, calculating loan payments, and estimating project costs. **Database software** helps you enter, find, organize, update, and report information stored in a database. **Office productivity software** is generally defined as software that integrates word processing, spreadsheet, database, drawing, and presentation capabilities.

■ Document production software can be classified as one of three types:

Word processing software is used to produce documents, such as reports, letters, and manuscripts. See **Figure C-13**. Microsoft Word is an example of word processing software.

Desktop publishing software (DTP) provides tools for word processing and graphic design. Although many of today's word processing programs offer page layout and design features, desktop publishing programs provide more sophisticated features to help you produce professional-quality output for publications. QuarkXPress is an example of destktop publishing software.

Web authoring software is used to design and develop Web pages that can be published electronically on the Internet. Web authoring software provides easy-to-use tools for composing the text for a Web page, assembling graphical elements, and automatically generating HTML tags. Macromedia Dreamweaver is an example of Web authoring software.

■ A **spreadsheet** uses rows and columns of numbers to create a model or representation of data when it is based in numbers. Spreadsheet software provides tools to create electronic

spreadsheets. Spreadsheet software can turn your data into a variety of colorful graphs and charts. Spreadsheet software is useful for answering what-if questions, such as, "What if I take out a 30-year mortgage at 5.0% interest? Or a 15-year mortgage at 4.5% interest? How will my payments change? How will the interest I pay over the life of the loan differ?"

■ You use spreadsheet software to create an on-screen **worksheet** like the one shown in **Figure C-14**. A worksheet is based on a grid of columns and rows. Each **cell** in the grid can contain a value, label, or formula and has a unique **cell reference**, or "address," derived from its column and row location. For example, A1 is the cell reference for the upper-left cell in a worksheet because it is in column A and row 1. You can select any cell and make it active by clicking it. Once a cell is active, you can enter data into it. A **value** is a number that you want to use in a calculation. A **label** is any text that is used to describe data.

■ A **database** is a collection of data that is stored electronically. A database can contain any sort of data, such as a university's student records, a library's card catalog, a store's inventory, an individual's address book, or a company's customer information. Database software is used to

Figure C-13: Microsoft Word

Even after you type an entire document, adjusting the size and placement of tabs and margins is simple

As you type, the spelling checker compares your words with a list of correctly spelled words; words not included in the list are marked with a wavy line as possible misspellings

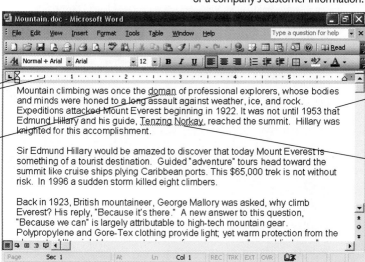

Document production software uses word wrap to fit your text automatically within the margins

Proper nouns and scientific, medical, and technical words are likely to be flagged as misspelled even if you spell them correctly because they do not appear in the spelling checker's dictionary

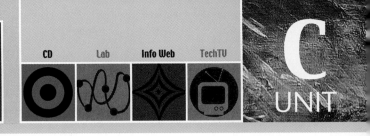

CD   Lab   Info Web   TechTV

C UNIT

Figure C-14: An on-screen worksheet

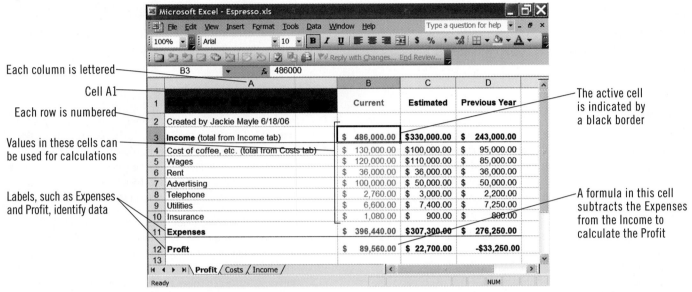

Each column is lettered

Cell A1

Each row is numbered

Values in these cells can be used for calculations

Labels, such as Expenses and Profit, identify data

The active cell is indicated by a black border

A formula in this cell subtracts the Expenses from the Income to calculate the Profit

create a database that stores data as a series of records. A **record** holds data for a single entity—a person, place, thing, or event. A record is composed of fields. A **field** holds one item of data relevant to a record. You specify the fields for the database, as shown in **Figure C-15**. You can envision a record as a Rolodex or index card with all the fields, and a series of records as a **table**. Database software can help you print reports, export data to other programs (such as to a spreadsheet, where you can graph the data), convert the data to other formats (such as HTML so that you can post the data on the Web), and transmit data to other computers.

■ The visual presentation of output from spreadsheets, databases, and documents has different purposes and is determined by the layout of the content and the way the content is formatted. **Layout** refers to the physical position of each element on a page, in a spreadsheet, or in a report from a database. A **header** is text that you specify to appear in the top margin of every page automatically. A **footer** is text that you specify to appear in the bottom margin of every page. The **format** for a document refers to how text, pictures, titles, and page numbers look on the page. The look of your document will depend on formatting factors such as font style, paragraph style, and page layout. You can vary the font style by selecting different fonts, such as Arial and Comic Sans MS, and character formatting attributes, such as bold, italic, underline, superscript, and subscript. You can also select a color and size

for a font. A **table** is a grid-like structure that can hold text or pictures, such as **clip art**, which is a collection of pictures and drawings. For printed documents, tables are a popular way to provide easy-to-read columns of data and to position graphics. For Web pages, tables provide one of the few ways to position text and pictures precisely.

Figure C-15: An on-screen database

Record   Field

Defining graphics software

The term **graphics** refers to any picture, drawing, sketch, photograph, image, or icon that appears on your computer screen or your printed output. **Graphics software** is designed to help you create, display, modify, manipulate, and print graphics. Many kinds of graphics software exist, and each one is typically used with a particular type of graphic. Individuals who work with graphics will undoubtedly use more than one graphics software package.

- **Paint software** (sometimes called "image editing software") provides a set of electronic pens, brushes, and paints for painting images on the screen. A simple program called Microsoft Paint is included with Windows. More sophisticated paint software products include JASC Paint Shop Pro and Procreate Painter. Graphic artists, Web page designers, photographers, and illustrators use paint software as their primary computer-based graphics tool.

- **Photo editing software**, such as Adobe Photoshop, includes features specially designed to improve the quality of photos by modifying contrast and brightness, cropping unwanted objects, and removing "red eye." While photos can be edited using paint software, photo editing software typically provides tools and wizards that simplify common photo editing tasks.

- **Drawing software** provides a set of lines, shapes, and colors that can be assembled into diagrams, corporate logos, and schematics. The drawings created with this type of software tend to have a "flat" cartoon-like quality, but they are very easy to modify and look good at just about any size. **Figure C-16** provides more information on paint, photo editing, and drawing software.

- **3-D graphics software** provides a set of tools for creating "wire-frames" that represent three-dimensional objects. A wireframe acts much like the framework for a pop-up tent. Just as you would construct the framework for the tent and then cover it with nylon fabric, 3-D graphics software can cover a wireframe object with surface texture and color to create a graphic of a 3-D object. See **Figure C-17**.

Figure C-16: Images created using photo editing and drawing software

Photo editing software includes special features for touching up photographs

Toolbars change to provide ready access to formatting commands, selection tools, and text tools

Palettes provide tools for working with colors, layers, and other image features

Drawing software provides tools for creating and manipulating graphics

This toolbar allows artists to select colors and shading

This toolbar contains tools for selecting parts of an image and adding text

This toolbar allows artists to select brush sizes and styles

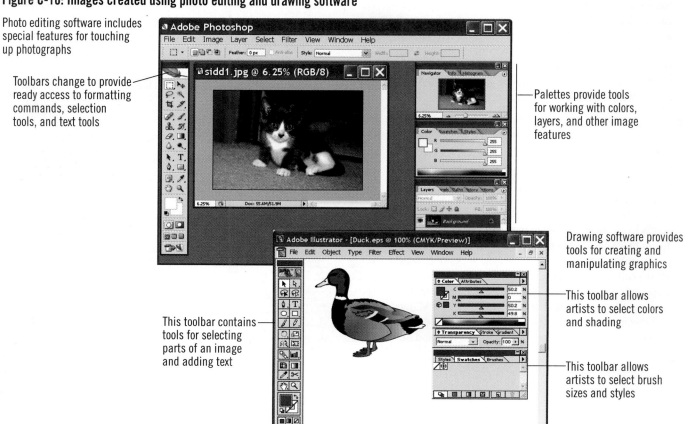

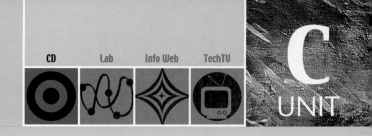
Figure C-17: Images created using 3-D graphics tools

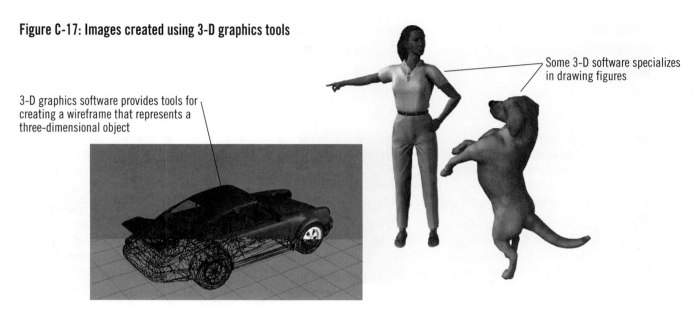

3-D graphics software provides tools for creating a wireframe that represents a three-dimensional object

Some 3-D software specializes in drawing figures

■ **CAD (computer-aided design) software** is a special type of 3-D graphics software designed for architects and engineers who use computers to create blueprints and product specifications. Scaled-down versions of professional CAD software provide simplified tools for homeowners who want to redesign their kitchens, examine new landscaping options, or experiment with floor plans.

■ **Presentation software** provides all of the tools you need for combining text, graphics, graphs, animations, and sound into a series of electronic **slides**. See **Figure C-18**. Presentation software, such as Microsoft PowerPoint, is often included with office productivity software. You can display the electronic slides on a color monitor for a one-on-one presentation, or you can use a computer projection device for group presentations. You can also output the presentation as overhead transparencies, paper copies, or 35-mm slides.

Figure C-18: A computer-based presentation

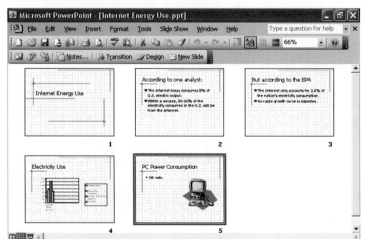

A computer-based presentation consists of a series of slides, created with presentation software

Defining entertainment and education software

The computer can provide entertainment in many formats, including listening to music, watching videos, and playing games. Computer games are the most popular type of entertainment software. Software classified as educational can also be entertaining. When these software categories often overlap, the product is called edutainment.

■ **Audio editing software**, such as iTunes and Sound Recorder (see **Figure C-19**), is used to make digital voice and music recordings that can be stored on a computer. Audio editing software typically includes playback as well as recording capabilities. A specialized version of this software, called karaoke software, integrates music files and on-screen lyrics.

A variety of software allows you to convert music from commercial CDs for use on computers and portable audio players. **CD ripper software** pulls a track off an audio CD and stores it in "raw" digital format on your computer's hard disk. **Audio encoding software** (sometimes called an "audio format converter") converts the raw audio file into a format such as MP3. **MP3** is a music compression file format that stores digitized music in such a way that the sound quality is excellent, but the file size remains relatively small—small enough to be easily downloaded from the Web. After the file is converted, you can listen to it on your computer, or you can transfer it to a portable MP3 player. To listen to MP3 music on your computer, you need an **MP3 player**. Versions of MP3 player software are available for many handheld computers and for personal computers running Windows, Mac OS, and Linux.

■ **Ear training software** is used mainly by musicians and music students who want to learn to play by ear, develop tuning skills, recognize notes and keys, and develop other musical skills. **Notation software** is the musician's equivalent of a word processor. It helps musicians compose, edit, and print the notes for their compositions. For non-musicians, **computer-aided music software** is designed to generate unique musical compositions simply by selecting the musical style, instruments, key, and tempo. **MIDI**

sequencing software and software synthesizers are an important part of the studio musician's toolbox. They are great for creating sound effects and for controlling keyboards and other digital instruments.

■ **Video editing software** provides a set of tools for transferring video footage from a camcorder to a computer, deleting unwanted footage, assembling video segments in any sequence, adding special visual effects, and adding a sound track. See **Figure C-20**. Video editing software allows desktop video authors to transfer their productions to DVDs and watch them on standard DVD players connected to television sets or projectors. Just like commercial movies, desktop videos can now include menu selections, such as Play Movie, Scene Selection, and Special Features.

■ **Educational software** helps users learn and practice new skills. For the youngest students, educational software teaches basic arithmetic and reading skills. Instruction is presented in game format, and the levels of play are adapted to the player's age and ability. For older students and adults, software is available for educational endeavors such as learning languages, training yourself to use new software, learning how to play the piano or guitar, preparing for standardized tests, improving keyboarding skills, and even learning managerial skills for a diverse workplace.

■ **Reference software** provides you with a collection of information and a way to access the information. The reference software category spans a wide range of applications from encyclopedias and medical references to map software, trip planners, cookbooks, and telephone books. An encyclopedia on CD-ROM or the Web has

Figure C-19: Audio editing software

Menus provide additional digital editing features, such as speed control, volume adjustments, clipping, and mixing

Rewind to beginning

Fast Forward to end   Play   Stop   Record

Audio editing software, such as Sound Recorder, provides controls much like a tape recorder

Figure C-20: Video editing software

Video editing software, such as Adobe Premiere, helps you import a series of video clips from a camera or VCR, arrange the clips in the order of your choice, add transitions between clips, and add an audio track

Use the timeline to indicate the sequence for your video clips and transitions

Arrange the audio tracks to synchronize with each video clip

The video and sound clips that you import for the project are displayed in a list so that you can easily select them in sequence

Preview your video to see how the clips, transitions, and soundtrack all work together

several advantages over its printed counterpart. For example, in addition to containing text, graphics, and audio, it might also contain video clips and interactive timelines. Finding information is easier, since you can search using keywords or click hyperlinks to access related articles.

- Computer games are generally classified into subcategories, such as multiplayer, role-playing, action, adventure, puzzles, simulations, and strategy/war games. Multiplayer games provide an environment in which two or more players can participate in the same

game. Players can use Internet technology to band together in sophisticated visual environments. Massively multiplayer games operate on multiple Internet servers, each one with the capacity to handle thousands of players at peak times. Since it was established in 1994, the Entertainment Software Rating Board (ESRB) has rated over 12,000 video and computer games. ESRB ratings have two parts: rating symbols that suggest what age group the game is best suited for and content descriptors that tell you about content elements that may be of interest or concern. Rating symbols, shown in **Figure C-21**, can usually be found on the game box.

Figure C-21: ESRB ratings and symbols

 **EARLY CHILDHOOD** Suitable for ages 3 and older. Contains no material that parents would find inappropriate.

 TEEN Suitable for 13 and older. May contain violent content, mild or strong language, and/or suggestive themes.

 **ADULTS ONLY** Content suitable only for adults. May include graphic depictions of sex and/or violence.

 **EVERYONE** Suitable for ages 6 and older. May contain minimal violence, some comic mischief, or crude language.

 MATURE Suitable for 17 and older. May contain mature sexual themes or more intense violence or language.

 **RATING PENDING** Product has been submitted, but a rating has not yet been assigned.

Defining business and science software

The terms business software and science software provide a broad umbrella for several types of software that are designed to help businesses and organizations accomplish routine or specialized tasks. These types of software provide a structured environment dedicated to a particular number-crunching task such as money management, mathematical modeling, or statistical analysis.

- **Accounting and finance software** helps you keep a record of monetary transactions and investments. In this software category, **personal finance software** is geared toward individual finances. **Tax preparation software** is a specialized type of personal finance software designed to help you gather your annual income and expense data, identify deductions, and calculate your tax payment.

- Some accounting and finance software is geared toward business. If you are an entrepreneur, **small business accounting software** can be a real asset. These easy-to-use programs do not require more than a basic understanding of accounting and finance principles. This type of software helps you invoice customers and keep track of what they owe. It stores additional customer data such as contact information and purchasing history. Inventory functions keep track of the products that you carry. Payroll capabilities automatically calculate wages and deduct federal, state, and local taxes.

- **Vertical market software** is designed to automate specialized tasks in a specific market or business. Examples include patient management and billing software specially designed for hospitals, job estimating software for construction businesses, and student record management software for schools. Today, almost every business has access to some type of specialized vertical market software designed to automate, streamline, or computerize key business activities.

- **Horizontal market software** is generic software that can be used by any business. **Payroll software** is a good example. Almost every business has employees and must maintain payroll records. No matter what type of business uses it, payroll software must collect similar data and make similar calculations in order to produce payroll checks and W2 forms. Accounting software and project management software are additional examples of horizontal market software. **Accounting software** helps a business keep track of the money flowing in and out of various accounts. **Project management software** is an important tool for planning large projects, scheduling project tasks, and tracking project costs.

What is a software suite?

A software suite is a collection of application software sold as a single package. Suites are available in many application categories. For example, office suites such as Microsoft Office, Star Office, Open Office, and WordPerfect Office typically include applications (such as word processing, spreadsheet, database, presentation, drawing, and e-mail) to boost basic productivity. Graphics suites such as Adobe Creative Suite, Macromedia Studio, and CorelDRAW Graphics Suite typically include paint, draw, animation, and Web graphics tools. Media suites such as InterVideo MediaOne provide tools for creating music CDs and video DVDs. Business suites, bundled by companies such as Microsoft, Netsuite, and Computer Associates, provide all the tools a small business needs in one software suite.

Purchasing a software suite is usually much less expensive than purchasing each application in the suite separately. Another advantage is usability. Because all the applications in a suite are produced by the same software publisher, they tend to have similar user interfaces and provide an easy way to transport data from one application to another. The disadvantage of a software suite is that it might include applications you do not need. If that is the case, you should calculate the price of the applications you do need and compare that to the cost of the suite.

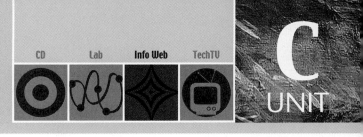
■ **Groupware**, another umbrella term in the world of business software, is designed to help several people collaborate on a single project using network or Internet connections. It usually provides the capability to maintain schedules for all group members, select meeting times for the group, facilitate communication by e-mail or other channels, distribute documents according to a prearranged schedule or sequence, and allow multiple people to contribute to a single document.

■ **Statistical software** helps users analyze large sets of data to discover relationships and patterns. It is a helpful tool for summarizing survey results, test scores, experiment results, or population data. Most statistical software includes graphing capability so that data can be displayed and explored visually.

■ **Mathematical modeling software**, such as MathCAD and Mathematica, provides tools for solving a wide range of math, science, and engineering problems. See **Figure C-22**. Students, teachers, mathematicians, and engineers, in particular, appreciate how this software helps them recognize patterns that can be difficult to identify in columns of numbers.

Figure C-22: Mathematical modeling software

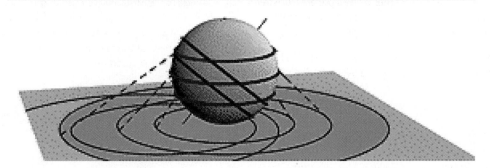

Mathematical modeling software helps you visualize the result of complex formulas

Using data responsibly

Many business and science software programs use databases. Whether you print, import, copy, save, or transmit the data in databases, worksheets, or documents, it is your responsibility to use the data appropriately. Never introduce inaccurate information into a database, worksheet, or document. Respect copyrights, giving credit to the person or organization that compiled the data. You should always respect the privacy of the people who are the subject of the data. Unless you have permission to do so, do not divulge names, social security numbers, or other identifying information that might compromise someone's privacy.

Understanding utilities

Utility software (often referred to as "utilities") is a type of system software that is designed to perform a specialized task, such as system maintenance or security. Unlike the application software discussed in the last few lessons, this category of software provides essential tools for maintaining the health of your computer. If your computer is working optimally, you can complete tasks such as creating documents, graphics, or spreadsheets, or sending and receiving e-mail. It is important to include some of these utilities in your software arsenal so you can run the applications without problems. The computer's operating system supplies a variety of utilities that help you manage files, get help, and customize the user interface. For example, **Table C-1** lists some Windows operating system utilities. In addition to utilities that come with your operating system, other utilities are available, such as those discussed next.

■ **Third-party utilities** are designed for the same tasks handled by the operating system. Computer owners typically use utilities from third-party vendors for one of two reasons. First, operating system utilities are sometimes not as comprehensive as third-party utilities designed by companies that specialize in system maintenance or security. In addition, some operating system utilities do not provide as many features as third-party versions.

■ **Compression utilities** reduce file size for quick transmission or efficient storage. The Windows operating system comes with a file compression utility, but many computer owners prefer to use third-party utilities, such as WinZip, WinAce, IZArc, QuickZip, or PKZIP because these utilities offer a variety of compression options.

■ **FTP (file transfer protocol) utilities** are used to upload or download files from another computer or a Web site. Even though many Web sites offer automated downloads, users often prefer FTP (File Transfer Protocol) utilities such as WSFTP or CuteFTP because they provide a wide variety of file transfer utilities to help users manage the file transfer process.

■ **Security utilities**, such as antivirus software, help the user control nuisance ads, intrusion attempts, and spam. Third-part utilities, such as pop-up ad blockers, personal firewalls, and spam filters, have also become best sellers. Other security-related utilities include file-encryption software, such as PGP, that scrambles file content for storage or transmission. You can also buy utilities that remove the trail of Web sites from a computer. These utilities remove Internet history lists, files, and graphics from locations that can be scattered in many parts of the hard disk. Filtering software is used by parents to block their children from access to objectionable Web sites.

Table C-1: Examples of Windows operating system utilities

UTILITY	USED TO	DESCRIPTION
Windows Explorer	Manage files	Allows you to view a list of files, move them to different storage devices, copy them, rename them, and delete them
Help system	Get help	Provides information on how the various commands work; you can search using keywords, through a topic index, or table of contents
Control Panel	Customize the user interface	Accessible from the Start menu, provides utilities that help you customize your screen display and work environment; also provides access to utilities that help you set up and configure your computer's hardware and peripheral devices

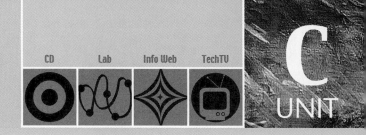

- **Skins utilities** are used to customize screen-based desktops with screensavers that display clever graphics when the machine is idle. Skins utilities that customize the look and feel of media players and DVD burners are also popular utilities. See **Figure C-23**.

- **Document reader utilities**, such as the popular Acrobat Reader, transform all kinds of files into a portable format that can be created and read by any computer on which they are installed. Acrobat Reader is especially handy for viewing documents created using expensive desktop publishing software that is not likely to be installed on many people's computers.

- **System utilities**, such as Norton System Works and System Mechanic PowerToys, provide disk maintenance functions including tracking down and fixing disk errors and corrupted files. These utilities can also give your PC a performance-enhancing tune-up.

- **Hard disk utilities** are used for backing up, securing, permanently deleting, and cleaning up files on hard disks. These utilities help computer owners maintain the integrity of their hard disks. These utilities include security features for shredding files so they cannot be recovered. Utilities such as Recover My Files, VirtualLab, and R-Undelete can help you recover files deleted by mistake.

Figure C-23: Skins

Skins, such as the ones shown here, change the appearance of Windows Media Player; skins are an example of a popular utility

Buying utilities

Third-party utilities as well as antivirus programs, such as Norton AntiVirus and McAfee VirusScan, are commercial packages that can be purchased in any store that carries computers or office supplies. They can also be purchased online. Many utilities, including several antivirus packages, can be downloaded from the Web site for free and used on a trial basis for a short period of time. If you want to continue using utilities you downloaded for a trial period, you can make an online payment as instructed in the readme.doc file or pop-up registration menu that appears at the end of the trial period.

Understanding licenses and copyrights

Once you purchase a software package, you might assume that you can install it and use it in any way that you like. In fact, your "purchase" entitles you to use the software only in certain prescribed ways. In most countries, computer software, like a book or movie, is protected by a copyright. In addition to copyright protection, computer software is often protected by the terms of a software license. Copyright laws provide fairly severe restrictions on copying, distributing, and reselling software. However, a license agreement may offer some rights to consumers as well.

- A **software license**, or "license agreement," is a legal contract that defines the ways in which you may use a computer program. For personal computer software, you will find the license on the outside of the package, on a separate card inside the package, on the CD packaging, or in one of the program files.

- An **EULA (end-user license agreement)** is displayed on the screen when you first install the software. After reading the software license on the screen, you can indicate that you accept the terms of the license by clicking a designated button usually labeled "OK," "I agree," or "I accept."

- Typically, computer owners purchase the right to use software that is distributed under a **single-user license** that limits use of the software to only one person at a time. Schools, organizations, and businesses sometimes purchase a site license, multiple-user license, or concurrent-use license, which allows more than one person to

use the software. A **site license** is generally priced at a flat rate and allows software to be used on all computers at a specific location. A **multiple-user license** is priced per user and allows the allocated number of people to use the software at any time. A **concurrent-use license** is priced per copy and allows a specific number of copies to be used at the same time.

- Most legal contracts require signatures before the terms of the contract take effect. This requirement becomes unwieldy with software; imagine having to sign a license agreement and return it before you can use a new software package. To circumvent the signature requirement, software publishers typically use two techniques to validate a software license: shrink-wrap licenses and installation agreements. When you purchase computer software, the distribution media, such as CDs or DVDs, are usually sealed in an envelope, plastic box, or shrink wrapping. A **shrink-wrap license** goes into effect as soon as you open the packaging. See **Figure C-24**.

Figure C-24: A shrink-wrap license

When software has a shrink-wrap license, you agree to the terms of the software license by opening the package; if you do not agree with the terms, you should return the software in its unopened package

Software licenses are often lengthy and written in legalese, but your legal right to use the software continues only as long as you abide by the terms of the software license. Therefore, you should understand the software license for any software you use. When you read a software license agreement, look for answers to the following questions: Am I buying the software or licensing it? When does the license go into effect? Under what circumstances can I make copies? Can I rent the software? Can I sell the software? What if the software includes a distribution CD and a set of distribution media? Does the software publisher provide a warranty? Can I loan the software to a friend?

■ A **copyright** is a form of legal protection that grants the author of an original work an exclusive right to copy, distribute, sell, and modify that work, except under special circumstances described by copyright laws. Exceptions include the purchaser's right to copy software from a distribution disk or Web site to a computer's hard disk in order to install it; to make an extra, or backup, copy of the software in case the original copy becomes erased or damaged; and to copy and distribute sections of a software program for use in critical reviews and teaching.

■ Most software displays a **copyright notice**, such as "© 2007 eCourseWare," on one of its screens. However, because this notice is not required by law, programs without a copyright notice are still protected by copyright law. People who circumvent copyright law and illegally copy, distribute, or modify software are sometimes called software pirates, and their illegal copies are referred to as pirated software.

Reviewing software copyright protections by software classifications

Commercial software is typically sold in computer stores or at Web sites. Although you buy this software, you actually purchase only the right to use it under the terms of the software license. A license for commercial software typically adheres closely to the limitations provided by copyright law, although it might give you permission to install the software on a computer at work and on a computer at home, provided that you use only one of them at a time.

Shareware is copyrighted software marketed under a try-before-you-buy policy. It typically includes a license that permits you to use the software for a trial period. To use it beyond the trial period, you must send in a registration fee. A shareware license usually allows you to make copies of the software and distribute them to others. If they choose to use the software, they must send in a registration fee as well. These shared copies provide a low-cost marketing and distribution channel for shareware developers.

Registration fee payment relies on the honor system, so unfortunately many shareware authors collect only a fraction of the money they deserve for their programming efforts. Thousands of shareware programs are available, encompassing just about as many applications as commercial software.

Freeware is copyrighted software that is available without a fee. Because the software is protected by copyright, you cannot do anything with it that is not expressly allowed by copyright law or by the author. Typically, the license for freeware permits you to use the software, copy it, and give it away, but does not permit you to alter it or sell it. Many utility programs, device drivers, and some games are available as freeware.

Open source software makes the uncompiled program instructions available to programmers who want to modify and improve the software. Open source software may be sold or distributed free of charge, but it must, in every case, include the uncompiled source code. Linux is an example of open source software, as is FreeBSD, a version of UNIX designed for personal computers.

Public domain software is not protected by copyright because the copyright has expired or the author has placed the program in the public domain, making it available without restriction. Public domain software may be freely copied, distributed, and even resold. The primary restriction on public domain software is that you are not allowed to apply for a copyright on it.

Tech Talk Installing Software

No matter how you obtain a new software package, you must install it on your computer before you can use it.

Printed on the software package or on the software publisher's Web site are the **system requirements**, which specify the operating system and minimum hardware requirements for a software product to work correctly. When you **install** software, the new software files are placed in the appropriate folders on your computer's hard disk, and then your computer performs any software or hardware configurations necessary to make sure the program is ready to run.

Windows software typically contains a **setup program** that guides you through the installation process. **Figure C-25** shows you what to expect when you use a setup program.

Downloadable software can be provided in several different formats. Some automatically install themselves, whereas others require manual procedures. A downloadable file typically is set up as a self-installing executable file, self-executing zip file, or nonexecuting zip file. **Figure C-26** shows you what to expect when you download a program to install.

Figure C-25: Installing software using distribution media

1.

Insert the distribution disk, CD, or DVD. The setup program should start automatically. If it does not, look for a file called *Setup.exe* and then run it.

2.

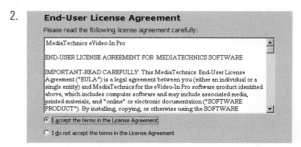

Read the license agreement, if one is presented on the screen. By agreeing to the terms of the license, you can proceed with the installation.

3.

- ◉ **Full Installation**
- ○ **Custom Installation**

Select the installation option that best meets your needs. If you select a full installation, the setup program copies all files and data from the distribution medium to the hard disk of your computer system. A full installation provides you with access to all features of the software.

If you select a custom installation, the setup program displays a list of software features for your selection. After you select the features you want, the setup program copies only the selected program files, support programs, and data files to your hard disk. A custom installation can save space on your hard disk drive.

4.

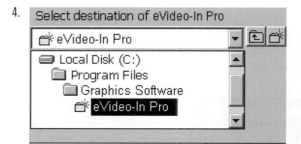

Follow the prompts provided by the setup program to specify a folder to hold the new software program. You can use the default folder specified by the setup program or a folder of your own choosing. You can also create a new folder during the setup process.

5.

If the software includes multiple distribution CDs or DVDs, insert each one in the specified drive when the setup program prompts you.

6.

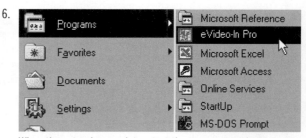

When the setup is complete, start the program you just installed to make sure it works.

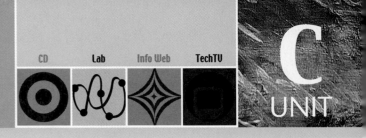
Figure C-26: Installing downloaded software

1.

At the distribution Web site, locate any information pertaining to installing the software. Read it. You might also want to print it.

2.

Click the download link.

3.

If you are downloading from a trusted site and have antivirus software running, click the Open button in the File Download dialog box.

4.

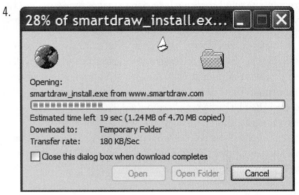

Wait for the download to finish.

5.

Select Destination Folder

Destination Folder

C:\SmartDraw6

- c:\
- Backups
- Data Manager
- HPFonts

c:

OK   Cancel

Specify a folder to hold the new software program. You can use the default folder specified by the setup program or a folder of your own choosing. You can also create a new folder during the setup process.

6.

Installing

Copying SmartDraw Trial Libraries:
C:\SmartDraw6\Library\Standard\Fun\Fun.sdl

75%

Cancel

Wait for the setup program to uncompress the downloaded file and install the software in the selected directory. During this process, respond to license agreement and other prompts. When the installation is complete, test the software to make sure it works.

To combat piracy, many software publishers require users to type in a validation code to complete an installation. A **validation code** is a long sequence of numbers and letters that is typically supplied separately from the software itself. It is not the serial number that you sometimes see in the About dialog box—that number can exist electronically even if the software is a pirated copy. Validation codes are not part of the software. Instead they can usually be found on distribution media packaging. They might also be sent to you via e-mail. To use a validation code, you simply enter it when instructed during the installation process.

Installing a software update is not that different from installing the original version. A new version update usually installs in a manner similar to the way you installed the original version, by activating a setup program, displaying a license agreement, and adding updated entries to your computer's Start menu. **Patches** and **service packs** are usually distributed over the Internet and automatically install themselves when you download them.

From time to time, you might also want to uninstall some of the software that exists on your computer. Operating systems, such as Windows and Mac OS, provide access to an **uninstall routine** that deletes the software's files from various directories on your computer's hard disk. The uninstall routine also removes references to the program from the desktop and from operating system files, such as the file system and, in the case of Windows, from the Windows Registry.

Computers in Context Journalism

The news business is all about gathering and disseminating information as quickly as possible (see **Figure C-27**). In the ancient world, news spread by word of mouth, relayed by bards and merchants who traveled from town to town—in essence, they were the first reporters to "broadcast" the news. Throughout history, technology has played a major role in how news reporting has evolved into the modern 24-hour "live" news networks. Johann Gutenberg's movable-type printing press (ca. 1450), the first technological breakthrough in the news business, made it feasible to publish news as printed notices tacked to walls in the town square. As paper became more economical, resourceful entrepreneurs sold broadsheets to people eager for news, and the concept of a newspaper was born.

But the news spread slowly. In the early 1800s, it took four weeks for newspapers in New York to receive reports from London. With the advent of the telegraph in 1844, however, reporters from distant regions could "wire" stories to their newspapers for publication the next day. The first radio reporters in the 1920s offered live broadcasts of sports events, church services, and variety shows. Before the 1950s, black-and-white newsreels shown in movie theaters provided the only visual imagery of news events; and it was television that gave viewers news images on a nightly basis.

"In the old days, we had time to think before we spoke. We had time to write, time to research and time to say, 'Hey, wait a minute.' Now we don't even have the time to say, 'Hey, wait a nanosecond.' Just because we can say it or do it, should we?" observes Jeff Gralnick, former executive producer for ABC News. Technology has given journalists a powerful arsenal of tools for gathering and reporting the news, but it has also increased their accountability for accurate, socially responsible reporting.

Technology has benefited print journalism in many ways. For decades, typesetters transferred reporters' handwritten stories into neatly set columns of type. Today, reporters use computers and word processing software to type their stories and run a preliminary check of spelling and grammar. Stories are submitted via a computer network to editors, who use the same software to edit stories so they fit space constraints. The typesetting process has been replaced by desktop publishing software and computer-to-plate (CTP) technology. Digital pages produced with desktop publishing software are sent to a raster image processor (RIP), which converts the pages into dots that form words and images. A platesetter uses lasers to etch the dots onto a physical plate, which is then mounted on the printing press to produce printed pages. CTP is much faster and more flexible than typesetting, so publishers can make last-minute changes to accommodate late-breaking stories.

Personal computers have added a new dimension to the news-gathering process. Reporters who were once limited to personal interviews, observation, and fact gathering at libraries can now make extensive use of Internet resources and e-mail. Web sites and online databases provide background information on all sorts of topics. Other resources include newsgroups, blogs, and chat rooms, where reporters can monitor public opinion on current events and identify potential news sources.

Most major television networks maintain interactive Web sites that offer online polls and bulletin boards designed to collect viewers' opinions. Although online poll respondents are not a representative sample of the population, and the statistics are not scientifically valid, they can help news organizations gauge viewer opinions and determine whether news coverage is comprehensive and effective.

E-mail has changed the way reporters communicate with colleagues and sources. It is often the only practical method for contacting people in remote locations or distant time zones, and it is useful with reluctant sources who feel more comfortable providing information under the cloak of anonymous Hotmail or Yahoo! accounts. "Vetting" e-mail sources—verifying credentials such as name, location, and occupation—can be difficult, however, so reporters tend not to rely on these sources without substantial corroboration.

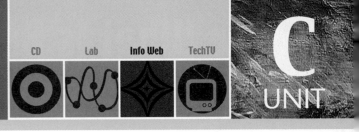
For broadcast journalism, digital communications play a major role in today's "live on the scene" television reporting. Most news organizations maintain remote production vans, sometimes called "satellite news gathering (SNG) trucks," that travel to the site of breaking news. These complete mobile production facilities include camera control units, audio and video recording equipment, and satellite or microwave transmitters. They need only to raise their antennas to begin broadcasting.

On-the-scene reporting does not always require a truck full of equipment. Audiovisual editing units and video cameras have gone digital, making them easier to use and sized to fit in a suitcase. A new breed of "backpack journalists" carries mini-DV cameras, notebook computers, and satellite phones. Jane Ellen Stevens, a pioneer backpack journalist specializing in science and technology, has reported since 1997 from remote locations such as a space camp in Russia. Backpack journalists can connect their minicams to notebook computers with a firewire cable, transfer their video footage to the hard disk, and then edit the footage using consumer-level video editing software. The resulting video files, compressed for transmission over a satellite phone, are sent to newsroom technicians, who decompress and then broadcast them— all in a matter of seconds. One drawback of backpack journalists' use of minicams and compression is that the video quality usually is not as crisp as images filmed with studio cameras. News organizations with high standards were hesitant to use this lower-quality video, but they have found that viewers would rather see a low-quality image now than a high-quality image later. To many viewers, a few rough edges just make the footage seem more compelling, more "you are there."

Computers, the Internet, and communications technology make it possible to instantly broadcast live reports across the globe, but live reporting is not without controversy. A reporter who arrives at the scene of a disaster with microphone in hand has little time for reflection, vetting, and cross-checking, so grievous errors, libelous images, or distasteful video footage sometimes find their way into news reports.

"In the old days, we had time to think before we spoke. We had time to write, time to research and time to say, 'Hey, wait a minute.' Now we don't even have the time to say, 'Hey, wait a nanosecond.' Just because we can say it or do it, should we?" observes Jeff Gralnick, former executive producer for ABC News. Technology has given journalists a powerful arsenal of tools for gathering and reporting the news, but it has also increased their accountability for accurate, socially responsible reporting.

Figure C-27

Issue What Is Being Done about Software Piracy?

Software is easy to steal. You do not have to walk out of a Best Buy store with a Quicken Deluxe box under your shirt. You can simply borrow your friend's distribution CDs and install a copy of the program on your computer's hard disk. It seems so simple that it could not be illegal. But it is. Software piracy takes many forms. End-user piracy includes friends loaning distribution disks to each other and installing software on more computers than the license allows.

Counterfeiting is the large-scale illegal duplication of software distribution media and sometimes even its packaging. According to Microsoft, many software counterfeiting groups are linked to organized crime and money-laundering schemes that fund a diverse collection of illegal activities. Counterfeit software is sold in retail stores and online auctions—often the packaging looks so authentic that buyers have no idea they have purchased illegal goods.

Internet piracy uses the Web as a way to illegally distribute unauthorized software. Some pirated software has even been modified to eliminate serial numbers, registration requirements, expiration dates, or other forms of copy protection. The Business Software Alliance (BSA) estimates that more than 800,000 Web sites illegally sell or distribute software. According to a BSA and IDC 2005 Piracy Study, $59 billion was spent on software worldwide, but software worth $90 billion was installed during the year. In many countries, including the United States, software pirates are subject to civil lawsuits for monetary damages and criminal prosecution, which can result in jail time and stiff fines. Nonetheless, software piracy continues to have enormous impact.

> According to a BSA and IDC 2005 Piracy Study, $59 billion was spent on software worldwide, but software worth $90 billion was installed during the year.

A small but vocal minority of software users, such as members of GNU (which stands for "Gnu's Not UNIX"), believes that data and software should be freely distributed. Richard Stallman writes in the GNU Manifesto, "I consider that the golden rule requires that if I like a program I must share it with other people who like it. Software sellers want to divide users and conquer them, making each user agree not to share with others. I refuse to break solidarity with other users in this way. I cannot in good conscience sign a nondisclosure agreement or a software license agreement."

As a justification of high piracy rates, some observers point out that people in many countries simply might not be able to afford software priced for the U.S. market. The BSA and IDC reported about 35% of the software currently in use is pirated. (Source: BSA/IDC Global Piracy Report 2005.) Most countries with a high incidence of software piracy, however, have strong economies and respectable per capita incomes. To further discredit the theory that piracy stems from poverty, India—which has a fairly large computer-user community, but a per capita income of only $1,600—is not among the top 10 countries with high rates of software piracy.

Although the rate of business software piracy might be declining, total piracy appears to be growing one or two percentage points each year. Analysts fear that the Internet is a major factor in piracy growth. As Internet access becomes available to subscribers in developing countries, piracy could skyrocket. To make matters worse, increased access to high-speed Internet connections makes it much easier to quickly download large software files.

Who cares if you use Microsoft Office without paying for it? Is software piracy really damaging? Software piracy is damaging because it has a negative effect on the economy. Software production makes a major contribution to the United States economy, employing more than 2 million people and accounting for billions of dollars in corporate revenue. Software piracy in the United States is responsible for tens of thousands of lost jobs, millions in lost wages, and lost tax revenues. Decreases in software revenues can have a direct effect on consumers, too. When software publishers must cut corners, they tend to reduce customer service and technical support. As a result, you, the consumer, get put on hold when you call for technical support, find fewer free technical support sites, and encounter customer support personnel

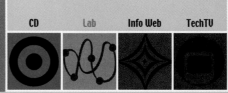

C UNIT

who are only moderately knowledgeable about their products. The bottom line—software piracy negatively affects customer service. As an alternative to cutting support costs, some software publishers might build the cost of software piracy into the price of the software. The unfortunate result is that those who legitimately license and purchase software pay an inflated price.

If economic factors do not account for the pervasiveness of software piracy, what does? Some analysts suggest that people need more education about software copyrights and the economic implications of piracy. Other analysts believe that copyright enforcement must be increased by implementing more vigorous efforts to identify and prosecute pirates.

Interactive Questions

☐ Yes   ☐ No   ☐ Not Sure   **1.** Do you believe that software piracy is a serious issue?

☐ Yes   ☐ No   ☐ Not Sure   **2.** Do you know of any instances of software piracy?

☐ Yes   ☐ No   ☐ Not Sure   **3.** Do you think that most software pirates understand that they are doing something illegal?

☐ Yes   ☐ No   ☐ Not Sure   **4.** Should software publishers adjust software prices for local markets?

Expand the Ideas

1. Do you believe that software piracy is a serious issue? Write a two-page paper supporting your position. Include the opposing side's arguments in your report. Be sure to include your resources.

2. Do you think there are ways that software publishers can control piracy in the United States? In other countries? Do you know of any recent attempts at doing so? Work in a small group to brainstorm ideas and research recent trends or events. Compile your ideas and findings into a short presentation to give to the class. Include handouts for the audience and cite any sources you used.

3. Do you think that most software pirates understand that they are doing something illegal? Design a marketing campaign that could be used to educate the public about the issue. Create a poster that could be used in the campaign.

4. Should software publishers try to adjust software pricing for local markets? How would you propose such a pricing structure? How would these policies be enforced? Can you think of any other industry that adjusts prices for local markets? Write a two-page paper discussing your proposals and explaining your findings. Be sure to cite your sources.

End of Unit Exercises

Key Terms

3-D graphics software

Accounting and finance software

Accounting software

Application software

Audio editing software

Audio encoding software

Bootstrap program

CAD software

CD ripper software

Cell

Cell reference

Clip art

Compiler

Compression utility

Computer-aided music software

Computer-aided design software

Computer language

Computer program

Computer programmer

Concurrent-user license

Copyright

Copyright notice

Database

Database software

Desktop operating system

Desktop publishing software

Drawing software

Document reader utility

Document production software

DOS

Ear training software

Educational software

EULA (end-user license agreement)

Executable file

Field

Footer

Format

Freeware

FTP (File Transfer Protocol)

Graphical user interface (GUI)

Graphics

Graphics software

Groupware

Hard disk utility

Header

High-level language

Horizontal market software

Install

Interpreter

Kernel

Label

Layout

Linux

Mac OS

Machine language

Mathematical modeling software

Microsoft Windows

MIDI sequencing software

MP3

MP3 player

Multiple-user license

Multitasking

Multithreading

Multiuser operating system

Network operating system

Notation software

Object code

Office Productivity Software

Open source software

Operating system

Paint software

Palm OS

Patch

Payroll software

Personal finance software

Photo editing software

Presentation software

Program data file

Programming language

Project management software

Public domain software

Record

Reference software

Resource

Security utility

Server operating system

Service pack

Setup program

Shareware

Shrink-wrap license

Single-user license

Single-user operating system

Site license

Skins utility

Slide

Small business accounting software

Software

Software license

Software suite

Source code

Spreadsheet

Spreadsheet software

Statistical software

Support program

Symbian OS

System requirements

System software

System utility

Table (database)

Table (layout)

Tax preparation software

Third-party utility

Uninstall routine

UNIX

Utilities

Validation code

Value

Vertical market software

Video editing software

Web authoring software

Windows Mobil OS

Windows XP Tablet Edition

Word processing software

Worksheet

Unit Review

1. Use your own words to define each of the bold terms that appear throughout the unit. List 10 of the terms that are least familiar to you and write a sentence for each of them.

2. Make sure that you can list and describe the three types of files that are typically supplied on software distribution media.

3. Explain the difference between a compiler and an interpreter.

4. List three types of system software and at least five categories of application software.

5. Describe how an operating system manages resources.

6. List three types of office productivity software that you might use and describe how you might use each one.

7. List three types of third-party utility software that you might use and describe how you might use each one.

8. Describe when you would use each type of graphics software covered in this unit.

9. Create a list of the different categories of operating systems discussed in this unit. Write a brief summary of each category listing the significant and distinguishing features, then give an example of a current operating system for each category.

10. In your own words, explain what each of the ESRB ratings means and how it would help you purchase software.

End of Unit Exercises

Fill in the Best Answer

1. Software can be divided into two major categories: application software and _____ software.

2. Software usually contains support programs and data files, in addition to a main _____ file that you run to start the software.

3. Instructions that are written in a(n) _____ -level language must be translated into _____ language before a computer can use them.

4. A(n) _____ translates all of the instructions in a program as a single batch, and the resulting machine language instructions are placed in a new file.

5. To run more than one program at a time, the operating system must allocate specific areas of _Memory_ for each program.

6. A(n) _____ user interface provides a way for a user to interact with the software using a mouse and graphical objects on the screen.

7. A(n) _Many_ operating system is designed to deal with input, output, and processing requests from many users.

8. A(n) _Network_ operating system provides communications and routing services that allow computers to share data, programs, and peripheral devices.

9. Palm OS and Windows Mobile OS are two of the most popular operating systems for _handout_ computers.

10. Linux is an example of open _source_ software.

11. If you need to either send files or get files from another computer or a Web site, you could use a(n) _FTP_ utility, even though many Web sites offer automated downloads.

12. _graphic_ software helps you work with wireframes, CAD drawings, photos, and slide presentations.

13. _Skin_ customize the look and feel of media players and DVD burners.

14. _vertical_ market software is designed to automate specialized tasks in a specific market or business.

15. To combat piracy, many software publishers require users to type in a(n) _____ code—a long sequence of numbers and letters typically supplied separately from the software itself—to complete an installation.

16. _MP3_ is a music compression file that stores digitized music in such a way that quality is excellent but the file size is relatively small.

17. _copyright_ laws provide software authors with the exclusive right to copy, distribute, sell, and modify their work, except under special circumstances.

18. _shareware_ is copyrighted software that is marketed with a "try before you buy" policy.

19. A(n) _site_ license is generally priced at a flat rate and allows software to be used on all computers at a specific location.

20. Public _Domain_ software is not copyrighted, making it available for use without restriction, except that you cannot apply for a copyright on it.

Practice Tests

When you use the Interactive CD, you can take Practice Tests that consist of 10 multiple-choice, true/false, and fill-in-the blank questions. The questions are selected at random from a large test bank, so each time you take a test, you will receive a different set of questions. Your tests are scored immediately, and you can print study guides to determine which questions you answered incorrectly. If you are using a Tracking Disk, save your test scores.

INDEPENDENT CHALLENGE 1

There are so many software packages on the market today that making a wise purchasing decision can be overwhelming. The breadth of software available in each category is quite large, and no two packages offer all the same features. Do you base your decision to buy a new application package on word of mouth? Reviewer comments in professional magazines? Trying it out? To complete this independent challenge, you will review the software that is installed on your computer and then research a type of software package that you intend to purchase. You will complete the independent challenge by writing a short summary discussing the issues raised below.

1. What software is installed on your computer? How did you acquire the software? What type of software does each package fall into, based on the categories outlined in this unit? Which operating system do you use?

2. Assume you will add a software program to your computer, determine the type of package you want to select (for example, office productivity, graphics, Web development, e-mail, or perhaps a utility).

3. Locate vendor ads either on the Internet or in local papers or trade magazines that sell or discuss the software.

4. Read comparison reviews of the products. Create a chart detailing the features and prepare a competitive analysis of the three top candidates for your purchase.

5. Write a short summary of your findings, indicating which package you would buy and why.

INDEPENDENT CHALLENGE 2

When you use a software package, it is important to understand the legal restrictions on its use. Is the software free? Do you have to pay for using it? Can you try it first, then pay after a trial period? For this independent challenge, make a photocopy of the license agreement for any software package. Read the license agreement, then answer these questions:

1. In your own words, explain the differences between commercial software, shareware, open source software, freeware, and public domain software. Which of these types would you prefer to use? Why would you select one type over the other?

2. Review the license agreement that you copied. Is this a shrink-wrap license? Why or why not? Does the license specify if this is commercial software, shareware, open source software, freeware, or public domain software?

3. After you pay your software dealer for the program covered by this license, who owns the program?

4. Can you legally have one copy of the program on your computer at work and another copy of the program on your computer at home, if you use the software only in one place at a time?

5. Can you legally sell the software? Why or why not?

6. Under what conditions can you legally transfer possession of the program to someone else?

7. If you were the owner of a software store, could you legally rent the program to customers if you were sure they did not keep a copy after the rental period was over?

8. Can you legally install this software on one computer, but give more than one user access to it?

9. If you use this program for an important business decision and later find out that a mistake in the program caused you to lose $500,000, what legal recourse, if any, is provided by the license agreement?

End of Unit Exercises

INDEPENDENT CHALLENGE 3

 Copyrights and software piracy are very relevant issues for software users, developers, and educators. There is constant debate among all stakeholders as to the best models for software distribution, and how developers, publishers, or programmers should be compensated. To begin this project, log on to the Internet and use your favorite search engine or consult the Copyright and Piracy InfoWeb to get an in-depth overview of the issue. Armed with this background, select one of the following viewpoints and argue for or against it:

Viewpoints:

a. Free software advocates: As an enabling technology, software should be freely distributed, along with its modifiable source code.

b. Librarians: Copyright laws, especially the Digital Millennium Copyright Act, minimize the needs of the public and go too far in their efforts to protect the rights of software authors.

c. Software Publishers Association: Strong copyright laws and enforcement are essential for companies to publish and support high-quality software.

Directions:

1. Write a two- to five-page paper about this issue, based on information you gather from the Internet.

2. Be sure to cite your sources and list them as part of the paper.

3. Follow your instructor's instructions for formatting and submitting your paper.

INDEPENDENT CHALLENGE 4

 The Computers in Context section of this unit focused on computer and communications technology used by reporters and journalists. Technology has had a major effect on "backpack journalists" who use small-scale digital devices to gather and report the news.

Log on to the Internet and use your favorite search engine to collect information on the advantages and disadvantages of backpack journalism. In your research, you should explore technical issues such as the cost of equipment, video quality, and transmission capabilities. Also explore ethical issues pertaining to on-the-spot news reporting.

1. Create an outline of the major points you researched.

2. Summarize your research in a two- to four-page paper. Make sure you cite sources for your material.

3. Follow your instructor's instructions for formatting and submitting your paper.

C UNIT

LAB: Using the Windows Interface

1. Start the interactive part of the lab. Insert your Tracking Disk if you want to save your QuickCheck results. Perform each of the lab steps as directed and answer all of the lab QuickCheck questions. When you exit the lab, your answers are automatically graded and your results are displayed.

2. Draw a sketch or print a screenshot of the Windows desktop on any computer that you use. Use ToolTips to identify all of the icons on the desktop and the taskbar.

3. Use the Start button and Accessories menu to start an application program called Paint. (If Paint is not installed on your computer, you can use any application software, such as a word processing program.) Draw a sketch or print a screenshot of the Paint (or other application) window and label the following components: Window title, title bar, Maximize/Restore button, Minimize button, Close button, menu bar, toolbar, and scroll bar.

4. Look at each of the menu options provided by the Paint software (or other application). Make a list of those that seem to be standard Windows menu options.

5. Draw a sketch of the Paint program's Print dialog box (or another application's Print dialog box). Label the following parts: buttons, spin box, pull-down list, option button, and check boxes.

LAB: Installing and Uninstalling Software

1. Start the interactive part of the lab. Insert your Tracking Disk if you want to save your QuickCheck results. Perform each of the lab steps as directed and answer all of the lab QuickCheck questions. When you exit the lab, your answers are automatically graded and your results are displayed.

2. Browse the Web and locate a software application that you might like to download. Use information supplied by the Web site to answer the following questions:

    a. What is the name of the program and the URL of the download site?

    b. What is the size of the download file?

    c. According to the instructions, does the download file appear to require manual installation, is it a self-executing zip file, or is it a self-installing executable file?

3. On the computer that you typically use, look through the list of programs (click Start, then select Programs to see a list). List the names of any programs that include their own uninstall routine.

4. On the computer that you typically use, open the Control Panel and then open the Add/Remove Programs dialog box. List the first 10 programs that are currently installed on the computer.

Student Edition Labs

Student Edition Labs

Reinforce the concepts you have learned in this unit through the **Using Windows, Word Processing, Spreadsheets, Databases, Presentation Software, Installing and Uninstalling Software,** and **Advanced Spreadsheets** Student Edition Labs, available online at the Illustrated Computer Concepts Web site.

SAM Labs

SAM

If you have a SAM user profile, you have access to additional content, features, and functionality. Log in to your SAM account and go to your assignments page to see what your instructor has assigned for this unit.

End of Unit Exercises

Visual Workshop

Figure C-28 shows images of the Palm OS, the Windows Mobile OS, and the Symbian OS, respectively. These operating systems are used in handheld computers and smartphones. The image beneath the three images is the Windows operating system designed specifically for tablet PCs.

Figure C-28

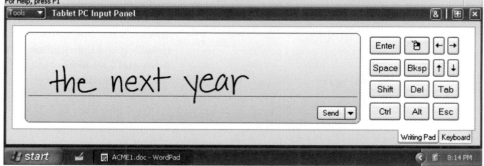

Log on to the Internet. Find Web sites that discuss each of the operating systems shown above.

1. In your research, find five facts about each of the operating systems. Write a brief statement explaining the similarities and differences among these operating systems.

2. Which devices are supported by each of these operating systems?

3. Which utilities are built into these operating systems? Are the utilities similar to utilities you find in desktop computer operating systems? Explain the differences.

4. List three applications that are supported by these operating systems. Are the applications available for personal computer desktop computers also? If so, list one major difference, if any, in the functionality of the software.

Digital Electronics and File Management

CD

Lab

Info Web

TechTV

D
UNIT

Discuss digital data representation

Introduce integrated circuits

Explore processors

Introduce computer memory: RAM

Explore computer memory

Introduce computer file basics

Examine file locations

Introduce file management

Explore file management

Examine file storage

Tech Talk: How a Processor Executes Instructions

Computers in Context: Banking

Issue: Can Online Voting Be Fair and Secure?

Overview

In this unit, you will learn how data representation and digital electronics work together. You will learn about two important components in a computer—the processor and memory. You will learn how they work and how they affect computer performance. You will learn about the different types of memory and how memory works to store and process data. You will get a general introduction to computer files and learn practical information about file management, such as techniques for naming your computer files and for organizing them so that they are easy to access and update. You will also learn how an operating system stores, deletes, and tracks files. The Tech Talk explains the details of how a processor executes instructions. You will have the opportunity to look at computers in the context of banking. The Issue discusses online voting and its impact on the future of elections.

Discussing digital data representation

Data representation refers to the form in which information is conceived, manipulated, and recorded. Because a computer is an electronic digital device, it uses electrical signals to represent data. A **digital device** works with discrete data or digits, such as 1 and 0, "on" and "off," or "yes" and "no." Data exists in the computer as a series of electronic signals represented as 1s and 0s, each of which is referred to as a **bit**. Most computer coding schemes use eight bits to represent each number, letter, or symbol. A series of eight bits is referred to as a **byte**. This lesson looks more closely at the coding schemes used in digital data representation.

■ Just as Morse code uses dashes and dots to represent the letters of the alphabet, computers use sequences of bits to represent numbers, letters, punctuation marks, music, pictures, and videos. **Digital electronics** makes it possible for a computer to manipulate simple "on" and "off" signals to perform complex tasks. The **binary number system** allows computers to represent virtually any number simply by using 0s and 1s, which translate into electrical "on" and "off" signals.

Digital computers use many different coding schemes to represent data. The coding scheme used by a computer depends on whether the data is numeric or character-based.

■ **Numeric data** consists of numbers representing quantities that might be used in arithmetic operations. For example, your annual income is numeric data, as is your age. Computers represent numeric data using the binary number system, also called "base 2." The binary number system has only two digits: 0 and 1. See **Figure D-1**. Notice that the

decimal system uses ten symbols (0, 1, 2, 3, 4, 5, 6, 7, 8, and 9) to represent numbers, but the binary number system uses only two symbols (0 and 1) to represent numbers. For example, the number 3 cannot be used in the binary number system; so instead of *3* you would use *11— one one, not eleven*. These binary digits can be converted to electrical "ons" or "offs" inside a computer.

■ **Character data** is composed of letters, symbols, and numerals that will not be used in arithmetic operations. Examples of character data include your name, address, and hair color. Character data is also represented by a series of 1s and 0s.

■ Several types of codes are used to represent character data, including ASCII, EBCDIC, and Unicode. **ASCII (American Standard Code for Information Interchange)** requires only seven bits for each character. Most personal computers use **Extended ASCII code**, a superset of ASCII, which uses eight bits to represent each character. For example, the Extended ASCII code for an uppercase "A" is 01000001. See **Figure D-2**. Extended ASCII provides codes for 256 characters including uppercase letters, lowercase letters, punctuation symbols, numerals, and additional characters, which are usually boxes, circles, and other graphical symbols. **EBCDIC (Extended Binary-Coded Decimal Interchange Code)** is an alternative 8-bit code, usually used by older IBM mainframe computers, that can also represent 256 characters. **Unicode** uses 16 bits and provides codes for 65,000 characters, including characters from all current written languages.

■ Because computers represent numeric data with binary equivalents, ASCII codes that represent numbers might seem unnecessary. Computers, however, sometimes distinguish between numeric data and numerals. For example, you do not use your social security number in calculations, so a computer considers it to be character data composed of numerals, not numbers.

Figure D-1: Comparing decimal and binary numbers

DECIMAL (BASE 10)	BINARY (BASE 2)
0	0
1	1
2	10
3	11
4	100
5	101
6	110
7	111
8	1000
9	1001
10	1010
11	1011
1000	1111101000

■ To work with pictures and sounds, a computer must **digitize** the information that makes up the picture (such as the colors) and the information that makes up the sound (such as the notes) into 1s and 0s. Computers convert colors and notes into bits and stores them in files as a series of 1s and 0s.

■ Your computer needs to know whether to interpret those 1s and 0s as ASCII code, binary numbers, or the code for a picture or sound. Most computer files contain a **file header**, which is data at the beginning of the file that computers can interpret and that provides information on the code that was used to represent the file data. A file header is stored along with the file and can be read by the computer; it never appears on the screen.

Figure D-2: A sample of Extended ASCII code

The Extended ASCII code uses a series of eight 1s and 0s to represent 256 characters, including lowercase letters, uppercase letters, symbols, and numerals; the first 63 ASCII characters are not shown in this table because they represent special control sequences that cannot be printed

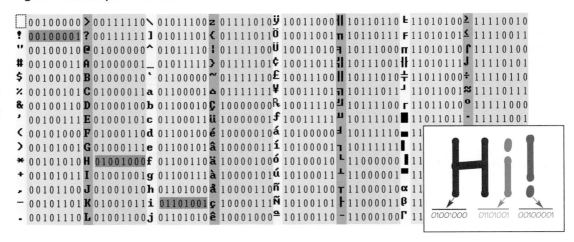

Quantifying bits and bytes

A bit is one binary digit and a byte is eight bits. The word "bit" can be abbreviated as a lowercase "b" and byte can be abbreviated as an uppercase "B."

Bits and bytes are used in different ways. Data transmission speeds are usually expressed in bits, whereas storage space is usually expressed in bytes. The speed 56 Kbps means 56 kilobits per second; the capacity 8 GB means 8 gigabytes. "Kilo" is usually a prefix that means 1,000. For example, $50 K means $50,000. However, when it refers to bits or bytes, a "kilo" is 1,024 because computer engineers measure everything in base 2, and 2^{10} in base 2 is 1,024, not 1,000. So a **kilobit** (abbreviated Kb or Kbit) is 1,024 bits and a **kilobyte** (abbreviated KB or Kbyte) is 1,024 bytes. The prefix "mega" refers to a million, or in the context of bits and bytes, precisely 1,048,576 (the equivalent of 2^{20}). Mb or Mbit is the abbreviation for **megabit**. MB or Mbyte is the abbreviation for **megabyte**.

The prefix "giga" refers to a billion, or precisely 1,073,741,824. A **gigabit** (Gb or Gbit) is approximately one billion bits. A **gigabyte** (GB or Gbyte) is approximately one billion bytes. Gigabytes are typically used to refer to RAM and hard disk capacity. Tera- (trillion), peta- (thousand trillion), and exa- (quintillion) are prefixes for large amounts of data. **Figure D-3** summarizes the commonly used terms to quantify computer data.

Some computer scientists have proposed alternative terminology to dispel the ambiguity in terms such as "kilo" that can mean 1,000 or 1,024. They suggest the following prefixes: Kibi =1,024, Mebi = 1,048,576, and Gibi = 1,073,741,824.

Figure D-3

Bit	One binary digit
Byte	8 bits
Kilobit	1,024 or 2^{10} bits
Kilobyte	1,024 or 2^{10} bytes
Megabit	1,048,576 or 2^{20} bits
Megabyte	1,048,576 or 2^{20} bytes
Gigabit	2^{30} bits
Gigabyte	2^{30} bytes
Terabyte	2^{40} bytes
Petabyte	2^{50} bytes
Exabyte	2^{60} bytes

Introducing integrated circuits

If it were not for digital electronics, computers would be huge, and the inside of a computer's system unit would contain a jumble of wires and other electronic components. Today's computers contain relatively few parts. Computers are electronic devices that use electrical signals and circuits to represent, process, and move data. Bits take the form of electrical pulses that can travel over circuits. An **integrated circuit (IC)** is a super-thin slice of semiconducting material packed with microscopic circuit elements such as wires, transistors, capacitors, logic gates, and resistors. The terms *computer chip*, *microchip*, and *chip* are all synonymous with the term *integrated circuit*.

■ A computer's system unit contains circuit boards, storage devices, and a power supply that converts current from an AC wall outlet into the DC current used by computer circuitry. See **Figure D-4**. The integrated circuit is essential to a computer system.

■ Integrated circuits are made from **semiconducting materials** (or "semiconductors"), such as silicon and germanium. The conductive properties of selective parts of the semiconducting material can be enhanced to create miniature electronic pathways and components, such as transistors.

Figure D-4: Inside a typical desktop computer

Power supply
CD-ROM drive
Floppy disk drive
Fan
Hard disk drive
Processor
Cables that transfer data from storage devices to the motherboard
Main circuit board (motherboard)
Expansion cards

Which companies produce most of today's popular processors?

A typical computer ad contains a long list of specifications describing a computer's components and capabilities. Most computer specifications begin with the processor brand, type, and speed. Intel is the world's largest chipmaker and supplies a sizeable percentage of the processors that power PCs. In 1971, Intel introduced the world's first processor, the 4004. In 1974, the Intel 8088, a descendant of the 4004, was developed; it became the cornerstone of the processor revolution for personal computers. The company has continued to produce a steady stream of new processor models.

AMD (Advanced Micro Devices) is Intel's chief rival in the PC chip market. It produces processors that work just like Intel's chips, but at a lower price.

AMD's Athlon and Opteron processors are direct competitors to Intel's Pentium and Itanium lines and have a slight performance advantage according to some benchmark tests. Historically, Motorola and IBM were the main chip suppliers for Apple computers, but Apple began a transition to Intel chips in 2005. IBM produces RISC-based POWER processors for servers and other high-performance computers.

The processors that are marketed with today's computers will handle most business, educational, and entertainment applications. While it is technically possible to upgrade your computer's processor, the cost and technical factors discourage processor upgrades.

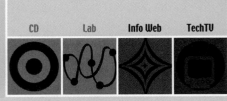
- Integrated circuits can be used for processors, memory, and support circuitry. Integrated circuits are classified by the number of miniaturized components they contain—from small-scale integration (SSI) of less than 100 components per chip to ultra large-scale integration (ULSI) of more than 1 million components per chip.

- Each processor, memory module, and support circuitry chip is packaged in a protective carrier or "chip package." Chip carriers vary in shape and size including small rectangular **DIPs (dual in-line packages)** with caterpillar-like legs protruding from a black, rectangular body; long, slim **DIMMs (dual inline memory modules)**; pin-cushion-like **PGAs (pin-grid arrays)**; and cassette-like **SEC (single-edge contact) cartridges**. See **Figure D-5**. The pins on each chip package provide the electronic connection between the integrated circuit and other computer components.

Figure D-5: Integrated circuits

  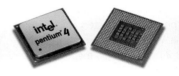 

A DIP has two rows of pins that connect the IC circuitry to a circuit board

A DIMM is a small circuit board containing several chips, typically used for memory

A PGA is a square chip package with pins arranged in concentric squares, typically used for processors

An SEC cartridge houses a circuit board and processor chip

- Integrated circuits are connected to the computer's main circuit board, called a **motherboard** or main system board. The motherboard provides sockets for chips, slots for small circuit boards, and the circuitry that connects all these components. See **Figure D-6**. Some chips are permanently soldered in place. Other chips are plugged into special sockets and connectors, which allow chips to be removed for repairs or upgrades. When multiple chips are required for a single function, such as generating stereo-quality sound, the chips all might be connected to a separate small circuit board, such as a sound card, which can be plugged into a special slot-like connector on the motherboard.

- A **processor** (sometimes referred to as a microprocessor) is an integrated circuit designed to process instructions. It is the most important component of a computer, and usually the most expensive single component. Looking inside a computer, you can usually identify the processor because it is the largest chip on the motherboard. Most of today's processors are housed in a PGA (pin grid array) chip package. A processor is a very complex integrated circuit, containing as many as 400 million miniaturized electronic components.

Figure D-6: The motherboard

Expansion card

Expansion slots hold additional expansion cards, such as a modem or sound card

Battery powers the computer's real-time clock

Circuitry transports data from one component to another

ROM chip

Processor

DIMM module containing memory chips

Connectors for storage device cables

Connector for power supply

Exploring processors

All processors have two main parts: the arithmetic logic unit (ALU) and the control unit. To process data, each of these units performs specific tasks. A processor's performance is affected by several factors including clock speed, word size, cache size, instruction set, and processing techniques. This lesson looks at the two main parts of a processor and the factors that affect processor performance.

- The **arithmetic logic unit (ALU)** is the circuitry that performs arithmetic operations, such as addition and subtraction. It also performs logical operations, such as comparing two numbers using the logical operators less than (<), greater than (>), or equal to (=). Logical operations also allow for comparing characters as well as sorting and grouping information. The ALU uses **registers** to hold data that is being processed. **Figure D-7** illustrates how the ALU works.

- The processor's **control unit** fetches each instruction, as illustrated in **Figure D-8**. A processor executes instructions that are provided by a computer program. The list of instructions that a processor can perform is called its **instruction set**. These instructions are hardwired into the processor's circuitry and include basic arithmetic and logical operations, fetching data, and clearing registers. A computer can perform very complex tasks, but it does so by performing a combination of simple tasks from its instruction set.

- How efficiently the ALU and the control unit work are determined by different performance factors. Processor speed is one of the most important indicators in determining the power of a computer system. The **processor clock** is a timing device that sets the pace (the **clock speed**) for executing instructions. The clock speed of a processor is specified in **megahertz (MHz)**—millions of cycles per second or **gigahertz (GHz)**—billions of cycles per second. A cycle is the smallest unit of time a processor can recognize. The faster the clock, the more instructions the processor can execute per second. A specification such as 2.8 GHz means that the processor's clock operates at a speed of 2.8 billion cycles per second.

- **Word size**, another performance factor, refers to the number of bits that a processor can manipulate at one time. Word size is based on the size of the registers in the ALU and the capacity of circuits that lead to those registers. A processor with a 32-bit word size, for example, has 32-bit registers, processes eight bits at a time, and is referred to as a 32-bit processor. Processors with a larger word size can process more data during each processor cycle. Today's personal computers typically contain 32-bit or 64-bit processors.

- **Cache**, sometimes called RAM cache or cache memory, is high-speed memory that a processor can access more rapidly than memory elsewhere on the system board. A Level 1 cache (L1) is built into the processor chip, whereas a Level 2 cache (L2) is located on a separate chip, and so it takes a processor more time to get data from L2 cache to the processor. Cache capacity is usually measured in kilobytes. The amount of cache memory, as well as its location, affects performance.

Figure D-7: How the ALU works

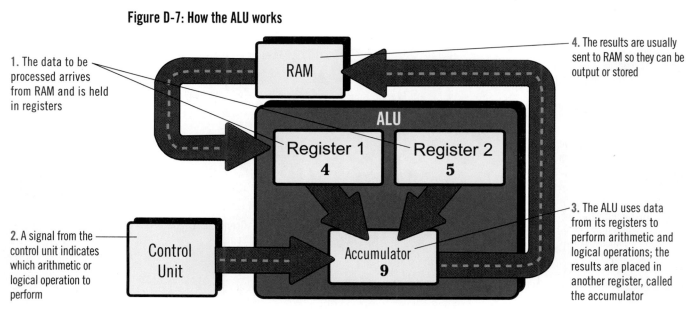

1. The data to be processed arrives from RAM and is held in registers

RAM

4. The results are usually sent to RAM so they can be output or stored

ALU

Register 1
4

Register 2
5

2. A signal from the control unit indicates which arithmetic or logical operation to perform

Control Unit

Accumulator
9

3. The ALU uses data from its registers to perform arithmetic and logical operations; the results are placed in another register, called the accumulator

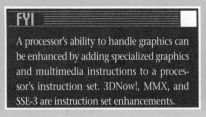
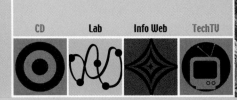

Figure D-8: How the control unit works

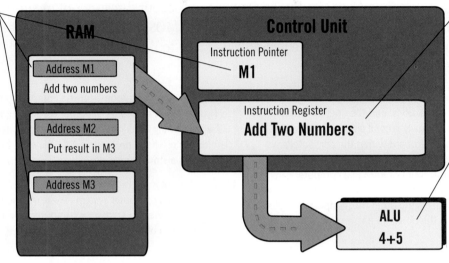

1. The RAM address of the instruction is kept in the instruction pointer; when the instruction has been executed, the address in the instruction pointer changes to indicate the RAM address of the next instruction to be executed

RAM

Address M1
Add two numbers

Address M2
Put result in M3

Address M3

Control Unit

Instruction Pointer
M1

Instruction Register
Add Two Numbers

ALU
4+5

2. The control unit retrieves an instruction from RAM and puts it in the instruction register; the control unit interprets the instruction in its instruction register

3. Depending on the instruction, the control unit will get data from RAM, tell the ALU to perform an operation, or change the memory address of the instruction pointer

■ The instruction set used by a processor also affects performance. As chip designers developed various instruction sets for processors, they tended to add increasingly more complex instructions, each of which required several clock cycles for execution. A processor with a very complex set of instructions uses **CISC (complex instruction set computer)** technology. A processor with a limited set of simple instructions uses **RISC (reduced instruction set computer)** technology. Processors in most PCs use CISC technology.

■ Performance is also affected by the processing technique used in the processor. With **serial processing**, the processor must complete all of the steps in the instruction cycle before it begins to execute the next instruction. However, using a technology called **pipelining**, a processor can begin executing a second instruction before it completes the previous instruction. Many of today's processors also perform **parallel processing**, in which multiple instructions are executed at the same time. **Hyper-Threading** refers to a technology that enables processors to execute multiple instructions in parallel. As an alternative to using more than one processor, some computers have a **dual core processor**, which is a single chip containing the circuitry for two processors. A dual core processor is faster than a single core processor. To gain maximum speed when using a dual core processor, however, your computer's operating system and software should be optimized for dual core processing.

Benchmarking

All things being equal, a computer with a 3.8 GHz processor is faster than a computer with a 2.4 GHz processor—and a computer with a processor that has a larger word size can process more data during each processor cycle than a computer with a processor that has a smaller word size. Furthermore, all things being equal, a computer with Level 1 cache is faster than a computer with the same amount of Level 2 cache. But all things are not equal. So how do you tell the overall performance of a computer and its processor? Various testing laboratories run a series of tests called **benchmarks** to gauge the overall speed of a processor. These results can be used to compare the results to other processors. The results of benchmark tests are usually available on the Web and are published in computer magazine articles.

Introducing computer memory: RAM

Memory is the electronic circuitry linked directly to the processor that holds data and instructions when they are not being transported from one place to another. Computers use four categories of memory: random access memory (RAM), virtual memory, read-only memory (ROM), and CMOS memory. Each type of memory is characterized by the type of data it contains and the technology it uses to hold the data.

- **RAM (random access memory)** is a temporary holding area for data, application program instructions, and the operating system. In a personal computer, RAM is usually several chips or small circuit boards that plug into the motherboard within the computer's system unit. Next to the processor, RAM is one of the most expensive computer components. The amount of RAM in a computer can, therefore, affect the overall price of a computer system. Along with processor speed, RAM capacity is the other most important factor in determining and comparing the power of a computer system.

- RAM is the "waiting room" for the computer's processor. Refer to **Figure D-9**. It holds raw data that is waiting to be processed and the program instructions for processing that data. In addition, RAM holds the results of processing until they can be stored more permanently on a storage medium.

- RAM also holds operating system instructions that control the basic functions of a computer system. These instructions are loaded into RAM every time you start your computer, and they remain there until you turn off your computer.

Figure D-9: What RAM does

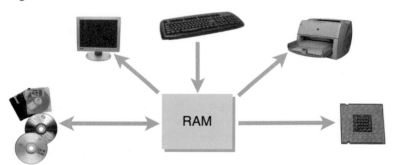

RAM contains portions of the operating system and portions of application programs that are waiting to be stored, processed, or printed

What are SDRAM and RDRAM?

Most of today's personal computers use SDRAM. SDRAM (synchronous dynamic RAM) is fast and relatively inexpensive. Recent innovations, such as dual-channel technology and double data rate (DDR) have increased SDRAM speed. SDRAM is the most popular type of RAM in today's computers. It is typically available on a small circuit board called a DIMM (dual inline memory module), as shown in **Figure D-10**.

Another type of RAM is RDRAM (rambus dynamic RAM), which was first developed for the popular Nintendo 64® game system and adapted for use in personal computers in 1999. While SDRAM can deliver data at a maximum speed of about 100 MHz, RDRAM can transfer data at up to 800 MHz. However, because it is more expensive than SDRAM, RDRAM is usually found in high-performance workstations rather than in personal computers.

Figure D-10

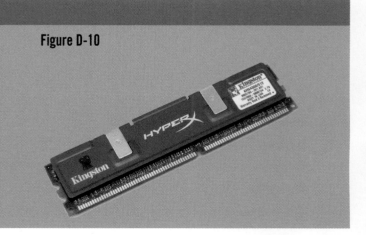

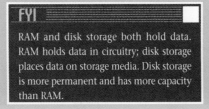

FYI

RAM and disk storage both hold data. RAM holds data in circuitry; disk storage places data on storage media. Disk storage is more permanent and has more capacity than RAM.

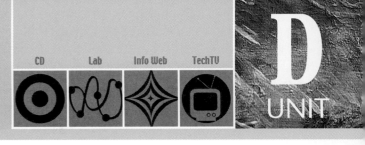

CD   Lab   Info Web   TechTV

D

UNIT

■ In RAM, electronic parts called **capacitors** hold the bits that represent data. You can visualize the capacitors as microscopic lights that can be turned on or off. Refer to **Figure D-11**. A charged capacitor is "turned on" and represents a "1" bit. A discharged capacitor is "turned off" and represents a "0" bit. You can visualize the capacitors as being arranged in banks of eight. Each bank holds eight bits, or one byte, of data.

■ Each RAM location has an address and holds one byte of data. A RAM address at each location helps the computer locate data as needed for processing.

■ In some respects, RAM is similar to a chalkboard. You can use a chalkboard to write mathematical formulas, erase them, and then write an outline for a report. In a similar way, RAM can hold numbers and formulas when you balance your checkbook, then hold the text of your English essay when you use word processing software. The content of RAM can be changed just by changing the charge of the capacitors, which is done as you input data and the computer processes that data. Unlike a chalkboard, however, RAM is volatile, which means that it requires electrical power to hold data. If the computer is turned off, or if the power goes out, all data stored in RAM instantly and permanently disappears.

■ The capacity of RAM is usually expressed in megabytes (MB). Today's personal computers typically feature between 128 MB and 2 GB of RAM. The amount of RAM needed by your computer depends on the software that you use. RAM requirements are routinely specified on the outside of a software package. If it turns out that you need more RAM, you can purchase and install additional RAM up to the limit set by the computer manufacturer.

■ RAM components vary in speed. RAM speed is often expressed in **nanoseconds**, or billionths of a second. Lower numbers mean faster transmission, processing, and storage of data. For example, 8 ns RAM is faster than 10 ns RAM. RAM speed can also be expressed in MHz (millions of cycles per second). Just the opposite of nanoseconds, higher MHz ratings mean faster speeds. For example, 533 MHz RAM is faster than 400 MHz RAM.

Figure D-11: How RAM works

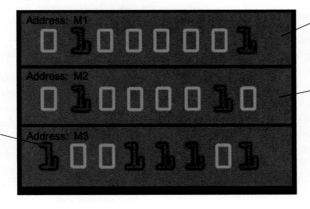

The two charged capacitors at this RAM address represent the letter "A"

A different sequence of charged capacitors represents the letter "B"

Each bank of capacitors holds eight bits of data

Exploring computer memory

In addition to RAM, a computer uses three other types of memory: virtual memory, ROM, and CMOS. This lesson looks at these types of computer memory and how all computer memory types work together.

■ If you want to work with several programs and large graphics at the same time, personal computer operating systems are quite adept at allocating RAM space to multiple programs. If a program exceeds the allocated space, the operating system uses an area of the hard disk called **virtual memory** to store parts of a program or data file until they are needed. By selectively exchanging the data in RAM with the data in virtual memory, your computer effectively gains almost unlimited memory capacity.

One disadvantage of virtual memory is reduced performance. Too much dependence on virtual memory can have a negative effect on your computer's performance because getting data from a mechanical device, such as a hard disk, is much slower than getting data from an electronic device, such as RAM. Installing as much RAM as your computer system allows will help your computer speed through all of its tasks.

■ **ROM (read-only memory)** is a type of memory circuitry that holds the computer's startup routine. ROM is housed in a single integrated circuit, usually a fairly large, caterpillar-like DIP package that is plugged into the motherboard.

While RAM is temporary and volatile, ROM is permanent and non-volatile. ROM circuitry holds "hard-wired" instructions that remain in place even when the computer power is turned off. This is a familiar concept to anyone who has used a hand-held calculator, which includes various "hard-wired" routines for calculating square roots, cosines, and other functions. The instructions in ROM are permanent, and the only way to change them is to replace the ROM chip.

■ When you turn on your computer, the processor receives electrical power and is ready to begin executing instructions. But, because the power was off, RAM is empty and contains no instructions for the processor to execute. Now ROM plays its part. ROM contains a small set of instructions called the **ROM BIOS (basic input/output system)**. These instructions tell the computer how to access the hard disk, find the operating system, and load it into RAM. Once the operating system is loaded, the computer can understand your input, display output, run software, and access your data. While ROM BIOS instructions are accomplished mainly without user intervention or knowledge, the computer will not function without the ROM chip and the BIOS instructions.

■ In order to operate correctly, a computer must have some basic information about storage, memory, and display configurations. For example, your computer needs to know how much memory is available so that it can allocate space for all of the programs that you want to run. RAM goes blank when the computer power is turned off, so configuration information cannot be stored there. ROM would not be a good place for this information either because it holds data on a permanent basis. For example, if you added more memory modules, you could not update the memory specification information in ROM, which means the new memory would not be recognized by your computer system. To store some basic system information, your computer needs a type of memory that is more permanent than RAM but less permanent than ROM.

CMOS (complementary metal oxide semiconductor) memory, pronounced "SEE moss," is a type of memory that requires very little power to hold data. CMOS memory is stored on a chip that can be powered by a small, rechargeable battery plugged into the motherboard. The battery trickles power to the CMOS chip so that it can retain vital data about your computer system configuration even when your computer is turned off.

When you change the configuration of your computer system by adding RAM, for example, the data in CMOS must be updated. Some operating systems recognize such changes and automatically perform the update; or you can manually change CMOS settings by running the CMOS setup program. See **Figure D-12**. To access the CMOS setup program, press and hold down the F1 key as your computer boots. But be careful! If you edit these settings and make a mistake, your computer might not be able to start.

■ Even though virtual memory, ROM, and CMOS have important roles in the operation of a computer, it is really RAM capacity that makes a difference you can notice. The more data and programs that can fit into RAM, the less time your computer will spend moving data to and from virtual memory. With lots of RAM, you will find that documents scroll faster and that many graphics operations take less time than with a computer that has less RAM capacity.

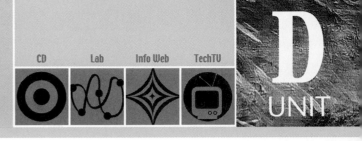

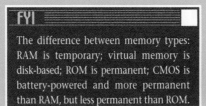

CD   Lab   Info Web   TechTU

Figure D-12: CMOS setup program

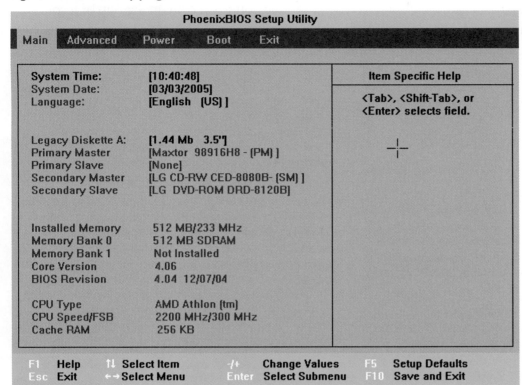

PhoenixBIOS Setup Utility				
Main	Advanced	Power	Boot	Exit

		Item Specific Help
System Time:	[10:40:48]	
System Date:	[03/03/2005]	<Tab>, <Shift-Tab>, or
Language:	[English [US]]	<Enter> selects field.
Legacy Diskette A:	[1.44 Mb 3.5"]	
Primary Master	[Maxtor 98916H8 - [PM]]	
Primary Slave	[None]	
Secondary Master	[LG CD-RW CED-8080B- [SM]]	
Secondary Slave	[LG DVD-ROM DRD-8120B]	
Installed Memory	512 MB/233 MHz	
Memory Bank 0	512 MB SDRAM	
Memory Bank 1	Not Installed	
Core Version	4.06	
BIOS Revision	4.04 12/07/04	
CPU Type	AMD Athlon [tm]	
CPU Speed/FSB	2200 MHz/300 MHz	
Cache RAM	256 KB	

F1	Help	↑↓ Select Item	-/+	Change Values	F5	Setup Defaults
Esc	Exit	←→ Select Menu	Enter	Select Submenu	F10	Save and Exit

CMOS holds computer configuration settings, such as the date and time, hard disk capacity, number of floppy disk drives, and RAM capacity

Understanding memory specified in computer ads

Most ads specify RAM capacity, speed, and type. When you see the specification "2 GB 533 MHz SDRAM (max. 4 GB)" in a computer ad similar to the one in **Figure D-13**, you know that the advertised computer comes with 2 gigabytes of installed RAM (plenty to run most of today's software), that it operates at 533 megahertz (fairly fast), and that it uses SDRAM (a little slower and less expensive than RDRAM). You will also have important information about the maximum amount of RAM that can be installed in the computer—4 GB, which is needed for memory-intensive graphic programs and games.

Figure D-13

- Intel Pentium EE 840 64-bit dual core processor 3.2 GHz with Hyper-Threading
- 2 MB L2 cache
- 2 GB 533 MHz SDRAM (max. 4 GB)
- 160 GB SATA HD (7200 rpm)
- 48X CD-RW+16X DVD+RW/+R with double-layer write capable

Introducing computer file basics

A **computer file** or simply "file" is defined as a named collection of data that exists on a storage medium, such as a hard disk, floppy disk, solid state storage device, CD, DVD, or tape. A file can contain a group of records, a document, a photo, music, a video, an e-mail message, or a computer program. This lesson looks at several common characteristics of computer files—type, filename, and format.

■ There are several categories of files, such as data files, executable files, configuration files, and drivers. A computer file is classified according to the data it contains, the software that was used to create it, and the way the computer uses it. See **Table D-1**.

■ Every file has a filename. The filename has two parts—the filename itself and the filename extension.

■ A **filename** is a unique set of characters and numbers that identifies a file and should describe its contents. When you save a file, you must provide it with a valid filename that adheres to specific rules, referred to as **filenaming conventions**. Each operating system has a unique set of filenaming conventions. See **Table D-2** for rules for both Windows and Mac OS.

If an operating system attaches special significance to a symbol, you might not be able to use it in a filename. For example, Windows uses the colon (:) and the backslash (\) to separate the device letter from a filename or folder, as in C:\Music. A filename such as Report:\2004 is not valid because the operating system does not allow the use of the colon and backslash in filenames; the operating system would not recognize a file that was named using a colon and backslash.

Some operating systems also contain a list of **reserved words** that are used as commands or special identifiers. You cannot use these words alone as a filename. You can, however, use these words as part of a longer filename. For example, the Windows XP operating system would not recognize a file with the filename Nul, but it would recognize a file with a filename such as Nul Committee Notes.doc.

■ A **filename extension** (or file extension) is separated from the main filename by a period, as in Paint.exe. A filename extension further describes the file contents. Generally, the software application you are using automatically assigns the filename extension when you save a file. If you do not see a filename extension when you use the Save, Save As, or Open dialog box or when using Windows Explorer, Windows is set to hide (but not erase) filename extensions. To view filename extensions, open Windows Explorer, click Tools on the menu bar, click Folder Options, click the View tab, then click the Hide extensions for known file types check box to clear the mark.

Knowledge of filename extensions comes in handy when you receive a file on a disk or over the Internet but you do not know much about its contents. If you are familiar with filename extensions, you will know the file format and, therefore, which application to use when you want to open the file.

Table D-1: Types of files

TYPE OF FILE	DESCRIPTION	EXTENSION
Configuration file	Information about a program that the computer uses to allocate the resources necessary to run it	.cfg .sys .mif .bin .ini
Program data files	Contains data that is necessary for a task but that is not created by the user; such as a dictionary or help file	.dat .hlp .txt .bmp .hlp
Temporary file	Contains data while a file is open, but that data is discarded when the file is closed	.tmp
Program file	The main executable file for a computer program	.exe .com
Support files	Program instructions that are executed in conjunction with the main .exe file for a program	.ocx .vbx .vbs .dll
Data files	Documents, images, spreadsheets, databases, music, sound, video, Web page, any file created by a user with a program	.doc .bmp .jpg .gif .html .xls .mdb .mpg .pdf .fla

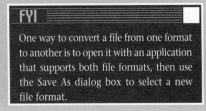
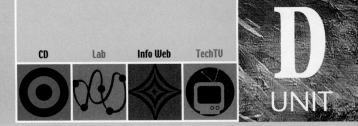

Table D-2: Filenaming conventions

WHAT IS THE CONVENTION FOR...?	FOR WINDOWS THE RULE IS...	FOR MAC OS THE RULE IS...
Filename length	Filename and extension cannot exceed 255 characters	Maximum 31 characters (no extension)
Spaces	Allowed	Allowed
Numbers	Allowed	Allowed
Characters not allowed	* \ : < > l " / ?	:
Filenames not allowed	Aux, Com1, Com2, Com3, Com4, Con, Lpt1, Lpt2, Lpt3, Prn, Nul	Any filename is allowed
Using upper or lowercase	Not case sensitive	Not case sensitive

■ A filename extension is usually related to the **file format**, which is defined as the arrangement of data in a file and the coding scheme that is used to represent the data. Files that contain graphics are usually stored using a different file format than files containing text. Hundreds of file formats exist, and you will encounter many of them as you use a variety of software. As you work with a variety of files, you will begin to recognize that some filename extensions, such as .txt (text file) or .jpg (graphics file), indicate a file type and are not specific to application software.

You will also recognize that other filename extensions, such as .doc (Word), .xls (Excel), and .zip (WinZip), can help you identify which application was used to create the data file. These filename extensions

indicate the **native file format**, which is the file format used to store data files created with that software program. For example, Microsoft Word stores data files in doc format. A software application can typically open files that exist in its "native" file format, plus several additional file formats. When using a software application such as Microsoft Word to open a file, the program displays any files that have the filename extension for its native file format, as shown in **Figure D-14**. Microsoft Word opens files in its native document (.doc) format, and files in formats such as HTML (.htm or .html), text (.txt), and rich text format (.rtf). Within the Windows environment, you can discover which formats a particular software program can open by looking at the Files of type list in the Open dialog box.

Figure D-14: Filename extensions

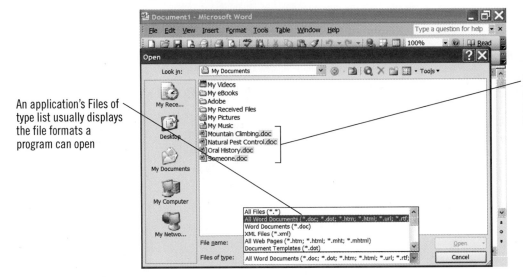

An application's Files of type list usually displays the file formats a program can open

Files with the native file extension are displayed in the Open, Save, and Save As dialog boxes

Examining file locations

Programs and data files have unique names and locations to ensure that the computer can find them. To designate a file's location, you must specify where the file is stored on the storage medium. This lesson looks more closely at file locations—how to assign them and the information about each file that is available at the file's location.

■ The Windows operating system labels storage devices with letters, such as A: and C:. See **Figure D-15**. If the PC has a floppy disk drive, it is usually assigned device letter A and is referred to as "drive A." A device letter is usually followed by a colon, so drive A could be designated as A: or as 3½" Floppy (A:). The main hard disk drive is usually referred to as "drive C" or as Locak Disk (C:). Additional storage devices can be assigned letters from D through Z. Although most PCs use the standard of drive A for the floppy disk drive and drive C for the hard disk drive, the device letters for CD, Zip, and DVD drives are not standardized. For example, the DVD/CD-RW on your computer might be assigned device letter E, whereas the DVD/CD-RW on another computer might be assigned device letter R.

Figure D-15: Labeling storage devices

Name	Type
Hard Disk Drives	
Local Disk (C:)	Local Disk
Devices with Removable Storage	
3½ Floppy (A:)	3½-Inch Floppy Disk
DVD/CD-RW Drive (D:)	CD Drive
Network Drives	
files on 'Mtcnas' (H:)	Network Drive

■ An operating system maintains a list of files called a **directory** for each storage medium. The main directory of a disk is referred to as the **root directory**. On a PC, the root directory is typically identified by the device letter followed by a backslash. For example, the root directory of the hard disk drive would be C:\.

■ A root directory is often subdivided into smaller **subdirectories**. When you use Windows, Mac OS, or a Linux graphical file manager, these subdirectories are depicted as **folders** because they work like the folders in a filing cabinet to store related files. Each folder has a name. For example, you could use a folder called My Documents to hold reports, letters, and so on. You could use another folder called My Music to hold your MP3 files. Because folders can be created within other folders, you might create a folder called Jazz within your My Music folder to hold your jazz collection and another folder called Reggae within your My Music folder to hold your reggae collection.

■ A computer file's location is defined by a **file specification** (sometimes called a **path**), which begins with the drive letter and is followed by the folder(s), filename, and filename extension. A folder name is separated from a drive letter and other folder names by a special symbol. In Windows, this symbol is the backslash (\). For example, the path to the folder for your reggae music (within the My Music folder on drive C) would be written as C:\My Music\Reggae. The path to the folder for the jazz collection would be C:\My Music\Jazz. By storing files in folders, you assign each file a place in an organized hierarchy of folders. Suppose that you have stored an MP3 file called Marley One Love in the Reggae folder on your hard disk drive. Its file specification would be C:\My Music\ Reggae\Marley One Love.mp3, as shown in **Figure D-16**.

Figure D-16: A file specification

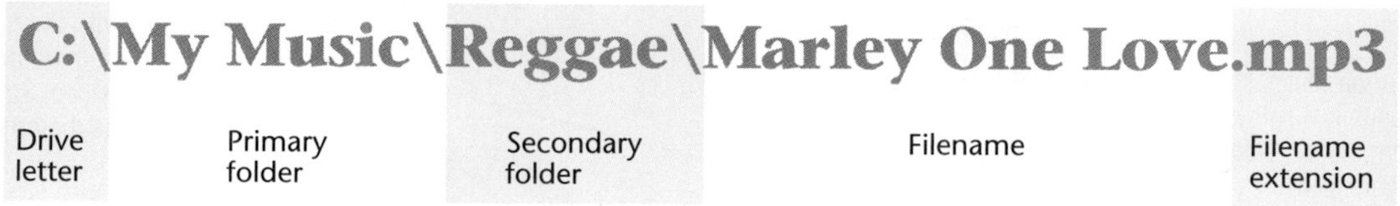

C:\My Music\Reggae\Marley One Love.mp3

| Drive letter | Primary folder | Secondary folder | Filename | Filename extension |

■ A file contains data, stored as a group of bits. The more bits, the larger the file. **File size** is usually measured in bytes, kilobytes, or megabytes. Knowing the size of a file can be important, especially when you are sending a file as an e-mail attachment. Your computer's operating system keeps track of file sizes.

■ Your computer keeps track of the date on which a file was created or last modified. The **file date** is useful if you have saved a file using slightly different filenames each time and you want to know which is the most recent.

■ The operating system keeps track of file locations, filenames, filename extensions, file size, and file dates. See **Figure D-17**. This information is always available to you through a file management utility, which will be discussed in the next lesson.

Figure D-17: File sizes and dates

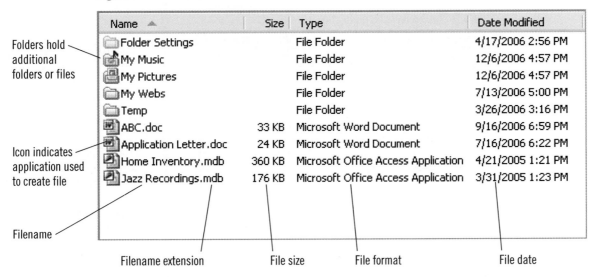

Folders hold additional folders or files

Icon indicates application used to create file

Filename

Filename extension   File size   File format   File date

Name ▲	Size	Type	Date Modified
Folder Settings		File Folder	4/17/2006 2:56 PM
My Music		File Folder	12/6/2006 4:57 PM
My Pictures		File Folder	12/6/2006 4:57 PM
My Webs		File Folder	7/13/2006 5:00 PM
Temp		File Folder	3/26/2006 3:16 PM
ABC.doc	33 KB	Microsoft Word Document	9/16/2006 6:59 PM
Application Letter.doc	24 KB	Microsoft Word Document	7/16/2006 6:22 PM
Home Inventory.mdb	360 KB	Microsoft Office Access Application	4/21/2005 1:21 PM
Jazz Recordings.mdb	176 KB	Microsoft Office Access Application	3/31/2005 1:23 PM

Deleting files

You may have noticed when using Windows that when you delete a file it is moved to the Recycle Bin. The Windows Recycle Bin and similar utilities in other operating systems are designed to protect you from accidentally deleting files stored on your hard disk drive that you actually need. The operating system moves the file to the Recycle Bin folder. The "deleted" file still takes up space on the disk, but does not appear in the usual directory listing. The file does, however, appear in the directory listing for the Recycle Bin folder, and you can undelete any files in this listing. It is important to remember that only files you delete from your hard disk drive are sent to the Recycle Bin; files you delete from a removable storage medium, such as a floppy disk, USB device, CD, or DVD, are not sent to the Recycle Bin.

To delete data from a disk in such a way that no one can ever read it, you can use special file shredder software. You might find this software handy if you plan to donate your computer to an organization and you want to make sure that your personal data is no longer on the hard disk nor able to be recovered from the hard disk.

Introducing file management

File management encompasses any procedure that helps you organize your computer-based files so that you can find and use them more efficiently. Depending on your computer's operating system, you may be able to organize and manipulate your files from within an application program or by using a special file management utility provided by the operating system.

■ Application software provides file management capabilities for files created within the application. For example, an application software program provides a way to open files and save them in a specific folder on a designated storage device. Most application software provides access to file management tasks through the Save and Open dialog boxes. These dialog boxes allow you to do more than just save a file. You can use them to perform other file management tasks such as rename a file, delete a file, or create a new folder, as shown in **Figure D-18**.

Figure D-18: The Save As dialog box

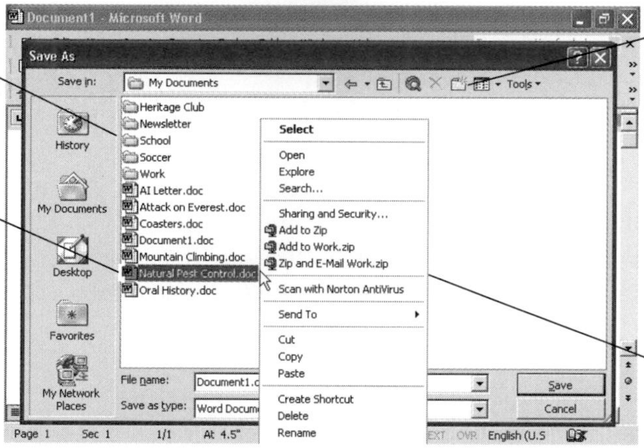

To rename or delete a folder, right-click it and then use one of the options on the shortcut menu

To rename or delete a file, right-click the filename, then select a command from the shortcut menu that appears; in addition to the Rename and Delete options, this menu might also include options to print the file, e-mail it, or scan it for viruses

Click this button to create a new folder

Click any option on the shortcut menu to work with the selected file

Save vs. Save As dialog box

Knowing how to save a file is a crucial file management skill. The Save As command is generally an option on the File menu. In addition to the Save As option, the menu also contains a Save option. The difference between the two options is subtle, but useful. The Save As option allows you to select a name and storage device for a file, whereas the Save option simply saves a file using its current name and to its current location. When you try to use the Save option for a file that does not yet have a filename, your application will open the Save As dialog box, even though you selected the Save option. The flowchart in **Figure D-19** will help you decide whether to use the Save or the Save As command.

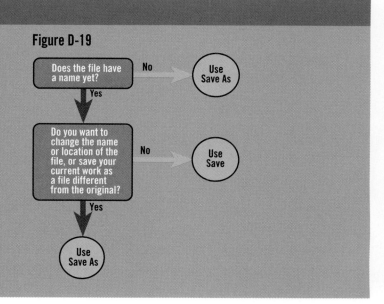

Figure D-19

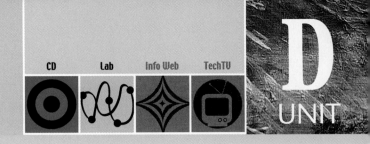
■ At times, however, you might want to work with groups of files, or perform other file operations that are inconvenient to perform within the Save or Open dialog boxes. For these tasks, most operating systems provide **file management utilities**, shown in **Figure D-20**, that give you the "big picture" of the files you have stored on your disks and help you work with them. File management utilities are designed to help you organize and manipulate the files that are stored on your computer. Most file management operations begin with locating a particular file or folder. A file management utility should make it easy to find what you are looking for by drilling down through your computer's hierarchy of folders and files.

Windows provides a file management utility called **Windows Explorer** that can be accessed from the My Computer icon or from

the Windows Explorer command on the Start menu. On computers running Mac OS, the file management utilities are called the **Finder** and **Spotlight**. These utilities help you view a list of files, find files, move files from one place to another, make copies of files, delete files, discover file properties, and rename files.

■ In addition to utilities that help you find or access information in files and folders, there are utilities, called **desktop search tools**, that help you find and access information stored in e-mails, Web pages, and contact lists. Desktop search tools are offered by third party vendors such as Google and Yahoo! and are also being included in the most recent operating system utilities.

Figure D-20: File management utilities

The Windows file management utility can be tailored to show files as icons (top) or as a list (below)

Mac OS provides a file management utility called the Finder

Exploring file management

Creating, opening, saving, renaming, and starting are all actions that you perform on files as you work with software. A file management utility provides tools and procedures to help you keep track of your program and data files, but these tools are most useful when you have a logical plan for organizing your files and when you follow some basic file management guidelines. The filing cabinet is a popular metaphor for computer storage. In this metaphor, each storage device of a computer corresponds to one of the drawers in a filing cabinet. The drawers hold folders and the folders hold files.

■ The Windows Explorer window is divided into two "window panes." The pane on the left side of the window lists each of the storage devices connected to your computer, plus several important system objects, such as My Computer, Network Neighborhood, the Desktop, folders, or files. See **Figure D-21**.

■ If a storage device or system object contains additional information (such as folders or files), it is preceded by a plus sign. Clicking a plus-sign icon "expands" the view to show the next level of information (the sublevel folders and files) in the pane on the right side of the Windows Explorer window. Any folders can contain files or subfolders. Subfolders can be further expanded by clicking their plus-sign icons. You continue expanding folders in this manner until you reach the file you need. Selecting an item in the right pane displays the content of that item in the left pane.

Figure D-21: Windows Explorer

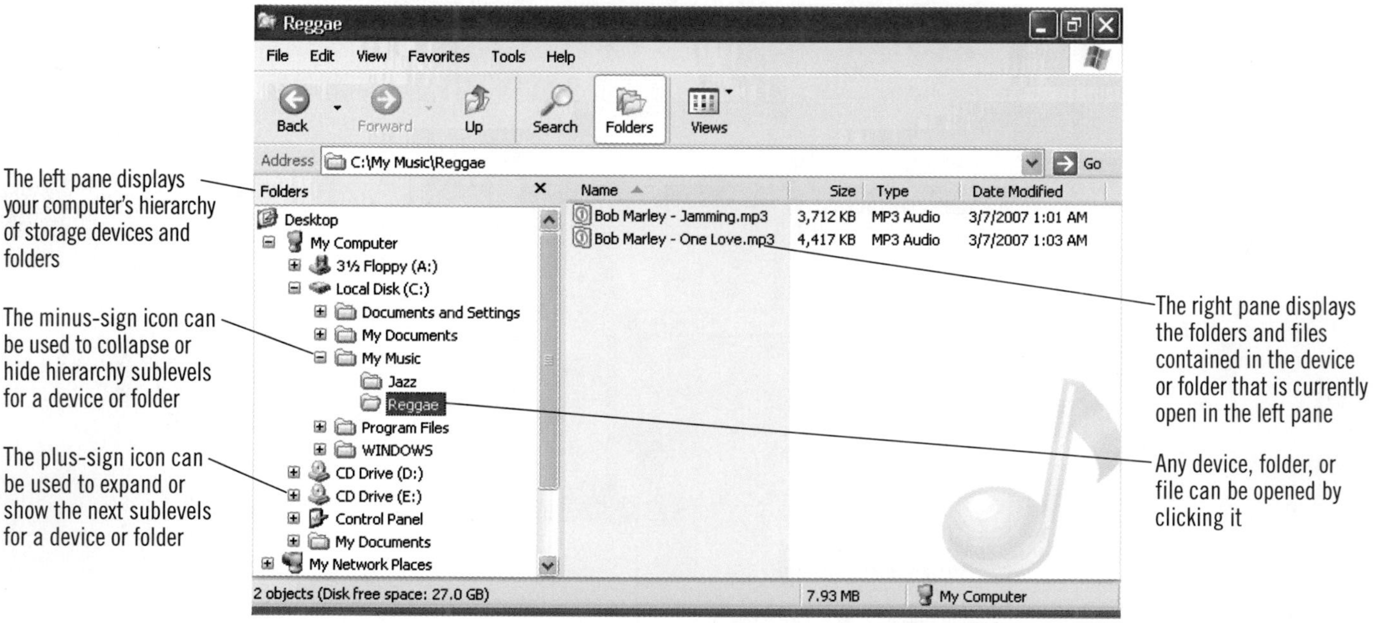

The left pane displays your computer's hierarchy of storage devices and folders

The minus-sign icon can be used to collapse or hide hierarchy sublevels for a device or folder

The plus-sign icon can be used to expand or show the next sublevels for a device or folder

The right pane displays the folders and files contained in the device or folder that is currently open in the left pane

Any device, folder, or file can be opened by clicking it

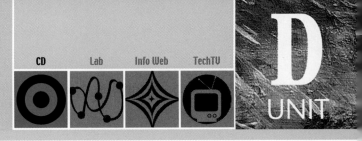
■ Once a storage device or system object has been expanded, it is preceded by a minus sign. Clicking a minus-sign icon collapses the device or the system object so that level of the hierarchy is hidden, and a plus-sign icon again appears next to the device or system object.

■ In addition to locating files and folders, Windows Explorer provides a set of file management tools that will help you manipulate files and folders. Refer to **Table D-3**. To work with either a file or a folder, you must select it. Windows Explorer highlights each item that you select. Once a folder or file is highlighted, you can work with that object, such as copying, moving, renaming, or deleting it. You can select more than one folder or file at a time. One way to do that is to press and hold the Ctrl key while clicking each file or folder you want to select. Once the files and folders are selected, you can work with them just as you would work with a single object.

■ The following tips pertain to managing files on your own computer.

• Use descriptive names. Give your files and folders descriptive names when you save or create them, and avoid using cryptic abbreviations.

• Maintain filename extensions. When renaming a file, keep the original file extension so that you can easily open it with the correct application software.

• Group similar files. Separate files into folders based on subject matter. For example, store your creative writing assignments in one appropriately named folder and your MP3 music files in another appropriately named folder.

• Organize your folders from the top down. When devising a hierarchy of folders, consider how you want to access files and back them up. A backup is a copy of your files made for safekeeping. For example, it is easy to specify one folder and its subfolders for a backup. If your important data is scattered in a variety of folders, however, making backups is more time consuming.

Table D-3: What you can do with files and folders

FILE OR FOLDER COMMAND	DESCRIPTION	EXAMPLES AND NOTES
Rename	Change the name of a file or folder to better describe its contents	Change letter.doc to Letter to Pam 10-6.doc; when renaming a file, you should be careful to keep the same filename extension so that you can open it with the correct application software
Copy	Create a copy of a file or folder on another medium or in a new folder; the file remains in the original location and a duplicate file is added to a different location	Copy several large photograph image files from your hard disk to a flash drive to give to a friend or colleague; copy a document file to a new folder so that you can revise the content in the copy and leave the original content intact
Move	Move a file or folder from one folder to another, or from one storage device to another	Move a folder to a new folder to better organize your hard drive; when you move a file or folder with files, it is erased from its original location, so make sure that you remember the new location of the file
Delete	Remove the file from the folder and place it in the Recycle Bin	Delete a file or folder with files when you no longer need it; be careful when you delete a folder because most file management utilities also delete all the files (and subfolders) that the folder contains

Examining file storage

An operating system like Windows can help you organize files and folders. The structure of files and folders that you see in Windows Explorer is called a "logical" model because it helps you create a mental picture of how files are created, saved, and retrieved. What actually happens to a file when you save it is called physical file storage.

■ When a storage medium is formatted (usually at the factory), it is being prepared for physical file storage. When the storage medium such as a hard disk drive or a CD is formatted, it is divided into **tracks**, and each track is divided into wedge-shaped **sectors**. On CDs and DVDs, one or more tracks spiral out from the center of the disk; on floppy, Zip, and hard disks, tracks are arranged as concentric circles. See **Figure D-22**.

■ To speed up the process of storing and retrieving data, a disk drive usually works with a group of sectors known as a **cluster** or a "block." The number of sectors that form a cluster varies depending on the capacity of the disk and how the operating system works with files. Tracks and sectors are numbered; the numbering scheme depends on the storage medium and the operating system. The numbering system provides addresses for each data cluster.

■ A file system's primary task is to maintain a list of clusters and to keep track of which ones are empty and which ones hold data. The operating system uses a **file system** to keep track of the names and locations of files that reside on a storage medium such as a hard disk. Different operating systems use different file systems. Most versions of Mac OS use the Macintosh Hierarchical File System (HFS). Linux uses Ext2fs (extended 2 file system) as its native file system. Windows NT, Windows 2000, and Windows XP use a file system called New Technology File System (NTFS). Windows versions 95, 98, and ME use a file system called FAT32. If your computer uses the

FAT32 file system, for example, this special file is called the **File Allocation Table (FAT)**. If your computer uses NTFS, it is called the **Master File Table (MFT)**.

■ Each storage medium contains its own index file so that information about its contents is always available when the storage medium is in use. Unfortunately, storing this crucial file on the storage medium also presents a risk because if the index file is damaged, for example by a hard disk head crash or scratch, you will generally lose access to all the data stored on the storage medium. Index files become damaged all too frequently, so it is important to back up your data.

When you save a file, your PC's operating system looks at the index file to see which clusters are empty. It selects one of these clusters, records the file data there, and then revises the index file to include the filename and its location. A file that does not fit into a single cluster spills over into the next contiguous cluster, unless that cluster already contains data. When contiguous clusters are not available, the operating system stores parts of a file in noncontiguous (nonadjacent) clusters. **Figure D-23** helps you visualize how an index file, such as the MFT, keeps track of filenames and locations.

When you want to retrieve a file, the OS looks through the index for the filename and its location. It moves the disk drive's read-write head to the first cluster that contains the file data. Using additional data from the index file, the operating system moves the read-write heads to each of the clusters containing the remaining parts of the file.

Figure D-22: Tracks and sectors on storage media

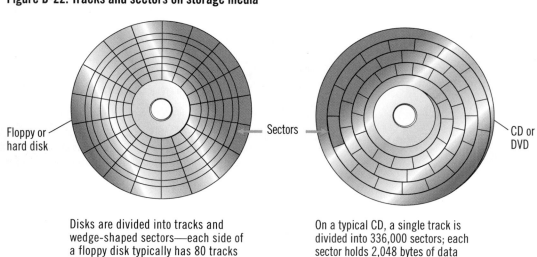

Floppy or hard disk

Sectors

CD or DVD

Disks are divided into tracks and wedge-shaped sectors—each side of a floppy disk typically has 80 tracks divided into 18 sectors; each sector holds 512 bytes of data

On a typical CD, a single track is divided into 336,000 sectors; each sector holds 2,048 bytes of data

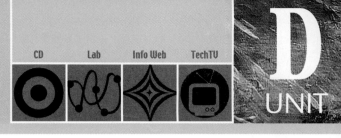
Figure D-23: How the MFT works

Each colored cluster on the disk contains part of a file; the file Bio.txt is stored in contiguous clusters; the file Jordan.wks is stored in noncontiguous clusters; the computer locates and displays the Jordan.wks file by looking for its name in the Master File Table (MFT)

MASTER FILE TABLE		
FILE	**CLUSTER**	**COMMENT**
MFT	1	Reserved for MFT files
DISK USE	2	Part of MFT that contains list of empty sectors
Bio.txt	3, 4	Bio.txt file stored in clusters 3 and 4
Jordan.wks	7, 8, 10	Jordan.wks file stored noncontiguously in clusters 7, 8, and 10
Pick.wps	9	Pick.wps file stored in cluster 9

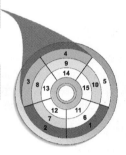

■ When you click a file's icon and then select the Delete option, the operating system simply changes the status of the file's clusters to "empty" and removes the filename from the index file. The filename no longer appears in a directory listing, but the file's data remains in the clusters until a new file is stored there. You might think that this data is as good as erased, but it is possible to purchase utilities that recover a lot of this "deleted" data—law enforcement agents, for example, use these utilities to gather evidence from "deleted" files on the computer disks of suspected criminals.

■ As a computer writes files on a disk, parts of files tend to become scattered all over the disk. These **fragmented files** are stored in noncontiguous clusters. Drive performance generally declines as the read-write heads move back and forth to locate the clusters that contain the parts of a file. To regain peak performance, you can use a **defragmentation utility** to rearrange the files on a disk so that they are stored in contiguous clusters. See **Figure D-24**.

Figure D-24: Defragmenting a disk

Defragmenting a disk helps your computer operate more efficiently; consider using a defragmentation utility a couple of times per year to keep your computer running in top form

Fragmented disk

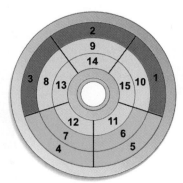

Defragmented disk

On this fragmented disk, the different colors represent files stored in noncontiguous clusters

When the disk is defragmented, the sectors of data for each file are moved to contiguous clusters

Tech Talk How a Processor Executes Instructions

Remarkable advances in processor technology have produced exponential increases in computer speed and power. In 1965, Gordon Moore, cofounder of chip-production giant Intel Corporation, predicted that the number of transistors on a chip would double every 18 to 24 months. Much to the surprise of engineers and Moore himself, "Moore's law" accurately predicted over 40 years of chip development. In 1958, the first integrated circuit contained two transistors. The Pentium III Xeon processor, introduced in 1999, had 9.5 million transistors. The Pentium 4 processor, introduced only a year later, featured 42 million transistors.

What is really fascinating, though, is how these chips perform complex tasks simply by manipulating bits. How can pushing around 1s and 0s result in professional-quality documents, exciting action games, animated graphics, cool music, street maps, and e-commerce Web sites? To satisfy your curiosity about what happens deep in the heart of a processor, you will need to venture into the realm of instruction sets, fetch cycles, accumulators, and pointers.

A computer accomplishes a complex task by performing a series of very simple steps, referred to as instructions. An instruction tells the computer to perform a specific arithmetic, logical, or control operation. To be executed by a computer, an instruction must be in the form of electrical signals, those now-familiar 1s and 0s that represent "ons" and "offs." In this form, instructions are referred to as machine code. They are, of course, very difficult for people to read, so typically when discussing them we use more understandable mnemonics, such as JMP (for jump), M1 (for the memory address), and REG1 (for register 1).

An instruction has two parts: the op code and the operands. An op code, which is short for "operation code," is a command for an operation such as add, compare, or jump. The operands for an instruction specify the data, or the address of the data, for the operation.

In the instruction JMP M1, the op code is JMP and the operand is M1. The op code JMP means jump or go to a different instruction. The operand M1 stands for the RAM address of the instruction to which the computer is supposed to go. The instruction JMP M1 has only one operand, but some instructions have more than one operand. For example, the instruction ADD REG1 REG2 has two operands: REG1 and REG2.

The list of instructions that a processor is able to execute is known as its instruction set. This instruction set is built into the processor when it is manufactured. Every task that a computer performs is determined by the list of instructions in its instruction set. For example, an instruction such as ADD adds the values in two registers and places the result in the accumulator, SUB subtracts the value in the second register from the value in the first register and places the result in the accumulator, and CMP compares the values in two registers and places 1 in the accumulator if the values are equal, or places 0 in the accumulator if the values are not equal.

The term **instruction cycle** refers to the process in which a computer executes a single instruction. Some parts of the instruction cycle are performed by the processor's control unit; other parts of the cycle are performed by the ALU. The steps in this cycle are summarized in **Figure D-25**.

When the computer completes an instruction, the control unit "increments" the instruction pointer to the RAM address of the next instruction and the instruction cycle begins again. So how does this all fit together? **Figure D-26** illustrates how the ALU, control unit, and RAM work together to process instructions.

Figure D-25: The instruction cycle

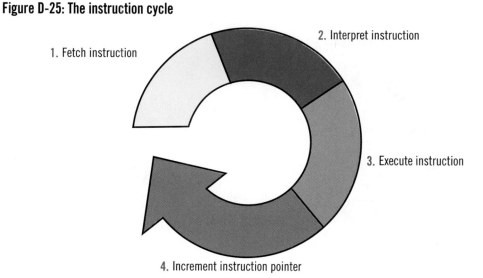

1. Fetch instruction
2. Interpret instruction
3. Execute instruction
4. Increment instruction pointer

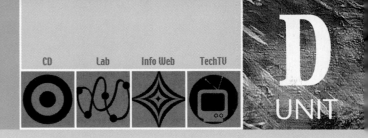

Figure D-26: The ALU, control unit, and RAM all work together to process instructions

1. The instruction pointer indicates the memory location that holds the first instruction (M1).

	Control Unit	ALU
M1 MMR M6 R1	Instruction Pointer	Accumulator
M2 MMR M7 R2	M1	
M3 ADD		
M4		R1
M5		
M6 100	Instruction Register	R2
M7 200		

2. The computer fetches the instruction and puts it into the instruction register.

	Control Unit	ALU
M1 MMR M6 R1	Instruction Pointer	Accumulator
M2 MMR M7 R2	M1	
M3 ADD		
M4		R1
M5		
M6 100	Instruction Register	R2
M7 200	MMR M6 R1	

3. The computer executes the instruction that is in the instruction register; it moves the contents of M6 into register 1 of the ALU.

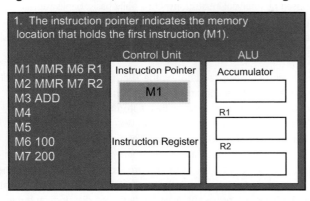

4. The instruction pointer changes to point to the memory location that holds the next instruction.

	Control Unit	ALU
M1 MMR M6 R1	Instruction Pointer	Accumulator
M2 MMR M7 R2	M2	
M3 ADD		
M4		R1
M5		100
M6 100	Instruction Register	R2
M7 200		

5. The computer fetches the instruction and puts it in the instruction register.

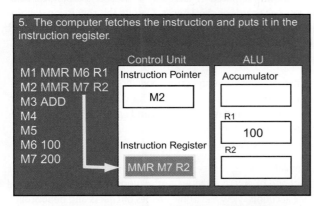

6. The computer executes the instruction; it moves the contents of M7 into register 2 of the ALU.

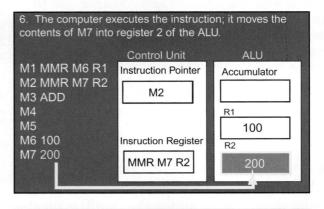

7. The computer fetches the instruction and puts it in the instruction register.

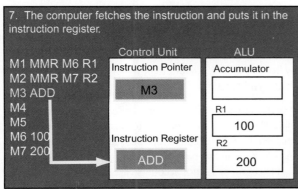

8. The computer executes the instruction. The result is put in the accumulator.

	Control Unit	ALU
M1 MMR M6 R1	Instruction Pointer	Accumulator
M2 MMR M7 R2	M3	300
M3 ADD		
M4		R1
M5		100
M6 100	Instruction Register	R2
M7 200	ADD	200

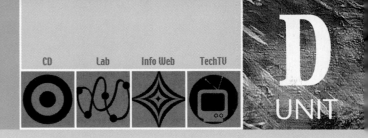

Computers in Context Banking

For most of history, banks used low-tech methods to track one of the world's most cherished commodities—wealth. Checking accounts were in widespread use as early as 1550, when wealthy Dutch traders began depositing money with cashiers for safekeeping. The use of printed checks became popular in England in the late 18th century—so popular that banks found it difficult to process a steadily increasing stream of checks, including those drawn on accounts from other banks.

An unverified story that has become part of bank lore describes the origin of a solution to the check processing problem. As the story goes, a London bank messenger stopped for coffee and got to talking with a messenger from another bank. Realizing that they were delivering checks drawn on each other's banks, the two messengers decided to exchange checks there in the coffee house. This event evolved into a system of check clearinghouses where representatives from various banks met periodically to exchange checks and reconcile totals in cash. By 1839, British clearinghouses were annually processing in excess of £954 million of checks—equivalent to U.S. $250 billion in today's money.

Bank clearinghouses were described in an essay "The Economy of Machinery and Manufactures" written by Charles Babbage in 1832. He also included a reference to the "possibility of performing arithmetical calculations by machinery" along with a description of the Difference Engine, then under construction in his workshop.

This dream of automated check clearing did not, however, become reality until more than a century later when S. Clark Beise, senior vice president at Bank of America, contracted with Stanford Research Institute (SRI) to develop a computer system to automate check processing. SRI completed a prototype in 1955 that used mechanical sorting equipment to queue up each check and MICR (Magnetic Ink Character Recognition) technology to read check numbers. In 1959, the first ERMA (Electronic Recording Machine-Accounting) system went into service. With ERMA handling calculations, nine employees could handle the job that once required 50 people. By 1966, 32 regional ERMA systems operated by Bank of America were processing more than 750 million checks per year.

Some people are concerned about the security of online banking.... Advances in technology continue to address issues such as authenticating users (is it really you accessing your money), paper trails (I paid that bill but there is no returned check), and fraud (where did my money go).

ERMA and similar check processing technologies quickly integrated with bank transaction processing systems to become the bedrock of today's banking technology. Output from check sorting machines can be submitted to the Automated Clearing House (ACH) network, which offers a secure, batch-oriented data exchange system that can be accessed by financial institutions. On a daily basis, banks submit check data and receive a report of balances due to other banks. These balances can be reconciled by electronic funds transfer over the Federal Reserve's FedWire telecommunications network.

An upswing in check fraud during the 1960s made it increasingly difficult to cash checks at local merchants. As an alternative to cashing checks at banks and local merchants, automatic teller machines (ATMs) were developed. The first ATMs were installed in the 1970s. A typical ATM connects to a bank's front-end processor—a computer that maintains account balances for in-network customers and monitors suspicious activity. The front-end processor is separated from the bank's main computer system for security. Some ATMs exchange data with the front-end processor by using dedicated dial-up telephone lines. Other ATMs use always-on leased lines. Legacy protocols, such as SNA and 3270 bisync, are being replaced by the standard Internet Protocol (IP) that can be routed through more affordable connections, such as cable, ISDN, DSL, or Internet VPN.

ATMs are expensive—about $50,000 to purchase one machine, install it, and operate it for one year. Banks have offset this cost by charging transaction fees and reducing the number of bank tellers. Once a promising entry-level occupation, bank tellers today earn comparatively low wages. Although tellers continue to accept deposits, process withdrawals, and cash payroll checks, they are increasingly pressed into customer service roles—opening new accounts, issuing ATM cards, resolving disputed transactions, and assisting customers who have lost bank cards or checkbooks. Despite this shift in job description, the number of bank teller jobs is expected to fall at least 10% by 2010. ATMs offer access to bank services from convenient locations where customers shop, eat, and hang out with friends.

The Internet takes banking convenience one step further and provides round-the-clock account access for customers from their personal computers. Today, most banks and credit unions offer some type of online banking (also called home banking, Internet banking, or electronic banking).

Basic online banking services allow customers to access checking account and bankcard activity, transfer funds between checking and savings accounts, view electronic images of checks and deposit slips, download and print monthly statements, and reorder checks. As competing banks offer more services to their customers, online banking has become a very large selling point. Almost all banks offer free bill paying services. After you set up your accounts, you can transfer money from your bank account to pay your bills by scheduling payment dates and amounts.

Many credit card and utility companies offer e-billing services that automatically forward electronic bills to customers' online banking accounts. For monthly fixed-amount bills, such as car loans, online banking offers automatic payment options that deduct funds from specified checking or savings accounts.

For managing assets more effectively, online banking sites also offer sophisticated tools including account aggregation, stock quotes, rate alerts, and portfolio management programs. Most online banking sites are also compatible with personal finance software, such as Managing Your Money, QuickBooks, Microsoft Money, and AOL BankNOW, so that transaction data can be shuttled between customer's local computers and their online banking services.

Customer support personnel work at online help desks for customers with questions about online banking. Webmasters, computer security specialists, and network technicians are also part of the banking industry's new job corps. Online banking services are typically housed on a secure Web server, and customers are not allowed direct access to the bank's transaction processing system. See **Figure D-27**. Customer privacy is maintained by the use of passwords and SSL connections that encrypt data as it is sent to and from customers' browsers.

Some people are concerned about the security of online banking. They worry about the security of their accounts and about privacy issues, especially related to identity. Advances in technology continue to address issues such as authenticating users (is it really you accessing your money), paper trails (I paid that bill but there is no returned check), and fraud (where did my money go).

Bank managers are increasingly working with business intelligence tools to look for trends in customer behavior, analyze competing financial institutions, and examine current business practices. Tools for these activities include data warehouses that collect and organize data, data mining software that organizes and analyzes data in a meaningful way, and statistical tools that formulate comparisons and trend lines.

Today, banking rests on multilayered technologies that incorporate check processing equipment, transaction processing systems, business intelligence software, ACH networks, FedWire, ATM networks, the Internet, and Web servers. Many banking practices originated from batch check processing, and only gradually have banks begun to move to more modern online transaction processing (OLTP) systems that store scanned images of checks and instantly update accounts when a purchase is made or a bill is paid.

Figure D-27

Issue Can Online Voting Be Fair and Secure?

Voting is an essential right for all citizens of any democratic nation. Throughout history and the world, finding ways to ensure that voting is accessible to all eligible citizens and that the ballots are counted accurately has been a challenge for each generation. From paper ballots to punch cards, countries find a way to administer elections. Advances in technology have had an impact on voting. Voting systems with touch-screen computerized voting machines have been developed. But these new direct-recording electronic voting machines have proven to be less than reliable. These systems are vulnerable to some of the same problems other systems using computer technology experience, including crashes, power-outages, viruses, and hacking. Another concern is the lack of a voter verifiable paper trail—that is, a permanent paper record of a user's vote if a manual recount or audit is needed.

A complex information system now in the planning stages would make it possible for Americans to vote online. The idea of online voting surfaced years ago as the Internet gained popularity. Early enthusiasts envisioned it as a technology solution to the problems of representative democracy. They expected the rapid emergence of a new e-democracy in which citizens had a direct vote in every issue with the ease of dashing off an e-mail or logging on to a Web site.

The term online voting usually refers to a remote voting system that allows voters to cast their ballots from any computer connected to the Internet—typically from personal computers, but possibly from other devices as well, such as interactive television, cell phones, handheld computers, or game machines.

In the early days of the Internet, online voting looked easy, but the feasibility of an easy solution died with the advent of viruses, worms, bots, denial-of-service attacks, unauthorized intrusion attempts, and the growing threat of cyberterrorism.

"Such attacks could occur on a large scale, and could be launched by anyone, including disaffected lone individuals to well-financed enemy agents outside the reach of U.S. law. These attacks could result in large-scale, selective voter disenfranchisement, privacy violations, vote buying and selling, and vote switching even to the extent of reversing the outcome of many elections at once, including the presidential election."

Computer scientists, systems analysts, security experts, and election officials now have a pretty good idea of the problems associated with online voting, but they disagree about the best solutions.

Whether a system is manual or electronic, there are six basic requirements for a voting system.

BASIC REQUIREMENTS FOR DEMOCRATIC VOTING SYSTEMS

- Encourage and allow voters to register
- Provide voters with an easy-to-understand ballot
- Allow voters to make their selections, review them, and revise them before casting their ballots
- Collect ballots and filter out those that are invalid or fraudulent
- Accurately tabulate votes from every valid ballot
- Allow officials to recount ballots if an election is challenged

Online voting meets some of these basic requirements better than current voting methods, but it faces challenges in adequately fulfilling other requirements. Online voting has several advantages. It is convenient. Voters can cast ballots from home or work, or even while on vacation. It is quick. Casting an online ballot does not require driving to a polling station and waiting in line. Because of its advantages, online voting has the potential to attract net-savvy young voters who historically have voted in lower numbers than other segments of the population. It might make the voting process more accessible for homebound voters. The convenience of online voting might also increase participation in local elections.

Online voting has the potential to decrease the number of ballots that are invalidated because of procedural problems, such as failing to completely punch out the "chad" on a ballot card or checking more than one candidate on a paper ballot. Voting software can prevent voters from erroneously selecting more than one candidate and can ensure that voters are able to revise their selections without invalidating their ballots.

In 2000, Arizona Democrats had the opportunity to vote online in the Democratic primaries. Although this online pilot program worked well, the state backed away from online voting in 2004. Michigan Democrats were given the opportunity to vote online in the 2004 primaries. More than 40,000 party members cast their votes over the Internet, apparently without any problems. The success of these online experiments is viewed by online voting supporters as evidence that Internet voting can be effective and secure.

Although online voting in Michigan and Arizona appeared to go without a hitch, a more comprehensive online voting project called Secure Electronic Registration and Voting Experiment (SERVE) was scrapped shortly before the 2004 presidential election. SERVE was initiated by the U.S. Department of Defense with a goal of offering online voting to overseas military personnel. The project expanded to include 50 counties in seven states and 100,000 American military personnel and civilians living abroad. The decision to scrap the project came shortly after a panel of security experts, the Security Peer Review Group (SPRG), analyzed SERVE and criticized its vulnerabilities. SPRG reported that Internet voting was susceptible to a variety of well-known cyber attacks that could alter votes, prevent votes from reaching a tabulating center, or stuff electronic ballot boxes with thousands of fraudulent votes.

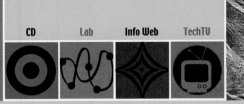

The report went on to say that "Such attacks could occur on a large scale, and could be launched by anyone, including disaffected lone individuals to well-financed enemy agents outside the reach of U.S. law. These attacks could result in large-scale, selective voter disenfranchisement, privacy violations, vote buying and selling, and vote switching even to the extent of reversing the outcome of many elections at once, including the presidential election."

The SPRG report also noted that successful attacks might go completely undetected, but even if attacks were detected and neutralized, they could have a devastating effect on public confidence in elections. Members of SPRG concluded that the vulnerabilities were not specific to the SERVE system, but rather were inherent to the Internet itself and the relatively unsecured personal computers used to access it.

In addition to technical issues with Internet security, online voting opponents have concerns about voter fraud and privacy. Voter fraud includes voting multiple times, stuffing the ballot box with ballots from nonexistent voters, and buying votes. To reduce voter fraud, registered voters must be verified to make sure they are eligible to vote and that they vote only once. When a person logs on to vote remotely, it is difficult to verify his or her identity. Passwords are not effective in controlling fraud because they can be shared and distributed. Biometric devices that offer more positive identification are not typically part of personal computer systems.

A partial solution might be for online voters to submit their names and Social Security numbers along with their votes. Computers at vote-tabulation centers could screen out duplicate voters. However, secret ballots are a cornerstone of democracy. In a physical polling place, voters provide identification at the door and are checked against voter registration records. Registered voters are allowed to proceed to voting booths where their votes are cast in secret. Nothing allows that vote to be traced back to the individual who voted.

Politically, skeptics of online voting are uncomfortable with its effect on voting demographics. Some Republican strategists are concerned about a sudden upswing in young voters—not a block of traditionally Republican supporters—who might take advantage of online polling. Democrats, on the other hand, have intimated that online voting would disproportionately increase the number of high-income voters because many economically deprived voters do not have access to a computer and an Internet connection.

For a democracy to function properly, its citizens should be confident that the electoral system is honest and that it works as intended. Online voting presents some sticky technological and social challenges. Although these challenges exist, secure technologies for online banking and e-commerce are working, so shouldn't it be possible to design an online voting system that is secure enough to conduct our elections?

Interactive Questions

☐ Yes   ☐ No   ☐ Not sure   **1.** Would you prefer online voting to voting at a polling place?

☐ Yes   ☐ No   ☐ Not sure   **2.** Do you think online voting will become the standard for voting in this country within the next 10 years?

☐ Yes   ☐ No   ☐ Not sure   **3.** Should online voting be available only to specific groups, such as elderly voters and military personnel stationed abroad, who currently have trouble reaching polling places?

Expand the Ideas

1. There are significant advantages in favor of exploring the use of online voting through the Internet. Write a list of the three major advantages you can see to continue the research in the use of online voting in general elections. Log onto the Internet and use your favorite search engine to research current issues and trends in online voting. Based on your research, do you think Internet voting will become the wave of the future?

2. Why are verified paper trails necessary? Do current electronic voting systems use voter-verifiable paper trails? Do you believe that we must insist on a paper trail? If we do, why bother with electronic or online voting at all?

3. There are significant concerns with Internet voting. Write a list of three major concerns you have regarding people voting via the Internet from remote locations. Log onto the Internet and research Internet voting. Visit the Electronic Frontier Foundation's Web site, the Verified Voting Web site, and other sites that discuss computerized and Internet voting. How have concerns about Internet voting been addressed? Did these sites address the concerns you recorded earlier? Based on your research, do you think Internet voting can be fair and secure?

End of Unit Exercises

Key Terms

ALU

ASCII

Benchmark

Binary number system

Bit

Byte

Cache

Capacitor

Character data

CISC

Clock speed

Cluster

CMOS memory

Computer file

Control unit

Data representation

Defragmentation utility

Desktop search tool

Digital device

Digital electronics

Digitize

DIMM

DIP

Directory

Dual core processor

EBCDIC

Extended ASCII code

File Allocation Table (FAT)

File date

File format

File header

File management

File management utility

File size

File specification

File system

Filename

Filename extension

Filenaming conventions

Finder

Folder

Fragmented file

Gigabit (Gb)

Gigabyte (GB)

Gigahertz (GHz)

Hyper-Threading

Instruction cycle

Instruction set

Integrated circuit (IC)

Kilobit (Kb)

Kilobyte (KB)

Master File Table (MFT)

Megabit (Mb)

Megabyte (MB)

Megahertz (MHz)

Motherboard

Nanosecond

Native file format

Numeric data

Parallel processing

Path

PGA

Pipelining

Processor

Processor clock

RAM

RDRAM

Register

Reserved word

RISC

ROM

ROM BIOS

Root directory

SDRAM

SEC cartridge

Sector

Semiconducting material

Serial processing

Spotlight

Subdirectory

Track

Unicode

Virtual memory

Windows Explorer

Word size

Unit Review

1. Review the bold terms in this unit. Then pick 10 terms that are most unfamiliar to you. Be sure that you can use your own words to define the terms you have selected.

2. Describe how the binary number system uses only 1s and 0s to represent numbers.

3. Describe the difference between numeric data, character data, and numerals. Then, list and briefly describe the four codes that computers typically use for character data.

4. Make sure that you understand the meaning of the following measurement terms: KB, Kb, MB, Mb, GB, Gb, Kbps, MHz, GHz, ns. What aspects of a computer system are they used to measure?

5. List four types of memory and briefly describe how each one works.

6. Describe how the ALU and the control unit work together to process data.

7. Describe the difference between the Save and the Save As commands.

8. Describe the kinds of file management tasks that might best be accomplished using a file management utility such as Windows Explorer.

9. Using a sample file specification from your own computer, describe a file specification and how it describes the location of files on the storage medium.

10. Make sure that you can describe what happens in the MFT when a file is stored or deleted.

End of Unit Exercises

Fill in the Best Answer

1. The _binary_ number system represents numeric data as a series of 0s and 1s.

2. ASCII is used primarily to represent _Character_ data.

3. Kilo is usually a prefix that means _____; therefore 50K means _____.

4. Digital _____ makes it possible for a computer to manipulate simple "on" and "off" signals to perform complex tasks.

5. An integrated _circut_ contains microscopic circuit elements, such as wires, transistors, and capacitors that are packed onto a very small square of semiconducting material.

6. The _ALU_ in the processor performs arithmetic and logical operations.

7. The _control unit_ in the CPU directs and coordinates the operation of the entire computer system.

8. The timing in a computer system is established by the _clock_.

9. In RAM, microscopic electronic parts called _____ hold the electrical signals that represent data.

10. The instructions for the operations your computer performs when it is first turned on are permanently stored in _ROm_.

11. System configuration information about the hard disk, date, and RAM capacity is stored in battery-powered _CMOS_ memory.

12. An operating system's filenaming _Conventions_ provide a set of rules for naming files.

13. A file _format_ refers to the arrangement of data in a file and the coding scheme that is used to represent the data.

14. The main directory of a disk is sometimes referred to as the _root_ directory.

15. A file's location is defined by a file _spec-file_, which includes the drive letter, folder(s), filename, and extension.

16. Windows XP maintains a File _allocation_ Table, which contains the name and location of every file on a disk.

17. The _____ command on an application's File menu allows you to name a file and specify its storage location.

18. Use the _____ command to change the name of an existing file or folder to better describe its contents.

19. On magnetic media, such as a hard disk, data is stored in concentric circles called _____, which are divided into wedge-shaped _____.

20. Windows Explorer is an example of a file _management_ utility.

Practice Tests

When you use the Interactive CD, you can take Practice Tests that consist of 10 multiple-choice, true/false, and fill-in-the blank questions. The questions are selected at random from a large test bank, so each time you take a test, you will receive a different set of questions. Your tests are scored immediately, and you can print study guides to determine which questions you answered incorrectly. If you are using a Tracking Disk, save your test scores.

INDEPENDENT CHALLENGE 1

 The leading manufacturers of processors are Intel and AMD. These companies manufacture processors for personal computers as well as other devices.

1. Based on what you read in this unit, list and describe the factors that affect processor performance. Create a table using the performance factors as column heads.

2. Use your favorite search engine on the Internet to research Intel and AMD as well as one other company that produce processors and that was not discussed in the unit.

3. List their Web sites and any other pertinent contact information for the companies that you chose.

4. List three of the models that each company produces as row labels in the table you created in Step 1. Complete the table to show how these models rate, that is, their specifications for each performance factor.

5. Write a brief statement describing any new research or new products that each company is developing.

INDEPENDENT CHALLENGE 2

 How quickly could you code a sentence using the Extended ASCII code? What is the history of coding and coding schemes? You can find a wealth of information about coding schemes that have been developed throughout the history of computing as well as coding used to transmit information.

1. Log onto the Internet, then use your favorite search engine to research the history of Morse code. Write a brief paragraph outlining your findings.

2. Use the International Morse Code alphabet to write your full name.

   The code is shown below.

3. Research the history of the ASCII code, and find and print a coding chart for extended ASCII.

4. Use the extended ASCII code to write your full name.

5. Research the history of the EBCDIC code, and find and print a coding chart for EBCDIC.

6. Use the extended EBCDIC code to write your full name.

7. Write a one-page summary of your findings. Include when one code might be used over another, and explain what difficulties, if any, you had writing your name using the various codes.

INTERNATIONAL MORSE CODE

1. A dash is equal to three dots.
2. The space between parts of the same letter is equal to one dot.
3. The space between two letters is equal to three dots.
4. The space between two words is equal to five dots.

A ● ▬	U ● ● ▬
B ▬ ● ● ●	V ● ● ● ▬
C ▬ ● ▬ ●	W ● ▬ ▬
D ▬ ● ●	X ▬ ● ● ▬
E ●	Y ▬ ● ▬ ▬
F ● ● ▬ ●	Z ▬ ▬ ● ●
G ▬ ▬ ●	
H ● ● ● ●	
I ● ●	
J ● ▬ ▬ ▬	
K ▬ ● ▬	1 ● ▬ ▬ ▬ ▬
L ● ▬ ● ●	2 ● ● ▬ ▬ ▬
M ▬ ▬	3 ● ● ● ▬ ▬
N ▬ ●	4 ● ● ● ● ▬
O ▬ ▬ ▬	5 ● ● ● ● ●
P ● ▬ ▬ ●	6 ▬ ● ● ● ●
Q ▬ ▬ ● ▬	7 ▬ ▬ ● ● ●
R ● ▬ ●	8 ▬ ▬ ▬ ● ●
S ● ● ●	9 ▬ ▬ ▬ ▬ ●
T ▬	0 ▬ ▬ ▬ ▬ ▬

1922 Chart of the Morse Code Letters and Numerals

NOTE: International Morse Code is composed of six elements:

short mark or dot (·)

longer mark or dash (-)

intra-character gap (between the dots and dashes in a character)

short gap (between letters)

medium gap (between words)

long gap (between sentences)

End of Unit Exercises

INDEPENDENT CHALLENGE 3

How will you organize the information that you store on your hard drive? Your hard disk will be your electronic filing cabinet for all your work and papers. You can create many different filing systems. The way you set up your folders will guide your work and help you keep your ideas and projects organized so that you can work efficiently with your computer. Take some time to think about the work that you do, the types of documents or files you will be creating, and then decide how you will create files and folders.

1. Read each of the following plans for organizing files and folders on a hard disk and comment on the advantages and disadvantages of each plan.

   a. Create a folder for each file you create.

   b. Store all the files in the root directory.

   c. Store all files in the My Documents folder.

   d. Create a folder for each application you plan to use and store only documents you generate with that application in each folder.

   e. Create folders for broad topics such as memos, letters, budget, art, and personal, then store all related documents and files within those folders.

   f. Create folders based on specific topics such as tax, applications, household, and school, then store all related documents and files within those folders.

   g. Create a new folder for each month and store all files or documents created in that month in that appropriate folder.

2. Write a summary of how you plan to organize your hard disk and explain why you chose the method you did.

INDEPENDENT CHALLENGE 4

You can use Windows Explorer or any file management program on your computer to explore and find specific files and folders on your hard disk.

1. Start Windows Explorer then expand the My Computer icon. List the devices under My Computer.

2. Open the My Documents folder on the Local Disk C: (if not available, find the folder that has your documents). List how many folders are in the My Documents folder (or alternate folder if you selected one) on your hard disk.

3. Open one of the folders in the My Documents folder (or alternate folder), then display the Details View. Are filename extensions showing? If so, list them and identify which programs would open those files.

4. How many different types of files can you find on your hard disk? List up to 10.

5. Make a list of five filenames that are valid under the filenaming conventions for your operating system. Create a list of five filenames that are not valid and explain the problem with each one.

6. Pick any five files on the computer that you typically use and write the full path for each one. Identify the programs that were used to create each of the files you found.

LAB: Working with Binary Numbers

1. Start the interactive part of the lab. Insert your Tracking Disk if you want to save your QuickCheck results. Perform each of the lab steps as directed and answer all of the lab QuickCheck questions. When you exit the lab, your answers are automatically graded and your results are displayed.

2. Using paper and pencil, manually convert the following decimal numbers into binary numbers. Your instructor might ask you to show the process that you used for each conversion.

a. 100	b. 1,000	c. 256	d. 27
e. 48	f. 112	g. 96	h. 1,024

3. Using paper and pencil, manually convert the following binary numbers into decimal numbers. Your instructor might ask you to show the process that you used for each conversion.

a. 100	b. 101	c. 1100	d. 10101
e. 1111	f. 10000	g. 1111000	h. 110110

4. Describe what is wrong with the following sequence:

   10 100 110 1000 1001 1100 1110 10000

5. What is the decimal equivalent of 2^0? 2^1? 2^8?

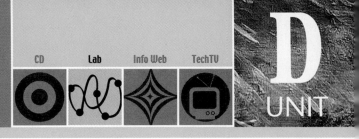

LAB: Benchmarking

1. Start the interactive part of the lab. Insert your Tracking Disk if you want to save your QuickCheck results. Perform each of the lab steps as directed and answer all of the lab QuickCheck questions. When you exit the lab, your answers are automatically graded and your results are displayed.

2. If Microsoft Word is available, use the System Info command that is available in Microsoft Word to analyze the computer that you typically use. Provide the results of the analysis along with a brief description of the computer that you tested and its location (at home, at work, in a computer lab, etc.).

3. Review the fictitious processor benchmarks below:

Processor	Quake III Arena	PCMark04
"Supernova EE"	548	5198
"Pulsar FX"	551	5020

Which processor appears to be faster at graphics processing? Which processor appears to be better at overall processing tasks?

4. Explain why you might perform a benchmark test on your own computer, but get different results from those that you read about in a computer magazine that tested the same computer with the same benchmark test.

5. Use a search engine on the Web to find benchmark ratings for Intel's Pentium 4 processors. What do these ratings show about the relative performance for 1.5 GHz, 2.4 GHz, and 3.8 GHz Pentium 4s?

LAB: Working with Windows Explorer

1. Start the interactive part of the lab. Insert your Tracking Disk if you want to save your QuickCheck results. Perform each of the lab steps as directed and answer all of the lab QuickCheck questions. When you exit the lab, your answers are automatically graded and your results are displayed.

2. Use Windows Explorer to look at the directory of the hard disk or any removable storage medium that currently contains most of your files. Draw a diagram showing the hierarchy of folders. Write a paragraph explaining how you could improve this hierarchy and draw a diagram to illustrate your plan.

3. Use a storage medium of your choice that does not contain important data. Create three folders: Music, Web Graphics, and Articles. Within the Music folder, create four additional folders: Jazz, Reggae, Rock, and Classical. Within the Classical folder, create two more folders: Classical MIDI and Classical MP3.

4. Use your browser software to connect to the Internet, then go to a Web site, such as www.zdnet.com or www.cnet.com. Look for a small graphic (remember, if you are using a floppy disk, you only have 1.44 MB of space!) and download it to your Web Graphics folder. Next, use a search engine like www.google.com or www.yahoo.com to search for "classical MIDI music." Download one of the compositions to the Music\Classical\Classical MIDI folder. Open Windows Explorer and expand all of the directories for the storage medium you are using. Open the Music\Classical\Classical MIDI folder and make sure that your music download appears. Capture a screenshot. Follow your instructor's directions to submit this screenshot as a printout or e-mail attachment.

Student Edition Labs

Reinforce the concepts you have learned in this unit through the **Understanding the Motherboard, Managing Files and Folders,** and **Binary Numbers** Student Edition Labs, available online at the Illustrated Computer Concepts Web site.

SAM Labs

If you have a SAM user profile, you have access to additional content, features, and functionality. Log in to your SAM account and go to your assignments page to see what your instructor has assigned for this unit.

End of Unit Exercises

Figure D-28 shows the inside of a typical desktop computer system unit. **Figure D-29** shows a typical motherboard for a desktop computer system. If you own a desktop computer, the components would be similar to those shown in these pictures.

Figure D-28

Figure D-29

1. Without looking back in the unit, identify each component in the picture. If you cannot identify the components, you can take a look back at Figures D-4 and D-6.

2. Write a brief description of each of the components in each picture. Describe what the component does and how it works inside the system unit as part of the computer.

3. Log onto the Internet or use any resource available to find one additional technology fact that was not discussed in the unit about each component identified in the picture.

Networks and the Internet

E
UNIT

Introduce networks

Classify networks

Introduce network topology

Explore network hardware

Explore communications channels

Transport data

Explore wired technology

Explore wireless technology

Introduce Internet connections

Introduce IP addresses and domain names

Connect to the Internet using POTS

Connect to the Internet using cable

Connect to the Internet without wires

Tech Talk: Install and Use a LAN

Computers in Context: Education

Issue: Free Wi-Fi? Why or Why Not?

Overview

Although network technology continues to evolve, the foundation of the technology has not changed. This unit discusses network building blocks and technologies. The unit discusses not only the technology of simple local area networks (LANs) but also the technology behind a complex network—the Internet. You will learn about the devices, connections, and protocols that make it possible to communicate over networks. The unit compares and contrasts various options for accessing the Internet and concludes with a Tech Talk on installing and using a LAN. You have the opportunity to read about computers in the context of education. The Issue discusses the implications of offering free Wi-Fi technology and how Wi-Fi affects public Internet access.

Introducing networks

A **communications network** is the combination of hardware, software, and connecting links that transport data. Networks offer **shared resources**—hardware, software, and data available to authorized network users. Network technology continues to evolve. In the past, a diversity of network technologies existed as engineers pioneered new ideas to make data transport faster, more efficient, and more secure. Today, networks are becoming more standardized, but some diversity remains necessary to accommodate networking environments that range from simple household networks to complex global networks.

■ In 1948, Claude Shannon, an engineer at the prestigious Bell Labs, published an article that described a communications system model. In this model, data from a source is "encoded," or changed from one form to another, and sent over a communications channel to its destination, where it is decoded. According to Shannon, effective communication depends on the efficiency of the coding process and the channel's resistance to interference, called noise. **Figure E-1** illustrates Shannon's communications system model.

■ Networks offer the following advantages:

Sharing networked hardware can

• Reduce costs. Networked peripheral devices can be accessed by any authorized network users. For example, a single expensive color printer, scanner, or plotter can be purchased and attached to a network, which allows authorized users working on networked computers to share the same printer instead of needing one printer for each computer.

• Provide access to a wide range of services. A network can allow multiple users to access Internet services through a single Internet connection.

Sharing networked software can

• Reduce costs. Software site licenses for network use are typically less expensive than purchasing single-user versions of a product for each network user. Purchasing and installing a single software copy for an entire network might be technically possible, but it is typically not allowed under the terms of a single-user license agreement.

• Facilitate data sharing. Networks can provide authorized users with access to data stored on network servers or workstations.

• Enable people to work together. Using groupware and other specialized network application software, several people can work together on a single document, communicate via e-mail and instant messaging, and participate in online conferences and Webcasts—all over the network. Internet teleconference technology links participants with visual and audio real-time interactivity from multiple geographical locations.

Figure E-1: Claude Shannon's communications system model

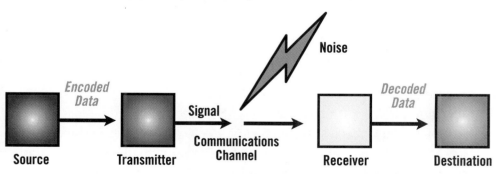

A communications system sends information from a source to a destination; the path between the source and the destination might appear to be straight as in the diagram, but the data may pass through several devices, which convert it to electrical, sound, light, or radio signals; beam it up to satellites; route it along the least congested links; or clean up parts of the signal that have been distorted by noise

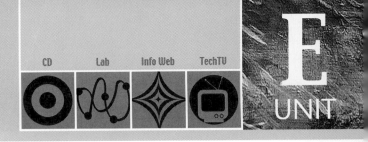
■ Two disadvantages of networks are the following:

- Vulnerability to unauthorized access. Whereas a stand-alone computer is vulnerable to on-premises theft or access, network computers are vulnerable to unauthorized access from many sources and locations. Through unauthorized use of a network workstation, intruders can access data stored on the network server or other workstations. Networks connected to the Internet are vulnerable to intrusions from remote computers in distant states, provinces, or countries. Wireless networks can be tapped from a specially equipped "snooping" computer, usually located in a car that is being driven by a hacker.

- Susceptibility to malicious code. Whereas the most prevalent threat to stand-alone computers is a disk-borne virus, networks are susceptible to an ever-increasing number of malicious online attacks such as worms, Trojan horses, and other threats.

■ Most computer owners are enthusiastic about the benefits provided by networks and believe that those benefits outweigh the risks of intrusions and viruses—especially if their computers can be protected. You will learn more about network security threats and countermeasures in Unit F.

■ In the early years of the personal computer's popularity, networks were scarce. Most personal computers functioned as stand-alone units, and computing was essentially a solitary activity in which one person interacted with a limited set of software tools. Some computer engineers, however, had the foresight to anticipate that personal computers could be networked to provide advantages not available with stand-alone computers. One of the most significant network ideas was conceived by Bob Metcalfe in 1976. His plan for transporting data between computers, shown in **Figure E-2**, has become a key element in just about every computer network, including the Internet.

Figure E-2: Bob Metcalfe's diagram of "Ethernet"

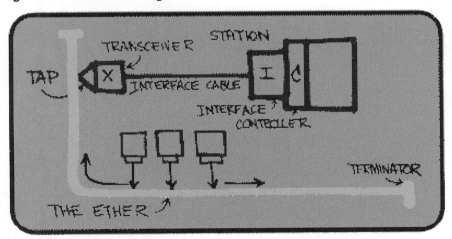

In 1976, Bob Metcalfe drew this diagram of a network technology, which he called "Ethernet"

Classifying networks

Networks exist in many variations because each one is constructed from a collection of technologies. To understand network classifications and make sense of the network options available for your computer, think of a network as several layers of technology. Networks can be categorized by distinguishing characteristics in each layer, such as their geographical structure, organizational structure, topology, links, bandwidth, and protocols. When discussing a network, it is often referred to by only one of the characteristics, even though that reference does not provide a complete description of the network and all the technologies it uses. Network characteristics important for classification are described in **Table E-1** and discussed in the next few lessons.

■ Geographical scope: From a geographic perspective, networks can be classified as PAN, LAN, NAN, MAN, or WAN.

- A **PAN (personal area network)** is a term sometimes used to refer to the interconnection of personal digital devices within a range of about 30 feet (10 meters) and without the use of wires or cables. For example, a PAN could be used to wirelessly transmit data from a notebook computer to a PDA or portable printer.

- A **LAN (local area network)** is a data communications network that typically connects personal computers within a very limited geographical area—usually a single building. LANs use a variety of wired and wireless technologies, standards, and protocols. School computer labs and home networks are examples of LANs.

- A **NAN (neighborhood area network)** provides connectivity within a limited geographical area, usually spread over several buildings. These networks are becoming popular as local coffee shops and computer hobbyists offer wireless Internet connections.

- A **MAN (metropolitan area network)** is a public high-speed network capable of voice and data transmission within a range of about 50 miles (80 km). Examples of MANs that provide data transport services include local ISPs, cable television companies, and local telephone companies.

- A **WAN (wide area network)** covers a large geographical area and typically consists of several smaller networks, which might use different computer platforms and network technologies. The Internet is the world's largest WAN. Networks for nationwide banks and superstore chains can be classified as WANs.

■ Organizational structure: Networks have an organizational structure that provides a conceptual model of the hierarchy of devices connected to the network. The two most prevalent network organizational structures are client/server and peer-to-peer.

Table E-1: Network technology

CATEGORY	DESCRIPTION	EXAMPLES
Geographical scope	The area in which network devices are located	PAN, LAN, NAN, MAN, WAN
Organizational structure	The hierarchy of devices connected to a network	Client/server, peer-to-peer
Physical topology	The physical layout and relationship between network devices	Star, ring, bus, mesh, tree
Communications channel	The technologies for cables and signals that carry data	Twisted-pair cable, coaxial cable, fiber-optic cable, RF signals, microwaves, infrared light, laser light, power line, phone line
Bandwidth	The capacity of a network for carrying data	Broadband, narrowband
Communications protocols	The transportation standards that provide an orderly way to package data and make sure data is not corrupted in transit	TCP/IP, SPX/IPX (Novell networks), NetBEUI/NetBIOS (Microsoft Networking), AppleTalk

CD   Lab   Info Web   TechTV

E UNIT

- A **client/server network** contains one or more computers configured with server software, and other computers configured with client software that access the servers. The computers running client software are referred to as **workstations**, or sometimes **client computers**. The server provides a centralized repository for data and a transfer point through which data traffic flows. Web sites, retail point-of-sale networks, school registration systems, online databases, and Internet-based multiplayer games typically use a client/server organizational structure. When your computer is running a browser and accessing a Web server, it is a client computer.

- **Peer-to-peer network (P2P)** treats every computer as an "equal" so that workstations can store network data, which can be transported directly to other workstations without passing through a central server. P2P technology forms the basis for file-sharing networks, such as Microsoft Networking provided with Windows. **Figure E-3** contrasts the client/server structure with the peer-to-peer structure.

Figure E-3: Comparing client/server and peer-to-peer networks

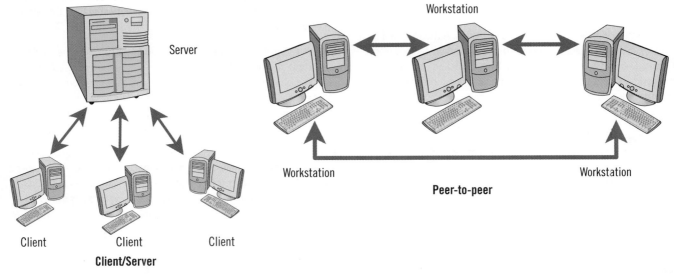

Server

Client   Client   Client

Client/Server

In a client/server network, a server is the most important resource

Workstation

Workstation   Workstation

Peer-to-peer

In a peer-to-peer network, every computer is treated as an equal resource

Understanding client/server terminology

A **server** refers to a computer that is connected to a network and that "serves" or distributes resources to network users. A server contains the software to manage and process files for other network nodes. E-mail servers, communications servers, file servers, and Web servers are some of the most common servers on today's networks. A **host computer**, or "host," usually refers to any computer that provides services to network users. The terms "host" and "server" are often used interchangeably, but "host" is more commonly used in the context of the Internet. "Server" is used both in the context of the Internet and LANs.

A workstation usually refers to a personal computer connected to a network. In a client/server network, the computers accessing the server are workstations, which are sometimes referred to as client computers. The term client refers to software on a computer that allows a user to access the services of a server. While the terms client and workstation are sometimes used interchangeably, client is commonly used in the context of a personal computer that is connected to the Internet and workstation is more often used to refer to a computer connected to a network.

Introducing network topology

Networks connect different devices. Each connection point on a network is referred to as a **node**. A network node is typically one of the following: a **server**, which is a computer responsible for storing data and programs; a **workstation**, which is any personal computer connected to a network; a **networked peripheral**, which is any hardware, such as a printer or scanner, connected to a network; and a **network device** used to broadcast network data, boost signals, or route data to its destination. The pathways shown between nodes can be linked by physical cables or wireless signals. The physical arrangement of devices, wires, and cables on a network is called its **physical topology**.

- **Figure E-4** illustrates the five common network topologies: star, ring, bus, mesh, and tree—each named for its inherent shape.

- A **star topology** features a central connection point for all workstations and peripherals. Many home networks are arranged in a star topology. The advantage of this topology is that any link can fail without affecting the rest of the network. Its primary disadvantage is that it requires quite a bit of cable to link all the devices—a disadvantage that disappears with wireless networks. Although the failure of a link does not affect the rest of the network, you can see from **Figure E-4** that a device with a failed link would be cut off from the network; it would be unable to communicate with other devices on the network or to use the network resources.

- A **ring topology** connects all devices in a circle, with each device having exactly two neighbors. Data is transmitted from one device to another around the ring. This topology minimizes cabling, but failure of any one device can take down the entire network. Ring topologies, once championed by IBM, are infrequently used in today's networks.

- A **bus topology** uses a common backbone cable to connect all network devices. The backbone cable functions as a shared communication link, which carries network data. The backbone cable stops at each end of the network with a special device called a "terminator." Bus networks work best with a limited number of devices. Bus networks with more than a few dozen computers are likely to perform poorly, and if the backbone cable fails, the entire network becomes unusable.

- A **tree topology** is essentially a blend of star and bus networks. Multiple star networks are connected using a backbone cable to form a bus configuration. Tree topologies offer excellent flexibility for expansion—for example, a single link to the backbone cable can add an entire group of star-configured devices. Most of today's school and business networks are based on tree topologies.

- A **mesh topology** connects each network device to many other network devices. Data traveling on a mesh network can take any of several possible paths from its source to its destination. These redundant data pathways make a mesh network very robust. Even if several links fail, data can follow alternative functioning links to reach its destination—an advantage over networks arranged in a star topology.

How to interconnect various networks

Two similar networks can be connected by a device called a bridge, which simply transfers data without regard to its format. Networks that use different topologies and technologies can be interconnected by using gateways, a generic term for any device or software used to join two dissimilar networks by converting data sent from one network into a format that is compatible with the receiving network. A gateway can be implemented using only software, only hardware, or using a combination of the two. The most commonly used gateway is a router, an electronic device that joins two or more networks. A router provides an access point from one network to another network, allowing it to shuttle data from one network to another network. For example, a home network can use a router and a modem to connect the home's LAN to the Internet. A router accepts incoming data transmissions and distributes them to devices attached to the network. Routers make decisions about the best route for data based on the data's destination and the state of the available communications channels.

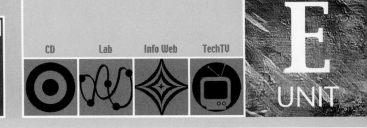
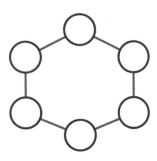

Figure E-4: Network topologies

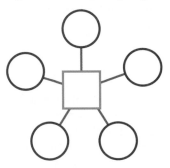

Star topology

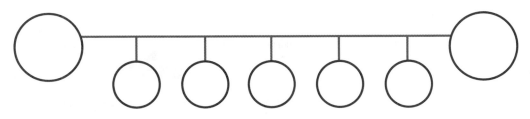

Bus topology

Ring topology

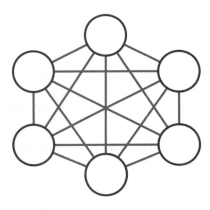

Mesh topology

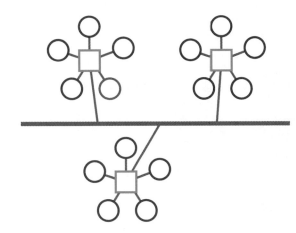

Tree topology

Using addressing to identify network devices

Every node on a network, whether it is a computer or a network device, has an address. Every packet of data that travels over a network also has an address, which helps to route a packet to its destination, much like the address on a letter. A physical address is built into the circuitry of most network devices at the time they are manufactured. A device's physical address, however, is not always in a format that can be used by a particular network. If that is the case, a network device is assigned a logical address. Network software keeps track of which physical address corresponds to each logical address.

Exploring network hardware

Even though networks come in many sizes and configurations, and use different software, they all require some basic network hardware components. A variety of devices connect computers over a network, either individually or in combination. These devices include modems, network interface cards, transceivers, hubs, repeaters, routers, and gateways.

■ A **modem** is a network device connected to a computer that converts the digital signals from a computer into signals that can travel over a network, such as the telephone system or the Internet. The term modem is derived from the words "modulate" and "demodulate." In communications terminology, **modulation** means changing the characteristics of a signal, as when a modem changes a digital signal into an analog audio signal. **Demodulation** means changing a signal back to its original state, as when a modem changes an audio signal back to a digital signal. When you send data, your modem modulates the signal that carries your data; a modem at the other end of the transmission demodulates the signal. See **Figure E-5**.

Figure E-5: How a modem works

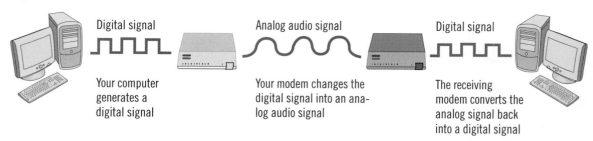

Digital signal

Your computer generates a digital signal

Analog audio signal

Your modem changes the digital signal into an analog audio signal

Digital signal

The receiving modem converts the analog signal back into a digital signal

Figure E-6: Cable modem

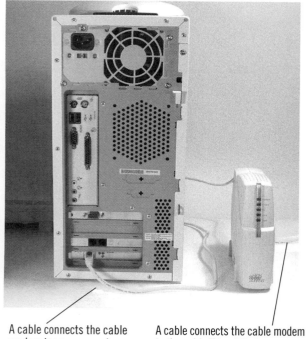

A cable connects the cable modem to your computer

A cable connects the cable modem to the cable TV wall jack

■ A **cable modem** (**Figure E-6**) is one type of modem. Many people get their television programming signal from their local cable television (CATV) company because cable TV provides a clearer picture, less reception interruptions, and more channels. People who have cable TV can also get a high-speed connection to the Internet from their cable provider through the same cable. Other types of modems include voiceband and wireless.

■ A **network interface card (NIC)** or "network adapter" is a small circuit board that converts the digital signals from a computer into signals that can travel over a network. NICs send data to and from network devices such as workstations or printers over the network, and usually use cables. A NIC designed to support Ethernet protocols is called an **Ethernet card**. You will learn about Ethernet protocols in a later lesson. Many desktop, notebook, and tablet computers include a preinstalled Ethernet card. Ethernet circuitry is also included in some printers and other peripheral devices. Add-on Ethernet cards for desktop computers fit into a slot inside the system unit; those for notebook and tablet computers are designed to fit in a PCMCIA slot. See **Figure E-7**.

Figure E-7: Ethernet NICs

NIC for a desktop computer that plugs into an expansion slot on the motherboard

NIC for notebook fits in a PCMCIA slot

- Instead of cables, a wireless network sends and receives data using a **transceiver** (a combination transmitter and receiver) that is equipped with an antenna. On a wireless network, every network device, including the hub (discussed next), must be equipped with a transceiver, which sends and receives data. See **Figure E-8**.

- The central connection point is not necessarily a server—more typically it is a network device called a **hub**, which is designed to broadcast data to workstations and peripherals. A **hub** is a network device that connects several nodes of a LAN. All of the devices that attach to a hub are part of the same LAN. A hub should have enough ports to accommodate the number of devices you plan to connect to the network. A five-port or an eight-port hub is typical for home networks. A 16-port hub, such as the one in **Figure E-9**, might be used in a small business. An Ethernet hub or combination hub/router features a collection of ports for connecting servers, workstations, and peripheral devices. Multiple hubs can be linked to expand a LAN. Today, most hubs also serve as **routers**, which connect one network to another network. Most networks require the use of hubs, routers, and gateways (hardware and software that make data compatible across networks).

- Some hubs are also repeaters. A **repeater** is a network device that amplifies and regenerates signals so that they can retain the necessary strength to reach their destinations. A repeater can boost the strength of the signal that carries data over any network topology when the distance between two nodes exceeds the carrying capacity of their connecting links.

Figure E-8: Wireless devices

Wireless network card for workstation

Wireless hub

Figure E-9: Ethernet hub

Exploring communications channels

A **communications channel**, or "network link," is a physical path or a frequency for a signal transmission. Data in a **wired network** travels from one device to another over cables. Data in a **wireless network** travels through the air, eliminating the need for cables. Computer networks use a variety of communications channels to carry data between nodes; the most common are wired communications channels including twisted-pair cable, coaxial cable, fiber-optic cable, power line, and phone line. Wireless communications channels include RF signals, microwaves, infrared light, and laser light.

■ Many networks use **twisted-pair cables** for data communications. See **Figure E-10**. Twisted-pair cables are similar to the telephone wiring in a house and can be shielded or unshielded. **STP (shielded twisted pair)** encases its twisted pairs with a foil shield, which reduces signal noise that might interfere with data transmission. **UTP (unshielded twisted pair)** contains no shielding and is less expensive than shielded cable, but is more susceptible to noise. UTP is commonly used for small networks.

■ **Coaxial cable**, shown in **Figure E-11**, is often called coax cable or co-ax. It is the same type of cable used for cable television; its high capacity allows it to carry cable modem signals as well as signals for more than 100 television channels simultaneously.

■ **Fiber-optic cable**, shown in **Figure E-12**, is a bundle of extremely thin tubes of glass. Each tube, called an optical fiber, is much thinner than a human hair. Fiber-optic cables do not conduct or transmit electrical signals; instead, miniature lasers convert data into pulses of light that flash through the cables. Fiber-optic cables are an essential part of the Internet backbone, and they are increasingly being used on business and campus networks.

■ **USB**, **serial**, **parallel**, **SCSI**, and **FireWire** cables can also be used as communications channels to transport data between a computer and a network or communications device. For example, you might use a USB cable to connect your computer to a cable modem, or a serial cable to connect your computer to a voiceband modem. Some home networks allow you to make use of existing electrical wiring, using special adapters that connect computers to electrical wall outlets.

■ In addition to wired communication channels, computer data can also travel via wireless communications channels. **RF signals (radio frequency signals)**, commonly called radio waves, are sent and received by a transceiver, which is equipped with an antenna. **Microwaves** have more carrying capacity than radio waves. They can be aimed in a single direction and work best when a clear path exists between the transmitter and receiver. Microwaves cannot penetrate metal objects. Radio and microwave transmissions cannot bend around the surface of the earth, so earth-orbiting **communications satellites** play an important role in long-distance communications. A signal can be relayed from a ground station to a communications satellite. A **transponder** on the satellite receives, amplifies, and retransmits the signal to a ground station on earth. Satellite transmissions are a key technology for the Internet backbone and provide a way for individuals to connect personal computers to the Internet. RF signals provide data transport for small home networks, campus networks, and business networks. Microwave installations typically provide data transport for large corporate networks and form part of the Internet backbone.

■ Other wireless communications channels include infrared light, laser light, and airborne data transmission. **Infrared light** can carry data signals, but only for short distances and with a clear line of sight. At the present time, its most practical use is for transmission of data between a notebook computer and a printer or between a PDA and a desktop computer, and in remote controls to change television channels. **Laser light** can stay focused over a larger distance than other wireless options, but requires a clear line of sight—no trees, snow, fog, or rain. Airborne data transmission is currently in the experimental stage.

What Is HomePNA? What Is HomePLC?

A HomePNA network utilizes existing telephone wiring to connect network devices. The HomePNA network standard uses a special NIC and cable to connect each computer to a standard telephone wall jack. The NIC contains circuitry that eliminates the need for a hub. When your computer is connected to a HomePNA network, you can typically use the phone to make a call and send information over the network at the same time because the network frequency is different from the voice frequency.

A HomePLC network, or "power line network," uses a special NIC to connect a computer to a standard electrical outlet. Data, transmitted as low-frequency radio waves, travels along the electrical wiring until it reaches another network device. Unfortunately, power line fluctuations caused by fluorescent lights, baby monitors, dimmer switches, amateur band radios, air-conditioning units, or other major appliances can disrupt the signal and cause momentary loss of network connections.

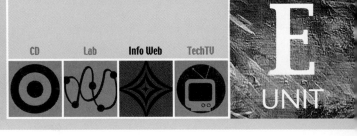
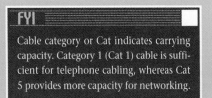

CD   Lab   **Info Web**   TechTU

Figure E-10: Twisted-pair cable

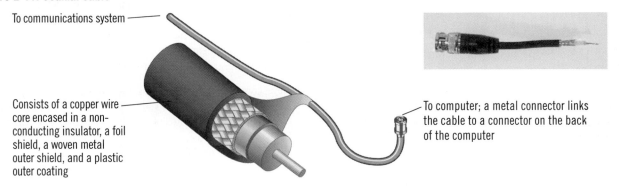

Each of the four pairs of copper wires is independently insulated and then twisted around each other

Twisted-pair cables typically terminate with plastic RJ-11 plugs for telephones or RJ-45 plugs for computer networks

To communications system

A plastic sheath protects the bundled wires

To computer

Figure E-11: Coaxial cable

To communications system

Consists of a copper wire core encased in a non-conducting insulator, a foil shield, a woven metal outer shield, and a plastic outer coating

To computer; a metal connector links the cable to a connector on the back of the computer

Figure E-12: Fiber-optic cable

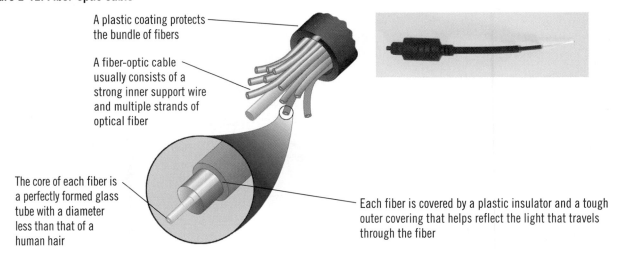

A plastic coating protects the bundle of fibers

A fiber-optic cable usually consists of a strong inner support wire and multiple strands of optical fiber

The core of each fiber is a perfectly formed glass tube with a diameter less than that of a human hair

Each fiber is covered by a plastic insulator and a tough outer covering that helps reflect the light that travels through the fiber

Defining broadband and narrowband

Bandwidth is the transmission capacity of a communications channel. The bandwidth of a digital channel is usually measured in bits per second (bps). The bandwidth of an analog channel is typically measured in hertz (Hz). A high-bandwidth communications channel can carry more data than a low-bandwidth channel. High-bandwidth communications systems, such as cable, are sometimes referred to as broadband; systems with less capacity, such as the telephone system, are referred to as narrowband. A dial-up connection, which allows speeds up to 56 Kbps, is an example of narrowband. A typical LAN, such as a college computer lab, might provide 100 Mbps bandwidth and is an example of broadband.

Transporting data

Protocols are rules that ensure the orderly and accurate transmission and reception of data. Protocols start and end transmission, recognize errors, send data at the appropriate speed, and identify the correct senders and recipients. For example, TCP/IP is the protocol that regulates Internet data transport.

■ **Table E-2** lists some common communications protocols.

Table E-2: Common communications protocols

PROTOCOL	MAIN USE
TCP/IP	Internet
NetBEUI/NetBIOS	Microsoft networks
AppleTalk	Macintosh networks
SPX/IPX	Novell networks

■ Protocols perform several important network functions, including dividing messages into packets, affixing addresses to packets, initiating transmission, regulating the flow of data, checking for transmission errors, and acknowledging receipt of transmitted data.

■ Protocols help two network devices negotiate and establish communications through a process called **handshaking**. The transmitting device sends a signal to a receiving device, and then waits for a signal from the receiving device. The two devices then negotiate a transmission speed that both can handle.

■ When you send a file or an e-mail message over a network, the file is actually broken up into small pieces called packets. A **packet** is a "parcel" of data that is sent across a computer network. See **Figure E-13**. The technology of dividing a message into several packets that can be routed independently to their destination to avoid out-of-service or congested links is called **packet switching**. Packet switching uses available bandwidth efficiently because packets from many different messages can share a single communications channel, or "circuit." Packets are shipped over the circuit on a "first-come, first-served" basis. If some packets from a message are not available, the system does not need to wait for them. Instead, the system moves on to send packets from other messages, resulting in a steady stream of data.

■ Some communications networks, such as the telephone system, use a technology called **circuit switching**, which essentially establishes a dedicated, private link between one telephone and another for the duration of a call. Packet-switching technology is a more efficient alternative to circuit switching. Today, packet switching is the technology used for virtually every computer network.

Figure E-13: Sending a file or an e-mail message over a network

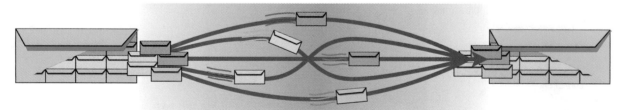

A copy of a message is divided into packets; each packet contains the address of its sender, the destination address, a sequence number, and some data; dividing messages into equal-size packets makes them easier to handle than an assortment of different-sized files

When a packet reaches an intersection in the network's communications channels, a router examines the packet's address; the router checks the address in a routing table and then sends the packet along the appropriate link toward its destination

As packets arrive at their destination, they are reassembled into a replica of the original file

 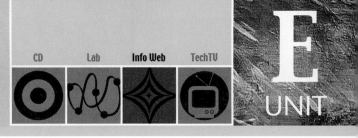

CD   Lab   **Info Web**   TechTU

■ The best-known protocol is TCP/IP—popular because it is the protocol that regulates Internet data transport. **TCP/IP** is a suite of protocols that includes TCP, IP, and others. **TCP (Transmission Control Protocol)** breaks a message or file into packets. **IP (Internet Protocol)** is responsible for addressing packets so that they can be routed to their destinations. TCP/IP is also used on LANs and WANs. TCP/IP is not the only Internet protocol. Protocols used on the Internet are summarized in **Table E-3**.

Table E-3: Protocols used on the Internet

PROTOCOL	NAME	FUNCTION
TCP/IP	Transmission Control Protocol/Internet Protocol	Breaks messages into packets and addresses them for transmission over the Internet
HTTP	Hypertext Transfer Protocol	Exchanges information over the Web
FTP	File Transfer Protocol	Transfers files between local and remote host computers
POP	Post Office Protocol	Transfers mail from an e-mail server to a client Inbox
SMTP	Simple Mail Transfer Protocol	Transfers e-mail messages from client computers to an e-mail server
IMAP	Internet Mail Access Protocol	An alternative to POP
TELNET	Telecommunications Network	Allows users who are logged on to one host to access another host
SSL	Secure Sockets Layer	Provides secure data transfer over the Internet

What is VoIP?

Packet switching can even work for tasks once performed by circuit switching networks, for example, by carrying voice conversations. This technology, called Voice over IP (VoIP) or Internet telephony, uses Internet packets to transmit voice. When your computer is connected to your ISP using a standard dial-up connection, data is transmitted over the same frequencies that are normally used for voice conversations. If you have only one telephone line, you cannot pick up your telephone receiver, dial your friend, and carry on a voice conversation while you are connected to your ISP. You can, however, use the Internet to carry voice signals from your computer's microphone through the dial-up connection to the sound card of another computer. VoIP allows you to play games over the Internet and chat about your moves, all while you are online.

Exploring wired technology

Despite challenges from other technologies, Ethernet has emerged as the leading technology for wired networks, and it is one of the most widely implemented LAN standards today. Ethernet's success is attributable to several factors; Ethernet networks are easy to understand, implement, manage, and maintain. As a nonproprietary technology, Ethernet equipment is available from a variety of vendors, and market competition keeps prices low. Current Ethernet standards allow extensive flexibility in network topology to meet the needs of small and large installations.

■ LAN technologies are standardized by the Institute of Electrical and Electronics Engineers (IEEE) *Project 802 – Local Network Standards*. IEEE standards are available for most types of commercial networks. An IEEE designation number, such as IEEE 802.3, is sometimes used to refer to a network standard. IEEE designation numbers help identify compatible network technologies.

■ In 1980, **Ethernet** became commercially available. Ethernet simultaneously broadcasts data packets to all network devices. A packet is accepted only by the device to which it is addressed. See **Figure E-14**. Today, the term Ethernet refers to a family of LAN technologies that offer various data transmission rates over fiber-optic and twisted-pair cables arranged in a bus or star topology.

Figure E-14: How Ethernet networks work

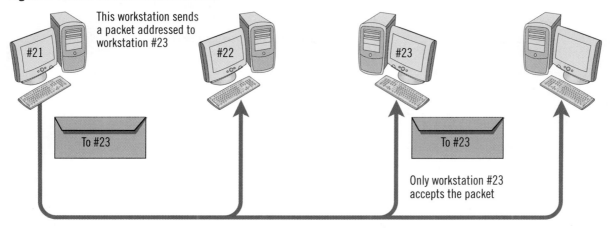

This workstation sends a packet addressed to workstation #23

#21   #22   #23

To #23

To #23

Only workstation #23 accepts the packet

The packet is broadcast to every device

What are some legacy wired technologies?

Historically, several LAN standards have experienced popularity, including ARCnet, Token Ring, and FDDI. Introduced in 1977, **ARCnet (Attached Resource Computer network)** is one of the oldest, simplest, and least expensive wired LAN technologies. A special advantage of ARCnet permits twisted-pair, coax, and fiber-optic cables to be mixed on the same network to connect up to 255 workstations. ARCnet technology is now only deployed for applications such as industrial control, building automation, transportation, robotics, and casino gaming. A **Token Ring network**, defined by the IEEE 802.5 standard, passes data around a ring topology using a signal called a "token" to control the flow of

data. Although some Token Ring networks are still operational today, many have been replaced by new network technologies that offer faster and less expensive networking solutions. **FDDI (Fiber Distributed Data Interconnect)** offers 100 Mbps speeds over fiber-optic cables. As defined by the IEEE 802.8 standards, an FDDI network supports up to 500 devices and is cabled as a dual ring; the second ring provides redundancy in case the first ring fails. Like Token Ring networks, FDDI uses a token to control data transmission. In an FDDI network, routers and servers are connected using a double ring topology; workstations are then connected to a router rather than to the ring.

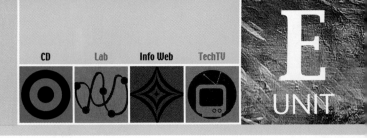
■ An integral part of Ethernet technology relies on **CSMA/CD protocol (Carrier Sense Multiple Access with Collision Detection)**. CSMA/CD takes care of situations in which two network devices attempt to transmit packets at the same time.

See **Figure E-15**. A "collision" occurs as two signals travel over the network. CSMA/CD protocol detects the collision, deletes the colliding signals, and resets the network.

Figure E-15: How Ethernet's CSMA/CD works to avoid collisions

On an Ethernet network, data travels on a first-come first-served basis; if two workstations attempt to send data at the same time, a collision occurs and that data must be resent

Data is sent from this workstation

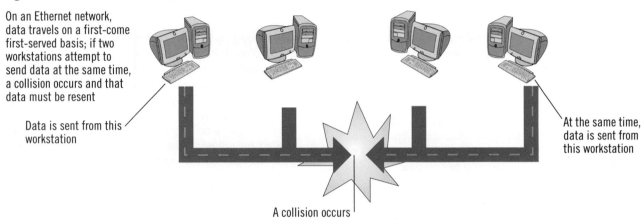

At the same time, data is sent from this workstation

A collision occurs

■ The original Ethernet standard carried data over a coaxial cable bus topology at 10 Mbps. Ethernet standards are 10BaseT Ethernet, Fast Ethernet, Gigabit Ethernet, and 10 Gig Ethernet. Of the Ethernet standards shown in **Table E-4**, Fast Ethernet is currently the most popular for small to medium LANs, such as you might find in homes and small businesses.

■ In a basic Ethernet network, each workstation and any peripheral device that is attached directly to the network requires an Ethernet card—a type of network interface card (NIC) designed to support Ethernet protocols. A home Ethernet network also requires a link between network nodes—typically Cat 5 twisted-pair cable. These

cables link workstations and peripherals to a central connection point called an Ethernet hub. Today, most Ethernet hubs also serve as routers. Ethernet hubs are available in many configurations offering various numbers of ports.

■ Large Ethernet networks typically stretch over a sizable geographic area and connect hundreds or thousands of workstations. A simple step up from a basic single-hub network is to connect several hubs using an **uplink port**. A repeater can boost signals between distant workstations. A bridge can be used to connect two smaller Ethernet segments. Enterprise devices called concentrators allow network builders to add modules containing Ethernet ports to a rack-like case.

Table E-4: Ethernet standards

ETHERNET STANDARD	IEEE DESIGNATION	SPEED	CABLE
10BaseT Ethernet	IEEE 802.3	10 Mbps	Cat 3 or Cat 5
Fast Ethernet	IEEE 802.3u	100 Mbps	Cat 5 or fiber-optic
Gigabit Ethernet	IEEE 802.3z	1 Gbps	Cat 5 or fiber-optic
10 Gig Ethernet	IEEE 802.3ae	10 Gbps	Fiber-optic

Exploring wireless technology

Wireless networks are popular because of the absence of wires and cables running through walls and between floors. Wireless networks are desirable for notebook and tablet computers that do not otherwise need to be tethered to electrical outlets. Whereas the frequencies used for broadcast TV, radio, and cable TV require a license from the FCC (Federal Communications Commission), wireless networks require no license. Despite security concerns and other potential drawbacks, wireless networks are becoming increasingly popular in corporate, school, and home networks. Wireless networks use **Wi-Fi (Wireless Fidelity)** technology, which refers to a set of wireless networking technologies defined by IEEE 802.11 standards that are compatible with Ethernet.

■ When compared to wired networks, Wi-Fi has three disadvantages: slower speed (transmission rate), distance limitations and susceptibility to interference, and lack of security.

- Speed: A **Wi-Fi network** transmits data as radio waves over predefined frequencies, much like cordless telephones. Wi-Fi networks operate at 2.4 or 5 GHz. Wi-Fi standards are listed in **Table E-5**. The fastest Wi-Fi standards operate at a maximum speed of 54 Mbps, but actual throughput is about half the maximum speed. Throughput is the rate at which a computer or network sends or receives data.

- Distance: In a typical office environment, Wi-Fi's range varies from 25 to 150 feet, depending on the standard being used. Considerably more range is possible with additional equipment. Thick cement walls, steel beams, and other environmental obstacles can, however, drastically reduce this range to the point that signals cannot be reliably transmitted. Wi-Fi signals can also be disrupted by interference from electronic devices operating at the same frequency, such as 2.4 GHz cordless telephones.

- Security: Because Wi-Fi signals travel through the air, they are easy to intercept by any suitably equipped receiving device within the network's range of service. A practice called **war driving** or

LAN-jacking occurs when hackers cruise around with a Wi-Fi-equipped notebook computer that is set up to search for Wi-Fi signals coming from home and corporate Wi-Fi networks. War drivers can access and use unsecured Wi-Fi networks; some war drivers do this to hack into files and gain unauthorized access to larger, wired networks—an act which is both unethical and, in most cases, illegal. Another threat to wireless network users is called an "evil twin." Users think they are logging onto a legitimate network, but its signals are being jammed by hackers who can extract passwords and credit card information from unsuspecting users.

■ Encrypting data using **WEP (Wired Equivalent Privacy)** is an essential step in making Wi-Fi-transmitted data useless to intruders. The WEP algorithm used to encrypt data has been broken, however, so although it is adequate for a typical home network, corporations must establish additional security measures.

■ As with a wired Ethernet network, every workstation and network peripheral requires a NIC or network adapter. **Figure E-16** shows Wi-Fi cards and an adapter. A **Wi-Fi card** includes a transmitter, receiver, and antenna to transmit signals.

Table E-5: Wi-Fi standards

IEEE DESIGNATION	FREQUENCY	SPEED	RANGE	PROS/CONS
IEEE 802.11b	2.4 GHz	11 Mbps	100–300 feet	Original standard
IEEE 802.11a	5 GHz	54 Mbps	25–75 feet	Not compatible with 802.11b
IEEE 802.11g	2.4 GHz	54 Mbps	100–150 feet	Faster than, but compatible with, 802.11b
IEEE 802.11n	2.4/5 GHz	200 Mbps	100–150 feet	Faster than 802.11b and compatible with b and g

Figure E-16: Wi-Fi cards

Wi-Fi NIC plugged into notebook computer

Wi-Fi NIC plugged into expansion slot in a desktop computer; antenna protrudes out the back

A wireless adapter converts a standard Ethernet port into a wireless port

■ A **wireless access point** (**Figure E-17**) provides a central point for data transmitted over a wireless network by broadcasting signals to any devices with compatible Wi-Fi cards. This is the same function as a hub or router in a wired Ethernet network. Many wireless access points also include a port for connecting to a wired Ethernet network or cable modem, allowing the network to extend beyond the set of workstations and peripherals on the wireless network.

■ **Bluetooth** is a short-range wireless network technology that is designed to make its own connections between electronic devices—without wires, cables, or any direct action from a user. Unlike Wi-Fi, Bluetooth is not typically used to connect a collection of workstations. Instead, Bluetooth connectivity replaces the short cables that would otherwise tether a mouse, keyboard, or printer to a computer. Bluetooth can also be used to link devices in a PAN, connect home entertainment system components, and synchronize PDAs with desktop base stations. Bluetooth-enabled devices automatically find each other and strike up a conversation without any user input at all. Bluetooth operates at the same 2.4 GHz frequency as Wi-Fi, but offers peak transmission rates of only 1 Mbps over a range of about 30 feet.

Figure E-17: A Wi-Fi access point

A Wi-Fi access point provides a central point for data transmitted over a wireless network

Introducing Internet connections

Even people who have not used the Internet know about it from watching the news, reading magazines, and watching movies. With several hundred million nodes and more than 500 million users, the Internet is huge. Although exact figures cannot be determined, it is estimated that Internet traffic exceeds 100 terabytes each week—about 100 trillion bytes. That is approximately ten times the amount of data stored in the entire printed collection of the U.S. Library of Congress. The Internet lets you browse Web sites, shop at the Net mall, send e-mail, and chat online. How does this one network provide so much information to so many people?

■ The Internet is not "owned" or operated by any single corporation or government. It is a data communications network that grew over time as networks connected to other networks. The Internet backbone provides the main high-speed routes for data traffic and consists of high-speed fiber-optic links connecting high-capacity routers that direct network traffic. Backbone links and routers are maintained by **Network Service Providers (NSPs)**, such as AT&T, MCI, Qwest, Sprint, and UUNET. NSP equipment and links are tied together by network access points (NAPs). For example, data that

begins its journey on an AT&T link can cross over to a Sprint link, if necessary, to reach its destination.

■ To access the Internet, you do not typically connect your computer directly to the Internet backbone. Instead, you connect to an ISP that in turn connects to the backbone. An **ISP (Internet Service Provider)** operates network devices that handle the physical aspects of transmitting and receiving data from your computer. Your computer connects to the Internet in one of two ways, as shown in **Figure E-18**.

Figure E-18: Connecting your computer to the Internet

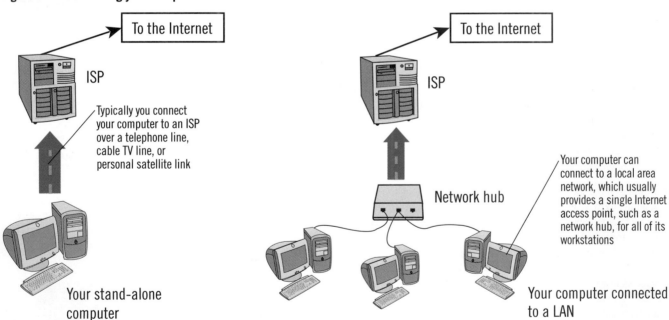

To the Internet

ISP

Typically you connect your computer to an ISP over a telephone line, cable TV line, or personal satellite link

Your stand-alone computer

To the Internet

ISP

Network hub

Your computer can connect to a local area network, which usually provides a single Internet access point, such as a network hub, for all of its workstations

Your computer connected to a LAN

■ Internet pathways can be checked to be sure that they are open to Internet traffic. A software utility called **Ping (Packet Internet Groper)** sends a signal to a specific Internet address and waits for a reply. If a reply arrives, Ping reports that the computer is online and displays the elapsed time, or latency delay, for the round-trip message. Ping is useful for finding out if a site is up and running. Ping is also useful for determining whether the connection is adequate for online computer games, VoIP, or videoconferencing.

Good quality VoIP and videoconferencing require ping rates of 200 ms or less. Ping also shows whether packets were lost in transmission. Packets can become lost when signal interference or network congestion overwhelms Internet servers and routers. Lost packets can cause jitter in VoIP communications and videoconferencing. Too many lost packets during an online gaming session can cause the game to stutter or stall. And if packets do not arrive in the correct order, your game character might seem to act randomly for a few seconds.

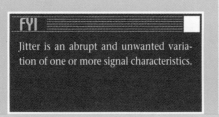
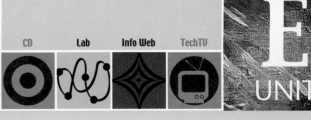
FYI

Jitter is an abrupt and unwanted variation of one or more signal characteristics.

■ Data traveling over the Internet can be traced. A software utility called **Traceroute** records a packet's path, including intermediate routers, from your computer to its destination. Using Ping or Traceroute, you can discover how long data is in transit from point A to point B. On average, data within the continental United States arrives at its destination 110-120 ms (milliseconds) after it is sent. Overseas transmissions usually require a little more time.

■ An ISP operates network devices that handle the physical aspects of transmitting and receiving data from your computer. For example, an ISP that offers telephone modem connections must maintain a bank of modems that answer when your computer dials the ISP's access number. Many ISPs operate e-mail servers to handle incoming and outgoing mail for their subscribers, and Web servers for subscriber Web sites. ISPs can also maintain servers for chat groups, instant messaging, music file sharing, FTP, and other file transfer services. Customers arrange for service for which they pay an installation charge and a monthly fee. **Figure E-19** illustrates the equipment at a typical ISP.

Figure E-19: ISP equipment

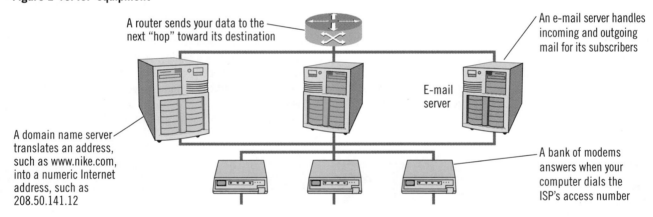

A router sends your data to the next "hop" toward its destination

An e-mail server handles incoming and outgoing mail for its subscribers

E-mail server

A domain name server translates an address, such as www.nike.com, into a numeric Internet address, such as 208.50.141.12

A bank of modems answers when your computer dials the ISP's access number

How fast is a modem?

When modems were a new technology, their transmission speed was measured as **baud rate**, the number of times per second that a signal in a communications channel varies, or makes a transition between states. Since a change between states can involve more than a single bit of data, the **bits per second (bps)** unit of measurement has replaced baud rate as a better expression of data transmission speed. This is actually a measure of capacity, but everyone calls it "speed."

Actual data-transfer speeds are affected by factors such as the quality of your local loop connection to your ISP. Even with a "perfect" connection, a 56 Kbps

voiceband modem used for connecting via dial-up tops out at about 44 Kbps. Many Internet connection methods provide faster downstream (data received) transmission rates than upstream (data sent) rates. Dial-up connections are no exception: 44 Kbps is a typical downstream speed for a 56 Kbps modem; upstream, the data rate drops to about 33 Kbps, or less. Most **DSL modems** are rated for 1.5 Mbps downstream, compared to standard 56 Kbps for a dial-up connection. Cable modems are rated at 1.5 Mbps and wireless modems range from 500 Kbps for satellite to 268 Mbps for WiMAX.

Introducing IP addresses and domain names

An organization called **ICANN (Internet Corporation for Assigned Names and Numbers)** is recognized by the United States and other governments as the global organization that coordinates the technical management of the Internet's domain name system, the allocation of IP addresses, and the assignment of protocol parameters. Computers on the Internet are identified using IP addresses. The "IP" part of TCP/IP defines the format for the IP addresses.

- Every ISP controls a unique pool of IP addresses, which can be assigned to subscribers as needed. An **IP address** is a series of numbers, such as 204.127.129.001. When written, an IP address is separated into four sections by periods, for the convenience of readers. The number in a section cannot exceed 255. Each section is called an octet. In binary representation, each section of an IP address requires 8 bits, so the entire address requires 32 bits. The four sections are used to create classes of IP addresses where each part is assigned based on the size, type of network, and other Internet functions.

- A permanently assigned IP address is called a **static IP address**. As a rule of thumb, computers that need a permanent IP address are servers or "hosts" on the Internet, for example, ISPs, Web sites, Web hosting services, or e-mail servers. Computers with static IP addresses usually are connected to the Internet all the time. For example, the computer that hosts the Course Technology Web site has a permanent address so that Internet users can always find it.

- A temporarily assigned IP address is called a **dynamic IP address**. Dynamic IP addresses are typically assigned by ISPs for most dial-up connections and some DSL, ISDN, or cable modem connections. When you use a dial-up connection, for example, your ISP assigns a temporary IP address to your computer. When you end a session, that IP address goes back into a pool of addresses so it can be distributed to other subscribers when they log in. Your computer will rarely be assigned the same IP address it had during a previous dial-up session. Dynamic IP addresses are generally assigned to computers that are running client software that will access the Internet for activities such as surfing the Web, sending and receiving e-mail, listening to Internet radio, or participating in chat groups.

- An ISP can assign its subscribers a static IP address, a dynamic address each time you connect, or a semi-permanent address that lasts for several months. Because your ISP assigns IP addresses, you usually do not need to know the IP address assigned to your computer. However, if you need to identify how your computer is connected to the Internet or troubleshoot your connection, you can see your computer's IP address by reviewing the Internet configuration settings.

How to register a domain name

The domain name system is based on a distributed database. This database is not stored as a whole in any single location; it exists in parts all over the Internet. Your Internet connection is set up to access one of the many domain name servers that reside on the Internet. When you enter a domain name or URL, it is sent to your designated domain server, which can either send back the IP address that corresponds to the domain name, or if your domain name server does not have a record of the domain name, it can contact another domain name server and request the IP address. The servers in the domain name system supply IP addresses in a matter of milliseconds. Organizations or individuals can select a domain name and register it by using an online registration service, as shown in **Figure E-20**.

The first step in registering a domain name is to find out whether the name is currently in use or reserved for future use. Some domain names are not currently in use, yet they are not available because they are reserved. If a domain name is not available, consider using a different top-level domain, such as biz instead of com. After you have found an available domain name you like, you can continue the registration process by filling out a simple online form.

Figure E-20

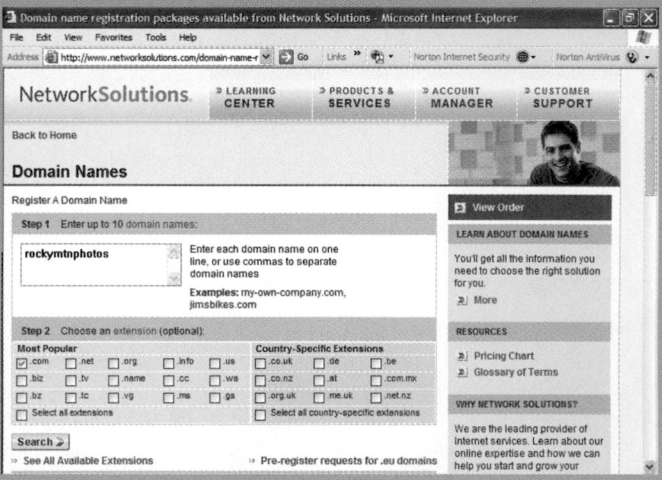

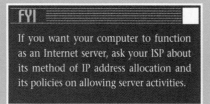
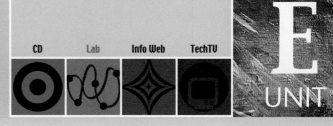

CD   Lab   Info Web   TechTV

E
UNIT

■ IP addresses work well for communication between computers, but people often have difficulty remembering a series of numbers. As a result, many host computers have an easy-to-remember name that translates directly to the computer's IP address. This name is the "fully qualified domain name" (FQDN), but most people just refer to it as a **domain name**. Every domain name corresponds to a unique IP address that has been entered into a database called the **domain name system**. When you type a domain name into your browser, a domain name request is routed through your ISP to your designated domain name server, which then searches through its database to find a corresponding IP address. Computers that host this database are referred to as **domain name servers**. A domain name must be converted into an IP address before any packets can be routed to it.

■ A domain name is a key component of URLs and e-mail addresses. It is the Web server name in a URL and the e-mail server name in an e-mail address. For example, in the URL www.course.com, the domain name is course.com. In the e-mail address emilyb@course.com, the domain name is course.com.

■ A domain name ends with an extension that indicates its **top-level domain**. For example, in the domain name course.com, "com" indicates that the host computer is maintained by a commercial business, in this case, Course Technology. Top-level domains and their uses are listed in **Table E-6**. Other domains are also in use. For example, country codes also serve as top-level domains. Canada's top-level domain is ca; the United Kingdom's is uk; Australia's is au. Another domain with growing popularity is .tv, which is available for a fee to media-related Web sites.

Table E-6: Top-level domains

DOMAIN	DESCRIPTION
biz	Unrestricted use; usually for commercial businesses
com	Unrestricted use; usually for commercial businesses
edu	Restricted to North American educational institutions
gov	Restricted to U.S. government agencies
info	Unrestricted use
int	Restricted to organizations established by international treaties
mil	Restricted to U.S. military agencies
net	Unrestricted use; traditionally for Internet administrative organizations
org	Unrestricted use; traditionally for professional and nonprofit organizations

Connecting to the Internet using POTS

The most difficult aspect of the Internet is getting connected. Many high-speed Internet access options, such as cable modems, DSL, personal satellite dishes, and ISDN are available, however, most people's first experience connecting to the Internet begins with a **dial-up** connection. A dial-up connection uses **POTS (plain old telephone service)** to transport data between your computer and your ISP. Although the standard equipment provided by telephone companies limits the amount of data that you can transmit and receive over a voiceband modem, the copper wire that runs from your wall jacks to the switching station actually has a fair amount of capacity.

■ The telephone communications system uses a tiered network to transport calls locally, cross-country, and internationally. At each level of the network, a switch creates a connection so that a call eventually has a continuous circuit to its destination. The first tier of this network uses a star topology to physically connect each telephone in a city to a switch in a "switching station," "local switch," or "central office." The second tier of the telephone network links several local switching stations. Connections then fan out to switches that are maintained by many different local and long-distance telephone companies. The telephone network uses a technology called circuit switching. See **Figure E-21**.

■ When you use a dial-up connection, your computer's modem places a regular telephone call to your ISP. Your call is routed through the telephone company's local switch and out to the ISP. When the ISP's computer answers your call, a dedicated circuit is established between you and your ISP, just as if you had made a voice call and someone at the ISP had picked up the phone. The circuit remains connected for the duration of your call and provides a communications link that carries data between your computer and the ISP. As your data arrives at the ISP, a router sends it out over the Internet.

The signals that represent data exist in your computer as digital signals. The telephone system, however, expects to work with human voices, so the data that it carries must be in the format of analog audio tones. A **voiceband modem**, usually referred to as a modem, converts the digital signals from your computer into signals that can travel over telephone lines.

Figure E-21: Packet switching compared to circuit switching

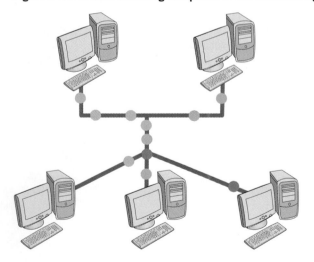

Packet switching

Divides a message into several packets that can be routed independently to their destinations

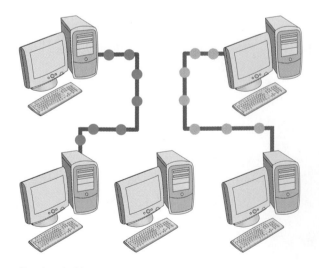

Circuit switching

Provides callers with a direct pipeline over which streams of voice data can flow; circuit switching is inefficient, for example, when someone is "on hold," no communication is taking place—because the circuit is reserved and cannot be used for other communications

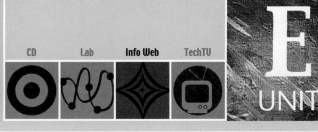

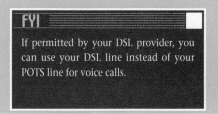

■ Although telephone companies "went digital" long ago, their digital switches kick into action only after your call arrives at the local switching station. The technology between your telephone and your local switch is designed to carry analog voice signals. To transport data over this loop, the digital signals from your computer must be converted into analog signals that can travel over the telephone lines to your local switch. When these signals arrive at the local switch, they are converted into digital signals. See **Figure E-22**.

Figure E-22: Dialing in to the Internet

When you use an ISP to access the Internet, your data travels through the local telephone switch to your ISP, which sends it onto the Internet

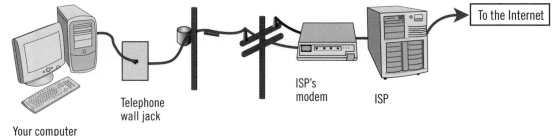

To the Internet

Your computer and modem

Telephone wall jack

ISP's modem

ISP

■ **DSL (Digital Subscriber Line)** is a high-speed, digital, always-on Internet access technology that uses standard phone lines to transport data. It is one of the fastest Internet connections affordable to the individual consumer. Several variations of DSL technology exist, including ADSL (asymmetric DSL with downstream speed faster than upstream speed), SDSL (symmetric DSL with the same upstream and downstream speed), HDSL (high-rate DSL), and DSL lite. This entire group of DSL technologies is sometimes called xDSL.

DSL is digital, so data does not need to be changed into analog form and then back to digital, resulting in fast data transmission over standard copper telephone cable. **Figure E-23** illustrates how voice and data signals travel over DSL to a special device at the local telephone switching station, where they are divided and routed either to an ISP or to the regular telephone network.

In many areas, DSL is a joint venture between the telephone company and the DSL provider. The telephone company is responsible for the physical cabling and voice transmission. The DSL provider is responsible for data traffic. The speed of a DSL connection varies according to the characteristics of your telephone line, your proximity to the switching station (the further you get from the station, the poorer the signal), the equipment at your local switch, and your DSL provider.

■ **ISDN (Integrated Services Digital Network)** connections move data faster than a dial-up connection, but not as fast as DSL or cable modems. ISDN is an all-digital service with the potential to carry voice and data. ISDN service is typically regarded as a high-speed Internet connection option for businesses that maintain small local area networks. The service is usually obtained from a local telephone company or a dedicated ISDN service provider.

■ T1, T3, and T4 services are dedicated, leased lines that offer fast, high-capacity data transmission. Speed ranges from 1.544 Mbps to 274 Mbps. T3 and T4 lines provide many of the links on the Internet backbone. T1, T3, and T4 lines are leased from the telephone company and are not usually shared by other customers. These high speed services are usually too expensive for individuals.

Figure E-23: How DSL carries voice and data

Digital data and analog voice signals travel over the DSL line to the local switching station; data signals are interpreted by special equipment called a DSLAM (DSL Access Multiplexor)

Switching Station

DSL line

DSLAM

Data is routed over high-speed lines to a DSL provider or directly to the Internet

POTS SWITCH

Voice signals are transferred to the telephone company's regular lines

Connecting to the Internet using cable

The cable television system was originally designed for remote areas where TV broadcast signals could not be received in an acceptable manner with an antenna. These systems were called "community antenna television," or CATV. The CATV concept was to install one or more large, expensive satellite dishes in a community, catch TV signals with these dishes, and then send the signals over a system of cables to individual homes. This system has been adapted and now provides Internet service to many homes.

■ The satellite dish "farm" where television broadcasts are received and retransmitted for cable connections is referred to as the head-end. From the head-end, a cabling system branches out and eventually reaches consumers' homes. When your cable TV company becomes your Internet service provider, your computer becomes part of a neighborhood local area network, as shown in **Figure E-24**. A router and high-speed connection from the head-end to the Internet provide the potential for Internet connectivity over every cable in the system.

■ To offer both television and Internet access, the cable's bandwidth is divided among three activities. As shown in **Figure E-25**, a CATV cable must provide bandwidth for television signals, incoming data signals, and outgoing data signals. Even dividing the bandwidth among these activities, the lowest-capacity coaxial cable used by the CATV system has a far greater carrying capacity than a POTS line.

■ When you configure your computer to access the Internet with a cable modem, you are essentially connecting to an Ethernet-style LAN that connects a neighborhood of cable subscribers. The two requirements of a cable connection are a NIC with circuitry to handle Ethernet protocols and a cable modem, which converts your computer's signal into one that can travel over the CATV network. If the cable modem includes Ethernet circuitry, it can be connected to a computer using only a USB cable.

■ Most cable subscribers have only one CATV cable, so a splitter is used to connect both the cable modem and a television to that one CATV cable. If a subscriber has multiple CATV cables available, the cable modem can be connected directly to any one of them.

Figure E-24: The topology of CATV

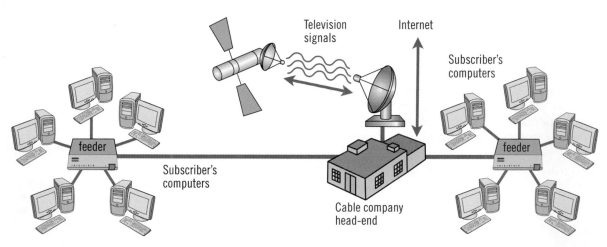

Cables from the CATV head-end extend out as a series of "trunks;" the trunks are then connected to "feeders" that serve neighborhoods; the connection from a feeder to a subscriber's home is referred to as a "drop"

Figure E-25: CATV cable

CATV cable has enough bandwidth to support TV channels and data flowing downstream, as well as data flowing upstream

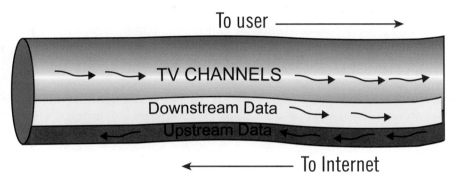

To user

TV CHANNELS

Downstream Data

Upstream Data

To Internet

■ When your cable connection is up and running, two issues become significant: bandwidth and security.

- Bandwidth: A communications channel like your CATV cable carries packets at a constant speed. The CATV cable also has a certain amount of bandwidth. As more and more neighbors use the service, data transport might seem to get slower.

- Security: Most cable companies use DOCSIS-compliant cable modems that block "crossover" traffic between subscribers.

■ **DOCSIS (Data Over Cable Service Interface Specification)** is a security technology that filters packets to certain ports, including the port the Windows operating system uses for networking. DOCSIS secures your computer from your neighbors, but it does not close up all the security holes that are opened when you use an always-on connection.

Security and always-on connections

Unlike a dial-up connection, which is only connected for the duration of your "call" or connection, an **always-on connection** is always connected whenever your computer is powered up. With an always-on connection, you might have the same IP address for days, or even months, depending on your ISP. A hacker who discovers that your computer is always on can easily find your computer again, and its high-speed access makes it a very desirable target.

When your computer is turned off, it is not vulnerable to attack. Therefore, it is a good idea to shut down your computer when you are not using it. Putting your computer into sleep mode or activating a screen saver is not sufficient protection. Your computer must be shut down and turned off. Additional steps you can take to protect yourself from security breaches through your cable connection to the Internet are discussed in Unit F.

Connecting to the Internet without wires

You do not need wires to connect to the Internet; you can connect a computer to the Internet using wireless technology. You can also use a mobile wireless Internet connection to surf the Web and check your e-mail. Devices such as cell phones, PDAs, notebook computers, and tablet computers can be configured for mobile Internet access. Currently, the most popular option for mobile Internet access is a public Wi-Fi network.

- Satellite connections include digital satellite service and fixed wireless service. Both of these services are relatively expensive; but in some areas, particularly remote rural areas, they might be the only high-speed option available.

- **Digital satellite service (DSS)** uses a geosynchronous or low-earth satellite to transmit television, voice, or computer data directly to and from a satellite dish, or "base station," owned/leased by an individual. See **Figure E-26**. A satellite Internet modem connects the satellite dish to a computer. Satellite transmission and reception can be blocked by adverse weather conditions, which makes this type of data transport less reliable than most wired options. Satellite data transport is subject to latency delays of one second or more, which occur as your data is routed between your computer and a satellite that orbits 22,200 miles above the earth. Latency can become a showstopper for interactive gaming that requires quick reactions.

- **Fixed wireless Internet service** is designed to offer Internet access to homes and businesses by broadcasting RF data signals over areas large enough to cover most cities and outlying areas. Wireless technologies such as **WiMAX** have less latency than DSS and can offer connection speeds suitable for online gaming and teleconferencing. WiMAX is an Ethernet-compatible network technology that is essentially wide-area Wi-Fi, with a range of 30 miles.

- A **public Wi-Fi network** is a wireless LAN that provides open Internet access to the public. Public Wi-Fi networks are popping up in places such as bookstores, coffee shops, airports, hotels, and restaurants. The range of network coverage is called a **Wi-Fi hotspot**. Any Wi-Fi-equipped device that enters a hotspot can gain access to the network's services. Some Wi-Fi public networks offer free service; others require a subscription or one-time use fee. A company that maintains a public Wi-Fi network is sometimes referred to as a WISP (wireless ISP).

Figure E-26: Connecting to the Internet via satellite

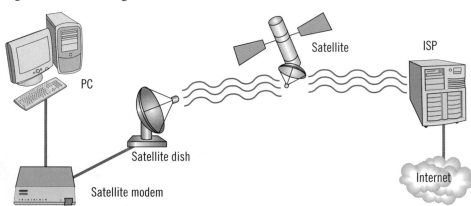

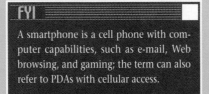

FYI

A smartphone is a cell phone with computer capabilities, such as e-mail, Web browsing, and gaming; the term can also refer to PDAs with cellular access.

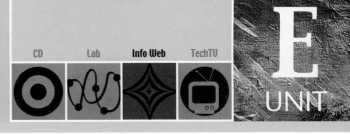

CD   Lab   **Info Web**   TechTU

E

UNIT

■ **WAP (Wireless Access Protocol)** is a communications protocol that provides wireless Internet access from handheld devices, such as cell phones and PDAs. WAP-enabled devices contain a microbrowser that simplifies Web and e-mail access on a small, low-resolution screen. See **Figure E-27**. You can obtain WAP-enabled devices and services from many mobile telecommunications providers, such as T-Mobile, Verizon, and CellularOne.

■ Some cell phones connect to your computer and act as a wireless modem to transmit data over the Internet. **Cellular-ready modems** are packaged as PC cards that slip easily into the PCMCIA port of a notebook or tablet computer. Data transfer speeds using basic cell phone service top out at 14.4 Kbps or less—only a fraction of the speed of a dial-up connection. Some cellular carriers, however, offer special data transfer services that match or exceed 56 Kbps dial-up speeds. These services are fairly expensive. Cell phone and notebook combinations are practical only for mobile computer users who want to use their notebook computers in areas not serviced by Wi-Fi hotspots or cable connections.

■ The best Internet connection depends on your budget and what is available in your area. If several Internet connection services are available to you, evaluate their requirements, upload and download speeds, monthly costs, installation costs, and overall advantages and disadvantages.

Figure E-27: WAP-enabled devices

The advantage of WAP-enabled devices is their portability; the disadvantage is their small, low-res screens; although various schemes for scrolling over a full-sized Web page have been tried, most WAP users stick to Web sites specially designed for small screen devices

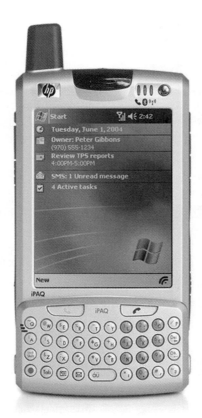

What features should I look for in a handheld device that connects to the Internet?

When shopping for a handheld device to access the Internet, you should consider screen size, keypad functionality, and network connection options. Color screens are essential for a look similar to your desktop browser. Cellular service providers offer dual-band, tri-band, and quad-band phones. The "band" refers to the radio frequency used to transmit calls. You benefit from a dual-band phone if you use your phone outside big cities. If you plan to use your phone in Europe, you might consider a tri-band phone. Try to find a device that offers cellular, Wi-Fi, and Bluetooth connectivity.

Cellular technology is evolving rapidly and generates technologies with acronyms such as G1, AMPS, CDMA, GSM, and GPRS. Within each technology are subcategories offering different features ranging from basic cellular service to e-mail and Web browsing. Additional features include short message service or SMS (also known as text messaging), multimedia messaging (MMS), camera phones that take still photos and/or videos that can be sent to other mobile phones or to e-mail addresses, music fingerprinting, games, stocks, news, weather, and city guides.

A LAN provides a cost-effective way to share one Internet connection among several computers. For example, a single cable Internet, DSL, ISDN, or satellite connection can be shared via your home LAN, which means it can be accessed by all the workstations on your LAN. However, before connecting multiple computers to a single Internet connection via your LAN, be sure to check with your Internet Service Provider, because some have restrictions on sharing connections. Typically, routers are configured to automatically distribute IP addresses to LAN workstations using DHCP (Dynamic Host Configuration Protocol). Most Windows computers are configured to request an IP address using DHCP, so the computer and router can work together to establish a connection for each computer. To establish LAN Internet access, you will need the following: a wired or wireless LAN, a router or a hub with router capabilities, a high-speed Internet connection, and a modem that corresponds to your Internet connection type. Remember that networks typically use always-on connections, so it is important to implement security measures to protect data on network servers and workstations. The Tech Talk provides an overview of Ethernet and Wi-Fi setup. See **Figure E-28**.

Installing a LAN

Figure E-28: Installing a LAN

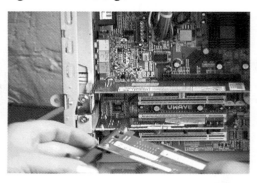

1. To begin, make sure every computer and peripheral you'll connect to the network contains a NIC; if a card is not built in, you must install one

Devices you intend to connect using cables require Ethernet cards; devices slated for wireless connections require Wi-Fi cards

2. Place the hub or router in a central location and plug it in

If you are planning to link your LAN to the Internet, connect the hub or router to your Internet connection

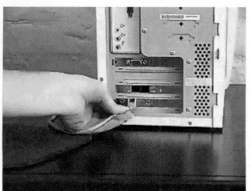

3. For an Ethernet network, run cables from the hub or router to the NIC in each device

Turn on network devices one at a time; Windows should automatically detect the NICs and establish a connection to the network

Use the Windows Start menu to access the Control Panel; from there, select the Network Setup Wizard to complete the installation process

Using a LAN

How do you access network resources? If you use Windows, it automatically detects the network any time you turn on a workstation. Even once the network is recognized, you might be asked to log in by entering a user ID and password, depending on your network setup. Once access is established, you can use any shared resources for which you have been given authorization.

How do you specify which resources can be shared by other workstations? Workstation owners can specify whether files and locally attached printers can be accessed from other workstations on the network.

Windows allows you to designate a special folder for files you want to share with others. You can allow others to view and edit these files, or you can limit access only to viewing. You can also allow other network users to access your computer's entire hard disk or locally connected printer. For example, you can use My Computer to access shared resources listed under the My Network Places icon, or you can use **drive mapping** to assign a drive letter to a storage device located on a different workstation. See **Figure E-29**.

Figure E-29

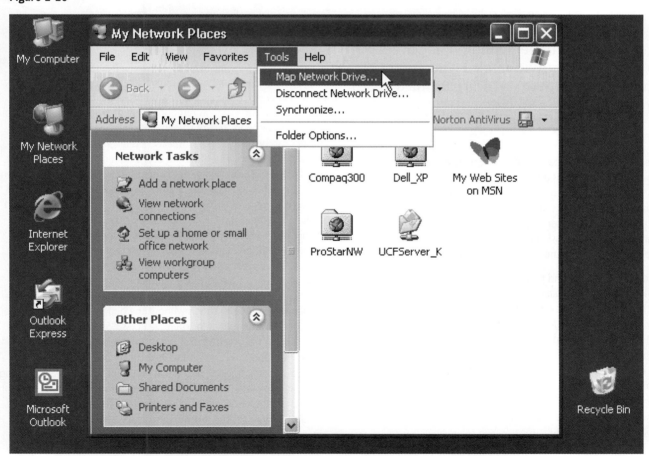

In this drive mapping example, a server's drive C will be mapped as drive F by a workstation; after the mapping is complete, the server's hard disk will appear in the workstation's directory as drive F so it can be used just as though it were a drive connected directly to the workstation

Computers in Context Education

The first educational application of computers emerged in the 1960s, when huge mainframes with clunky interfaces introduced students to computer-aided instruction (CAI). CAI uses basic drill and practice: The computer presents a problem, the student responds, and the computer evaluates the response. Studies in the 1970s indicated that CAI systems, such as PLATO (Programmed Logic for Automated Teaching Operations), improved student test scores, but students found the mainframe's monochrome display (see **Figure E-30**) and the CAI's regimented drill format boring. More recent versions of CAI use colorful graphics and arcade formats to grab learners' attention.

Educators looking for ways to harness the computer's interactive and programmable nature arrived at the idea of computer-based training (CBT). CBT is formatted as a series of tutorials, beginning with a pretest to see whether students have the prerequisite skills, followed by drill and practice, then ending with a CAI-style test to determine whether students can move on to the next tutorial segment.

> Most educators believe that computers can help create an individualized and interactive learning environment, which can make learning more effective and efficient.

Another educational approach, called computer-aided learning (CAL), uses the computer more as a source of information than an assessment mechanism. Students using CAL make decisions about their level of expertise, what material is relevant, and how to pace their own learning. Exploratory CAL environments included Seymour Papert's Logo programming language; using Logo, students investigated geometry concepts to program the movement of a graphical turtle on-screen.

In addition to CAI, CBT, and CAL, simulations were developed as an educational tool. In a simulation, the computer mimics a real-world situation through a narrative description or with graphics. Students are given options and respond with a decision or an action. The computer evaluates each response and determines its consequences. Oregon Trail, a simulation popular with elementary school students, describes events that beset a group of pioneers traveling in a wagon train. Students respond to each event, while learning bits of history, money-handling skills, conservation, and decision making. Even though this was one of the earliest simulations, it has kept up with advances in technology and is still popular today.

Figure E-30

Most educators believe that computers can help create an individualized and interactive learning environment, which can make learning more effective and efficient. Although 99% of American public schools have computers and 93% of students use them in some way, these statistics can be deceiving. The reality falls far short of the ideal situation, which is every student having access to a computer throughout the school day. The challenge is to figure out how to realize the potential of computers in an educational setting. Solutions have been tried with varying degrees of success. Some schools have installed learning labs where students go for scheduled "lab time." In elementary schools, often a few computers are placed in special work areas of classrooms and used for small group projects or individual drill and practice. Some schools have relegated most computers to the library, where they are connected to the Internet and used for research. In some classrooms, a single computer can be used as an effective presentation device. A few schools without the budget for enough desktop computers have opted for inexpensive PDAs. "Students need to use technology just as you and I do, not just one hour a day," says one teacher in support of PDAs. Students use standard PDA software for educational tasks: tracking nutritional intake for health class, collecting data from experiments in biology class, graphing functions in math class, translating phrases for French class, and maintaining to-do lists. The biggest drawback to more widespread educational use of PDAs, however, is a lack of software specifically designed for education.

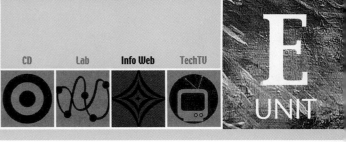
As another option, some schools—primarily colleges— have confronted the problem of computer access by requiring all incoming first-year students to purchase notebook computers. Many colleges, for example, provide Internet connections in dorm rooms and library study carrels or offer campus-wide Wi-Fi service. Students can tote their notebook computers, for example, either to class to take notes or outside for use with a study group. See **Figure E-31**. They can contact instructors via e-mail, use the Internet as a research resource, and run educational software.

Figure E-31

Another educational use of computers can be seen in distance education (DE) or distance learning (DL) courses. Historically, distance education meant correspondence study or courses delivered by radio or television, but the meaning has been broadened to encompass any educational situation in which students and instructors are not in the same place. Therefore, most DE courses today require students to have access to a computer and an Internet connection. DE courses are offered to K-12 students, college students, military personnel, business people, and the general public. Most students who choose DE courses do so because they want to learn at their own pace, at a convenient time, and in a location close to home. For example, single parents who must deal with the realities of day care, working professionals who cannot relocate to a college town, and physically disabled students all find DE to be an acceptable alternative to traditional school-based learning. DE has the potential of increasing the pool of students for a course by making the course financially feasible; for example, an advanced Kanji course could be offered at a Midwestern university with only 10 on-campus Japanese majors if enough DE students can boost enrollment.

The Internet hosts a wide variety of DE courses, both credit-earning and noncredit courses. Several course management systems (CMSs), such as Blackboard and WebCT, help teachers prepare and manage DE courses. These systems are popular with degree-granting institutions that offer credit-earning DE courses in their course catalogs (subject to the usual course fees and requirements). Course management software typically runs from a server maintained by a school system, college, or university. Using Web browsers, teachers access the CMS to post an online syllabus, develop Web pages with course content, create a database of questions for online assessment, manage e-mail, set up online discussion groups, and maintain a grade book. Students using Internet-connected computers and standard Web browsers can access course materials, submit assignments, interact with other students, and take tests.

Computers and the Internet have opened opportunities for life-long learning.

Computers and the Internet have opened opportunities for life-long learning. Prospective students can use a search engine to easily find non-credit courses and tutorials for a wide range of topics, including pottery, dog grooming, radio astronomy, desktop publishing, and drumming. Some tutorials are free, and others charge a small fee. Several Web sites, such as Barnes & Noble University and OnlineLearning.com, offer a good choice of fee-based or free courses. In a society that promotes learning as a lifelong endeavor, the Internet has certainly made it possible for students of all ages to pursue knowledge and skills simply by using a computer and an Internet connection.

Issue Free Wi-Fi? Why or Why Not?

How would you like high-speed Internet access that requires no cables, no modem, and best of all—no subscription fees? Free community wireless access in cities as diverse as San Francisco, Miami, New York, Prague, and Amsterdam is made possible by free WLANs (wireless LANs). Dubbed "renegade WLANs" by some members of the press, these free networks are operated by public-spirited individuals who like to tinker with technology and want to provide a useful community service. Free WLAN operators typically subscribe to a DSL or cable provider for high-speed Internet access. They pay their monthly fees, but instead of curtailing access to their own personal use, they distribute their connections to friends, neighbors, and just about anyone who passes by with the right computer equipment.

Free WLANs are based on Wi-Fi technology, which uses the 802.11b networking standard to create wireless Ethernet-compatible LANs. The technology itself is not inherently renegade; in fact, it is used for many mainstream applications. Wi-Fi networks are popular in corporations and universities where users are mobile and the flow of information typically requires broadband capacity.

If your neighbor sets up a free WLAN that becomes popular with customers in a nearby coffeehouse, your previously sedate network neighborhood might suddenly become an overcrowded metropolis with major Internet access traffic jams.

The 802.11b standard uses an unlicensed telecommunications spectrum, so it is perfectly legal to set up an antenna to transmit and receive Wi-Fi signals without obtaining a broadcast license or paying any fees to the Federal Communications Commission. Not only is it legal, setting up a Wi-Fi antenna is simple and inexpensive. A basic Wi-Fi antenna can be created with a few wires and an empty container. Using a Wi-Fi network is even cheaper and easier than setting one up. Many notebook computers have built-in Wi-Fi transceivers and software. If a transceiver is not built into your computer, you can add one for less than $100. With a Wi-Fi-ready computer, you can literally walk down the street, and your computer will look for and connect to any available (that is, unsecured) Wi-Fi network.

Some free WLAN advocates envision a nationwide web of interconnected Wi-Fi networks that will form "a seamless broadband network built by the people, for the people." In this vision of a world connected by free WLANs, libraries could offer Internet access to people in low income neighborhoods. Local schools could get wired without exorbitant cabling expenses. Parents, kids, and grandparents, as well as corporate executives, could exchange e-mail and instant messages from locations that include the kitchen table, the corner coffee shop, and the Little League field.

But some broadband providers, such as AT&T and Time Warner Cable, fear that every user of a free wireless network is one less paying customer. According to one industry analyst, "The telecom industries are addicted to the one-wire, one-customer philosophy."

Sharing an Internet connection that is intended for single-user access does not coexist with this philosophy. Most subscriber agreements contain wording that limits use of a broadband connection to one user and perhaps immediate family members. Although wording varies from one provider to another, most agreements expressly prohibit subscribers from using their connections for commercial purposes. Some free WLAN operators do not believe that sharing is commercial use. "I'm sharing it with people," says one free WLAN provider, "I'm not selling it. I'm not making a profit off it."

Whether or not free WLANs are legal, their benefits are tempered by several potentially negative repercussions. For example, tightening up subscriber agreements to eliminate the sharing loophole could affect many broadband subscribers who currently operate private wired or wireless networks that link several computers to a single Internet connection. Broadband providers could force private network operators to purchase more expensive multi-user licenses—an option that might be too expensive for many home networks.

Most free WLANs are operated as a hobby. Some operators are very conscientious, but others have a laid-back attitude toward quality of service. Consequently, free WLAN access can be unreliable; but users cannot really complain when the network does not work if they are not paying for the service. If broadband providers threaten to pull out of areas where free WLANs are popular, community members might have to choose between unreliable free WLAN service offered by hobbyists and more reliable, but more costly, services supplied by for-profit providers.

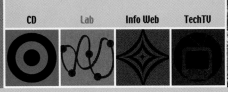

| CD | Lab | Info Web | TechTV |

The wisdom of unregulated network availability is called into question by resulting ethical, security, and privacy issues. A publicly accessible LAN that requires no passwords or accounts can be used anonymously for a variety of illegal and dangerous activities. Like drug dealers who use public telephones to avoid taps and traces, terrorists and other criminals can simply walk into a free WLAN zone, tap into the Internet, and walk away without leaving a trace.

Widespread distribution of free WLANs can reduce the bandwidth available to paying customers. If your neighbor sets up a free WLAN that becomes popular with customers in a nearby coffeehouse, your previously sedate network neighborhood might suddenly become an overcrowded metropolis with major Internet access traffic jams.

Despite possible repercussions, the free WLAN movement appears to be growing and becoming more controversial. Some industry analysts expect a battle similar to the one that ensued when Napster's peer-to-peer music-sharing network was attacked by the music industry. The free WLAN controversy could pit a group of telecommunications giants against a rag-tag alliance of free WLAN advocates. The outcome has the potential to affect broadband subscribers everywhere.

Interactive Questions

☐ Yes   ☐ No   ☐ Not sure   **1.** Have you ever accessed a free WLAN?

☐ Yes   ☐ No   ☐ Not sure   **2.** Do you believe that pirated WLANs can survive alongside for-profit broadband ISPs?

☐ Yes   ☐ No   ☐ Not sure   **3.** Are broadband providers justified in limiting the terms of their service agreements to "one subscription, one customer"?

Expand the Ideas

1. Research Wi-Fi technology. Write a brief description of what it is and how it works. Then consider: Is it ethical to set up a free Wi-Fi? Is it ethical to use one? Research two articles that present both viewpoints, for and against the unregulated use of free WLANs. Compare the viewpoints and then summarize the findings. Draw your own conclusion at the end of a short paper.

2. Do you believe that pirated WLANS can provide service alongside for-profit broadband ISPs? Why might one group prefer to use one service over the other? Might a for-profit broadband ISP consider offering Wi-Fi service? How could that be beneficial for the consumer? Write a short description of your ideas.

3. Are broadband ISPs justified in limiting the terms of their service agreements to "one subscription, one customer"? Relate broadband ISP services to other services such as telephone, cable TV, software licenses, radio, and print media. How are the services similar? How are they different? Does the difference justify the "one subscription, one customer" service agreements? Should exceptions be made for the following: same family users, same dwelling users, or home network users? Explain your position in a media presentation.

End of Unit Exercises

Key Terms

Always-on connection
ARCnet (Attached Resource Computer network)
Bandwidth
Baud rate
Bluetooth
Bits per second (bps)
Bridge
Broadband
Bus topology
Cable modem
Cellular-ready modem
Circuit switching
Client computer
Client/server network
Coaxial cable
Communications channel
Communications network
Communications satellite
CSMA/CD
Demodulation
Dial-up
Digital satellite service (DSS)
DOCSIS (Data Over Cable Service Interface Specification)
Domain name
Domain name server
Domain name system
Drive mapping
DSL

DSL modem
Dynamic IP address
Ethernet
Ethernet card
Extranet
FDDI
Fiber-optic cable
FireWire
Fixed wireless Internet service
Gateway
Handshaking
HomePLC
HomePNA
Host computer
Hub
ICANN
Infrared light
Internet Service Provider (ISP)
Internet telephony
Intranet
IP (Internet Protocol)
IP address
ISDN
LAN (local area network)
LAN-jacking
Laser light
Logical address
MAN (metropolitan area network)
Mesh topology
Microwaves

Modem
Modulation
NAN (neighborhood area network)
Narrowband
Network device
Network interface card (NIC)
Network Service Provider (NSP)
Networked peripheral
Node
Packet
Packet switching
PAN (personal area network)
Parallel
Peer-to-peer network
Physical address
Physical topology
Ping
POTS
Protocols
Public Wi-Fi network
Repeater
RF signals
Ring topology
Router
SCSI
Serial
Server
Shared resource
Star topology

Static IP address
STP (shielded twisted pair)
TCP (Transmission Control Protocol)
TCP/IP
Token Ring network
Top-level domain
Traceroute
Transceiver
Transponder
Tree topology
Twisted-pair cable
Uplink port
USB
UTP (unshielded twisted pair)
Voice band modem
Voice over IP (VoIP)
WAN (wide area network)
WAP (Wireless Access Protocol)
War driving
WEP (Wired Equivalent Privacy)
Wi-Fi (Wireless Fidelity)
Wi-Fi card
Wi-Fi hotspot
Wi-Fi network
WiMAX
Wired network
Wireless access point
Wireless network
Workstation

Unit Review

1. Use your own words to define bold terms that appear throughout the unit. List the 10 terms that are least familiar to you and write a sentence for each of them.

2. List the five classifications for networks based on geographical structure and explain each classification. Then list the two network classifications based on organization structure and explain each classification.

3. Create a table listing communications channels. Include advantages, disadvantages, relative speed/capacity, and quality of connection for each channel.

4. Explain three advantages and three disadvantages of wireless technology. List three wireless technologies discussed in this unit and write a brief explanation of each.

5. Make a list of the networks discussed in this unit, and then briefly describe each.

6. Make a list of four of the network hardware devices discussed in this unit. Explain how each device works within the network.

7. Draw diagrams of star, ring, and bus network topologies. What are the advantages and disadvantages of each topology?

8. Explain the differences between dynamic IP addresses, static IP addresses, and domain names.

9. What devices can you use to connect to the Internet? What services are available? Briefly describe each method that you can use to access the Internet and include its advantages and disadvantages.

10. Describe the technologies available for wireless Internet access. What are the advantages and disadvantages of each technology?

Fill in the Best Answer

1. A communications _____ is the combination of hardware, software, and connecting links that transport data.

2. From a geographic perspective, networks can be classified as _____, _____, _____, _____, and _____.

3. A local area network that uses TCP/IP is called a(n) _____ *intranet* and is popular with businesses that want to store information as Web pages but not provide them for public access.

4. A bundle of extremely thin tubes of glass used to carry data is called _____ *fiber* cable.

5. The _____ *bandwith*, or capacity, of a digital channel is usually measured in bps.

6. The _____ topology of a network refers to the layout of cables, devices, and connections.

7. A technology called _____ switching divides messages into small parcels and handles them on a first-come, first-served basis.

8. _____ is one of the most widely used network technologies, and uses a protocol called CSMA/CD to deal with collisions.

9. _____ *bluetooth* is a short-range wireless network technology that is designed to make its own connections between electronic devices, without wires, cables, or any direct action from a user.

10. Protocols help two network devices negotiate and establish communications through a process called _____.

11. When you use a dial-up connection, your ISP gives you a temporary address, called a(n) _____ IP address, for use as long as you remain connected.

12. The database that keeps track of the names that correspond to IP addresses is called the _____ *Domain* name system.

13. In communications terminology, _____ means changing the characteristics of a signal, whereas _____ means changing a signal back to its original state.

14. Although the speed of a modem was once measured by _____ *baud* rate, today's modem transmission speeds are measured in bps.

15. A software utility called _____ *Ping* sends a signal to a specific Internet address and waits for a reply.

16. Technology for carrying conversations, called Internet telephony or _____, uses Internet packets to transmit voice.

17. DSS service uses a low-earth _____ to send television, voice, or computer data directly to a dish owned by an individual.

18. A(n) _____ network uses radio frequencies, not cables, to send data from one node to another.

19. _____ is a communications protocol that provides Internet access from handheld devices, such as cell phones and PDAs.

20. _____ *.gov* is a top-level domain for use by government agencies and _____ *.edu* is a top level domain for use by educational institutions.

Practice Tests

When you use the Interactive CD, you can take Practice Tests that consist of 10 multiple-choice, true/false, and fill-in-the-blank questions. The questions are selected at random from a large test bank, so each time you take a test, you will receive a different set of questions. Your tests are scored immediately, and you can print study guides to determine which questions you answered incorrectly. If you are using a Tracking Disk, save your test scores.

End of Unit Exercises

INDEPENDENT CHALLENGE 1

 You have decided to network a few computers in your home and set up an Internet connection. You can connect to the Internet in a variety of ways, including dial-up connections, cable modem connections, DSL service, ISDN service, and digital satellite service. The Internet connection service you choose may be based more on availability than on which technology is considered the fastest and the best. This is the first time you have been put to this task, so you have to research and develop a plan for the project.

1. Describe the number, type, and location of the computers that will form your network.

2. Decide what type of network technology you want to use: Ethernet, HomePNA, wireless, or HomePLC.

3. Create a diagram showing the location of each computer, the wiring path (for Ethernet), the location of electrical outlets (for HomePLC), the location of telephone outlets (for HomePNA), or potential signal interference (for wireless).

4. Create a shopping list of the network components that you will need to purchase. Research prices for each item on your list. Be sure to include any software that you would have to purchase for the network.

5. Write a brief statement explaining your Internet needs. Be sure to include whether you are planning to use the Internet for research, shopping, or business, how often you need to log on, and if you need mobile access or high-speed access.

6. Research Internet connection options available in your area.

7. Create a table that lists the vendors for each available option and compares the options in terms of their setup cost, monthly fees, maximum speed upstream, and maximum speed downstream. Provide a summary of which Internet access options would be your first and second choices and why.

INDEPENDENT CHALLENGE 2

 The domain name system contains a vast array of names for businesses, organizations, and institutions. When you see a URL in an advertisement or a book, you often know immediately what the company or organization is and what the site will be about when you get to the page.

1. Use your favorite search engine to research top-level domains, or you might start by visiting the ICANN Web site.

2. Find out the latest information about the new top-level domains (TLD).

3. Think about a URL that you might want to register, for example, yourname.com or something else that is important to you personally. Also think about a business venture that you might want to begin. What URL would you want for that business?

4. Find out if these URLS are available. Track your research. If the first choice was not available, list how you went about finding a URL that you could use. For example, if your name is Tasha Simone, would you want tashasimone.com? If that is not available, would you go for tsimone.com? or tashasimone.biz?

5. Submit a paper detailing your quest and the results you achieved.

INDEPENDENT CHALLENGE 3

Wireless services are available and expanding. You can get mobile news, e-mail, text messaging, and mobile access to the Internet. Wireless communication is already having an impact on the way people work. More and more people are working at least part-time from a remote location such as a satellite office or a home office. As this becomes the emerging business model, employees are finding that being connected is a necessity, not just a convenience.

1. Write a brief statement explaining your position and opinions on each of the following:

    a. how wireless e-mail is changing the way business is conducted

    b. how wireless e-mail is changing the relationship between employer and employee

    c. how wireless e-mail is affecting personal relationships

2. Wireless e-mail raises societal questions such as privacy issues, employer expectations versus employee responsibilities, and impact on family life. Choose one societal issue impacted by wireless e-mail. Research the issue and write a paper presenting your findings.

3. Write a short summary of your findings. In your conclusion, compare your research findings with the opinions you expressed when you answered Question 1 above.

4. Be sure to include references and resources for your research.

INDEPENDENT CHALLENGE 4

 The Bluetooth wireless technology is a standard for low-cost, personal area network connection among mobile computers, mobile phones, and other devices. Using a globally available frequency range, Bluetooth eliminates the need for cables and provides secure, radio-based transmission of data and voice. You will write a short research paper that includes information about Bluetooth.

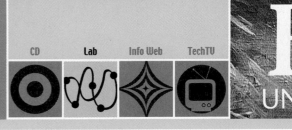

1. Log onto the Internet and go to the official Bluetooth Web site. You can also research Bluetooth technology on related sites. To introduce your paper, be sure to find answers to the following questions: Who developed the Bluetooth wireless technology? When was it developed? What were the goals or reasons for developing the technology? What is the origin of the name "Bluetooth" and why was it so named?

2. Bluetooth technology is being included in many new applications. As part of your paper, be sure to list two applications that are discussed on the Web site.

3. Bluetooth technology is being incorporated into many different products. Research the products that currently support Bluetooth. Name at least two products from three different categories. Describe how the product uses the technology and how it benefits the user.

4. Find the Web site of one of the companies using Bluetooth technology in its products. Describe one of the applications. Be sure to cite your sources.

LAB: Tracking Packets

1. Start the interactive part of the lab. Insert your Tracking Disk if you want to save your QuickCheck results. Perform each of the lab steps as directed and answer all of the lab QuickCheck questions. When you exit the lab, your answers are automatically graded and your results are displayed.

2. Use the Ping utility that is supplied by Windows to ping www.abcnews.com. Record the IP address for the ABC News site, plus the minimum, maximum, and average times. For each time, indicate whether it would be considered poor, average, or good.

3. Use the Tracert utility that is supplied by Windows to trace a packet between your computer and the Web. Print the Traceroute report. Circle any pings on the report that indicate high latency.

4. Locate a Web-based Ping utility and use it to ping www.gobledegok.com. Include the URL for the Web site where you found the Ping utility. Explain the results of the ping.

5. Connect to the Internet Traffic Report Web site, make a note of the date and time, and then answer the following questions:

   a. What is the traffic index for Asia?

   b. How does the index for Asia compare with the traffic index for North America?

   c. During the previous 24 hours in Europe, what was the period with the worst response time?

LAB: Securing Your Connection

1. Start the interactive part of the lab. Insert your Tracking Disk if you want to save your QuickCheck results. Perform each of the lab steps as directed, and answer all of the lab QuickCheck questions. When you exit the lab, your answers are automatically graded and your results are displayed.

2. Use the Netstat utility to scan any computer that you typically use. Write out the Netstat report or print it. To print the report, copy it to Paint or Word, and then print. Explain what the Netstat report tells you about the security of that computer.

3. Connect to the grc.com site and access the Shields Up! tests. Test the shields and probe the ports for the same computer that you used for Assignment 2. Explain the similarities and differences between the Shields Up! report and the Netstat report for this computer. Which report indicates more security risks? Why?

4. In the lab, you learned which dialog boxes to use for disabling Windows file and print sharing, plus a technique for unbinding TCP from file and print sharing. Without actually changing the settings, use the dialog boxes to determine whether file and print sharing is active or disabled on your computer. Also, discover if file and print sharing is bound to TCP on your computer. Report your findings and indicate if these settings are appropriate in terms of network access and security.

Student Edition Labs

Student Edition Labs

Reinforce the concepts you have learned in this unit through the **Protecting Your Privacy Online**, **Connecting to the Internet**, **Getting the Most Out of the Internet**, **Networking Basics**, and **Wireless Networking** Student Edition Labs, available online at the Illustrated Computer Concepts Web site.

SAM Labs

If you have a SAM user profile, you have access to additional content, features, and functionality. Log in to your SAM account and go to your assignments page to see what your instructor has assigned for this unit.

Visual Workshop

The ping command is defined in the Windows XP Help system (See **Figure E-32**) as a command that "Verifies IP-level connectivity to another TCP/IP computer by sending Internet Control Message Protocol (ICMP) Echo Request messages. The receipt of corresponding Echo Reply messages is displayed, along with round-trip times. Ping is the primary TCP/IP command used to troubleshoot connectivity, reachability, and name resolution."

Figure E-32

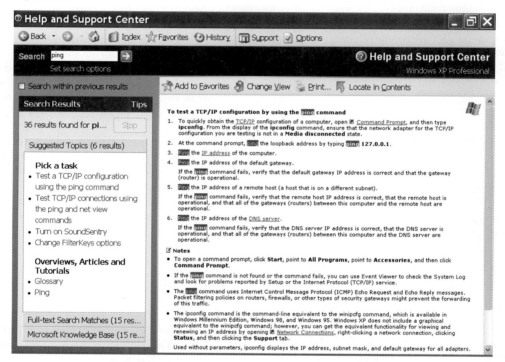

1. Open the Windows Help system, search on PING, then print the pages.

2. Follow the instructions in the Help system for pinging at least two Web sites, one should be a major site, one should be a site in another country, and one should be a small or local site. Discuss the different results.

3. The ping command also has parameters. Search the Windows Help system to find out about the parameters. Execute a ping with one of the parameters. Explain your results.

Data Security

CD

Lab

Info Web

TechTV

F UNIT

- Know what can go wrong
  Protect systems
- Introduce computer viruses
- Learn how viruses spread
  Introduce bots
- Use antivirus software
- Introduce data backup
- Examine backup procedures
- Explore backup media and software

Tech Talk: Internet Access Security
Computers in Context: Law Enforcement
Issue: What Are Professional Ethics?

Overview

Understanding how to create, organize, and interpret your data is very important. However, if your data is not secure, it could be lost. This unit discusses factors that may work against you to destroy your data and ways to secure your computer and data. The unit begins with a discussion about what can go wrong and how to avoid data loss; later lessons discuss computer viruses and the potential attacks that affect files and disrupt computer operations. You will learn how to restrict access by unauthorized users and how to use antivirus software to protect or recover your computer data. You will also learn one of the most important aspects of computing—how to back up your data. The Tech Talk discusses ways to secure stand-alone computers as well as local area networks when connecting to the Internet. You will have the opportunity to read about computers in the context of law enforcement. The Issue examines ethics, provides a discussion of real-world ethical dilemmas, and reviews basic ethical principals for the computer professional.

Knowing what can go wrong

In the context of computer systems, **risk management** is the process of identifying potential threats to computer equipment and data, implementing plans to avoid as many threats as possible, and developing steps to recover from unavoidable disasters. Although it might not be cost-effective or even possible to protect a computer system from all threats, a good risk management plan provides a level of protection that is technologically and economically feasible. Part of risk management is knowing what can go wrong. Computer systems are vulnerable to a variety of threats including hardware breakdowns, power outages, software failures, human error, and computer viruses. Less common threats but ones that still create devastating effects occur when computer systems are harmed by natural disasters, acts of war, security breaches, malicious hackers, or even theft.

■ Hardware failure. The effect of a hardware failure depends on which component fails. Most hardware failures are simply an inconvenience. For example, if your monitor fails, you can obtain a replacement monitor, plug it in, and get back to work. A hard disk drive failure, however, can be a disaster because you might lose all your data. Although an experienced computer technician might be able to recover some of the files on the damaged hard disk drive, it is more often the case that all programs and data files stored on the hard disk are permanently lost. Much of the computer hardware that fails does so within the first hours or days of operation. If this period passes without problems, hardware can be expected to work fairly reliably until it nears the end of its useful life. The risk of a hardware failure increases as a hardware component ages. Many devices are rated with a **mean time between failures (MTBF)** statistic. For example, an MTBF rating of 125,000 hours means that, on average, a device could function for 125,000 hours before failing. MTBF ratings are averages, so a device with a 125,000 MTBF rating might actually operate for only 10 hours before it fails.

■ Power problems. Power outages can be caused by natural disasters, overloaded power grids, planned brownouts, rolling blackouts, and even human error. See **Figure F-1**. Because computers are powered by electricity, they are susceptible to power failures, spikes, and surges. A **power failure** is a complete loss of power to the computer system, usually caused by something over which you have no control. Even a brief interruption in power can force your computer to reboot and lose all data in RAM. Although a power failure results in loss of data in RAM, it is unlikely to result in loss of data stored on the storage media.

Two common power-related problems are **power spikes** or **voltage spikes** and **power surges**. Both of these can damage sensitive computer components. Spikes and surges can be caused by malfunctions in the local generating plant or the power distribution network, and they are potentially more damaging than a power failure. Both can destroy the circuitry that operates your hard disk drive or they can damage your computer's motherboard.

Figure F-1: The North American blackout of 2003

The 2003 North American blackout was a massive power outage that occurred throughout parts of the northeastern United States and eastern Canada on August 14, 2003; its cause was traced to human error

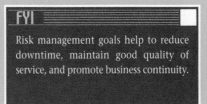

FYI

Risk management goals help to reduce downtime, maintain good quality of service, and promote business continuity.

CD   Lab   **Info Web**   TechTU

F

UNIT

■ Human error. Human error or **operator error** refers to a mistake made by a computer operator or programmer. Common errors within a computing system include entering inaccurate data and failing to follow required procedures. Despite the sometimes sensational press coverage of computer criminals and viruses, the most common cause of lost and/or inaccurate data is a mistake made by a computer user—such as entering the wrong data or deleting a file that is still needed. One of the most well-known failures due to human error was the loss of the Mars Climate Orbiter in 1999. See **Figure F-2**.

■ Software failures. Software failure can be caused by bugs or flawed software design. A flaw might be undetectable in a small computing system, but it can be disastrous on a system consisting of hundreds or thousands of computers. Other bugs may cause security leaks. For example, hackers continue to discover bugs in Microsoft software that allow unauthorized access to servers.

■ Computers can be stolen, and in many cases the data proves to be the most valuable component of the computer system. Security breaches might be the result of physical intrusions or deliberate sabotage; those who commit security breaches are often looking to steal or compromise data. With a recent increase in terrorism, all computers (civilian, government, and commercial) are considered targets. **Cyberterrorism**, the term used to describe terrorist acts committed via the Internet, uses viruses and worms to destroy data and otherwise disrupt computer-based operations. These operations include critical national infrastructures such as power grids and telecommunications systems, so the risks from cyberterrorism can be significant.

Figure F-2: Computer-related failure caused by human error

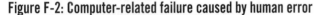

In the fall of 1999, the Mars Orbiter crashed rather than landed on Mars. Investigators determined that the cause of the crash was human error. Data critical to the computer-controlled maneuvers required to place the Orbiter in the proper Mars orbit was miscalculated because one NASA team of scientists used English measurements (e.g., inches, feet) while the other team responsible for navigation of the Orbiter used metric measurements. The data was incorrect because the measurements were not converted to the same unit of measure. Because the incorrect data was used to navigate the Orbiter, it crashed. Since this incident, NASA has established safeguards to help prevent human error and, as a result, has successfully landed spacecraft on Mars, such as the Spirit and Opportunity Orbiters.

What if disaster strikes?

Despite the best risk-prevention measures, disasters that destroy data can and do occur. For example, on March 28, 2000, a tornado touched down in downtown Fort Worth, Texas, traveling over a mile through some of the densest parts of the downtown area and causing more than $400 million in damage. Many small businesses lost their entire computer systems in this disaster. One of the most destructive disasters in history was the attack on the World Trade Center and subsequent collapse of the Twin Towers on September 11, 2001. Although the human and personal toll was staggering, very few companies affected by the disaster experienced critical data loss. Most companies were able to rebuild their computer systems because they had developed and implemented disaster recovery plans that included remote offsite data backup servers or services. A disaster recovery plan is a step-by-step plan that describes the methods used to secure data against disaster, and explains how an organization will recover lost data if and when a disaster occurs. Kemper Insurance, located on the 35th and 36th floors of the north tower of the World Trade Center, designed a disaster recovery plan after the 1993 bombing of the Twin Towers. Kemper's disaster recovery plan not only detailed what to do in case of disaster, it also required a mock disaster recovery exercise at least once a year. In these exercises, Kemper IT employees went through the process of reconstructing the company's computer system from scratch at an off-site location. They configured new hardware, installed the required software, and restored data from backup tapes. In response to the 9/11 catastrophe, Kemper IT employees followed the disaster recovery plan and recreated the computer system at another Kemper Insurance site. Kemper Insurance was up and running by 4:00 a.m. on September 12th—less than 24 hours after one of the largest and most devastating disasters in U.S. history.

Protecting systems

No computer system can be completely risk-free, but several proactive procedures can protect computer systems from threats. Preventive countermeasures shield the computer system from attack or reduce the impact if an attack occurs. These countermeasures can be grouped into three categories: deterrents, detection activities, and corrective procedures.

■ Deterrents. Deterrents are preventive countermeasures that reduce the likelihood of deliberate attack, hardware failure, or data loss. Deterrents include devices that protect computer systems as well as devices and procedures that restrict access to computer systems.

- Provide power protection. There are several devices that can help protect computer systems from power problems. See **Figure F-3**. A **UPS (uninterruptible power supply)** offers the best protection against power problems. A UPS is a device containing a battery that provides a continuous supply of power and other circuitry to prevent spikes and surges from reaching your computer. A UPS gives you enough time to save your files and exit your programs safely in the event of a power outage. As a low-cost alternative, you can plug your computer into a **surge strip** (also called a **surge protector** or **surge suppressor**), an appliance designed to protect electrical devices from power surges and voltage spikes. Unlike a UPS, a surge strip does not protect the data in RAM if the power fails, because it does not contain a battery to keep the computer running.

- Establish user rights. Restricting the access of users—especially those who are logging in from sites thousands of miles away—is a critical step in data security. One way to limit access is to assign **user rights**, which are rules that limit the directories and files that each user can access. They can restrict a user's ability to erase, create, write, read, and find files. For example, when you receive a user ID and password for a password-protected system, the system administrator gives you rights that allow you to access and perform specified tasks only on particular directories and files on the host computer or file server. Assigning user rights helps prevent both accidental and deliberate damage to data. How do user's rights help? If users are granted limited rights, a hacker who steals someone's password has only the same access as the person from whom the password was stolen.

- Stop mistakes before they happen. Some companies establish procedures, which, if followed, can reduce operator error. Many organizations have reduced the incidence of operator error by using a **direct source input device**, such as a bar code reader, to collect data directly from a document or object. Computer software

Figure F-3: Devices used to provide power protection

A UPS

A surge protector

Securing your computer and data

A computer can be an attractive target for thieves, but the value of a stolen computer often is determined not by the hardware that makes up the system but rather by the data contained in the computer system. Using data (such as your bank account numbers, credit card numbers, and PINs) stolen from your computer, a thief can wipe out your checking and savings accounts and can go on a spending spree with your credit cards. Even worse, a criminal can use stolen data to assume your identity, run up debts, get into legal trouble, ruin your credit rating, and cause you no end of trouble.

When you carry a notebook computer, never leave it unattended. To thwart a thief who breaks into your home or dorm room, anchor your computer to your desk with a specially designed lock you can buy at most electronics stores. If a thief steals your computer, you can make your data difficult to access by setting up your computer system to require a password before allowing access to data on the system. In this situation, a thief might be able to boot the Windows desktop, but the thief would not be able to access the data in your folders. Many new computers are shipped with a standard administrator password that everyone knows. Be sure to create a secure password for this account as soon as you get your new computer system. If you are the only person using your computer, you can use the administrator account for your day-to-day computing. Your computer might also include a preset guest account with an unsecure password such as "guest." You should disable this guest account or assign it a secure password.

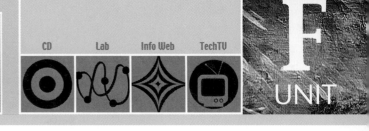

FYI

When you shop for a surge strip, do not mistakenly purchase a power strip, which offers no protection.

CD   Lab   Info Web   TechTV

F

UNIT

designers can also help prevent operator error by designing products that anticipate mistakes users are likely to make and that provide features to help users avoid those mistakes.

- Restrict access. Physical deterrents for restricting access include providing only limited access to critical servers. If potential criminals cannot get to a computer or a terminal, stealing or damaging data becomes more difficult. Keep in mind, however, that restricting physical access will not prevent a determined criminal from stealing data. Passwords are a first line of defense against unauthorized access and a basic method for restricting access. Security features such as password protection and **authentication**—verifying that the person accessing the data is really the person who has access—help to identify authorized users. Examples of some devices used to authenticate users are shown in **Figure F-4**.

■ Detection activities. Detection activities recognize attacks and trigger preventive countermeasures or corrective procedures. Theft or vandalism can be detected by periodic hardware inventories. Antivirus software detects viruses entering a system, and can be configured to

automatically clean the system or quarantine infected files. Viruses will be discussed in detail in this unit. In addition, monitoring software that tracks users, file updates, and changes to critical systems can be used to detect unwanted activity. Firewalls—software that prevents unauthorized access to a system—can be used to detect what computers are trying to access another computer. Data collected from monitoring software and firewalls are effective preventive countermeasures.

■ Corrective procedures. Corrective procedures reduce the impact of an attack. Data backups, disaster recovery plans, and the availability of redundant hardware devices all are examples of corrective procedures. Another corrective procedure is to carry proper insurance. Insurance companies will provide coverage to replace lost or damaged hardware, and some provide extra coverage for the data on your computer. With this type of coverage, you would receive a sum of money to compensate you for the time it takes to reload your data on a replacement computer. While this coverage will provide compensation for data recovery, lost data cannot be recovered without an up-to-date backup tape or disk. Backups and redundancy are the best insurance, and will be discussed in detail in this unit.

Figure F-4: Examples of devices used to authenticate users

Retinal scanner   Identity card reader

Ways to restrict physical access

Three methods of personal identification are used to restrict access: something a person carries, something a person knows, or some unique physical characteristic. Each of these methods has the potential to positively identify a person, and each has a unique set of advantages and disadvantages.

Something a person carries: An identity badge or pass card featuring a photo, or perhaps a magnetic strip or bar code with unique coded information, remains a popular form of personal identification. Because an identity badge can be lost, stolen, or duplicated, however, it works best when used on site where a security guard verifies that the face on the badge is the face of the person wearing the badge. Without visual verification, the use of identity badges from a remote site is not secure, unless combined with a password or PIN (personal identification number) that is coded on the badge.

Something a person knows: User IDs and passwords fall into this category of personal identification. When you work on a multiuser system or network,

you generally must have a user ID and password. Data security on a computer system that is guarded by user IDs and passwords depends on password secrecy. If users give out their passwords, choose obvious passwords, or write them down in obvious places, hackers can break into the system. The method of trying every word in an electronic dictionary to steal a password decreases in effectiveness if a password is based on two words, a word and number, or a nonsense word that does not appear in a dictionary.

Some unique physical characteristic: This third method of personal identification, called biometrics, bases identification on some physical trait, such as a fingerprint, hand print, or the pattern of blood vessels in the retina of the eye. Unlike passwords, biometric data cannot be forgotten, lost, or borrowed. Such technologies include hand-geometry scanners, voice recognition, face recognition, fingerprint scanners, and retinal scanners. Refer again to **Figure F-4** for examples of authentication systems used to restrict physical access.

Introducing computer viruses

Computer viruses invade all types of computers, including mainframes, servers, personal computers, and even handheld computers. Spreading a virus is a crime. Although the term virus technically refers to a type of program that behaves in a specific way, it has become a generic term that refers to a variety of destructive programs. To defend your computer against viruses, you should understand what they are, how they work, and how to use antivirus software.

■ **Malicious code** refers to any program or set of program instructions that is designed to enter a computer without the user's knowledge or permission and disrupt its normal operations. Malicious code, including viruses, worms, and Trojan horses, is created and unleashed by individuals referred to as "hackers" or "crackers." The term hacker originally referred to a highly skilled computer programmer. Today, however, the terms **hacker** and **cracker** usually refer to anyone who uses a computer to gain unauthorized access to data, steal information, or crash a computer system.

■ A **computer virus** (often simply called **virus**) is a set of program instructions that attaches itself to a file, reproduces itself, and spreads to other files. It can corrupt files, destroy data, display an irritating message, or otherwise disrupt computer operations. A virus might deliver a **payload**, which could be as harmless as displaying an annoying message or as devastating as corrupting the data on your computer's hard disk. A **trigger event**, such as a specific date, can unleash some viruses. For example, the Michelangelo virus is designed to damage hard disk files on March 6, the birthday of artist Michelangelo.

■ Viruses that deliver their payloads on a specific date are sometimes referred to as "time bombs." Viruses that deliver their payloads in response to some other system event are referred to as "logic bombs." Viruses have the ability to lurk in a computer for days or months, quietly replicating themselves. While this is taking place,

you might not even know that your computer has a virus, which makes it is easy to spread infected files to other people's computers inadvertently.

■ A virus can be classified as a file virus, boot sector virus, or macro virus. A **file virus** infects application programs, such as games; its payload can overwrite sections of your hard disk. A **boot sector virus** infects the system files your computer uses every time you turn it on, causing widespread damage to your hard disk. A **macro virus** infects a set of instructions called a **macro**—a miniature program that usually contains legitimate instructions to automate document and worksheet production. The macro virus duplicates itself into the general macro pool, where it is picked up by other documents.

■ A **Trojan horse** is a computer program that seems to perform one function while actually doing something else. Trojan horses are notorious for stealing passwords using a **keylogger**—a type of program that records your keystrokes. For example, one Trojan horse arrives as an e-mail attachment named Picture.exe, which leads you to believe you have received some type of graphics software. If you open this file, however, it searches for America Online (AOL) user information and tries to steal your login and e-mail passwords. Trojan horses can also generate official-looking forms that are actually fake. These Trojan horses collect your credit card, banking, or online money transfer account numbers (such as those used with PayPal, an online payment service for transferring funds). See **Figure F-5**.

Figure F-5: A Trojan horse

A Trojan horse called Padodor watches your browser window for text strings such as "Sign in" and "Log in"; it then displays a fake login screen like the one shown here to collect your credit card numbers and ATM PIN code

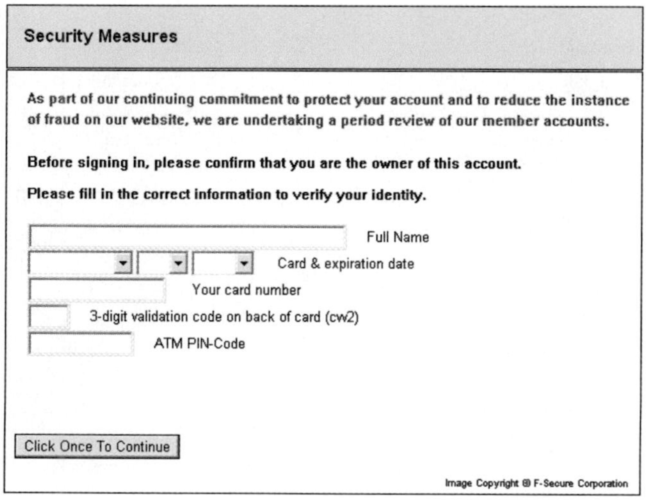

Security Measures

As part of our continuing commitment to protect your account and to reduce the instance of fraud on our website, we are undertaking a period review of our member accounts.

Before signing in, please confirm that you are the owner of this account.

Please fill in the correct information to verify your identity.

Full Name

Card & expiration date

Your card number

3-digit validation code on back of card (cw2)

ATM PIN-Code

Click Once To Continue

Image Copyright © F-Secure Corporation

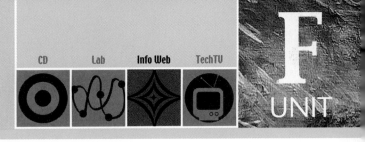
Many Trojan horses have backdoor capability, which allows unauthorized access to victims' computers. A **backdoor** allows remote hackers to download and execute files on your computer, upload a list of other infected computers, and use your computer as a relay station for breaking into other computers. Technically, a Trojan horse is not the same as a virus because it is not designed to make copies of itself, and most Trojan horses are stand-alone programs. Some Trojan horses contain a virus, however, which can replicate and spread. Other Trojan horses are carried by worms.

■ With the proliferation of network traffic and e-mail, worms have become a major concern. Unlike a virus, which is designed to spread from file to file, a **worm** is designed to spread from computer to computer. Most worms take advantage of communications networks (especially the Internet) to travel within e-mail and TCP/IP packets. See **Figure F-6**. Worms also deliver payloads that vary from harmless messages to malicious file deletions. Some worms are designed to generate a lot of activity on a network by flooding it with useless traffic—enough to overwhelm the network's processing capability and essentially bring all communications to a halt. These **denial-of-service (DoS) attacks** cut network users off from e-mail and Web browsing.

■ Virus experts use the term **blended threat** to describe threats that combine more than one type of malicious program. Common blended threats include Trojan-horse/virus combinations and worm/virus combinations.

Figure F-6: A simulated worm attack

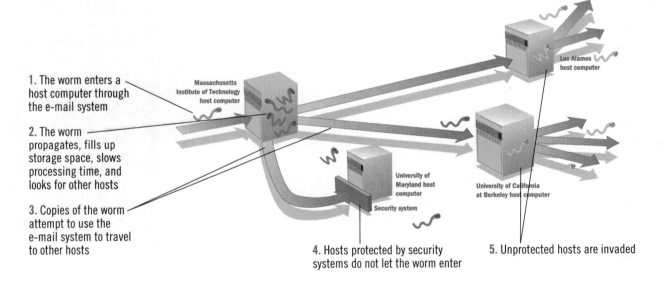

1. The worm enters a host computer through the e-mail system

2. The worm propagates, fills up storage space, slows processing time, and looks for other hosts

3. Copies of the worm attempt to use the e-mail system to travel to other hosts

Massachusetts Institute of Technology host computer

Los Alamos host computer

University of Maryland host computer

Security system

University of California at Berkeley host computer

4. Hosts protected by security systems do not let the worm enter

5. Unprotected hosts are invaded

What are the symptoms of a virus?

The symptoms depend on the virus. The following symptoms might indicate that your computer has contracted a virus, though some of these symptoms can have other causes: your computer displays vulgar or annoying messages; your computer develops unusual visual or sound effects; you have difficulty saving files, or files mysteriously disappear; your computer suddenly seems to work very slowly; your computer reboots unexpectedly; your executable files unaccountably increase in size; or your computer starts sending out lots of e-mail messages on its own.

It is important to remember, however, that some viruses, worms, and Trojan horses have no recognizable symptoms. Your computer system can contract a worm, for example, that never displays an irritating message or attempts to delete your files, but that replicates itself through your e-mail until it eventually arrives at a server where it can do some real damage to a network communications system. Your computer system can contract a Trojan horse known as a keylogger, which is designed to collect your keystrokes and send them to a hacker. Although your keystroke log is being sent to a hacker by e-mail, the Trojan horse has its own e-mail client and the messages going to the hackers will not appear in the outbox of your regular e-mail program. This means you might never discover that your computer has been compromised unless you scan it with antivirus software. You should use antivirus software to detect and remove viruses, worms, or Trojan horses in your computer.

Learning how viruses spread

Viruses spread because people distribute infected files by exchanging disks and CDs, sending e-mail attachments, and downloading software from the Web. A virus infects the files with .exe, .com, or .vbs filename extensions by attaching itself to them. When you open an infected file, the attached virus instructions also open. These instructions then remain in RAM, waiting to infect the next program that your computer runs or the next file that it opens.

■ Shared files are a common source of viruses. Removable storage media, noncommercial CDs, and Web sites that contain games are the most common sources of viruses. **Figure F-7** illustrates how a virus can easily infect many computers.

■ E-mail attachments are another common source of viruses. A seemingly innocent attachment can harbor a file virus or a boot sector virus. Typically, infected attachments look like executable files, usually with .exe filename extensions, although in some cases they can have .sys, .drv, .com, .bin, .vbs, .scr, or .ovl extensions. Infected files cannot infect your computer unless you open them, which then executes the virus code that they contain.

■ A **mass-mailing worm** spreads by sending itself to every address in the address book of an infected computer. Mass-mailing worms, such as Klez, Netsky, MyDoom, Sasser, and Bagle (also called Beagle), have made headlines and caused havoc on personal computers, LANs, and Internet servers. To make these worms difficult to track, the "From" line of the infected e-mail message sometimes contains a spoofed address of a randomly selected person—a valid address—from the address book rather than the address of the computer that actually sent the e-mail. Mass-mailing worms often include an attachment that contains the worm. Opening the attachment unleashes the worm. Some mass-mailing worms contain a Web link that installs a worm, Trojan horse, or virus. Sasser and other mass-mailing worms, however, require no user interaction to infect a computer.

Figure F-7: How a computer virus spreads

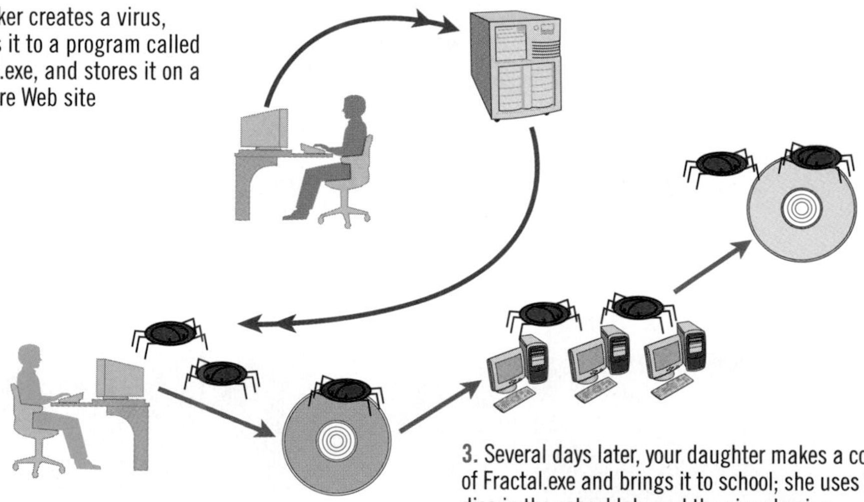

1. A hacker creates a virus, attaches it to a program called Gourmet.exe, and stores it on a shareware Web site

2. You download Gourmet.exe, thinking that it is a legitimate program; when you open it, the virus infects several programs on your hard disk, including two public domain programs: Proton.exe and Fractal.exe

3. Several days later, your daughter makes a copy of Fractal.exe and brings it to school; she uses the disc in the school lab, and the virus begins spreading to files on the computer she used

4. Any students who put discs in the lab computer and open a file have a good chance of contracting the virus on their discs; as these discs are used in other computers, the virus continues to spread

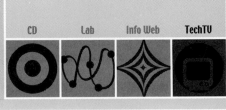

CD   Lab   Info Web   TechTU

F UNIT

■ In addition to problems with e-mail attachments, e-mail messages themselves can carry viruses to unsuspecting recipients. This is particularly true if you receive your e-mail in HTML format, which allows you to use different fonts and different font formatting features (such as colors and sizes) for your messages. E-mail in HTML format can harbor viruses and worms hidden in program-like scripts that are embedded in the HTML tags. These viruses are difficult to detect even for antivirus software. To avoid the threat to data security, many people stick with plain text, non-HTML e-mail format for sending and receiving e-mail messages.

■ Macro viruses can exist in documents created with Microsoft Word and spreadsheets created with Microsoft Excel. Infected files display the usual .doc or .xls filename extensions; there are no outward clues to the virus lurking within the file. Today, most software that executes macros includes security features that help protect your computer from macro viruses.

■ Web sites that contain games and music are also a common source of viruses. When you download files from these sites, the files often contain scripts that can harbor viruses. You should scan all files with up-to-date antivirus software before downloading files.

How can I know if my e-mail is safe?

You increase your chances of identifying "bad" e-mail attachments if you make sure that Windows is set to display all filename extensions. Never open a suspicious attachment without first checking it with antivirus software. If you do not want the attachment, simply delete the e-mail message to which it was attached. The conventional wisdom for avoiding e-mail-borne infections is not to open suspicious attachments—especially those with executable file extensions, such as .exe. Hackers use many tricks to get you to open e-mail attachments that contain worms. For example, **Figure F-8** appears to show a legitimate message about undelivered mail. In reality, it includes an attachment infested with the Mydoom worm. The message looks legitimate and has no particular characteristics that would warn you of the virus it harbors; the attachment is a zip file. In a situation like this one, you have to depend on your antivirus software to detect the malicious attachment.

You should also be wary of e-mails received from banks, ISPs, and commonly visited Web sites, such as Microsoft. A fake message from your bank, for example, might indicate that a charge has been made to your credit card. Clicking the link for more information takes you to a Web site that downloads a worm to your computer. If you are uncertain about any e-mail that seems to arrive from a reputable organization, open your browser and manually type in the organization's Web site address. Then search using the subject line of the e-mail message you received to see if the site provides any information about that e-mail; or use the contact us information to contact the organization and find out if they sent the e-mail.

Figure F-8

Returned Mail: see transcript for details - Message (Plain Text)

File Edit View Insert Format Tools Actions Help

Reply | Reply to All | Forward

You are now viewing this message in the Internet Zone.
Extra line breaks in this message were removed.

From: Mail Delivery Service   Sent: Tue 8/22/2006 9:49 AM
To: 'Misha Roberts' m2341rob@aol.com
Cc:
Subject: Returned Mail: see transcript for details

Attachments: Text.zip (851 B)

```
The original message was received Thurs, 24 August 2006 13:10:23 -0400
>From test net [89.163.189.142]

--------The following addresses had permanent fatal errors --------
sqstudent@aol.com

--------Transcript of session follows -------- ...while talking to
test.net
554 <sqstudent@aol.com>... Message is too large
554 <sqstudent@aol.com>... Service unavailable
```

Introducing bots

Any software that can automate a task or autonomously execute a task when commanded to do so is called an **intelligent agent**. Because an intelligent agent behaves somewhat like a robot, it is often called a **bot**. Good bots have been overshadowed by mounting publicity about bad bots launched and controlled by hackers.

- Good bots perform a variety of helpful tasks. They scan the Web to assemble data for search engines, such as Google. Some bots offer online help, while others monitor chat groups for prohibited behavior and language. Individuals can set up bots to track the best airfares or watch online databases for job openings in a specified career field.

- Bad bots were originally called remote-access Trojan horses because they allowed hackers to essentially sneak into a computer and control it without the owner's knowledge or authorization. Bot-infested computers are sometimes referred to as zombies because they carry out instructions from a malicious leader. Bad bots, such as Agobot, Mytob, Rbot, and Zotob, can be used to steal passwords, copy confidential data, launch attacks on other computers, and generate spam anonymously.

- Bots often gain access through operating system security holes that you have not patched. They can also use some of the same delivery methods used by worms, such as legitimate-looking

e-mail messages that contain infected attachments and e-mail links that direct you to a Web site that automatically downloads malicious code. See **Figure F-9**. Since Microsoft never puts links to software patches in e-mail messages, receiving an e-mail message like this should be a red flag that something is wrong.

- The person who controls many bot-infested computers can link them together into a network called a **botnet**. Botnets as large as 400,000 computers have been discovered by security experts. Botmasters who control botnets use the combined computing power of their zombie computers for many types of evil tasks. For example, an estimated 66% of spam circulating around the Internet is sent through botnets. Botmasters even rent out their botnets to professional spammers.

- Bots have become the biggest threat to computer security because of their ability to form botnets that can launch widescale denial-of-service attacks or distribute spam.

Figure F-9: Bot-delivered e-mail that links to malicious code

Bots can deliver e-mail messages that appear to be legitimate

Clicking the link in this e-mail message installs the Mytob bot on the computer

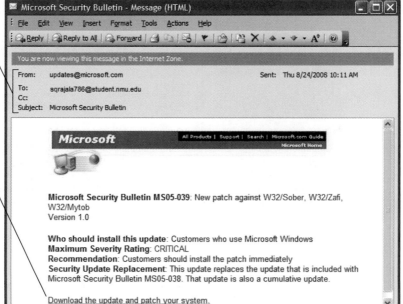

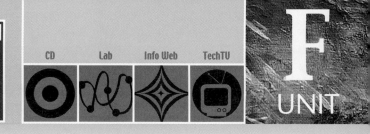

FYI
No legitimate software publisher ever puts links to software patches in e-mail messages, instead, they direct you to their Web site so you can take action from there.

CD   Lab   Info Web   TechTU

UNIT

F

■ Botnets can be used for other activities as well. For example, they can be used to carry out denial-of-service attacks against other computers. And some hackers have used the computation power of botnets to create a powerful virtual supercomputer for breaking into encrypted data.

■ Security experts are concerned about the potential for large botnets to launch destructive worms. A virus or worm launched from a single computer can spread relatively quickly, but antivirus publishers can typically identify such threats and distribute updates before damage is widespread. If a worm or virus is launched using a large botnet, however, it will spread quickly and possibly faster than antivirus publishers can counter it, which means its potential for doing damage is great.

■ Security experts say that bots are harder to detect than viruses or worms. They rarely damage files on your computer or show any noticeable signs of their existence. To keep your computer from being exploited in a botnet, make sure you install operating system security patches as they become available and keep your antivirus software up to date.

■ The current crop of viruses, Trojan horses, bots, and worms cause various problems, ranging from displaying harmless messages to bringing down Web sites. **Table F-1** summarizes the damage caused by malicious code.

Table F-1: Damage caused by malicious code

TYPE OF ATTACK	DESCRIPTION
Network traffic jam	Some malicious code, such as worms and bots, when it is active, generates traffic on LANs and the Internet. This causes service to deteriorate as download time increases for files, Web pages, and e-mail messages.
Denial-of-service (DoS) attack	Some malicious code is designed to generate a lot of activity on a network by flooding its servers with useless traffic—enough traffic to overwhelm the server's processing capability and essentially bring all communications to a halt. Successful DoS attacks have been launched against Microsoft, the White House, and the controversial Internet ad agency DoubleClick.
Browser reconfiguration	Some malicious code, usually worms, blocks users from accessing certain Web sites and can change the home page setting for that computer. It can also set up a redirection routine that downloads malicious code from an infected Web site, even when you enter a legitimate Web address.
Delete and modify files	Some malicious code, especially viruses, is designed to delete files on a personal computer's hard disk. Some malicious code modifies the Windows Registry and can cause system instability. Malicious code called ransomware encrypts documents and other files, then demands payment for the decryption key.
Access confidential information	Some malicious code, especially Trojan horses and bots, is notorious for using backdoors to steal passwords and credit card numbers. Some, usually worms, can scan files and Web sites for e-mail addresses.
Performance degradation	Some malicious code requires system resources to send e-mail and scan files. While the code, such as a virus or worm, is active, your computer might seem to perform slower than normal.
Disable antivirus and firewall software	Some malicious code, often called retro viruses, is designed to attack antivirus software by deleting the files that contain virus descriptions or corrupting the main executable virus-scanning program. One antivirus vendor calls them "anti-antivirus viruses."

Using antivirus software

Antivirus software is a set of utility programs that looks for and eradicates problems, such as viruses, bots, Trojan horses, and worms. Versions of antivirus software are available for handheld computers, personal computers, and servers. Considering the sheer number of existing viruses and the number of new viruses that debut every week, antivirus software is a must as part of your data security plan.

■ Antivirus software uses several techniques to find viruses. Some viruses insert themselves into unused portions of a program file. Therefore, one method used by antivirus software is to examine the bytes in an uninfected application program and calculate a checksum. A **checksum** is a number that is calculated by combining the binary values of all bytes in a file. Each time you run an application program, the antivirus software calculates the checksum and compares it with the previous checksum. If any byte in the application program has changed, the checksum will be different, and the antivirus software assumes that a virus is present. The checksum approach requires that you start with a copy of the program that is not infected with a virus. If the original copy is infected, the virus is included in the original checksum, and the antivirus software never detects it. Unfortunately, some viruses insert themselves in a program without changing the file length. In this case the checksum method does not work.

■ Antivirus software also identifies viruses by searching your files for a **virus signature**, a unique series of bytes that can be used to identify a known virus, much as a fingerprint is used to identify an individual. Most of today's antivirus software scans for virus signatures. The signature search technique is fairly quick, but it identifies only those viruses with a known signature.

■ Most antivirus software allows you to specify what to check and when to check it. See **Figure F-10**. You can, for example, start the program when you receive a suspicious e-mail attachment.

Or, you can set it to look through all of the files on your computer once a week. The best practice, however, is to keep your antivirus software running full-time in the background so that it scans all files the moment they are accessed and checks every e-mail message as it arrives.

■ Viruses try to escape detection in many ways. **Multi-partite viruses** are able to infect multiple types of targets. For example, a multi-partite virus might combine the characteristics of a file virus (which hides in .exe files) and a boot sector virus (which hides in the boot sector). If your antivirus software looks for that particular virus only in .exe files, the virus could escape detection by hiding in the boot sector as well. **Polymorphic viruses** mutate to escape detection by changing their signatures. **Stealth viruses** remove their signatures from a disk-based file and temporarily conceal themselves in memory.

■ The information your antivirus software uses to identify and eradicate viruses, bots, Trojan horses, and worms is stored in files referred to as **virus definitions**. New viruses and variations of old viruses are unleashed just about every day. To keep up with these newly identified viruses, antivirus software publishers provide virus definition updates, which are usually available as Web downloads. You should check your antivirus publisher's Web site for the latest updates of antivirus software every few weeks or when you hear of a new virus making headlines. See **Figure F-11**.

Figure F-10: Antivirus scanning options

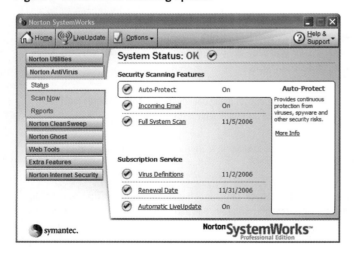

Figure F-11: Update the virus definitions

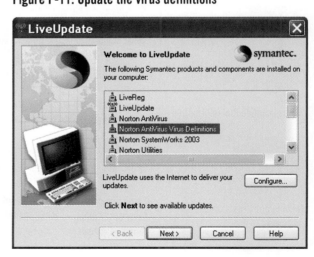

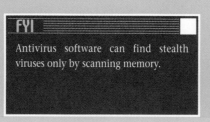

FYI

Antivirus software can find stealth viruses only by scanning memory.

CD   Lab   Info Web   TechTU

F

UNIT

■ Keeping a virus out of your computer and files is preferable to trying to eradicate a virus that has taken up residence. Once a virus infiltrates your computer, it can be difficult to remove, even with antivirus software. Certain viruses are particularly tenacious; just the process of booting up your computer can trigger their replication sequence or send them into hiding. As a result, antivirus software is not 100% reliable. On occasions, it might not identify a virus, or it might think that your computer has a virus when one does not actually exist. Despite these mistakes, the protection you get using antivirus software is worth the required investment of time and money. Tips for preventing your computer from becoming infected are listed in **Figure F-12**.

Figure F-12: Tips for preventing a computer from becoming infected

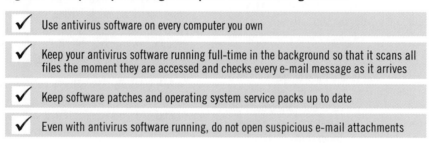

✓ Use antivirus software on every computer you own

✓ Keep your antivirus software running full-time in the background so that it scans all files the moment they are accessed and checks every e-mail message as it arrives

✓ Keep software patches and operating system service packs up to date

✓ Even with antivirus software running, do not open suspicious e-mail attachments

Virus hoaxes

Some viruses are very real, but you are likely to get e-mail about "viruses" that do not really exist. A virus hoax usually arrives as an e-mail message containing dire warnings about a supposedly new virus that is on the loose. The message typically suggests some strategy for avoiding the virus, and recommends that you forward the e-mail warning to all of your friends and colleagues. In most cases, however, the alleged virus does not exist, and the e-mail message is a prank designed to send people into a panic.

Bogus virus e-mail messages usually contain a long list of people in the To: and Cc: boxes; these messages have been forwarded many times. Most hoaxes include a recommended procedure for removing the virus, such as reformatting your computer's hard disk drive—a process that could cause more damage than the virus itself! Fake viruses are often characterized as being capable of bizarre acts. For example, check out the message about a phony virus in **Figure F-13**. If you follow the instructions in this e-mail, you will delete a legitimate program that debugs java programs.

When you receive an e-mail message about a virus, do not panic. Virtually all of them are hoaxes. If you are uncertain, check one of the many antivirus Web sites and look up the alleged virus by name to see if it is a hoax or if it is a real threat. If the virus is a real threat, the antivirus Web site will provide the information that you need to check your computer and download an update to your antivirus software.

Figure F-13

Virus Alert! - Message (Plain Text)

File Edit View Insert Format Tools Actions Help

Reply | Reply to All | Forward | ...

Extra line breaks in this message were removed.

From: Sent: Mon 7/26/2006 5:39 PM
To:
Cc:
Subject: Virus Alert!

A virus has been passed on to me by one of my contacts. The virus (called jdbgmgr.exe) is spreading rapidly on the Internet and is NOT detected by Norton or McAfee Anti-virus systems. The virus sits quietly for 14 days before exploiting an e-mail client weakness and damaging the system.

Here's how to check for the virus and get rid of it:

1. Locate the jdbgmgr.exe file on your C: drive. Do Not Open It!!
2. Delete this file.

IF YOU FIND THE VIRUS, YOU MUST CONTACT ALL THE PEOPLE IN YOUR ADDRESS BOOK, SO THAT THEY CAN ERADICATE IT FROM THEIR OWN ADDRESS BOOKS

Introducing data backup

Have you ever mistakenly copied an old version of a document over a new version? Has your computer's hard disk drive gone on the fritz? Did a virus wipe out your files? Has lightning "fried" your computer system? These kinds of data disasters are not rare; they happen to everyone. Since you cannot always prevent disasters from happening, you need a backup plan that helps you recover data that has been wiped out by operator error, viruses, or hardware failures. Computer experts universally recommend that you make backups of your data.

■ A **backup** is a copy of one or more files that has been made in case the original files become damaged. A backup is usually stored on a different storage medium from the original files. For example, you can back up files from your hard disk to a different hard disk, a writable CD or DVD, tape, Zip disk, solid state storage card, flash drive, or Web site. The exact steps that you follow to make a backup depend on your backup equipment, your backup software, and your personal backup plan. **Figure F-14** gives you a general idea of the steps that are involved in a typical backup session.

You **restore** data from a backup to the original storage medium or its replacement. As with the procedures for backing up data, the process that you use to restore data to your hard disk varies, depending on your backup equipment, backup software, and exactly what you need to restore. After a hard-disk crash, for example, you will probably need to restore all of your backup data to a new hard disk. On the other hand, if you inadvertently delete a file, or mistakenly

copy one file over another, you might need to restore only a single file from the backup. Most backup software allows you to select which files you want to restore.

A good backup plan allows you to restore your computing environment to its state before the data loss with a minimum of fuss. Unfortunately, no single backup plan fits everyone's computing style or budget. You must tailor your own backup plan to your particular computing needs. The checklist in **Figure F-15** outlines the factors you should consider as you formulate your own backup plan.

A **full backup** (also called a **full system backup**) contains a copy of every program, data, and system file on a computer. The advantage of a full backup is that you can easily restore your computer to its pre-disaster state simply by copying the backup files to a new hard disk. A full backup takes a lot of time, however, and automating the process requires a large-capacity storage device.

Figure F-14: Steps in a typical backup session

1. Insert the disk, CD, or tape on which you will store the backup.

2. Start the software you are using for the backup.

3. Select the folders and files you want to back up.

4. Give the "go ahead" to start copying data.

5. Insert additional disks, CDs, or tapes if prompted to do so.

6. Clearly label each disk, CD, or tape.

7. Test your backup.

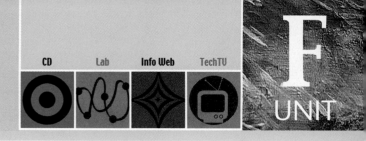

Figure F-15: Backup tips

✓ Decide how much of your data you want, need, and can afford to back up

✓ Decide what kind of storage device you will use to make backups

✓ Select software to handle backup needs

✓ Create a realistic schedule for making backups

✓ Make sure you have a way to avoid backing up files that contain viruses

✓ Find out what kind of boot discs you might need to get your computer up and running after a hard disk failure or boot sector virus attack

✓ Make sure you have a procedure for testing your restore procedure so that you can successfully retrieve the data that you have backed up

✓ Find a safe place to store your backups

An alternative is to back up your most important data files. By doing so, you make sure that your computer-based documents and projects are protected from data disasters. You can back up these files on floppy disks, Zip disks, removable hard disks, CDs, or DVDs. The disadvantage of this backup strategy is that because you backed up only data files, you must manually reinstall all of your software, in addition to restoring your data files if your entire system fails.

Some applications, such as financial software, create files and update them without your direct intervention. If you have the option during setup, make sure that these files end up in a folder you always backup, such as My Documents.

In addition to data files that you create, consider making backups of the following files:

- Internet connection information. Your ISP's phone number and TCP/IP address, your user ID, and your password are often stored in an encrypted file somewhere in the Windows\System folder. Your ISP can usually help you find this file.

- E-mail folders. If you are using POP e-mail software, your e-mail folder contains all of the e-mail messages that you have sent and received, but not deleted. Check the Help menu on your e-mail program to discover the location of these files.

- E-mail address book. Your e-mail address book might be stored separately from your e-mail messages. Find the file by using the Help menu for your e-mail program.

- Favorite URLs. Because it would be a hardship for you to try to remember, relocate the Web sites, and then resave all the URLs that you have collected in your Favorites or Bookmarks list, you might want to back up the file that contains this list.

- Downloads. If you paid to download any files, you might want to back them up so that you do not have to pay for them again. These files include software, which usually arrives in the form of a compressed .exe or .zip file that expands into several separate files as you install it. For backup purposes, the compressed file should be all that you need.

Backing up the Windows Registry

The Windows Registry is an important file that is used by the Windows operating system to store configuration information about all of the devices and software installed on a computer system. If the Registry becomes damaged, your computer might not be able to boot, launch programs, or communicate with peripheral devices. It is a good idea to have an extra copy of the Registry in case the original file is damaged.

Backing up the Registry can present a problem because the Registry file is always open while your computer is on. Some backup software will not copy open files, and if this is the type of backup software that you are using, the Registry will never make its way onto a backup. Windows users whose backup plans encompass all of the files on the hard disk must make sure that their backup software provides an option for including the Windows Registry. Even if a full-system backup is not planned, many experts recommend that you at least copy the Registry file to a separate folder on the hard disk or to any storage media. If you do so, it is necessary to update this copy whenever you install new software or hardware.

Examining backup procedures

One of the most distressing computing experiences is to lose all of your data. This problem might be the result of a hardware failure or a virus. Whatever its cause, most users experience only a moment of surprise and disbelief before the depressing realization sinks in that they might have to recreate their data and reinstall their programs. A backup can pull you through such trying times, making the data loss a minor inconvenience rather than a major disaster.

■ It is really frustrating when you restore data from a backup only to discover that the restored files contain the same virus that wiped out your data. If your antivirus software is not set to constantly scan for viruses on your computer system, you should run an up-to-date virus check as the first step in your backup routine.

■ A **full backup** (see **Figure F-16**) makes a copy of every file that exists in the folders on your computer. Because a full backup includes a copy of every file on a disk, it can take a long time to make one for a hard disk. Some users consider it worth the extra time, however, because this type of backup is easy to restore. You simply have the computer copy the files from your backup to the hard disk. It might, however, not be necessary to make a full backup every time you back up your data, especially if most of your files do not change from one backup session to another.

■ A **differential backup** makes a backup of only those files that were added or changed since your last full backup session. After making a full backup, you will want to make differential backups at regular intervals. You maintain two sets of backups: a full backup that you make infrequently (once a week); and a differential backup

that you make more frequently (once a day). It takes less time to make a differential backup than to make a full backup, but it is a little more complex to restore data from a differential backup. If you need to restore all of your files after a hard-disk crash, first restore the files from your full backup, then restore the files from your latest differential backup.

■ An **incremental backup** makes a backup of the files that were added or changed since the last backup, which might have been a full backup or an incremental backup. First you make a full backup, then when you make your first incremental backup, it will contain the files that have changed since the full backup. When you make your second incremental backup, it will contain only the files that changed since the first incremental backup. Incremental backups take the least time to make, and they provide better protection from viruses than other backup methods because your backup contains a series of copies of your files. They are, however, the most complex type of backup to restore. If you need to restore all of your files after a hard disk crash, first restore the files from the full backup, then restore the files from each incremental backup, starting with the oldest and working your way to the most recent. See **Figure F-17**.

Figure F-16: A full backup

A full backup is simply a copy of all files on your hard disk

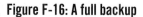
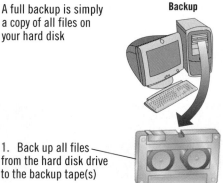

Backup   **Restore**

1. Back up all files from the hard disk drive to the backup tape(s)

2. If the hard drive fails, you can restore all of the files from the backup tape(s) to the hard disk drive

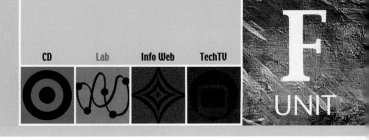
Figure F-17: An incremental backup

Of the three backup techniques, an incremental backup takes the least time, but is the most complex to restore

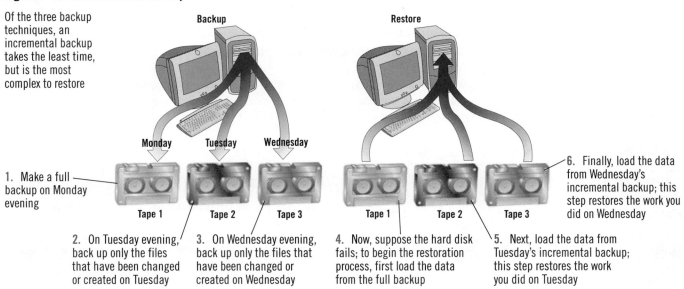

Backup

Monday   Tuesday   Wednesday

Restore

1. Make a full backup on Monday evening

Tape 1   Tape 2   Tape 3

Tape 1   Tape 2   Tape 3

2. On Tuesday evening, back up only the files that have been changed or created on Tuesday

3. On Wednesday evening, back up only the files that have been changed or created on Wednesday

4. Now, suppose the hard disk fails; to begin the restoration process, first load the data from the full backup

5. Next, load the data from Tuesday's incremental backup; this step restores the work you did on Tuesday

6. Finally, load the data from Wednesday's incremental backup; this step restores the work you did on Wednesday

■ Any data backup plan represents a compromise between the level of protection and the amount of time and resources you can devote to backup. Realistically you should perform backups at regular intervals (including copies of the Registry). The interval between backups will depend on the value of your data. If you are working on an important project, you might want to back up the project files several times a day. Under normal use, however, most people schedule a once-a-week backup.

■ As soon as you make a backup, test your backup to be sure you can restore your data. Also, make sure that you write the date of the backup on the media label so that you know which backup is the most recent. Then, store your backups in a safe place. Storing your backups at a different location is the best idea, but at least store them in a room apart from your computer.

■ Remote storage is also an option for your backup. If your computer is connected to a local area network, you might be able to use the network server as a backup device. Before backing up your data to a network server, you want to check with the network administrator to make sure that you are allowed to store a large amount of data on the server. If you want to limit access to your data, ask the network administrator to let you store your data in a password-protected area. Also make sure that the server is backed up on a regular basis and that you have access to the backups in case you need to restore data to your local computer.

■ Several Web sites offer fee-based backup storage space. When needed, you can download backup files from the Web site to your hard disk. These sites are practical for backups of your data files, but space limitations and download times make them impractical for a full-system backup. Experts suggest that you should not rely on a Web site as your only method of backup. If a site goes out of business or is the target of a denial-of-service attack, your backup data might not be accessible.

Exploring backup media and software

Choosing the storage media and software you use to create your backups depends on your backup plan. If you are simply copying a few data files to backup media, you can use the Copy command that is provided by your operating system or a file management utility, such as Windows Explorer. However, many types of backup storage media and software are available if you want to go beyond a simple file backup.

■ The hardware and media you use to backup your data is very important in determining the reliability and success of the procedure. The backup device that you select depends on the value of your data and your current computer configuration, equipment, and budget. There are several backup options available, some of which are detailed in **Table F-2**.

Table F-2: Storage capacities and costs of backup media

DEVICE	DEVICE COST*	MEDIA COST*	CAPACITY	COMMENTS
Floppy disk	$30 (average)	25¢	1.44 MB	Low capacity means that you have to wait around to insert disks when needed
Zip disk	$100 (average)	$9	750 MB	Holds much more than a floppy but a backup still requires multiple discs
External hard disk	$200 (average)	N/A	250 GB (average)	Fast and convenient
Removable hard disk	$130 (average)	$50	35 GB (average)	Fast, limited capacity, but disks can be removed and locked in a secure location
CD-R	$40 (average)	15¢	700 MB	Limited capacity, cannot be reused, long shelf life
CD-RW	$50 (average)	25¢	700 MB	Limited capacity, reusable, very slow
DVD-RW/ DVD+RW	$100 (average)	25¢	4.7 GB	Good capacity, reasonable media cost, higher capacity coming soon
Tape	$2,000 (average)	$80	200 GB (average)	Most convenient but expensive for capacity equal to today's hard drives
USB Flash drive	$15–$500	N/A	32 MB–4 GB	Convenient and durable, but high-capacity models are expensive
Web site	N/A	$15.00 per month	1 GB	Transfer rate depends on your Internet connection; security and privacy of your data might be a concern

*Approximate cost at the time this book was published

Creating a boot disc

If your computer's hard disk is out of commission, you might wonder how it can access the operating system files that are needed to carry out the boot process. If your hard disk failed, or a virus wiped out the boot sector files on your hard disk, you will not be able to use your normal procedures to boot your computer. A **boot disc** is a CD or DVD that contains the operating system files needed to boot your computer without accessing the hard disk.

A barebones boot disc simply loads the operating system kernel. You can make a boot disc using My Computer or Windows Explorer. The boot disc you create, however, boots DOS, not Windows. A more sophisticated boot disc—sometimes referred to as a **recovery CD**—loads hardware drivers and user settings as well as the operating system. Recovery CDs are sometimes included with new computer systems. Some computer manufacturer Web sites offer a download that creates a recovery CD. The operating system might also supply a method for creating recovery CDs. For example, the Windows XP Backup Utility creates a set of **Automated System Recovery** discs.

The contents and capabilities of recovery CDs vary. Some are designed to restore your computer to its "like new" state and will wipe out all your data. Others attempt to restore user settings, programs, and data. Before you depend on a recovery CD, make sure you know what it contains and how to use it in case of a system failure.

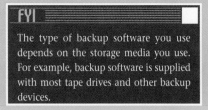

FYI

The type of backup software you use depends on the storage media you use. For example, backup software is supplied with most tape drives and other backup devices.

- **Backup software** is a set of utility programs designed to back up and restore files. Backup software usually provides options that make it easy to schedule periodic backups, define a set of files that you want to regularly back up, and automate the restoration process. Backup software differs from most copy routines because it typically compresses all the files for a backup and places them in one large file. Under the direction of backup software, this file can spread across multiple storage media if necessary. The file is indexed so that individual files can be located, uncompressed, and restored.

- Some versions of Windows include Microsoft Backup software (see **Figure F-18**), which you can usually find by clicking the Start button, and then selecting Accessories and System Tools. You can also purchase and download backup software from companies that specialize in data protection software.

- Backup software provides tools for scheduling backup dates and selecting the files you want to back up. The scheduling feature allows you to automate the backup process and reduces the chance that you will forget to make regular backups. Backup software can also save time and storage space by offering options for full, differential, or incremental backups.

- Whatever backup software you use, remember that it needs to be accessible when it comes time to restore your data. If the only copy of your backup software exists on your backup disks, you will be in a "Catch-22" situation. You will not be able to access your backup software until you restore the files from your backup, but you will not be able to restore your files until your backup software is running! Make sure that you keep the original distribution CD for your backup software or that you have a separate backup that contains any backup software that you downloaded from the Web. Also be sure to make the required recovery disks so that you can restore Windows and get your backup program running.

Figure F-18: Windows Backup Utility wizard

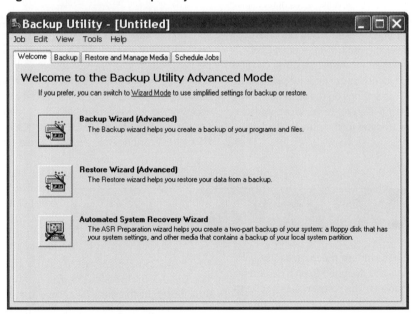

What is a data center?

The hardware and software for most enterprise and many high-performance computing systems are housed in a data center. A **data center** is a specialized facility designed to house and protect computer systems and data. A data center typically includes special security features such as fireproof construction, earthquake-proof foundations, sprinkler systems, power generators, secure doors and windows, and antistatic floor coverings. A typical data center may be located in the basement of a building or even underground—providing protection against extreme changes in surface temperature and some level of protection against natural disasters such as storms and fires. In general, data centers are not located in earthquake-, flood-, or tornado-prone areas. Data centers typically include equipment to keep computers functioning during power outages. A data center must also protect and maintain its own power grid. For example, fuel tanks must be protected against explosions or fire, and batteries must be kept at room temperature for proper functioning. Most data centers limit physical access via fingerprint identification systems, badges, or security guards. Steel doors divide the centers into secure areas. Motion detectors and automated alarm systems prevent unauthorized movement through the building.

Tech Talk Internet Access Security

Local area networks are susceptible to internal security breaches, such as when a person at one workstation gains unauthorized access to the files on another workstation. If a LAN is equipped with an always-on Internet connection, it also becomes vulnerable to external attacks. Security is an issue you must address if you are on a LAN or if you are using an ISP or a cable modem to connect to the Internet.

Any home network that is connected to an always-on Internet connection is vulnerable to intrusions. You should make sure that password protection is enabled on every workstation.

Whether you are connecting a stand-alone computer or a LAN, Internet connections pose two kinds of risks: malicious code and intrusions. To deal with malicious code, such as viruses and worms, it is important to run antivirus software on stand-alone computers and all network workstations. If you are the network administrator, you should make sure to stay up-to-date on security patches and service packs that apply to any network software providing network services or utilities, such as operating systems and browsers. A stand-alone computer with an always-on DSL, ISDN, or cable modem connection is particularly susceptible to intrusions. Hackers look for holes or vulnerabilities in Windows and Internet Explorer and work out ways to exploit them to gain unauthorized access to computers. As Microsoft develops security patches, they are posted at www.microsoft.com/security. Check the site frequently to download the most recent patches. You can also use Windows Automatic Updates to periodically check for patches. To configure Automatic Updates, use the settings on the Automatic Updates tab in the System folder in the Control Panel. When updates are available, you will see the New Updates icon on the taskbar, as shown in **Figure F-19**.

Figure F-19: Automatic update icon

For added protection, you might also want to purchase and install **personal firewall software**, which is designed to analyze and control incoming and outgoing packets. This software helps to keep your computer secure in several ways. It makes sure that incoming information was actually requested and is not an unauthorized intrusion. It blocks activity from suspicious IP addresses and, best of all, it reports intrusion attempts so that you can discover if any hackers are trying to break into your computer. Most firewall software allows you to set up various filters to control the type of packets that your workstation accepts. Most packages allow you simply to select a level of security, such as high, medium, or low. Windows XP includes firewall software called Internet Connection Firewall (ICF) or Windows Firewall. To activate and configure it, use the Control Panel's Network Connections option. For earlier Windows versions or non-Windows operating systems, Tiny Personal Firewall and BlackICE are popular personal firewall products.

If you are connected to the Internet using a cable modem, and if you have an Ethernet card in your PC, Windows automatically takes inventory of the local area network during boot-up. It looks for any computers on the network that have file and print sharing activated, and then lists them in the Network Places window. If your computer is connected to a LAN or used for access to a public Wi-Fi network, consider disabling file and printer sharing. When you turn off file and printer sharing (see **Figure F-20**), your files and printer cannot be accessed by other network users.

Unlike a dial-up connection that is only connected for the duration of your call, an always-on connection is connected continuously, and it is "on" whenever your computer is powered up. With an always-on connection, you might have the same IP address for days, or even months, depending on your ISP. A hacker who discovers that your computer has a security weakness can easily find it again, and its high-speed access makes it a very desirable target. To minimize risk, you can also use **network address translation (NAT)** as a line of defense. Your ISP typically assigns an IP address to your high-speed connection; that is the address that is visible to the rest of the Internet. Within your LAN, however, the workstations should use private Internet addresses. When the IP addressing scheme was devised, three ranges of addresses were reserved for internal or "private" use: 10.0.0.010.255.255.255, 172.16.0.0172.31.255.255, and 192.168.0.0192.168.255.255. These private IP addresses cannot be routed over the Internet. If you have assigned private IP addresses to your workstations, they are essentially hidden from hackers, who only see the IP address for your router.

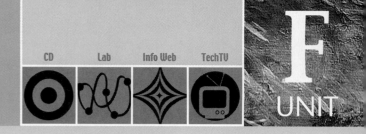

Figure F-20: Deactivating File and Printer Sharing

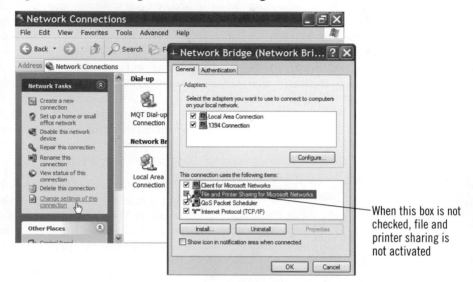

When this box is not checked, file and printer sharing is not activated

You might wonder how you can transmit and receive data from a workstation with a nonroutable address. Your router maintains a network address translation table that keeps track of the private IP addresses assigned to each workstation. For outgoing packets, the router substitutes its own address for the address of the workstation. When a response to a packet arrives, the router forwards it to the appropriate workstation. In that way, only the router's address is publicly visible. The router should, of course, be protected by antivirus software and firewall software.

When your computer is turned off, it is not vulnerable to attack. It is a good idea to shut down your computer when you are not using it. Putting your computer into sleep mode or activating a screen saver is not sufficient protection. Your computer must be shut down and turned off.

In addition to LAN users, it is sometimes necessary to secure connections for remote users. Many people need to access corporate LANs by using a remote connection from home or a customer's office. One way to secure these remote connections is by setting up a **virtual private network (VPN)**. Once a VPN is established, the remote user connects to his or her ISP as usual. After the connection is established, a second connection to the remote LAN server creates an encrypted channel for data transmission. Windows XP and several stand-alone products provide VPN software. **Figure F-21** illustrates how a VPN operates.

Figure F-21: Using VPN to secure remote access to a LAN

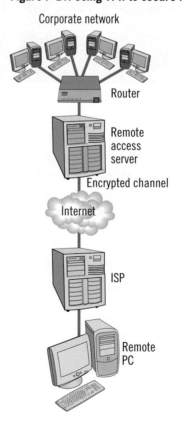

Corporate network

Router

Remote access server

Encrypted channel

Internet

ISP

Remote PC

Computers in Context
Law Enforcement

Mounted in the dashboard of marked and unmarked police cars, a mobile data computer resembles a notebook computer with its flat-panel screen and compact keyboard. See **Figure F-22**. Unlike a consumer-grade notebook, however, the computers in police cruisers use hardened technology designed to withstand extreme conditions, such as high and low temperatures in parked vehicles. The dashboard-mounted computer communicates with an office-based server using a wireless link, such as short-range radio, CDPD (cellular digital packet data) technology, or Wi-Fi. With this wireless link, police officers can access data from local, state, and national databases.

Figure F-22

With the increased use of computers in our society, computer crimes are escalating... Computer forensics is the scientific examination and analysis of data located on computer storage media, conducted to offer evidence of computer crimes in court.

One national database, the National Crime Information Center (NCIC), is maintained by the FBI and can be accessed by authorized personnel in local, state, and federal law enforcement agencies. The system can process more than 2.4 million queries per day related to stolen vehicles, wanted criminals, missing persons, violent gang members, stolen guns, and members of terrorist organizations. For example, the officers who pull over a speeding car might receive information from the NCIC that the car was stolen. If they do, they arrest the car's occupant and take him to the police station for booking. At the police station, digital cameras flash and the suspect's mug shot is automatically entered into an automated warrants and booking system. The system stores the suspect's complete biographical and arrest information, such as name, aliases, addresses, social security number, charges, and arrest date. The system also checks for outstanding warrants against the suspect. Booking agents assign the suspect to a cell, log his personal items, and print a photo ID or wrist band.

Automated warrants and booking systems have proven to increase police productivity. For example, New York City's system handles more than 300,000 bookings per year. Gains in productivity due to automated systems have put hundreds of the city's officers back into action investigating crimes and patrolling neighborhoods.

As part of the booking process, the suspect is fingerprinted. A standard fingerprint card, sometimes called a "ten-print card," contains inked prints of the fingers on each hand, plus name, date of birth, and other arrest information. Now, however, instead of using ink, a biometric scanning device can electronically capture fingerprints. See **Figure F-23**. Text information is entered via keyboard and stored with digital fingerprint images. The fingerprint information can be transmitted in digital format from local law enforcement agencies to the FBI's Automated Fingerprint Identification System (AFIS). This biometric identification methodology uses digital imaging technology to analyze fingerprint data. Using sophisticated algorithms, AFIS can classify arriving prints for storage and can search the collection of 600 million fingerprint cards for matching prints.

With the increased use of computers in our society, computer crimes are escalating. Computer crimes, also called **cybercrimes**, can be separated into two categories. The first includes crimes that use computers, such as transmitting trade secrets to competitors, reproducing copyrighted material, and distributing child pornography. The second includes crimes targeted at computers, such as denial-of-service attacks on servers, Web site vandalism, data theft, and destructive viruses. Conventional crimes, such as car thefts, are often solved by using standard investigative techniques with information from computer databases. To solve cybercrimes, however, often the special skills of computer forensic investigators are required. Computer forensics is the scientific examination and analysis of data located on computer storage media, conducted to offer evidence of computer crimes in court.

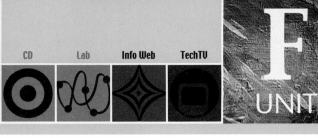
Figure F-23

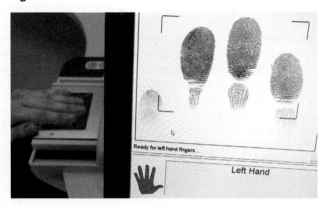

Computer forensics can be applied to both categories of computer crimes. Whether a computer is suspected as the origin of a cyber attack or it is suspected of holding evidence, the first step in the forensic process is to use disk imaging software to make an exact replica of the information stored on the hard disk. The disk image is then collected on a write-once medium that cannot be altered with "planted" evidence, and the forensic scientist begins analyzing the disk image data with simple search software that looks through files for keywords related to the crime. In the case of the "Gap-Toothed Bandit" who was convicted for robbing nine banks, analysis of the disk image of his personal computer revealed word processing files containing notes he handed to tellers demanding money. Criminals typically attempt to delete files with incriminating evidence, but a good forensic scientist can retrieve data from deleted files with undelete software or data recovery software. Temporary Internet or cache files can also yield evidence, pointing law enforcement officers to Web sites the suspect visited that might be fronts for illegal activity.

When a computer is a target of a cyber attack, forensic investigators use three techniques to track the source. The first option is to make an immediate image of the server's hard disk and look through its log files for evidence of activity coming from unauthorized IP addresses. A second technique is to monitor the intruder by watching login attempts, changes to log files, and file-access requests. Sophisticated intruders might be able to detect such monitoring, however, and cover their tracks. A third technique is to create a "honeypot"—an irresistible computer system or Web site containing fake information to lure any criminal activity. It allows investigators to monitor hackers until identification is possible.

Despite the many techniques and tools available to forensic investigators, they have three main constraints. First, they must adhere to privacy regulations and obtain warrants to set up wiretaps or gather information from ISPs about their customers. Second, they must scrupulously document their procedures so that the evidence they produce cannot be discredited in court as "planted" or fabricated. Third, forensic investigators must examine a wide range of alternatives pertaining to the crime, such as the chance that an IP or e-mail address used to commit a cybercrime does not belong to an innocent bystander being spoofed by the real hacker. Privacy, documentation, and evidentiary constraints cost forensic investigators time, and failure to adhere to strict standards can sometimes allow criminals to avoid conviction and penalties. But even within these constraints, careful forensic investigation is an important aspect of catching and convicting high-tech criminals.

Issue   What Are Professional Ethics?

The term **ethics** refers to the study of moral standards and how they affect how people conduct themselves in daily life. The term **professional ethics** refers to on-the-job choices and actions that reflect a person's values. Professional ethics encompass standards of conduct that specify how workers should behave, particularly in situations where doing the right thing might not seem to have short-term benefits, or when doing something of questionable legality seems to offer attractive benefits. Situations in which you ask yourself, "What is the right thing to do?" often require you to make ethical decisions. Professional ethics are derived from principles of right and wrong. In most modern societies, the foundation for ethical decisions and actions are based on values such as impartiality, fairness, objectivity, honesty, regard for privacy, commitment to quality, and respect for others.

Who decides what is ethical? Society's ethics are based on laws, which are documentation of permissible behavior according to the society that legislated the laws. As computers and digital technologies play a more central role in every aspect of daily life, laws are being created to deal with ethical issues related to computer uses and abuses. While it is important to consider applicable laws as you make decisions, it is also important to remember that all ethical behavior is not regulated by laws. Indeed, some actions that are unethical, such as lying about what time you arrived at work or claiming a sick day to go shopping, are not illegal.

Situations that require computer professionals to make ethical decisions often involve software copyrights, privacy, conflict of interest, use of work computers, software quality, hacking, and social responsibility.

Laws and court decisions sometimes conflict with regard to whether programmers and members of product development teams are responsible for the way their product is used. In the landmark case Sony Corp. vs. Universal City Studios, the U.S. Supreme Court set a precedent by ruling that Sony was not responsible when individuals used Sony Betamax recording technology to make and distribute illegal copies of movies. When applied to the IT industry, the Sony case seemed to absolve developers from any illegal actions taken by users. However, this position was negated by the Digital Millennium Copyright Act, which explicitly states that it is illegal to produce any product that allows individuals to circumvent copyright law or copy-protection methods. Therefore, a programmer who produces software to crack DVD copy protection technology can be held responsible when individuals use it to make illegal copies of DVDs. Hosts of peer-to-peer file sharing networks can be held accountable for users who illegally share copyrighted music and movies—especially if such illegal sharing is encouraged. Just like any other law, ignorance of the law is not an excuse for breaking it.

Ethical values such as honesty, fairness, respect, responsibility, and caring are universal. Decisions involving these values are encountered every day. Some decisions are easy to make and are made without even giving the decision a second thought. Other decisions are more difficult, perhaps because the consequences of the decision can have a negative impact. Decisions in the workplace that challenge ethical values must be made on a regular basis.

Situations that require computer professionals to make ethical decisions often involve software copyrights, privacy, conflict of interest, use of work computers, software quality, hacking, and social responsibility. Every day, computer professionals must cope with ethical dilemmas in which the right course of action is not entirely clear—or in which the right course of action is clear, but the consequences (such as getting fired) are not easy to face. Suppose, for example, that you are hired to manage a local area network in a prestigious advertising agency. On your first day of work, your employer hands you a box containing the latest upgrade for Microsoft Office and asks you to install it on all the computers in the business. When you ask if the agency owns a site license, your boss responds, "No, do you have a problem with that?" What would you reply? Would you risk your job by insisting that the agency order enough copies for all the computers before you install it? Or would you go ahead and install the software, assuming that your boss would take responsibility for this violation of the software license agreement? What is the ethical thing to do? How is it that software copyrights can become an ethical issue?

As this example points out, sometimes computer professionals are pressured to participate in activities that are clearly unethical and can even be illegal. These activities are sometimes justified with statements such as "Everyone does it" or "No one will know." Employees might be assured, "You won't be responsible" or "It's for the good of the company." Such justifications are not, however, always true or appropriate. And even if these statements were true, would the action in the example be any more justified because of these excuses?

Personnel in corporate IT departments and individual entrepreneurs sometimes get caught up in unethical activities because they make bad judgments or they have not done their homework regarding applicable laws and regulations. These individuals frequently face ethical decisions relating to software copyright laws. The previously described scenario is a classic example of how not understanding software copyright law and bad judgment might lead to unethical activities. As computer professionals it is critical to be familiar with the general principles of copyright law and the provisions of the Digital Millennium Copyright Act. It is critical to understand that it is illegal to make unauthorized copies of software and other copyrighted media, such as commercial music and movies. And, in fact, it is critical that programmers, Web designers, and other computer professionals respect intellectual property and adhere to copyright laws and license agreements as they are called upon to use intellectual property, such as installing software or using other people's graphics in their own work.

As an employee, it is not unusual, however, that you might find yourself in a software copyright dilemma like the one previously described in the advertising agency example. Business managers are not always familiar

with current copyright restrictions, or they might choose to ignore them. Because computer professionals are required to carry out the requests of management, they should stay up-to-date on current copyright law that applies to software and other digital media. It is important for companies to develop strict guidelines and to let management know the guidelines *before* the guidelines need to be used. For example, it is considered standard practice to ask for a copy of the End User License Agreement (EULA) before installing software. This document can sometimes resolve questions about the legality of copying software for use in multiple-user installations. Having it noted in writing that the EULA will be required before software can be installed can help eliminate ethical and even legal issues by insuring that both the management and the computer professionals are working from the same page.

Consider another example that raises ethical questions. Imagine that you are hired as a programmer for a local public school system. One day, the superintendent of schools calls you into her office and asks if you can write software that will monitor online access and provide reports to management. From your understanding of the school's network and Web access, you realize that it would be easy to write such monitoring software. You also realize, however, that the superintendent could use the software to track individual teachers and students as they visit Web sites. You ask the superintendent if faculty and students would be aware of the monitoring software, and she replies, "What they don't know won't hurt them." Should you write the program? Should you write the program, but start a rumor that monitoring software is being used to track faculty and student Web access? Should you pretend that it would be technically impossible to write such software? Having clear, detailed, written user guidelines of how the school network can be used by staff and students would help in the decision making. For example, if staff and students know right up front that their activity on the network is monitored and if they know what activities are acceptable and what activities are not acceptable, then writing the monitoring software does not pose an ethical dilemma. If staff and students have signed a written agreement, sometimes referred to as an Acceptable Use Policy, then they should be fully aware of what is permissible. In fact, the conversation suggested previously between you and the superintendent would not have taken place—other than to ask you if you could write the monitoring software.

Computer networking specialists sometimes encounter ethical issues related to privacy. For example, network technicians sometimes see the content of e-mail messages or personal files in the course of system maintenance or troubleshooting. Usually, computer professionals do not discuss or disclose what they see. However, computer professionals sometimes come across a file or an e-mail message that is troubling. It might be an e-mail message from an employee who is corresponding with a competing company about a job offer. More seriously, it might be an e-mail message divulging proprietary information to the competitor, harassing another employee, or outlining other illegal activities. If your employer has no guidelines for reporting suspicious activities, you will have to make your own decision about what kinds of information are serious threats.

So what do you do if you believe someone is violating a law in your place of work? You might find yourself in the position of becoming a **whistleblower**. A widely accepted definition of **whistleblowing** is the disclosure by an employee (or professional) of confidential information that relates to some danger, fraud, or other illegal or unethical conduct connected with the workplace, be it of the employer or of fellow employees. A whistleblower is someone in an organization who decides to speak out against on-the-job activities that are contrary to the mission of the organization or threaten the public interest. Generally, a whistleblower is making an ethical decision to address a situation or activities that are troubling to him or her.

Recently, whistleblowers have focused public attention on corporate abuses at large corporations, such as Enron and WorldCom, revealed major problems in the way the FBI investigated potential terrorists prior to 9/11, and uncovered defects in the body armor supplied to the U.S. combat troops. Although whistleblowing might seem effective, the consequences of whistleblowing can often be extreme. Whistleblowers are often fired or forced out of their jobs. If they keep their jobs, they might be excluded from promotions and shunned by coworkers. They are sometimes branded as tattletales and have difficulty finding other jobs in their career field. For example, a computer system administrator working for a state agency noticed his boss spent the majority of his time playing solitaire on his computer. After several e-mail messages up the chain of command were ignored, the system administrator installed Win-Spy software, which grabbed screenshots of his boss's computer several times per day over a period of several months. When the system administrator showed this evidence to his superiors, he was fired, even though he had 21 years of seniority. His boss received only a light reprimand. Were the actions of this system administrator ethical? Was it ethical for the system administrator to install the Win-Spy software? The system administrator probably thought that it was. He probably thought that with such tangible proof those above him would see how unproductive his boss was. But his superiors may have interpreted that action as unethical (that is, spying without permission on employees and as invading the privacy of others), and they may not have viewed playing cards on work time as being as serious an offense as spying.

Whistleblowing is risky under any circumstance, which is why the decision to blow the whistle is often grounded in ethical principles. But what one person considers ethical, may not be viewed the same way by others. Employee advocates have the following suggestions for reducing the risk of career repercussions so often experienced by whistleblowers.

■ **Examine your motives.** Make sure your cause is significant. Do not act out of frustration or because you feel underappreciated or mistreated.

■ **Try the normal chain of command.** Before you blow the whistle, try to correct the problem by reporting up the normal chain of command. Consider every possible way to work within the system before you take your concerns public.

- **Collect evidence to back up your accusations.** Gather documentary evidence that proves your case and keep it in a safe place before you draw attention to your concerns. Do not break any laws while collecting evidence.

- **Record events as they unfold.** Keep detailed, dated notes about events before and after you report the incident. Keep in mind that your notes might become public if the information is used as evidence in a trial.

- **Act ethically.** Do not embellish your case and do not violate any confidentiality agreements you may have. Engage in whistleblowing activities on your own time, not your employer's.

- **Be ready to accept repercussions.** Think through the effect your actions might have on your family. Be prepared for unemployment and the possibility of being blacklisted in your profession.

- **Establish a support network.** Seek out potential allies, such as elected officials, journalists, and activists that can support your cause.

- **Consult a lawyer.** Make sure you understand your rights as an employee.

- **Consider your strategy.** You might reduce the risk of repercussions if you lodge your complaint anonymously or as part of a group.

Computer professionals, like all professionals, must make ethical decisions as it relates to whistleblowing. They must be constantly on their guard regarding not only the legal but also the ethical implications of questionable activities.

Computer professionals can find themselves in compromising situations where they are asked to disclose confidential information gathered while employed in previous jobs.

As mentioned in the whistleblowing example, computers can be used to monitor employee activities. In the above example, software called Win-Spy was used to secretly capture images of a user's computer screen over a period of time. Although information from the screen captures can be used to monitor employee computer activities, new technologies that can be used to monitor employees are emerging. For example, RFID (Radio Frequency Identification) chips can be embedded in ID badges and used to keep track of employee locations in an office or manufacturing facility. Keystroke monitors, random samples of active programs, Web browsing history, network logs, and

e-mail logs can be used to monitor employee computing activities. Management defends the use of these monitoring systems as a way to make sure their employees are working productively. Privacy advocates question if these systems are ethical. They point out that while some surveillance is done with employee knowledge and consent, such as when it is clearly explained in an employment contract or company policy, other surveillance is surreptitious—done without the employee knowledge and done for unethical and perhaps even illegal activities.

Because surveillance is often set up by a programmer or network administrator, it is important for computer professionals to be familiar with laws and company policy applicable to privacy. Privacy laws differ from one country to the next, and most companies have unique privacy policies, so rather than assume you know the rules, make an effort to check applicable documents before you take action. Having this information in writing (both laws and company policies) will help guide you in making ethical and legal decisions.

In addition to privacy issues, computer professionals often must be concerned with confidentiality issues. Confidentiality is the obligation not to disclose any information obtained in confidence. Confidentiality rights apply to individuals and organizations. With respect to individuals, confidentiality means not disclosing names and associated data from databases and other information repositories. Laws in most countries restrict the disclosure of an individual's medical or financial information. In addition to the medical or financial professionals working with the individual, computer programmers often have access to this information, too. It is ethically imperative that all parties keep this information confidential. With respect to organizations, confidentiality means protecting proprietary information about company finances, procedures, products, and research that competitors would find valuable. Computer professionals can find themselves in compromising situations where they are asked to disclose confidential information gathered while employed in previous jobs.

Some individuals today skirt confidentiality issues and use information that individuals thought they had provided in confidence. For example, some people in marketing take advantage of gray areas in confidentiality laws to distribute names, addresses, and phone numbers collected "with consent" on forms, applications, and Web sites. The ethics of such marketing practices is doubtful.

So, faced with so many potentially unethical and illegal dilemmas, how do computer professionals stay grounded in their ethical judgments? One way is through the use of a Code of Ethics, which is a document designed to help computer professionals thread their way through a sometimes tangled web of ethical decisions. These codes are published by many professional organizations, such as the Association for Computing Machinery, the British Computer Society, the Australian Computer Society, and the Computer Ethics Institute. Each code varies in detail, but supplies a similar set of overall guiding principles for

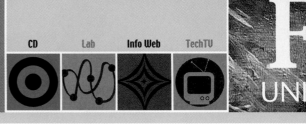
professional conduct. One of the shortest codes, which follows, is published by the Computer Ethics Institute:

1. Thou Shalt Not Use A Computer To Harm Other People.
2. Thou Shalt Not Interfere With Other People's Computer Work.
3. Thou Shalt Not Snoop Around In Other People's Computer Files.
4. Thou Shalt Not Use A Computer To Steal.
5. Thou Shalt Not Use A Computer To Bear False Witness.
6. Thou Shalt Not Copy Or Use Proprietary Software For Which You Have Not Paid.
7. Thou Shalt Not Use Other People's Computer Resources Without Authorization Or Proper Compensation.
8. Thou Shalt Not Appropriate Other People's Intellectual Output.
9. Thou Shalt Think About The Social Consequences Of The Program You Are Writing Or The System You Are Designing.
10. Thou Shalt Always Use A Computer In Ways That Insure Consideration And Respect For Your Fellow Humans.

© Copyright 1992 *Computer Ethics Institute*
Retrieved from http://www.brook.edu/its/cei/overview/Ten_Commandments_of_Computer_Ethics.htm

These 10 guidelines are short and to the point. Not all Codes of Ethics are short and snappy. For example, the ACM's Code of Ethics and Professional Conduct contains 21 guidelines, including "ACM members must obey existing local, state, province, national, and international laws unless there is a compelling ethical basis not to do so." But it goes on to say, "...sometimes existing laws and rules may be immoral or inappropriate and, therefore, must be challenged. Violation of a law or regulation may be ethical when that law or rule has inadequate moral basis or when it conflicts with another law judged to be more important. If one decides to violate a law or rule because it is viewed as unethical, or for any other reason, one must fully accept responsibility for one's actions and for the consequences."

A code of ethics can provide guidelines, but it might not offer ready answers to every dilemma that arises in the course of your career. When confronted with a difficult ethical decision, you should consider ethical guidelines, but also consider the policies of your workplace and relevant laws. These should support ethical decisions. You might also seek legal advice, consult the human resources advocate at your job, or ask advice from your union representative. Sometimes even talking to a trusted friend helps you recognize the correct course of action. Ethical decisions can be difficult and sometimes the results of your decision— good or bad—are not apparent right away. Ultimately, a decision about the right course of action is yours, and you must be willing to take responsibility for the consequences of your decision.

Interactive Questions

☐ Yes   ☐ No   ☐ Not sure   **1.** Do you think it is common to be ordered to install unlicensed software?

☐ Yes   ☐ No   ☐ Not sure   **2.** If you went ahead and installed software that was not properly licensed, and this installation was later discovered by the software publisher, do you think that you would be held responsible?

☐ Yes   ☐ No   ☐ Not sure   **3.** Is the use of monitoring software, even if the person is told that the software is in place, ethical?

Expand the Ideas

1. What might the conversation be regarding these two scenarios involving ethics? In the first scenario, you are a new employee at a company and your boss asks you to install software that you know is not properly licensed. Write a one-page dialog between you and your employer that reflects how this scenario might unfold. In the second scenario, you are the superintendent of schools and you are asking a new technical specialist to write software to monitor online access, to track the online activities of individuals and to provide reports to management. Write a short one-page dialog between you and your employee that reflects how this scenario might unfold.

2. Who is responsible for illegally installed software? Is it the organization or the individual? Are there any legal precedents to determine this? Research cases where action may have been brought against companies or individuals who illegally installed software. Summarize the case, then write a short paper supporting your opinion and the facts.

3. Do you agree with the code of ethics listed in this issue? If you were responsible for writing the code, what would it be? Write a code of ethics that you think is fair for computer users.

4. What is your opinion about whistleblowers? Do you believe that there should be strong legal protection in every field for whistleblowers? Do you think it is possible to protect those who are whistleblowers from the inevitable backlash from those who are "turned in"? How important is it to provide protection, under the law, for whistleblowers? Write a short paper explaining your position.

End of Unit Exercises

Key Terms

Antivirus software
Authentication
Automated System Recovery
Backdoor
Backup
Backup software
Biometrics
Blended threat
Boot disc
Boot sector virus
Bot
Botnet
Checksum
Computer virus
Cracker
Cybercrime
Cyberterrorism
Data center

Denial-of-service (DoS) attack
Differential backup
Direct source input device
Disaster recovery plan
Ethics
File virus
Full backup
Full system backup
Hacker
Incremental backup
Intelligent agent
Keylogger
Macro
Macro virus
Malicious code
Mass-mailing worm
Mean time between failures
   (MTBF)

Multi-partite virus
Network address translation
   (NAT)
Operator error
Payload
Personal firewall software
Polymorphic virus
Power failure
Power spike
Power surge
Professional ethics
Ransomware
Recovery CD
Restore
Retro virus
Risk management
Stealth virus
Surge protector

Surge strip
Surge suppressor
Trigger event
Trojan horse
UPS (uninterruptible power
   supply)
User rights
Virus
Virus definition
Virus hoax
Virus signature
Virtual private network (VPN)
Voltage spike
Whistleblower
Whistleblowing
Worm

Unit Review

1. Use your own words to define bold terms that appear throughout the unit. List 10 of the terms that are least familiar to you and write a sentence for each of them.

2. Create a chart to review the factors that cause data loss or misuse. List the factors you learned about in this unit in the first column. Then place an X in the appropriate column to indicate whether that factor leads to data loss, inaccurate data, stolen data, or intentionally damaged data. Some factors might have more than one X.

3. Summarize what you have learned about viruses, Trojan horses, bots, and software worms.

4. Make a checklist of steps to follow if you suspect that your computer is infected with a virus.

5. Define the term "bot." Explain how some bots can be harmless, and in fact can be used for good purposes. Explain what a botnet is and why it is a serious threat.

6. List the filename extensions of files that might typically harbor a virus.

7. Explain how antivirus software works and how it is able to catch new viruses that are created after the software is installed on your computer.

8. Explain the differences among the backup strategies discussed in this unit.

9. Define boot disc and describe how it might help you recover from a hard disk crash.

10. Devise a backup plan for the computer you use regularly. Explain how you would implement your plan.

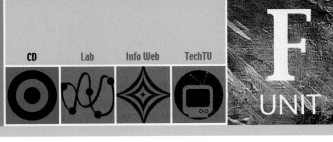
Fill in the Best Answer

1. A(n) _UPS_ is a device containing a battery that provides a continuous supply of power and other circuitry to prevent spikes and surges from reaching your computer.

2. Although a(n) _____ contains multiple outlets for power plugs, it does not contain the electronics necessary to filter out power spikes and surges.

3. The _____ is calculated by observing test equipment in a laboratory, then dividing the number of failures by the total number of hours of observation.

4. As part of a risk management program, preventive countermeasures can be grouped into three categories: deterrent measures, detection activities, and _____ procedures.

5. A method of personal identification called _____ bases identification on some physical trait, such as a fingerprint or the pattern of blood vessels in the retina of the eye.

6. User _rights_ are rules that limit the directories and files that each user can access.

7. A computer _____ is a program that attaches itself to a file and reproduces itself so it can spread from one file to another.

8. A boot _____ virus infects the system files that your computer uses every time you turn it on.

9. A Trojan _____ is a computer program that seems to perform one function while actually doing something else.

10. Viruses often attach themselves to a program file with a(n) _.exe_ extension so that when you run the program, you also run the virus code.

11. Unlike a virus, which is designed to spread from file to file, a(n) _____ is designed to spread from computer to computer.

12. A virus can enter a computer as an e-mail attachment or as a script in an e-mail message formatted as _____.

13. Antivirus software calculates a(n) _____ to make sure that the bytes in an executable file have not changed from one computing session to another.

14. The process of identifying potential threats to computer systems, implementing plans to avoid threats, and developing steps to recover from disasters is referred to as _____ management.

15. A virus that does not really exist is referred to as a virus _____ .

16. Virus experts use the term _____ threat to describe threats that combine more than one type of malicious program.

17. The three types of backup plans are full, differential, and _____ .

18. A(n) _____ CD contains the operating system files needed to start your computer without accessing the hard disk.

19. A(n) _data_ center is a facility specifically designed to house and protect computer systems and data.

20. Trojan horses are notorious for stealing passwords using a(n) _____ , which is a type of program that records your keystrokes.

Practice Tests

When you use the Interactive CD, you can take Practice Tests that consist of 10 multiple-choice, true/false, and fill-in-the-blank questions. The questions are selected at random from a large test bank, so each time you take a test, you will receive a different set of questions. Your tests are scored immediately, and you can print study guides to determine which questions you answered incorrectly. If you are using a Tracking Disk, save your test scores.

End of Unit Exercises

INDEPENDENT CHALLENGE 1

Do you have a plan for data recovery in place for your computer data? Are you working at a company that practices data backup and recovery on a regular basis? Is there antivirus software installed on the computer you use regularly? Assess the risk to the programs and data files stored on the hard disk drive of your computer.

Write a brief essay that answers the following questions:

1. What threats are likely to cause your data to be lost, stolen, or damaged?

2. What steps, if any, have you taken to prevent data loss?

3. How many of these data files are critical and would need to be replaced if you lost all of your data?

4. What would you need to do to reconstruct the critical files if the hard disk drive failed and you did not have any backups?

5. What measures could you use to protect your data from the threats you identified in Question 1? What is the cost of each of these measures?

6. Taking into account the threats to your data, the importance of your data, and the cost of possible protective measures, what do you think is the best plan for the security of your data?

INDEPENDENT CHALLENGE 2

 If you suspect that your computer has become infected with a virus, it is prudent to activate virus detection software to scan your files immediately. With the continued spread of viruses, virus detection software has become an essential utility in today's computing environment. Many virus detection software packages are available in computer stores, on computer bulletin boards, and on the Internet.

1. Log onto the Internet and use your favorite search engine to find information about three virus detection and removal software packages. Find at least one that is available as shareware. Write a brief report on each package, and compare and contrast their features and benefits.

2. Microsoft Word documents can harbor macro viruses. Using library or Internet resources, find symptoms for a Word macro virus. Write a one-page report describing a macro virus.

3. Bots have become a serious threat on the Internet. They also provide valuable tools. Use your favorite search engine to research bots. Explore and find specific information about

two good bots and two bad bots. Write a one-page report describing your findings.

INDEPENDENT CHALLENGE 3

An Internet worm created concern about the security of data on military and research computer systems, and it raised ethical questions about the rights and responsibilities of computer users. Select one of the following statements and use library resources to learn more about each viewpoint. Write a two-page paper that argues for or against the viewpoint you selected. Make sure that you support your viewpoint with facts and references to authoritative articles and Web pages, and include a bibliography of the resources you used.

1. People have the right to hone their computing skills by breaking into computers. As a computer scientist once said, "The right to hack is held higher than the right of someone to tell you not to. It's an inalienable right."

2. If problems exist, it is acceptable to use any means to point them out. The computer science student who created the Internet worm was perfectly justified in claiming that he should not be prosecuted because he was just trying to point out that security holes exist in large computer networks.

3. Computer crimes are no different from other crimes, and computer criminals should be held responsible for the damage they cause by paying for the time and cost of replacing or restoring data.

INDEPENDENT CHALLENGE 4

 Is it a good idea to use the Web to back up your data? Is this something that individuals as well as businesses should consider? At what point would a small business choose this option? What are the benefits and risks?

1. Log onto the Internet and then investigate a Web site that provides storage for data backups.

2. Find out the cost of using the site and investigate the site's terms and conditions for use. Try to discover if data stored at the site would be secure and private. Also try to determine whether the backup and restore procedures seem feasible. Try to determine whether a plan exists for notifying customers if the site is about to go out of business.

3. After completing your research, submit a two-page paper that explains whether or not you would use the site for storing your backups.

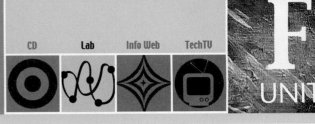

LAB: Backing Up Your Computer

1. Start the interactive part of the lab. Insert your Tracking Disk if you want to save your QuickCheck results. Perform each of the lab steps as directed and answer all of the lab QuickCheck questions. When you exit the lab, your answers are automatically graded and your results are displayed.

2. Describe where most of your data files are stored and estimate how many megabytes of data (not programs) you have in all of these files. Next, take a close look at these files and estimate how much data (in megabytes) you cannot afford to lose. Finally, explain what you think would be the best hardware device for backing up this amount of data.

3. Draw a sketch or capture a screenshot of the Microsoft Backup window's toolbar. Use ToolTips or the window's status bar to find the name of each toolbar button. Use this information to label the buttons on your sketch or screenshot.

4. Assume that you will use Microsoft Backup to make a backup of your data files. Describe the backup procedure you would use to specify the folders that you must include. It is not necessary to list individual files unless they are not within one of the folders that you would back up. Make sure that you indicate whether or not you would use password protection, the type of compression that you would select, and how you would handle the Windows Registry.

Student Edition Labs

Reinforce the concepts you have learned in this unit through the **Keeping Your Computer Virus-Free** and **Backing Up Your Computer** Student Edition Labs, available online at the Illustrated Computer Concepts Web site.

SAM Labs

If you have a SAM user profile, you have access to additional content, features, and functionality. Log in to your SAM account and go to your assignments page to see what your instructor has assigned for this unit.

End of Unit Exercises

Figure F-24 shows the first two pages of an acceptable-use policy published by the *U.S. Department of Education's Institute of Education Sciences National Center for Education Statistics*. Most educational institutions and places of work now have rules and regulations or acceptable-use policies detailing computer use. These rules often detail policies and rules relating to Internet use, privacy and confidentiality, e-mail accounts, general guidelines for e-mail access, appropriate Web content, and copyright restrictions. Most policies are made public and often have to be signed by the students or employees. It is imperative that you read and understand the policies and rules before signing the document.

Figure F-24

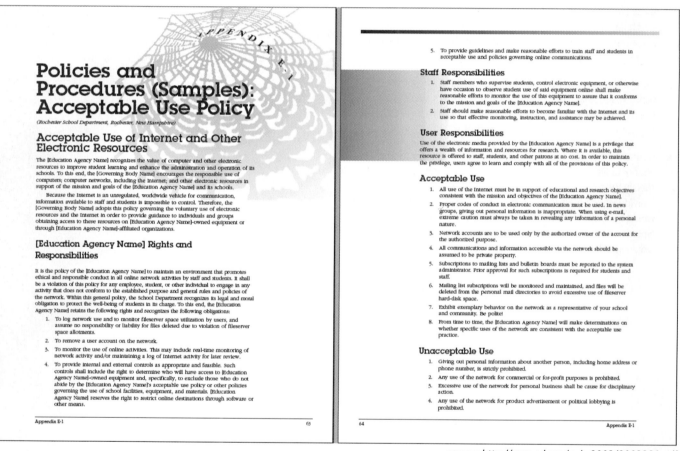

source: http://nces.ed.gov/pubs2003/2003381.pdf

If your school or workplace does not have a student/employee rules and regulations or an acceptable-use policy, use your favorite search engine to find examples of acceptable-use policies on the Internet. Read through at least two examples, then select one. Use the document you select to write a brief paper that answers the following questions:

1. To whom does the policy apply: students, faculty, staff, community members, others?

2. What types of activities does the policy specifically prohibit?

3. Does the policy state the penalties for computer crimes? If so, what are they?

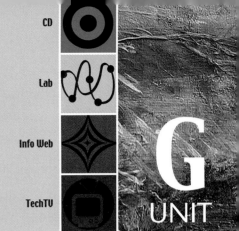

CD

Lab

Info Web

TechTU

The Web and E-commerce

G
UNIT

◎ Introduce Web technology
◎◆ Explore HTML
◆ Use Web browsers
   Create navigation elements
◎ Explain HTTP and Web servers
◆◆◼ Introduce Web page authoring
◎◆ Enhance Web pages
◎◆ Organize Web pages
◎◔◆◼ Introduce e-commerce
◎◆ Secure e-commerce transactions
◆◆◼ Avoid fraud when shopping online

◆ Tech Talk: Encryption
   Computers in Context: Politics
◎◆ Issue: Censorship on the Web

Overview

Unit G focuses on the Web and the variety of key technologies that make the Web what it is today. The unit begins with an introduction to the technologies that bring the Web to your computer screen. The unit continues by exploring the tools that make it possible to create and enhance Web pages while providing a consistent look across all pages in a Web site. You will also explore e-commerce topics and learn about buying and selling merchandise and services over the Web. The unit wraps up with a Tech Talk on encryption. You will read about computers in the context of politics. The Issue explores censorship on the Web.

Introducing Web technology

Although many people use the terms interchangeably, there is a difference between the Web and the Internet. The Internet is basically a collection of computers and cables that form a communications network. The Internet carries a variety of data, including e-mail, videoconferences, and instant messages. The Internet also carries text, graphics, video and audio that form Web pages. The Web is a collection of documents that can be accessed over the Internet and can be related by using links. This lesson discusses the technologies (HTTP, HTML, Web servers, URLs, and browsers) behind the Web.

- Three of the most important elements of the Web are **Hypertext Transfer Protocol (HTTP)**, **Hypertext Markup Language (HTML)**, and **URL (Uniform Resource Locator)**. HTTP is the communications protocol used to transport data over the Web. HTML is the set of specifications used to create Web pages. Both of these Web elements contain hypertext in their names. Hypertext is a key concept for understanding the Web. A URL is a unique address used to identify each Web page.

- The idea of hypertext originated before the Web, or even before the Internet. In 1945, an engineer named Vannevar Bush wrote the article

"As We May Think," which described a microfilm-based machine called the Memex that linked associated information or ideas through "trails." The idea resurfaced in the mid-1960s, when Harvard graduate Ted Nelson coined the term **hypertext** to describe a computer system that could store literary documents, link them according to logical relationships, and allow readers to comment and annotate what they read. Nelson sketched the diagram shown in **Figure G-1** to explain his idea. This early sketch of project Xanadu, a distant relative of the Web, used the terms links and web.

Figure G-1: Ted Nelson's early sketch of project Xanadu

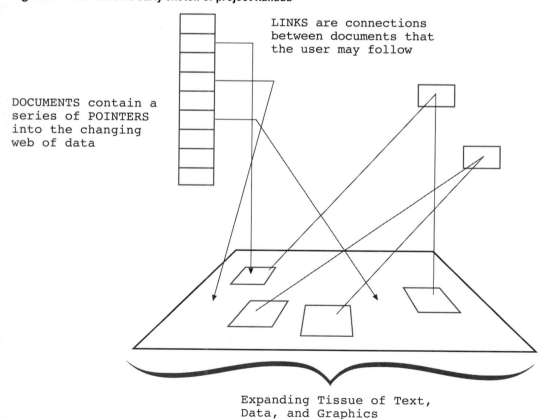

LINKS are connections between documents that the user may follow

DOCUMENTS contain a series of POINTERS into the changing web of data

Expanding Tissue of Text, Data, and Graphics

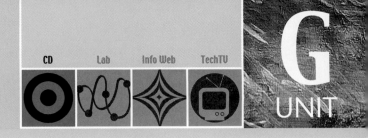
- In 1990, a British scientist named Tim Berners-Lee developed specifications for HTML, HTTP, and URLs. He hoped that these technologies would help researchers share information by creating access to a sort of web of electronic documents. In the words of Berners-Lee, "The Web is an abstract (imaginary) space of information. On the Net, you find computers; on the Web, you find documents, sounds, videos, and information. On the Net, the connections are cables between computers; on the Web, connections are hypertext links."

- A **Web server** stores one or more Web pages that form a Web site. Each page is stored as a file called an **HTML document**—a text or ASCII document with embedded HTML tags. Some tags specify how the document is to be displayed when viewed in a browser. Other tags contain **hypertext links** (or simply links) to related documents, graphics, and sound files that are also stored on Web servers. You can click a hypertext link—an underlined word, phrase, or graphic—to access related documents. In addition to storing these files, a Web server runs software that handles requests for specific Web pages.

- As an alternative to HTML documents, Web servers can also store Web page data in other types of files, such as databases. Data, such as product information, can be assembled into HTML format "on the fly" in response to Web page requests. In this way, a Web page is always current.

- Every Web page is a document stored on a Web server and identified by a URL. You use Web client software called a **browser** to view Web pages. To request the HTML document for the Web page that you want to view, you type a URL into the browser's address box. Your browser creates a request for the specified file using a command provided by the HTTP communications protocol. The request is sent to a Web server, which has been listening for HTTP requests. When your request arrives, the Web server examines it, locates the HTML document that you requested, and sends it back to your computer. If additional elements, such as a graphic, are needed to view the Web page correctly, your browser must issue a new request to the server for that element. The cycle continues until the Web page appears in your browser window. **Figure G-2** illustrates the entire process.

Figure G-2: How browsers and Web servers exchange HTTP messages

1. Using HTTP, the browser sends a request for an HTML document to a server

GET document.html

2. The server receives the browser's request and locates the requested HTML document

HTTP

document.html

4. The browser starts displaying the Web page according to the HTML tags embedded in the document

3. Using HTTP, the HTML document is sent to the browser, and then the server waits for more requests

Exploring HTML

HTML (Hypertext Markup Language) is a set of specifications for creating HTML documents that a browser can display as a Web page. HTML is called a **markup language** because authors mark up their documents by inserting special instructions called **HTML tags** that specify how the document should appear when displayed on a computer screen or printed. The original HTML specifications that were developed by Tim Berners-Lee in 1990 have been revised several times by an organization called the **World Wide Web Consortium (W3C)**. This lesson discusses how the current HTML specifications work to display the lines of text on your computer screen in the right color and size and to position graphics in your browser.

■ HTML has had several versions. **XHTML** is the version after HTML 4. XHTML, which includes all HTML 4 tags, can be extended by adding customized tags. To reflect its extensibility, the W3C preferred to name this new version XHTML 1.0, rather than calling it HTML 5, Today's Web operates according to XHTML standards, even though people commonly refer to the technology simply as HTML.

■ The term "source" is used to refer to the document that has the HTML tags. The term **Web page** refers to both the source HTML document and the corresponding Web page that is displayed by your browser. Most browsers include a menu option that allows you to view the source HTML document with its HTML tags. For example, when using the Internet Explorer browser, you can click View on the menu bar, then click Source to see the source code for the current Web page. See **Figure G-3**.

■ In an HTML document, HTML tags, such as <b> and <hr />, are enclosed in angle brackets. These tags are instructions to the browser. When your browser displays a Web page on your computer screen, it does not show the tags or angle brackets. Instead, it follows the tags' instructions. Most HTML tags work in pairs. An opening tag begins an instruction, which stays in effect until a closing tag appears. Closing tags always contain a slash. For example, the following sentence contains opening and closing bold tags: <b>Caterpillars</b> love sugar. When displayed by a browser, the word "Caterpillars" will be bold, but the other words in the sentence will not be bold.

■ Some tags are **self-closing tags**. which is a single tag that includes a closing "/" symbol. The <hr /> tag is a self-closing tag. It produces a horizontal line on a Web page. A space between the "hr" and "/" is included for maximum compatibility with various browsers. In self-closing tags such as <hr />, the slash comes at the end of the tag, whereas in a closing tag such as </b>, the slash comes at the beginning.

Figure G-3: Viewing the source HTML document

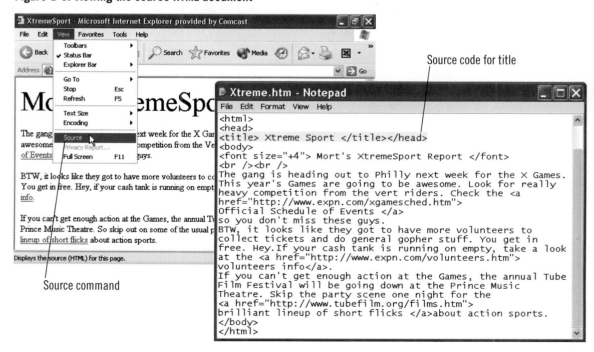

Source code for title

Source command

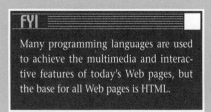

FYI

Many programming languages are used to achieve the multimedia and interactive features of today's Web pages, but the base for all Web pages is HTML.

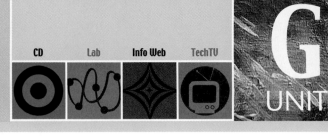

CD   Lab   **Info Web**   TechTV

G
UNIT

- HTML is not a case-sensitive language, but XHTML style requires tags to be lowercase so that they work on case-sensitive servers.

- HTML tags are used to create links to other Web documents. For example, the <a href> HTML tag contains both the URL for the linked page and the text that appears as an underlined link when the Web page is displayed in a browser. See **Figure G-4**.

Figure G-4: The components of the <a href> tag

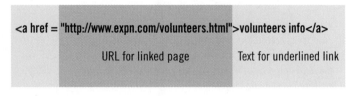

```
<a href = "http://www.expn.com/volunteers.html">volunteers info</a>
```

URL for linked page   Text for underlined link

- HTML documents contain no graphics. So, in addition to specifying how text should be formatted, HTML tags can be used to specify how to incorporate graphics on a page. A graphic on a Web page can be many different things. For example, a graphic might be a design element such as a horizontal line drawn by the browser as specified by a tag or it might be a graphic file of a sports car. The <img src> tag is used to specify the name and location of a graphic file that is to be displayed as part of a Web page. **Figure G-5** illustrates how browsers interpret HTML tags to display graphics.

- HTML includes hundreds of tags. For convenience, tags are classified into four groups. **Operational tags** specify the basic setup for a Web page, provide ways for users to interact with a page, and offer ways for Web pages to incorporate information derived from databases. **Formatting tags** change the appearance of text and work much like the formatting options in a word processor to create bold and italic text, adjust the size of text, change the color of text and backgrounds, arrange text in table format, or align text on a page. **Link tags** specify where and how to display links to other Web pages and e-mail addresses. **Media tags** specify how to display media elements, such as graphics, sound clips, or videos.

Figure G-5: Examples of graphics HTML tags

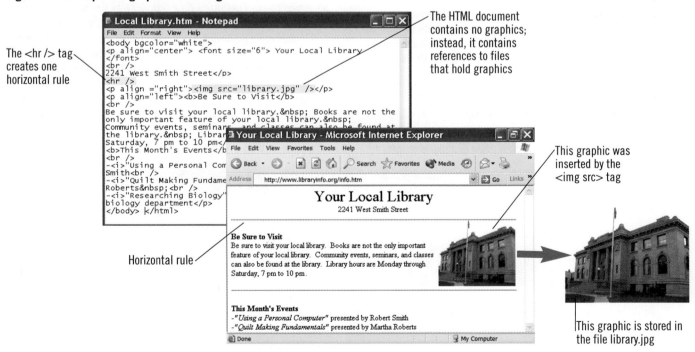

The <hr /> tag creates one horizontal rule

The HTML document contains no graphics; instead, it contains references to files that hold graphics

This graphic was inserted by the <img src> tag

Horizontal rule

This graphic is stored in the file library.jpg

Using Web browsers

A **Web browser**, usually referred to simply as a browser, is a software program that runs on your computer and helps you access Web pages. See **Figure G-6**. Technically, a browser is the client half of the client/server software that facilitates communication between a personal computer and Web server. The software on the Web server is the server side of the system. The browser is installed on your computer, and the Web server software is installed on a host computer on the Internet. This lesson gives an overview of the various browsers that are available, and explains how helper applications, plug-ins, and players work with your browser to display Web pages.

■ Your browser plays two roles in accessing and displaying Web pages. First, a browser uses HTTP to send messages to a Web server—usually a request for a specific HTML document. Second, when it receives an HTML document from a Web server, your browser interprets the HTML tags in order to display the requested Web page.

■ All browsers are designed to interpret HTML documents. Browsers also handle additional file formats, such as multimedia graphic file formats. However, if you click a link that leads to a file that your browser cannot handle, you will see a message that directs you to download the software necessary to read the file format. The software your browser uses to read nonnative file formats can be a helper application, plug-in, or player. A **helper application** is a program that understands how to work with a specific file format. When a helper application is installed, it updates your computer system so that your browser knows which file formats it can accept. Whenever your browser encounters a non-HTML file format, it automatically runs the corresponding helper application, which in turn opens the file. A helper application opens a new window for displaying the file.

For example, you might be directed to the Adobe Web site to download the Acrobat Reader software, which handles PDF (Portable Document Format) files and lets you view documents created from a

variety of desktop publishing applications uniformly on any system. To display animation, you might need Macromedia's Flash Player to display SWF files. For movies, you might need the Apple QuickTime player. For music or video, you might need Real Networks RealPlayer or Windows Media Player.

A **plug-in** is similar to a helper application, but it displays files within the browser window. Helper applications and plug-ins are very similar from the user's perspective. The current trend is to use the term **player** to refer to any helper application or plug-in that helps a browser display a particular file format. You can usually find a list of players installed for use with your browser. Your browser's list of players might include a PDF reader and spyware detectors used by your antivirus software.

■ It is a good idea to upgrade when a new version of your browser is available. You can get up-to-date browser functionality and often increased security simply by spending a few minutes downloading and installing an update. Because Web pages may depend on new HTML features that are supported only by the latest browser versions, you might encounter errors as your browser tries to display a page, but cannot interpret some of the HTML without the latest upgrade. In other cases, your browser might display the Web page without errors, but you will not see all of the intended effects.

Figure G-6: A Web page displayed in Internet Explorer, a popular Web browser

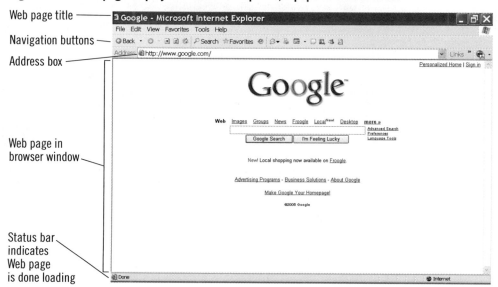

Web page title

Navigation buttons

Address box

Web page in browser window

Status bar indicates Web page is done loading

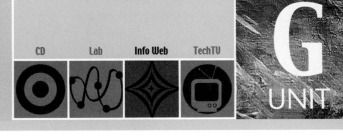
FYI

To view a list of players installed on your computer, look for a Manage Add-ons option on the Tools menu if you use Internet Explorer.

Another important reason to upgrade is increased security. As hackers discover and take advantage of security holes, browser publishers try to patch them. Upgrades typically contain patches for known security holes, though new features in the upgrade may open new security holes.

■ Popular browsers include Internet Explorer (IE), Mozilla Firefox, Netscape Navigator, and Opera. Internet Explorer and Netscape Navigator share similar features—perhaps because they evolved from the earliest graphical browser, Mosaic. Opera is an alternative that offers unique features such as a multidocument display, which IE and Navigator do not offer. Firefox provides more effective security measures, as well as tabbed browsing and live bookmarks. **Table G-1** provides a brief comparison of Web browsers.

Table G-1: A comparison of browsers

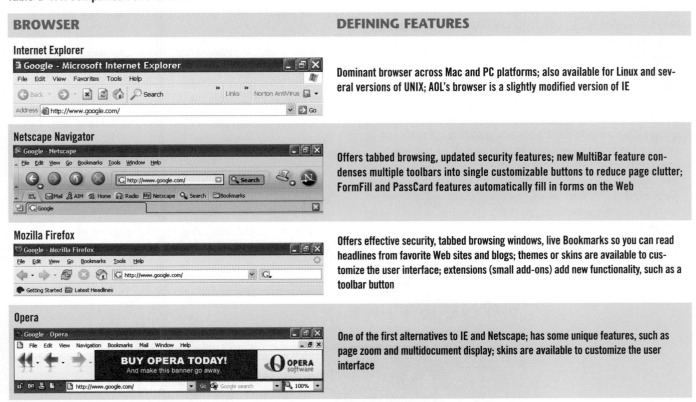

BROWSER	DEFINING FEATURES
Internet Explorer	Dominant browser across Mac and PC platforms; also available for Linux and several versions of UNIX; AOL's browser is a slightly modified version of IE
Netscape Navigator	Offers tabbed browsing, updated security features; new MultiBar feature condenses multiple toolbars into single customizable buttons to reduce page clutter; FormFill and PassCard features automatically fill in forms on the Web
Mozilla Firefox	Offers effective security, tabbed browsing windows, live Bookmarks so you can read headlines from favorite Web sites and blogs; themes or skins are available to customize the user interface; extensions (small add-ons) add new functionality, such as a toolbar button
Opera	One of the first alternatives to IE and Netscape; has some unique features, such as page zoom and multidocument display; skins are available to customize the user interface

Blocking adware, spyware, and pop-up ads

When you access Web sites, data is transferred to your computer and displayed by your browser. Most of this data is harmless, but malicious HTML scripts, adware, and spyware have the potential to search your computer for passwords and credit card numbers, install viruses, block your access to legitimate Web sites, or surreptitiously use your computer for illicit activities.

Adware is software that is bundled with a program that automatically displays or downloads advertising material to a computer after the program is installed or while the application is being used. It has been a way for programmers to recover development costs, and in some cases, it has allowed a program to be provided free of charge or at a reduced price. Adware is primarily advertising-supported; however, users may also be given the option to pay for a "registered" or "licensed" copy of a program to avoid the adware in the program. Adware does not track, report, or resell information about the user's activity.

Spyware is the most insidious threat. It often piggybacks on pop-up ads and activates if you click the ad window. Some spyware can begin its dirty work when you try to click what appears to be a Close button to get rid of an ad. The first line of defense is to never click anything or anywhere on pop-up ads—especially those that carry dire warnings about your computer being infected by a virus or spyware. To close an ad, right-click its button on the taskbar at the bottom of your screen, and then select the Close option from the menu that appears. Some browsers can be configured to block spyware and pop-up ads. Your antivirus software might offer similar options.

You can also install software specially designed to block adware, spyware, and pop-up ads. Some popular titles are Webroot, SpySweeper, Ad-Aware, Spybot S&D, SpyHunter, SpyRemover, Pest Patrol, Spykiller, and Pop-up Defender.

Creating navigation elements

For a Web page or Web site to be effective, visitors must be able to move intuitively to the information they want. Web pages should include clear and consistent navigation elements. This lesson looks at the techniques used to create navigation elements, such as hypertext links, graphics links, hot spots, and navigation bars, that help make navigating a Web page or Web site easy.

■ **Links** (also called **hyperlinks**) open a location in the same Web page, a different Web page, or a different Web site. Whether they are text or graphics, links provide the fundamental tools for navigating Web pages. An **internal link** (also called a local link or page link) links to other pages within the same Web site. An **external link** (also called a remote link) links to pages outside of the Web site. You can create links to any Web site in the world, but it is a good idea to check the site's policies on external links. An **interpage link** (also called an "anchor link") is a type of link usually used to jump to a different location within the current Web page. These links are handy for a long page divided into sections. For example, user group FAQs are often structured as a long page of questions and answers. The page begins with a list of questions, each of which is linked to its answer, which appears farther down the page. A **mailto link** automatically opens a preaddressed e-mail form that can be filled in and sent. These links are typically used to provide a method for contacting the Webmaster, the Web site's author, or a customer service representative.

■ Typically, a link appears on a Web page as underlined, blue text, but a link can also be a graphic such as a picture or a button. The arrow-shaped pointer changes, usually to a pointing hand, when it moves over any text or graphics link in the browser window.

■ The HTML tag that specifies a link typically has two parts: a destination and a label. See **Figure G-7**. The destination specifies a URL, usually the Web page that will appear as a result of clicking the link. The label is the wording for the underlined text that appears on the Web page as the clickable link.

You have probably encountered Web page links that open the linked page in a new window. That is because in addition to the information shown in **Figure G-7**, the <a href> tag can also allow a Web page author to specify whether the linked page will appear in the current browser window or in a new browser window. When used effectively, new windows help you easily return to previous pages. Newer browsers that offer tabbed browsing windows help organize all open windows. Even so, too many new windows can clutter your screen.

Figure G-7: A link to display another Web page

<a href = "http://www.e-course.com/instructions.html" > Click for instructions. </a>

Link destination   Link label that appears on the Web page

What is a broken link?

A Web page link only works as long as a file with the corresponding URL exists on the server. A nonfunctioning link is called a **broken link**. If a Webmaster moves, deletes, or changes the name of the requested file, the link will not function properly. If a link points to a nonexistent HTML document, your browser typically produces a 404 Page Not Found error. When a link points to a nonexistent graphic or other non-HTML format file, your browser typically displays a broken link icon (for example 🖻 or 🖻). When you see a response such as 404 Page Not Found error or a broken link icon, you know you have clicked a broken link.

It is the responsibility of Web page authors to check the links on their Web pages periodically to make sure they work. To test links, an author can click through them manually or use the link-checking feature of Web authoring software. Bad links must be removed or edited to reflect the correct URL for a destination page.

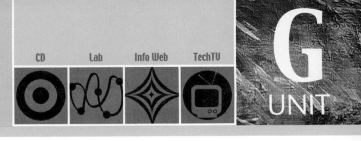

■ Instead of a text link, you can also use an image as a clickable link. These graphical links can connect to other Web pages or graphics. You might have encountered graphical links called **thumbnails** that expand in size when clicked. Graphical links can even look like buttons, complete with labels and icons. **Figure G-8** shows the HTML tag that creates a link using an image as the clickable object in a Web page. In this tag, the destination specifies a URL, usually the Web page that will appear as a result of clicking the link. The sports car image is the clickable link; the source for the sports car image is the file: sports car.jpg. When the link is clicked, the information contained in the file named features.html is displayed.

■ While browsing the Web, you have probably encountered graphics that are divided into several clickable areas. These images might be maps that allow you to click a geographic region to view a list of local attractions, businesses, or dealers. You also might encounter technical diagrams that link to information about the part that you click. You might even come across a Web site with a photo on the main page that is divided into areas representing different parts of the Web site.

A clickable map or diagram that has multiple "click points" for different parts of the map or diagram is referred to as an **image map**, and each of the links within the image map is sometimes referred to as a **hot spot**. See **Figure G-9**. To create an image map with a text editor, a Web page author uses a set of HTML tags that specify the coordinates and destination page for each clickable hot spot. A Web page authoring tool typically makes it easy to drag over an area of an image, then use menus and dialog boxes to specify the destination page for each hot spot.

Figure G-8: A graphic used as a link

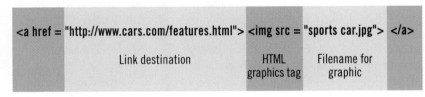

`<a href = "http://www.cars.com/features.html">`	`<img src = "sports car.jpg">`	`</a>`
Link destination	HTML graphics tag	Filename for graphic

Figure G-9: Web page with hot spots

Using Web page authoring software, hot spots can be defined by dragging over areas of the graphic; in this example, hot spots define areas of the solar system; clicking one of these hot spots displays information about that planet

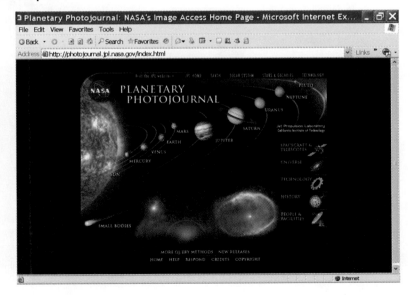

Courtesy NASA/JPL-Caltech

Explaining HTTP and Web servers

HTTP is a communications protocol that works in conjunction with the TCP/IP communications protocol to get Web resources to your computer. A **Web resource** is any data file that has a URL, such as an HTML document, a graphic, or a sound file. This lesson explains how HTTP works with Web servers to send and receive Web resources.

■ HTTP includes commands called **methods** that help browsers communicate with Web servers. GET is the most frequently used HTTP method and is typically used to retrieve the text and graphics files necessary for displaying a Web page. HTTP transports a request for a Web resource to a Web server, then transports the Web server's response back to a browser.

■ An HTTP communications transaction takes place over a pair of sockets. A **socket** is an abstract concept that represents one end of a connection. In an HTTP communications transaction, your browser opens a socket, connects to a similar open socket at the Web server, and issues a command like "GET an HTML document." The server receives the command, executes it, and sends a response back through the socket. The sockets are then closed until the

browser is ready to issue another command. **Figure G-10** illustrates how the messages flow between your browser and a Web server in order to retrieve an HTML document.

■ HTTP is classified as a **stateless protocol**, which generally allows one request and one response per session. As a result, your browser can request an HTML document during a session, but as soon as the document is sent, the session is closed, and the Web server does not retain the data that your browser ever made a request. To make additional requests, your browser must make another HTTP request. This is why assembling a complex Web page with several graphics, buttons, and sounds requires your browser to make many HTTP requests to the Web server.

Figure G-10: How HTTP messages flow between a browser and a Web server

1. The URL in the browser's Address bar contains the domain name of the Web server that your browser contacts

2. Your browser opens a socket and connects to a similar open socket at the Web server; next, your browser generates and sends an HTTP message through the socket

3. The server sends back the requested HTML document through the open sockets so you can view the page in your browser

4. After sending the response, the server closes its socket and the browser closes its socket

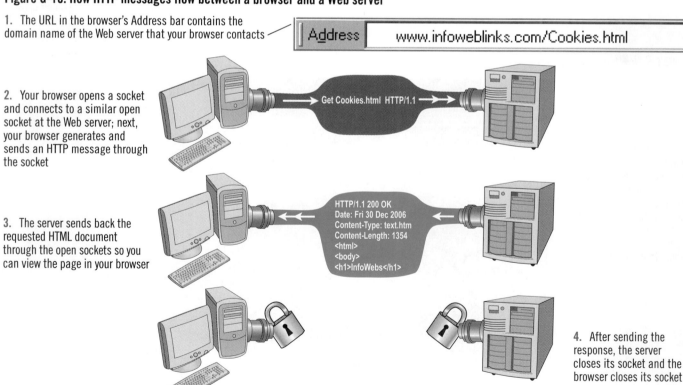

Address: www.infoweblinks.com/Cookies.html

Get Cookies.html HTTP/1.1

HTTP/1.1 200 OK
Date: Fri 30 Dec 2006
Content-Type: text.htm
Content-Length: 1354
<html>
<body>
<h1>InfoWebs</h1>

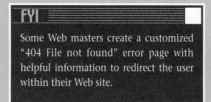
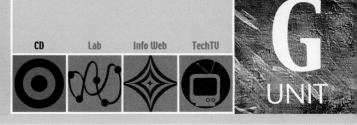

CD   Lab   Info Web   TechTU

G UNIT

■ A Web server's response to a browser's request includes an **HTTP status code** that indicates whether or not the browser's request can be fulfilled. You may have encountered the "404 Not Found" message that a browser displays when a Web server sends a 404 status code to indicate that the requested resource does not exist. Common HTTP status codes are summarized in **Table G-2**. Excessive demand can occur when special circumstances attract people to a Web site or when a worm launches a denial-of-service attack. When traffic exceeds capacity, a Web server can take a long time to fulfill Web page requests—some requests might even produce a "page not found" error.

Table G-2: Common HTTP status codes

CODE	MESSAGE	DESCRIPTION
200	OK	The request succeeded, and the resulting resource was sent
301	Moved Permanently	The resource was moved
302	Moved Temporarily	The resource is temporarily unavailable
303	See Other	The resource moved to another URL and should be automatically retrieved by the client
404	Not Found	The requested resource does not exist
500	Server Error	An unexpected server error, such as encountering a scripting error, occurred

■ A Web server is configured to include HTTP software, which is always running when the server is up and ready to fulfill requests. One of the server's ports is dedicated to listening for HTTP requests. When a request arrives, the server software analyzes the request and takes whatever action is necessary to fulfill it. The computer that runs Web server software might have other software running on it as well. For example, a computer might operate as a Web server, an e-mail server, and an FTP (File Transfer Protocol) server all at the same time! To handle these diverse duties efficiently, a computer devotes one port to HTTP requests (usually Port 80), another to handling SMTP e-mail (usually Port 25, or for Post Office Protocol e-mail, usually port 110), and a third to FTP requests (usually Port 20 or 21).

■ The way that a computer allocates one port to each service helps explain how it is possible for a Web service to be down when the Web server is still up and running. A Web server runs separate software for each service it offers. As long as the right software is running, the service is available.

■ A single port on a Web server can connect to many sockets carrying requests from browsers. The number of socket connections a port can handle depends on the server's memory and operating system, but at minimum, hundreds of requests can be handled at the same time. Most Web server software can be configured so that the server responds to requests addressed to more than one IP address or domain name. In such a case, one computer running one Web server program can act like multiple Web sites. This type of shared hosting is typically supplied to small Web sites that do not have enough traffic to justify the cost of a dedicated server.

■ Some large-volume sites, such as yahoo.com and amazon.com, have more traffic than any single Web server can handle. These sites tend to use a group of multiple servers, also known as a **server farm**, to handle the thousands of requests that come in each second. See **Figure G-11**.

Figure G-11: A server farm

Large-volume Web sites often use a server farm to handle thousands of Web page requests

Introducing Web page authoring

With today's Web page authoring tools, it is easy to create your own Web pages. You have several choices when it comes to Web page authoring tools. In this lesson, you will explore these different tools and get an overview of the basic components of a Web page.

■ At the most basic level, you can use a text editor such as NotePad to create Web pages. A **text editor** creates a plain text ASCII document with no hidden formatting codes. See **Figure G-12**. The only codes included in a document created with a text editor are the HTML tags you type, along with the text that you want your browser to display. Typed HTML codes produce various formats and effects.

When you save the document you create with a text editor, you must specify an appropriate filename extension, such as .htm or .html so that browsers will recognize it as an HTML document. If you want to create Web pages using a text editor, you will need a good HTML reference source for the HTML code.

■ Another way to create Web pages is to use the HTML conversion option included with many software applications. Microsoft Office applications, for example, allow you to create a standard file, such as a spreadsheet, document, or presentation, and then use the File menu's Save As Web Page option to convert the file into HTML format. To discover whether an application has an HTML option, click File on the menu bar, then click Save As or click Export. Converting a document into HTML format sometimes produces unexpected results because some of the features and formatting in your original document might not translate well into HTML format.

■ You can also create Web pages using online template-like Web page authoring tools provided by some ISPs and other companies that host Web pages. Working with these tools is typically quite simple. You type, select, drag, and drop elements onto a Web page. These simple tools are great for beginners, but they sometimes omit features that are included with more sophisticated authoring tools.

■ The most sophisticated way to create Web pages is to use a special category of software called **Web authoring software**, which provides tools specifically designed to enter and format Web page text, graphics, and links. Most Web authoring software includes features that help you manage an entire Web site, in addition to creating single Web pages. Web site management tools include the capability to link the pages within a site automatically and to easily change those links. They are also capable of checking all external links at a site to make sure that they still link to valid Web pages. Popular Web authoring software packages include Microsoft FrontPage (see **Figure G-13**) and Macromedia Dreamweaver.

■ The HTML document for a Web page is divided into two sections: the head and the body. If you create an HTML document using a text editor, you must manually enter the tags that begin and end these two sections. Refer again to **Figure G-12** to see the head and body tags. If you use Web authoring software, these tags are automatically entered for you.

Figure G-12: Notepad as a Web page authoring tool

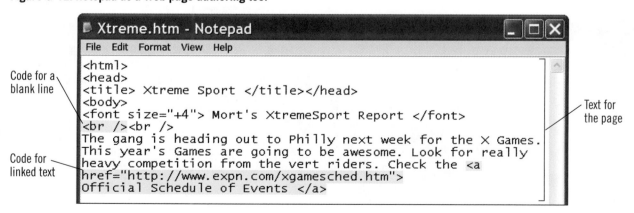

Code for a blank line

Code for linked text

Text for the page

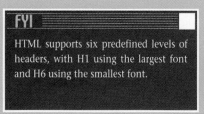
HTML supports six predefined levels of headers, with H1 using the largest font and H6 using the smallest font.

CD   Lab   Info Web   TechTV

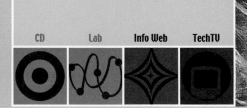

G
UNIT

Figure G-13: Web authoring software

When creating a Web page, you can type text without worrying about HTML tags; to format words, phrases, or paragraphs, simply use the formatting buttons on the toolbars

In HTML view, you can see all the HTML tags that were inserted into your text as a result of clicking the formatting buttons

In Normal view (shown here), the FrontPage window displays your Web page similar to how it will appear in a browser window

If you've done any word processing with Microsoft Word, most of the controls on the FrontPage toolbars should look familiar

■ The **head section** begins with the <head> HTML tag and contains information that defines some global properties for the document; this information it is not displayed by your browser. Information in the head section of an HTML document can include the title of your page as it will appear in the title bar of your browser window, global formatting information, information about your page that can be used by search engines, and scripts that add interactivity to your page.

■ The **body section** of an HTML document begins with the <body> HTML tag. It contains the text that you want the browser to display, the HTML tags that format the text, plus a variety of links, including links to graphics, other Web pages, and so on.

■ A **Web page header** or header is a subtitle shown in a different font size or color than the normal text on the page.

■ Other common characteristics of Web pages include navigation tools such as scroll bars and navigation bars, hyperlinks such as hypertext or graphics, Web page components such as search features, visual elements such as graphics, and multimedia elements such as video, audio, and animation.

■ Whether you create Web pages using a very basic text editor or a very sophisticated Web authoring program, all Web pages have common characteristics. **Figure G-14** illustrates the basic components of a typical Web page.

Figure G-14: Elements of a typical Web page

Web page title

Theme elements

Graphics

Graphic link

Text link

Navigation links

Body

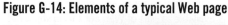
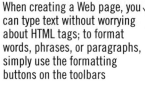

Enhancing Web pages

Web pages consist of visual elements that enhance the way the information is conveyed. Whether you are creating a single Web page or a Web site with several pages, it is important that these visual elements have a consistent look and feel. This lesson discusses styles, style sheets, themes, and sound and graphics that can enhance Web pages and create visual consistency.

■ A **style** is a combination of attributes—colors, sizes, and fonts—that specify the way text is displayed. When working with Web page authoring software, you can simply highlight the text that you want to format and select the formatting attributes from a list. When you create Web pages with a text editor, you can format text by inserting the appropriate HTML tags. **Table G-3** provides a list of basic HTML formatting tags.

Table G-3: Examples of HTML formatting tags

TAG	USE
<font size="xxx">	Specify a font size by inserting a number between the quotation marks
<font color="color">	Specify a color name or number between the quotation marks
<b> </b>	Bold text inserted between tags
<i> </i>	Italicize text inserted between tags
<u> </u>	Underline text inserted between tags
<align="direction">	Specify paragraph alignment by inserting right, center, or left between the quotation marks
<bgcolor="color">	Specify a background color for the entire page

■ A **style sheet**, also called a **cascading style sheet (CSS)**, acts as a template to control the layout and design of Web pages. Style sheets work in conjunction with HTML tags to make it easy to globally and consistently change the format of elements in a Web page. They allow Web page authors to separate the format specifications for an element from the element itself. A style sheet allows you simply to define the style for an element, such as a price list, one time, at the beginning of the HTML document. The style can then be applied by using a single HTML tag (if you are using a text editor) or by selecting the format from a list (if you are using Web page authoring software). You can also set up an **external style sheet** that contains formatting specifications for a group of Web pages. All Web pages in a Web site can use the external style sheet by means of a link placed in their head sections.

■ Style sheets make it easy to apply styles and change them consistently. For example, if you define the style for prices in a price list as centered, italic, and red, then every time this style is applied to the prices in a price list they will be centered, italic, and red. If later you decide to change the style associated with prices to different specifications, such as right-aligned, bold, and blue, you change the specifications for the prices style once in the style sheet, not each time the prices style is used. Changing the style in the style sheet causes the change to cascade through the entire Web page or Web site so that all occurrences associated with the prices style are changed.

■ In addition to styles, themes are often used to enhance Web pages. A **theme** is a collection of coordinated graphics, colors, and fonts applied to individual pages or all pages in a Web site. Themes are generally available as part of Web authoring software.

What are XML, XSL, Java, and ActiveX controls?

As you become more familiar with creating Web pages, you will discover many tools including programming languages that are available to help you create the look, feel, and features you want for your Web site. Among the resources you can use are XML, XSL, Java, and VBScript. Briefly defined, **XML (Extensible Markup Language)** is a method for putting structured data, such as spreadsheet cells or database records, into a text file. XML uses tags and attributes to mark a file to define fields of data. **XSL (Extensible Stylesheet Language)** is a technology that is similar to XML, but it can be used to create customized tags that control how the data displays in an XML document.

Java is a high-level programming language for Web-based projects. Small Java applications are called **Java applets** that a browser downloads and runs on a computer to perform specialized tasks. **JavaScript** and **VBScript** are popular scripting languages. Scripting languages allow Web pages to become more interactive and to incorporate activities that would otherwise require a computer program. For example, scripts enable e-commerce sites to verify credit card information. For security reasons, Java applets cannot open, modify, delete, or create files on a computer, make any network connections (except to the originating site), and they cannot start other programs.

An **ActiveX control** is a compiled computer program that can be referenced from within an HTML document, downloaded, installed on a computer, and executed within the browser window. Programmers and Web page authors use programming languages, such as C++ and Visual Basic, to create these controls, which can be applied in a wide variety of ways to make Web pages interactive.

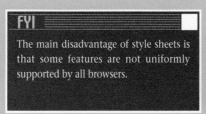
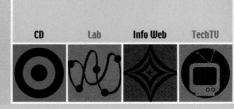

■ You can enhance Web pages by including sound files. The Web page can show a pop-up window containing sound controls, or the music can play in the background. The <a href> tag is used to create a link that visitors can click to hear the sound. You can use the <embed> tag to attach a sound file that starts to play "background sound" as soon as a browser displays the Web page.

■ Another way to enhance Web pages is through the use of graphics. The HTML document that your browser receives does not contain any graphics, but it does contain an HTML tag that references a graphic. If you use a text editor to create a Web page, you must enter the complete tag manually. For example, the tag <img src = "truck.gif"> includes the filename for the truck.gif graphic. When using Web page authoring software, you typically use a menu option to select the graphic from a list of files that are stored on your computer. **Figure G-15** illustrates how you insert a graphic when creating a Web page using FrontPage. Most of the graphics used for Web pages are stored in **GIF (Graphics Interchange Format)**, **JPEG (Joint Photographics Experts Group)**, or **PNG (Portable Network Graphics)** format. Keeping graphics files small helps Web pages download and appear quickly in the browser window.

■ Video is also used to enhance Web pages. Popular video formats, such as **QuickTime**, **MPEG**, and **AVI**, are used for Web-based and disk-based video playback. Variations of these formats are specially designed to handle the communications details for Web playback. To play video, your computer needs corresponding player software, usually specified at the Web site.

Figure G-15: Inserting a graphic in a Web page

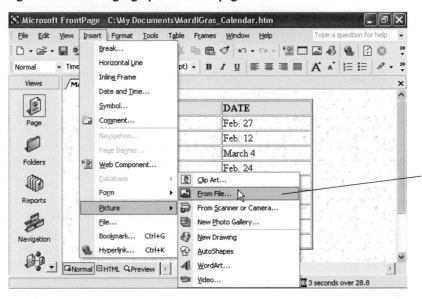

Click Insert on the menu bar, point to Picture, click From File to view a list of graphics stored on your hard disk, then select the one you want to use

Animating graphics

An *animated GIF* is a graphic file that consists of a sequence of frames or related images. When an animated GIF is displayed, your browser cycles through the frames, resulting in a simple, repeating animation. Animated GIFs are one of the easiest ways to add simple animation to a Web page. For example, the spacecraft shown in **Figure G-16** spins when clicked.

You can also use *Flash animation*, which is a proprietary technology developed by Macromedia. You have to download the Flash client software which is free and required for viewing Flash animation. Flash provides more flexibility than animated GIFs and can be used for more complex animations.

Figure G-16

Organizing Web pages

Tables and frames are tools you can use to help organize areas of text or graphics on a Web page. This lesson explains how to use tables and frames to layout the content on a Web page. Once you have finished your pages, you must test and publish them. **Table G-4** provides the basic steps for testing and publishing Web pages.

Table G-4: Steps for testing and publishing Web pages

STEPS	DESCRIPTION
Test each page locally	You must test your Web page locally to verify that every element is displayed correctly by any browsers that might be used by visitors to your Web page. You can accomplish this task without connecting to the Web. Simply open a browser, then enter the local filename for the HTML document that you created for your Web page. Because your hard disk drive is much faster than a dial-up connection, the text and graphics for your Web page will appear faster during your local test than when viewed over the Internet.
Transfer pages to a Web server	Whether you are publishing a single page, a series of pages, or an entire Web site, you must put your pages on a Web server. Although Web server software is available for your home computer, you probably will not want to leave your computer continually linked to the Internet. Instead, you should look for a Web hosting site that will host your pages, usually for a monthly fee.
Review all content and test all links	After you publish your pages on a Web server, make sure that all content appears as expected. Be sure to test the links between your pages, as well as the links to pages on other sites.
Update your site to keep it current	Periodically, you should review the information on your Web pages and verify that the links still connect to existing Web pages. You can easily change your pages and then test them offline before reposting them.

■ A **Web page table** (usually referred to simply as a "table") is a grid of cells that can be used as a layout tool for specifying the placement of text and graphics on a Web page. Tables are an important part of Web page design because HTML does not include a formatting feature for multiple columns. Without tables, authors have less control over the position of text and graphics displayed in the browser window. The effectiveness of tables is illustrated in **Figure G-17**, where one Web page uses tables and the other page does not.

Figure G-17: Using tables

This Web page uses a table to position graphics and text

Without a table, this Web page simply displays text and graphics in a single column

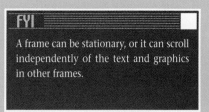
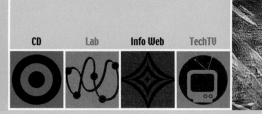
FYI

A frame can be stationary, or it can scroll independently of the text and graphics in other frames.

■ Web tables provide Web page designers with flexibility. For example, the table cells can contain text or graphics; columns and rows in a table can be different sizes. Individual cells can be sized according to the material they contain and their contents can be formatted individually. Many Web page designers put the entire contents of a Web page into one table.

■ Tables are easy to use, whether you create them with Web authoring software or with word processing software that converts documents into HTML format. You simply define the number of columns and rows for a table, then specify the size for each row and each column. You can merge two or more cells to create a larger cell, or you can split a cell to make smaller cells.

Creating tables with a text editor is more of a challenge. You use HTML tags to specify the beginning of the table, each row, and each cell in the row. What makes this task difficult is that you cannot see the table as you construct it. To view the table, you must preview your Web page using your browser.

■ In addition to Web tables, some designers use frames to create Web pages. An **HTML frame** (or simply "frame") scrolls independently of other parts of the Web page. The main advantage of frames is the ability to display multiple documents at once. A typical use of frames, shown in **Figure G-18**, is to display a stationary banner at the top of a page and a set of links on the left side of the screen that do not move as you scroll through the main text on the Web page.

Figure G-18: Using frames

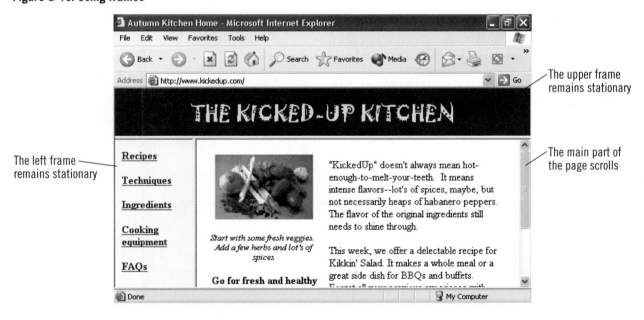

The upper frame remains stationary

The left frame remains stationary

The main part of the page scrolls

How does an HTML form work?

An **HTML form** (or "form") is a series of fill-in blanks created using the HTML <form> and <input> tags. Forms are used to collect user input for payment and shipping information in the checkout procedure of e-commerce orders, site registrations, opinion polls, and so on. See **Figure G-19**.

The information you enter into an HTML form is held in the memory of your computer, where your browser creates temporary storage bins that correspond to the input field names designated by the form's HTML tags. When you click a Submit button, your browser gathers the data from memory and sends it to a specially designated program on an HTTP server, where it can be processed and stored.

Figure G-19

Introducing e-commerce

The Internet was first opened to commercial use in 1991. Since that date, thousands of business Web sites have been posted, making online shopping a popular Web activity. The economics of the Web go beyond retail catalogs; even small businesses, individual artists, and isolated craftspeople can post Web pages that display their wares.

■ **E-commerce** is used to describe financial transactions conducted over a computer network. E-commerce activities include shopping, auctions, and stock trading. E-commerce includes many kinds of physical products (such as clothing and books), digital products (such as music, video, and software), and services (such as travel, Web hosting, and distance learning).

■ E-commerce activities fall into different categories depending on the seller and buyer. Most of the e-commerce activities that the typical Web surfer uses are classified as **B2C (business-to-consumer)** e-commerce. In the B2C model, businesses supply goods and services to individual consumers. In the **C2C (consumer-to-consumer)** e-commerce model, consumers sell to each other. This model includes online auctions and rummage sales. **B2B (business-to-business)** e-commerce involves one business buying goods or services from another business. **B2G (business-to-government)** e-commerce aims to help businesses sell to governments.

■ E-commerce seems simple from the perspective of a shopper who simply enters the URL for an online store in the browser address bar, connects to the online store, browses the text and images in the Web page catalog, selects merchandise, and then pays for it. Behind the scenes, e-commerce is based on a Web site and technologies that track shoppers' selections, collect payment data, guard customers' privacy, and protect credit card numbers. An e-commerce site usually includes some mechanism for customers to select merchandise and then pay for it. Most e-commerce businesses use as much automation as possible; their order-processing systems automatically update inventories, and then print packing slips and mailing labels. **Figure G-20** shows a typical e-commerce Web site home page.

Figure G-20: E-commerce Web site home page

You can find items by browsing through the catalog or by searching for specific items

A shopping cart keeps track of the merchandise you want to purchase; as you browse, you can drop items into your electronic shopping cart; at the checkout counter, you enter the information necessary to pay for the items you selected

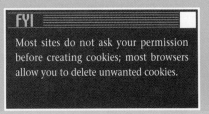 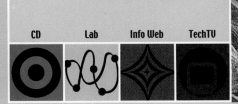 

CD   Lab   Info Web   TechTU

G

UNIT

■ An **online shopping cart** is a cyberspace version of the cart that you wheel around a store and fill with merchandise. Most shopping carts work by using cookies to store information about your activities on a Web site. A **cookie** is data generated by a Web server and stored in a text file on your computer. Cookies allow a Web site to store information on a client computer for later retrieval. Cookies can also be used to store information necessary to keep track of your preferences and activities while visiting a Web site. The cookie information can include a customer number, a shopping cart number, a part number, or any other data. An e-commerce site might use cookies as a storage bin for all of the items that you load into your shopping cart. Refer to **Figure G-21**.

Figure G-21: Storing shopping cart items in a cookie

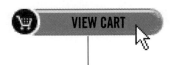

1. When you click the ADD TO CART button, the merchant's server sends a message to your browser to add that item number to the cookie, which is stored on your computer

ITEM #B7655

2. When you check out, the server asks your browser for all of the cookie data that pertains to your shopping cart items

3. Your browser sends those cookies along with a request for an order summary

Your order:
1 Blender   29.95
1 Wok   38.49

4. The Web server uses the cookies to produce a Web page listing the items you want to purchase

■ E-commerce enhances traditional business models by offering efficiency and opportunities for automation and computerization. As with a traditional "brick and mortar" business in a physical location, profit in an e-commerce business is the difference between income and expenses. E-commerce increases profit margins by cutting costs.

■ E-commerce merchants also gain income by hosting advertising space for banner and pop-up ads. A **banner ad** is an advertisement, typically embedded at the top of a Web page. A **pop-up ad** is an advertisement that appears in a separate window when you enter a Web site or connect to Web pages. See **Figure G-22**. When you click a banner or pop-up ad, your browser connects directly to the advertiser's Web site, where you can find product information and make a purchase. Banner and pop-up ads earn revenue for hosting merchants based on **click-through rate**—the number of times that site visitors click the ad to connect to the advertiser's site. The hosting merchant is paid a small fee for each click through. Click-through rates have declined in recent years because most consumers simply ignore the ads or install ad-blocking software to prevent ads from appearing on their screens.

Figure G-22: A pop-up ad

Pop-up ads appear as separate windows

Securing e-commerce transactions

After you wheel your cyber shopping cart over to the checkout line, you must verify the items you plan to purchase and you must pay for the merchandise online before your transaction can be completed. This lesson explores secure transactions and some of the ways you pay for merchandise and services you purchase on the Web.

■ Customers often worry about the security of their online transactions. They want to be sure their credit card and other personal information is secure. Several encryption technologies are used to secure online transactions. **Encryption** is the science of coding data. You will learn more about encryption in the Tech Talk in this unit.

■ A **packet sniffer** (also called a "protocol analyzer") is a computer program that monitors data as it travels over networks. A packet sniffer can observe and open any packet traveling on the network. Packet sniffers have legitimate uses in system maintenance, but hackers can also use them to pilfer data as it travels from customers' computers to e-commerce sites. To protect your data, you should engage in electronic transactions only over a secure connection. A **secure connection** encrypts the data transmitted between your computer and a Web site. Even if a hacker can capture the packets containing your payment data, this data must be decrypted before it can be used for illicit purposes. Technologies that create secure connections include SSL and S-HTTP.

■ **SSL (Secure Sockets Layer)** protocol encrypts the data that travels between a client computer and an HTTP server. This encryption protocol creates an SSL connection using a specially designated port, typically Port 443 rather than Port 80, which is used for unsecured HTTP communication. You will notice https: instead of http: in the URL of Web pages that provide an SSL connection.

■ **S-HTTP (secure HTTP)** is an extension of HTTP that encrypts the text of an HTTP message before it is sent. Although SSL and S-HTTP both use encryption techniques to transmit data securely, they are technically different. Whereas SSL creates a secure connection between a client and a server over which any amount of data can be sent securely, S-HTTP is designed simply to encrypt and transmit an individual message. From the consumer's perspective, however, either one of these security measures can do an excellent job of protecting the data you send over the Internet. Your browser helps you identify when you are using a secure connection. See **Figure G-23**.

Figure G-23: Identifying secure connections

When a secure connection is about to be activated, your browser usually displays a dialog box, such as this Security Alert

While a secure connection is active, the URL begins with *https://* and the status bar typically displays a padlock icon

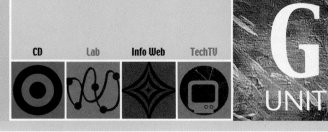

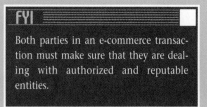
CD   Lab   Info Web   TechTV

- **SET (Secure Electronic Transaction)** is a security method that relies on cryptography and digital certificates to ensure that transactions are legitimate and secure. Consumers want to make sure that a merchant is legitimate. Merchants want to make sure that the credit card charges are authorized by the card's rightful owner. A **digital certificate** is a specially coded electronic attachment to a file that verifies the identity of its source. SET uses digital certificates and secure connections to transfer consumers' credit card numbers directly to a credit card processing service for verification.

- An **electronic wallet** (also called a digital wallet) is software that stores and handles the information a customer submits when finalizing an e-commerce purchase. It typically holds your name, shipping address, and the number, expiration date, and billing address for one or more credit cards. It might also hold a digital certificate that verifies your identity. You can create an electronic wallet by subscribing at the wallet provider's site. See **Figure G-24**. Most wallets implement SET. Even if a hacker gains access to your wallet file, the data it contains will be difficult to decode. Your wallet is protected by a password, which acts as a PIN to prevent unauthorized use.

Figure G-24: An electronic wallet

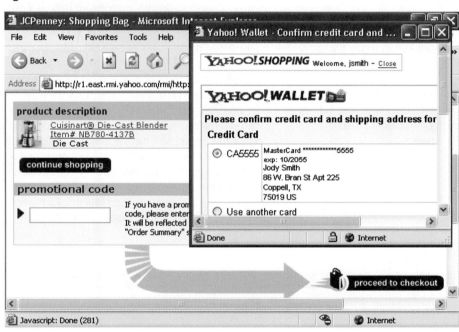

When you proceed to an online checkout, software on the merchant's server sends an HTTP message to your PC that looks for and activates compatible wallet software; by clicking a Submit button, your payment data is transferred from your electronic wallet to the server

Understanding transaction privacy and security

Web sites can secretly collect data about your browsing and purchasing habits. Merchants who market goods and services are eager to get the attention of prospective customers, but they sometimes use spyware that has the potential to compromise your privacy. In the context of the Web and e-commerce, spyware is any technology that secretly gathers information and relays it to advertisers or other interested parties. Web-based marketers use several spyware techniques, including ad-serving cookies and clear GIFs.

When you connect to a Web site, you expect it to store an innocuous cookie on your computer's hard disk. Some Web sites, however, feature banner ads supplied by third-party marketing firms. If you click the ad, this third party can create an ad-serving cookie and use it to track your activities at any site containing banner ads from that third party. The marketing firms that distribute ad-serving cookies maintain that this data is

simply used to select and display ads that might interest you, but privacy advocates are worried that shopper profiles can be compiled, sold, and used for unauthorized purposes.

A clear GIF or "Web bug" is typically a 1x1 pixel graphic on a Web page. Clear GIFs can be used to send cookies to third party Web sites. Unlike ad-serving cookies, you do not have to click a banner ad to receive a GIF-activated cookie. Simply viewing the page that contains a clear GIF sets the cookie. Cookies created with clear GIFs have the same uses and potential for misuse as ad-serving cookies.

Several software products are designed to block ad-serving cookies, clear GIFs, and other spyware—some even block banner and pop-up ads altogether. These products are quite popular, despite their tendency to slow the browser's response time slightly.

Avoiding fraud when shopping online

Fraud is a serious concern. Stolen credit card numbers can be used without the proper authorization. You may find yourself a victim of fraud even if you shop using traditional stores or through phone order services. Computers store credit card and shopping information for all businesses. This lesson explores several ways you might be the victim of fraud and how to protect yourself when shopping.

■ Security-conscious e-commerce merchants protect their databases by limiting access and encrypting data. Unfortunately, not all businesses follow these practices. Even when databases seem secure, hackers might find security holes and retrieve sensitive data. In fact, an increasing number of businesses report that their customer databases have been accessed without authorization. In some cases, thousands of credit card numbers have been stolen.

■ Secure connections differ from secure Web sites. A secure connection encrypts the data transmitted between your computer and a Web site. A secure Web site, such as an online banking site, uses password security to prevent unauthorized access to pages on the site. As a consumer, you cannot prevent database break-ins, but you can take steps to ensure that the credit card number stored in a merchant's database is of little use to a hacker.

■ An online break-in into the database of a merchant or credit card processing service is a fairly high-tech crime, but your credit card number can be compromised by low-tech methods as well. If a merchant collects your credit card number instead of routing it

directly to a credit card processing service, a dishonest employee who works for the merchant might be able to obtain your card number while processing your order. Individual consumers cannot do much to prevent this type of theft, but the likelihood of it occurring is low—you take a similar risk every time you pay for a meal by allowing a waiter to take your credit card back to a cashier station or give your credit card number over the phone.

■ A fake storefront appears to be an online store, but it is in fact a fraudulent Web site, designed exclusively for the purpose of collecting credit card numbers from unwary shoppers. These sites might have all the trappings of a real e-commerce site—they might even offer a secure connection for transmitting your credit card number. When your data is received, however, it is stored in a database that belongs to a hacker, who can use the data for illegitimate transactions. The URLs for fake storefronts often differ from the real thing by a single character. For example, hackers might create a fake storefront using the URL *www.ediebauer.com*—similar to the legitimate store at *www.eddiebauer.com*. See **Figure G-25** to see how you can use a search engine to protect yourself from fake storefronts.

Figure G-25: Avoiding fake storefronts

In a search engine such as Google, even if you mistype the store name, you can use the link provided to reach the site's home page

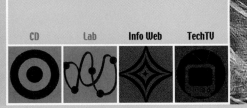

CD   Lab   Info Web   TechTV

■ Several credit card companies offer one-time-use credit card numbers, which allow consumers to make purchases while keeping their actual card numbers hidden. A one-time-use credit card number works for a single online purchase. Your credit card company tracks the purchases you incur with one-time-use numbers and adds the charges to your monthly credit card statement. One-time-use numbers cannot be used twice, so even if a hacker steals the number, it will not be accepted for any online or offline purchases.

■ A **person-to-person payment** (sometimes called an on-line payment) offers an alternative to credit cards. It can be used to pay for auction items and to wire money over the Internet. A service called PayPal pioneered person-to-person payments and has since been copied by several other service providers. The process begins when you open an account at a person-to-person payment service. As with a checking account, you deposit some money in your account by using your credit card. You receive a user ID and password that allows you to access your account to make purchases and deposit additional funds. Money can be sent to anyone who has an e-mail account, as shown in **Figure G-26**.

Figure G-26: Person-to-person payment service

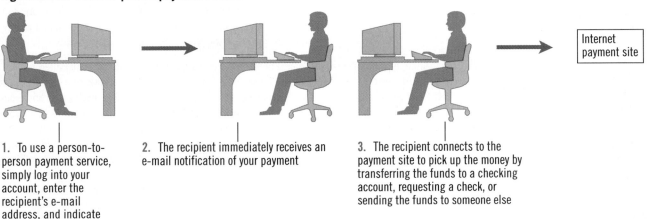

1. To use a person-to-person payment service, simply log into your account, enter the recipient's e-mail address, and indicate the payment amount

2. The recipient immediately receives an e-mail notification of your payment

3. The recipient connects to the payment site to pick up the money by transferring the funds to a checking account, requesting a check, or sending the funds to someone else

Internet payment site

How safe are cookies?

Cookies are a relatively safe technology and have several important privacy features. A cookie is data, not a computer program or script, so while a cookie is sent to your computer and stored there, it cannot be executed to activate a virus or worm. In addition, only the site that created the cookie can access it. Finally, a cookie can contain only as much information as you disclose while using the Web site that sets the cookie. For example, a cookie cannot rummage through your hard disk to find the password for your e-mail account, the number for your checking account, or the PIN number for your credit card. However, if you enter your credit card number in the process of making an online purchase, it is possible for the cookie to store that number. Most reputable Web sites do not store such sensitive information; you can read a Web site's privacy policy for more information on this important privacy and security topic.

Most browsers allow you to set your security level to block cookies. On many Web sites, cookies are the only mechanism available for tracking your activity or remembering your purchases. If you set the security level to block cookies, then you will not be able to access all the activities when you visit these Web sites.

A more sophisticated approach to cookie security is provided by **P3P (Platform for Privacy Preferences Project)**, which defines a standard set of security tags that become part of the HTTP header for every cookie. This header, called a **Compact Privacy Policy**, describes how cookie data is used by a Web site. Based on your security preferences, your browser can use this header data to decide whether or not to accept the cookie. Compact Privacy Policy headers are supported by recent versions of browsers.

Cookies can be deleted from your hard drive automatically or you can delete them manually. To delete cookies automatically, you let the cookie expire. When a cookie reaches the end of its predefined lifetime, your browser simply erases it. A cookie is programmed to time out by the Web site's developer. To delete cookies manually, you must know where the cookies are stored on your hard drive.

Tech Talk Encryption

Encryption is one of the most important technologies for maintaining your privacy and the security of important information, such as your credit card number. Encryption makes a message illegible to unauthorized users, and is designed to keep messages secret. Its purpose, therefore, is quite different from simple coding schemes, such as ASCII and EBCDIC, which are designed to transform data into formats that are publicly known and shared.

An original message that has not yet been encrypted is referred to as **plaintext** or cleartext. An encrypted message is referred to as **ciphertext**. The process of converting plaintext into ciphertext is called **encryption**. Reconverting ciphertext to plaintext is called **decryption**. In an e-commerce transaction, for example, your credit card number exists as plaintext, which is encrypted into ciphertext for its journey over a secure connection to the merchant. When the ciphertext arrives at its destination, it is decrypted back into the original plaintext credit card number.

Messages are encrypted using a cryptographic algorithm and key. A **cryptographic algorithm** is a specific procedure for encrypting or decrypting a message. A **cryptographic key** (usually just called a key) is a word, number, or phrase that must be known in order to encrypt or decrypt a message. An encryption method called simple substitution uses a transformation table like the one in **Figure G-27** to encrypt or decrypt messages.

Figure G-27: Simple substitution

Ciphertext letters:

D E F **G** H I J K L M N O P Q R S T U V W X Y Z A B C

Equivalent plaintext letters:

A B C **D** E F G H I J K L M N O P Q R S T U V W X Y Z

The simple substitution key is an example of **weak encryption**, because it is easy to decrypt even without the algorithm and key. **Strong encryption** is generally considered to be very difficult to break. Of course, with continuous advances in technology, strong encryption is a moving target. For example, several encryption methods that were considered impossible to break 10 years ago have recently been cracked using networks of personal computers. The encryption methods that are used for most e-commerce transactions are considered strong but not unbreakable. Unauthorized decryption is sometimes referred to as breaking or cracking a code.

Encryption methods can be broken by the use of expensive, specialized, code-breaking computers. The cost of these machines is substantial, but not beyond the reach of government agencies, major corporations, and organized crime. Encryption methods can also be broken by standard computer hardware—supercomputers, mainframes, workstations, and even personal computers. These computers typically break codes using a **brute force method**, which consists of trying all possible combinations.

Suppose that a criminal steals an ATM card. The card cannot be used, however, without the correct PIN. A four-digit PIN could be one of 10,000 possible combinations. If you are mathematically inclined, you will realize that each digit of the PIN could be one of 10 possibilities: 0, 1, 2, 3, 4, 5, 6, 7, 8, or 9, so 10^4 or 10x10x10x10 possible PINs exist. To discover a PIN number by brute force, a criminal must try, at most, 10,000 possibilities. Although it would take a person quite a long time to figure out and try all 10,000 possibilities, a computer could polish them off as quickly as the ATM would accept them.

The length of a computer-readable encryption key is measured in bits. Unlike the PIN example in which each digit could be one of 10 possible numbers, in a computer-readable encryption key, each digit can be one of two possible numbers: 0 or 1. Figuring out how many numbers you must try to break a computer code requires a calculation using powers of two rather than powers of 10. A 32-bit key, therefore, could be one of about 4.2 billion (2^{32}) numbers. Surprisingly, it would be possible to try all these numbers and discover the key in less than a day by using an average personal computer. To discover a 40-bit key, you would have to try about 1 trillion possible combinations—a week's worth of processing time on a personal computer. Two other encryption methods are 56-bit and 64-bit encryption. Once thought to be unbreakable by any computer in the private sector, 56-bit and 64-bit encryption methods require a lot of computing power, but have been broken by combining the power of many personal computers connected over the Internet. Most encryption today uses a 128-bit key; 128-bit encryption and 256-bit encryption are probably secure for several years. Another way to understand how the length of a key affects the strength of encryption is to consider this guideline: Beginning with a 40-bit key, each additional bit doubles the time it would take to discover the key. If a personal computer takes one week to crack a 40-bit key, it takes two weeks to crack a 41-bit key, four weeks to crack a 42-bit key, and eight weeks to crack a 43-bit key. A 128-bit key takes an unfathomable amount of time to crack. In fact the number used to describe the time it would take is larger than the estimated age of the universe.

The simple substitution encryption method is an example of **symmetric key encryption**, which is also called secret key or conventional encryption. With symmetric key encryption, the same key used to encrypt a message is also used to decrypt a message. Symmetric key encryption is often used to encrypt stationary data, such as corporate financial records. It is not, however, a very desirable encryption method for data that is on the move. The person who encrypts the data must get the key to the person who decrypts the data, without the key falling into the wrong hands. On a computer network, key distribution is a major security problem because of the potential for interception.

To eliminate the key-distribution problem, Whitfield Diffie and Martin Helman introduced a concept called **public key encryption (PKE)** in 1975. It uses asymmetric key encryption, in which one key is used to encrypt a message, but another key is used to decrypt the message. **Figure G-28** illustrates how public key encryption works. Public key encryption is a crucial technology for the Web and e-commerce. When you use an SSL (secure socket layer) connection to transmit your credit

card number, the server sends a public key to your browser, which uses this public key to encrypt the credit card number. Once encrypted, no one can use this public key to decrypt the message. The encrypted message is sent to the Web server, where the private key is used to decrypt it.

RSA (named for its inventors—Ron Rivest, Adi Shamir, and Leonard Adleman) is the most commonly used public key encryption algorithm. In addition to being the technology used for SSL connections, RSA is used to encrypt the data in most digital certificates. **DES (Data Encryption Standard)** is an encryption method based on an algorithm developed by IBM and the U.S. National Security Agency. It uses 56-bit symmetric key encryption. Although it was once the cornerstone of government encryption, DES is being replaced by AES, which offers stronger encryption. **AES (Advanced Encryption Standard)** is an encryption standard that uses three key sizes of 128, 192, or 256 bits. It is based on the Rijndael (pronounced "rain doll") encryption algorithm.

Figure G-28: Public key encryption

1. James sends the *public* key to JoBeth

2. JoBeth uses the public key to encrypt a message, which she sends back to James

If the message is intercepted by Draco, he cannot decrypt the message because he does not have the private key

3. James can decrypt the message using his *private* key

Computers in Context Politics

The word "politicians" conjures up images of candidates vying for votes during an election campaign, paid political advertising, and personal appearances. However, the Web has added a new dimension to today's political campaigns. Information technology, such as Web sites and e-mail, has become a valuable supplement to traditional campaign tools. According to Bruce Bimber, Director of the Center for Information Technology and Society at the University of California, Santa Barbara, "Rather than creating political attention as television can do, the Web serves to engage and sustain those already attentive."

Internet anthropologists credit Republican presidential candidate Bob Dole with using technology first when he announced the URL of his campaign Web site during a 1994 televised debate. These days, few campaigns would be complete without a Web site containing position statements and an easy way for supporters to donate money. A few candidates have experimented with mass e-mail solicitations, based on demographic databases similar to those telemarketers use. Because many voters view unsolicited e-mail as "spam," however, political strategists believe this approach is more likely to backfire than gain new supporters.

After they are elected to office, politicians at local, state, and national levels continue to use computer technology. Many state governments supply notebook computers to legislators, and some maintain information technology departments that offer computer training to lawmakers and their staffs. Lawmakers use notebook computers to do research, view bills, create amendments, communicate with colleagues, and correspond with constituents.

One politician describes the growing influence of e-mail: "Five years ago, it was 10 percent e-mail and 90 percent paper. Now, it's 10 percent paper and 90 percent e-mail. I still see literally dozens of people a day in my office, and nothing will ever replace personal contact on really personal issues, but, frankly, technology allows me to be a much more thorough legislator."

Government Web sites provide up-to-date information about the state and local governments. All states have Web sites with access to relevant information. Current governors and legislators use the Web to inform constituents about laws and regulations that are relevant to citizens. They also use the Web site to tout their successes and announce initiatives. During an election cycle, you can often find that Web sites are a venue for the incumbents to lobby for re-election.

You can also visit Web sites for information on your representatives. A quick look at the http://thomas.loc.gov/ site shows access to current bills, representatives and senators, and activities in Congress. You can browse the site for the current legislative agenda and the voting records of your representatives. See **Figure G-29**.

Figure G-29

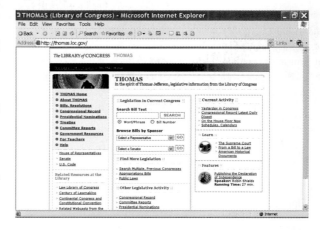

Political action groups, such as the ACLU and nonpartisan political organizations such as the League of Women Voters, maintain sophisticated Web sites to advance their political agendas and urge supporters to contact their local, state, or national officials regarding various issues and participate in government. In the past, many people did not know their legislators' names or addresses, but now they can enter a ZIP code at a political action group's Web site to find complete contact information. They can complete an online form to send a letter or they can download template letters that express concern about an issue—and then customize, print, and mail or fax these letters. The sites often provide a link to forward the form and information about the particular issue to friends in order to spread the word. Mass e-mail has allowed groups to disseminate information to their members quickly, cheaply, and effectively. If a vote is coming before the Congress, groups can get the message out quickly, calling for their members to call legislators and voice their opinions on the issue. **Figure G-30** shows a sample of an e-mail from a political action group, asking members to contact Congressional representatives to help stop passage of a bill that will cut the budget.

Constituents can gather political information from a variety of online sources. They can read the full content of pending and passed legislation posted on government Web sites. They can also read voter guides maintained by various organizations for information about elections, candidates, campaign funding, and other public issues. Some Web sites offer public forums and electronic "town hall" meetings where people can express their opinions and engage in debate. As with all information on the Web, be sure to consider and check the source before accepting the point of view expressed in any of these documents.

Figure G-30

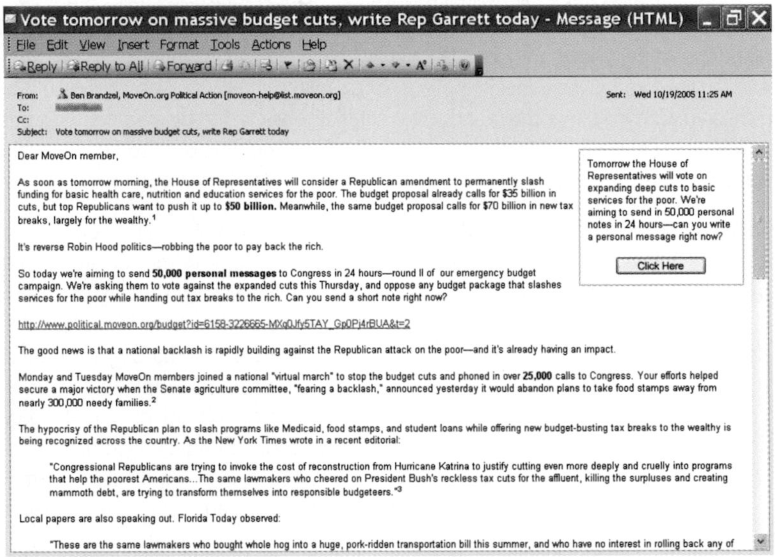
Vote tomorrow on massive budget cuts, write Rep Garrett today - Message (HTML)

File Edit View Insert Format Tools Actions Help

Reply | Reply to All | Forward

From: Ben Brandzel, MoveOn.org Political Action [moveon-help@list.moveon.org] Sent: Wed 10/19/2005 11:25 AM
To:
Cc:
Subject: Vote tomorrow on massive budget cuts, write Rep Garrett today

Dear MoveOn member,

As soon as tomorrow morning, the House of Representatives will consider a Republican amendment to permanently slash funding for basic health care, nutrition and education services for the poor. The budget proposal already calls for $35 billion in cuts, but top Republicans want to push it up to **$50 billion.** Meanwhile, the same budget proposal calls for $70 billion in new tax breaks, largely for the wealthy.[1]

It's reverse Robin Hood politics—robbing the poor to pay back the rich.

So today we're aiming to send **50,000 personal messages** to Congress in 24 hours—round II of our emergency budget campaign. We're asking them to vote against the expanded cuts this Thursday, and oppose any budget package that slashes services for the poor while handing out tax breaks to the rich. Can you send a short note right now?

http://www.political.moveon.org/budget?id=6158-3226665-MXq0Jfy5TAY_Gp0Pj4rBUA&t=2

The good news is that a national backlash is rapidly building against the Republican attack on the poor—and it's already having an impact.

Monday and Tuesday MoveOn members joined a national "virtual march" to stop the budget cuts and phoned in over **25,000** calls to Congress. Your efforts helped secure a major victory when the Senate agriculture committee, "fearing a backlash," announced yesterday it would abandon plans to take food stamps away from nearly 300,000 needy families.[2]

The hypocrisy of the Republican plan to slash programs like Medicaid, food stamps, and student loans while offering new budget-busting tax breaks to the wealthy is being recognized across the country. As the New York Times wrote in a recent editorial:

> "Congressional Republicans are trying to invoke the cost of reconstruction from Hurricane Katrina to justify cutting even more deeply and cruelly into programs that help the poorest Americans...The same lawmakers who cheered on President Bush's reckless tax cuts for the affluent, killing the surpluses and creating mammoth debt, are trying to transform themselves into responsible budgeteers."[3]

Local papers are also speaking out. Florida Today observed:

> "These are the same lawmakers who bought whole hog into a huge, pork-ridden transportation bill this summer, and who have no interest in rolling back any of

Tomorrow the House of Representatives will vote on expanding deep cuts to basic services for the poor. We're aiming to send in 50,000 personal notes in 24 hours—can you write a personal message right now?

Click Here

One only need look at the influence of blogs on politics to see the influence that the Web has had on the political process. Blogs have the power to expand the views of the average person beyond the coffee shop. Blogs take the media bias out of the opinion mill and place raw discussion on political topics within reach of anyone with a computer and the time to read and post to the blogs. There is no censorship of blogs; you post your opinion and nobody can alter what you post. Someone can strongly disagree with your viewpoint, and post a strong retraction, but your opinions are not changed.

Even with online access to information, interest in politics continues to decline in the United States. Voter turnout, for example, ranks among the lowest of the world's established democracies. Many political analysts expected that "cyberpolitics" might reverse this trend by improving access to political information and engaging citizens in interactive online political activities. Some observers hoped that information technology might increase levels of political knowledge and reduce the gap between the most and least engaged citizens. Studies leading up to the 2000 presidential election showed increasing use of the Internet to find political information. However, even citizens who specifically sought political information on the Internet were no more likely to vote than those who did not. More studies are needed to assess the current level of political interest and its relationship to new technologies.

Computer technology has also had a remarkable effect on the voting process. The 2000 presidential election "hanging chad" controversy highlighted problems with old optical ballot readers. Legislators swung into action and passed the Help America Vote Act in 2001, which provided $4 billion for new voting machines—computer kiosks called DREs (direct recording electronics) that use touch-screen technology similar to an ATM. One example of a DRE displays candidate names, numbers, and photos on-screen. Voters activate the machine with a one-time-use key card, similar to pass cards used for hotel door locks. Voters touch the screen to select a candidate; for voters with visual handicaps or those who cannot read, there is a voice-guided option. Voters can change and review selections until they are ready to activate the Cast Vote option. Votes are stored on the machine's hard disk and at least one removable device, such as a cartridge or SmartCard. When the poll closes, the removable storage device is extracted and transported to a central computer, which records, tallies, and combines the votes with those from other machines. To prevent hackers and viruses, the machines are not networked. Integrated backup battery power ensures continual service in case of a power outage.

Touch-screen voting machines are not without detractors, however. To recap, one complaint is that voting machine software is shrouded in secrecy, which prevents election officials from verifying the method for recording votes. Detractors fear that programmers at voting machine companies could surreptitiously insert code that shifts some votes from one party to another. According to voting machine company spokespeople, however, a simple pre-election test run can verify a machine's accuracy. Voting machine companies also state that maintaining secrecy about the software is a security measure to prevent outsiders from making unauthorized modifications that might invalidate votes.

Technology has had a profound effect on politics—from the ability to communicate instantly through e-mail and the Web, to being able to have uncensored open discussions through blogs, to being able to vote via the Internet and electronically. All these advances have changed the fundamental tools politicians can use to both get elected and govern. More importantly, these tools allow citizens a more active role in government. They provide citizens ready access to information on policy, the voting records and activities of their elected officials, and the ability to effectively communicate ideas and information to the officials as well as to other citizens.

Issue Censorship on the Web

The Internet offers instant access to information across national and cultural borders, but along with helpful information the Internet hosts a significant amount of provocative and disturbing material. Militias and hate groups use Web sites to recruit new members and spread their views. Hundreds of pornographic sites make a business of selling lewd images, and their material can be accessed by anyone—even children. Criminals, anarchists, and dissenters post guidebooks and tips on how to do all kinds of illegal activities, from making suitcase bombs to spreading computer viruses.

Some concerned "netizens" (a combination of the words "net" and "citizen" used to describe a member of the online community of the Internet) advocate cyber censorship to curtail irresponsible Web sites, blogs, and discussion groups. Cyber censorship typically means blocking access to Web sites, but it can also mean closing sites and removing them from host servers.

> As now-retired Justice Sandra Day O'Connor explained, "Cyberspace is malleable. Thus, it is possible to construct barriers in cyberspace and use them to screen for identity, making cyberspace more like the physical world and, consequently, more amenable to zoning laws."

Censorship advocates are opposed by free speech supporters who believe that the right to free expression should be unshackled by any laws or regulations. The controversy over censorship is not new. Guidelines from the pre-Internet era also shape the cyber-censorship-vs-free-speech debate. In most cases, words are acceptable, whereas actions can be punishable. Writing a mystery novel that describes how the main character cultivates botulism and then uses it to poison another character is acceptable; actually carrying out such an act would be against the law. This concept was applied to cyberspace when the U.S. Supreme Court upheld a law that pornography featuring real children was illegal, but ruled that child pornography featuring computer-generated children is not illegal because children were not harmed when it was created.

Cyberlaw is not yet totally consistent on the words vs. deeds precedent, however. In some cases, words are punishable. For example, the Digital Millennium Copyright Act makes it illegal to even disseminate information on how to bypass software, CD, and DVD copy restrictions. A second censorship guideline hinges on local standards of morality. Local communities can apply their own standards to determine whether material is obscene. Therefore, a raunchy magazine that you might find on a supermarket news stand in New York City might be limited to adult bookstore shelves in a conservative Tennessee community. Local standards, however, are difficult to sort out on the Internet, where a Web surfer in Tennessee can easily access Web sites, bulletin boards, and chat groups that originate from anywhere in the world.

Judges upheld the conviction of two system operators (sysops) whose California-based porn site distributed obscene material to individuals in Tennessee. The sysops claimed that the Internet required a more flexible definition of "community" to account for the Internet's global accessibility; otherwise Web sites would be forced to eliminate all materials objected to by anyone. Judges denied that claim, saying that technology could be used to filter out objectionable material based on age and location information provided by member registration data.

Underlying a group of decisions on cyber censorship, the U.S. Supreme Court seems to support the concept of cyberzones that limit Net access to certain materials in a way similar to how the adult sections of news stands restrict children from browsing through certain magazines. As now-retired Justice Sandra Day O'Connor explained, "Cyberspace is malleable. Thus, it is possible to construct barriers in cyberspace and use them to screen for identity, making cyberspace more like the physical world and, consequently, more amenable to zoning laws." As an example, AOL is trying to develop a family-friendly Internet portal by enforcing policies against offensive speech, but has been criticized by free-speech advocates for its policies. AOL responds that it is a private company and members who disagree with AOL terms of use are free to terminate their subscriptions.

In some countries, however, netizens have no choice but to use a government-controlled ISP. In many countries, free speech is not a basic right conferred to all citizens. Many dictatorial regimes want their citizens to receive news from the outside world only after it has been screened by a government censor. Rather than depend on legislation, officials in more than 20 countries use sophisticated tools to block sites, filter e-mail, and censor discussion groups.

China has some of the most rigorous Internet censorship in the world. The "Great Firewall of China," as it is sometimes called, blocks Internet content by preventing IP addresses of objectionable sites from being routed through its gateways into China. The system also selectively engages in DNS poisoning, a technique that tricks a DNS server into believing it has received authentic information when, in reality, it has not. So Web surfers in China who attempt to access the Electronic Frontier Foundation's Web site that advocates free speech might instead see a Chinese government site on social responsibility. In addition to blocking Web sites, the Chinese government filters e-mail, message boards, chat rooms, and blogs. In Iran, government censors monitor political and news Web sites, and block access to many pornographic Web sites, anonymizer tools, sites with gay and lesbian content, politically sensitive sites, and women's rights sites. If you tried to access *Rolling Stone* magazine's Web site from Saudi Arabia, you would find that access has been denied. The Saudi government claims it censors the Internet to preserve Islamic culture and heritage. This is an argument that in many ways reflects the concept of cyberzones that conform to local standards of ethics and morality. Even free-speech activists at the OpenNet Initiative (ONI) seem to agree, "We do think that information should be free," states one ONI technician, "but we do need to find a balance for respect for sovereign states to preserve their own culture."

FYI

Be sure to download the Podcast that is available for this Issue at www.course.com/Illustrated/concepts6.

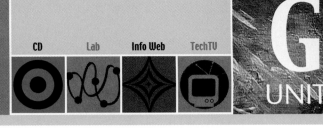

CD   Lab   Info Web   TechTV

G

UNIT

Despite such cultural sensitivity, technology giants such as Microsoft, Yahoo!, and Cisco Systems have been criticized for providing foreign governments with tools for blocking culturally objectionable sites. Critics question whether companies in a free society should aid foreign governments' attempts to censor cyberspace. For some people it is astonishing to realize that ideas such as liberty, equality, and women's rights would be subject to the same censorship attempts as pornography and hate speech. The solution to online censorship is still evolving as free speech comes into balance with cultural, ethical, and moral concerns in the global realm of cyberspace.

"We do think that information should be free," states one ONI technician, "but we do need to find a balance for respect for sovereign states to preserve their own culture."

Interactive Questions

☐ Yes   ☐ No   ☐ Not sure
1. Should governments be allowed to block access to Web sites based on local religion, politics, and customs?

☐ Yes   ☐ No   ☐ Not sure
2. Do you believe that a privately-held Internet Service Provider has the right to censor the data posted on Web sites it hosts?

☐ Yes   ☐ No   ☐ Not sure
3. Should companies like Microsoft, Yahoo!, and Cisco Systems provide blocking technology to foreign governments?

☐ Yes   ☐ No   ☐ Not sure
4. Would you use filtering software that was preprogrammed to block pornographic and nuisance Web sites?

Expand the Ideas

1. Do you believe that access to certain Web sites should be restricted in any way by government regulators? Do you think that public access facilities, such as a library, should have filters that restrict Web site access based on certain parameters? Would you use filtering software that was preprogrammed to block pornographic and nuisance Web sites at your home? Your office? Are they in use at your school? If so, what types of regulations or restrictions are in place on access, and why? Write a brief paper explaining your findings and viewpoints on these questions.

2. Do you believe that a privately-held Internet Service Provider has the right to censor the data posted on Web sites it hosts? If so, should access be blocked based on local religion, politics, and customs? How should the regulators be regulated? Who would determine the "acceptable" content that can filter through? Write a one-page dialog between two people with opposing viewpoints on this topic.

3. Should companies like Microsoft, Yahoo!, and Cisco Systems provide blocking technology to foreign governments? What other industries provide products they develop in one country but which are not in use or distributed for use in other countries?

4. On the Web, some sites contain pornography, bigotry, and terrorist rhetoric that many people would rather not be public. One of the cornerstones of democracy, however, is freedom of speech. Where do you draw the line when it comes to censoring and filtering on the Internet? Make sure you consider questions such as: Do parents have the right to monitor, screen, and filter their children's Web use? Are governments ever justified in regulating what their citizens can access? Should anyone be responsible for policing the Internet? Write a one-page paper explaining your views.

End of Unit Exercises

Key Terms

Ad-serving cookie	E-commerce	JPEG	Spyware
ActiveX control	Electronic wallet	Link	SSL
AES (Advanced Encryption	Encryption	Link tag	Stateless protocol
Standard)	External link	Mailto link	Strong encryption
Animated GIF	External style sheet	Markup language	Style
AVI	Flash animation	Media tag	Style sheet
B2B	Formatting tag	Method	Symmetric key encryption
B2C	GIF	MPEG	Text editor
B2G	Head section	Online shopping cart	Theme
Banner ad	Helper application	Operational tag	Thumbnail
Body section	Hot spot	P3P	URL
Broken link	HTML	Packet sniffer	VBScript
Browser	HTML document	Person-to-person payment	Weak encryption
Brute force method	HTML form	Plaintext	Web authoring software
C2C	HTML frame	Player	Web browser
Cascading style sheet	HTML tag	Plug-in	Web bug
Ciphertext	HTTP	PNG	Web page
Clear GIF	HTTP status code	Pop-up ad	Web page header
Click-through rate	Hyperlink	Public key encryption (PKE)	Web page table
Compact Privacy Policy	Hypertext	QuickTime	Web resource
Cookie	Hypertext link	RSA	Web server
Cryptographic algorithm	Image map	Secure connection	World Wide Web Consortium
Cryptographic key	Internal link	Self-closing tag	(W3C)
Decryption	Interpage link	Server farm	XHTML
DES (Data Encryption	Java	SET	XML (Extensible Markup
Standard)	Java applet	S-HTTP	Language)
Digital certificate	JavaScript	Socket	XSL (Extensible Stylesheet
			Language)

Unit Review

1. Use your own words to define bold terms that appear throughout the unit. List 10 of the terms that are least familiar to you and write a sentence for each of them.

2. Draw a multipanel cartoon that shows how a Web server and browser interact. Include the following terms: Web server, browser, HTTP, HTML, Port 80, socket, HTML document, graphic file, and URL.

3. In a short paragraph, explain the relationship between an HTML document and a Web page.

4. List and describe in your own words the classifications of HTML tags as presented in this unit.

5. List the port numbers that are traditionally used for HTTP traffic, SMTP e-mail, and FTP.

6. Describe how cookies work and list their major security and privacy features.

7. Explain how helper and plug-in applications work to enhance the experience of viewing a Web page. List two helper applications discussed in the unit and describe what they do.

8. List the various tools described in this unit for creating Web pages, then describe the advantages and disadvantages of each type of Web page development tool discussed in this unit.

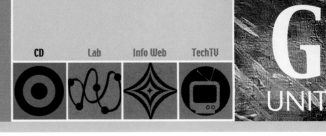
9. Locate a Web page, print it out, and then identify the following parts of the Web page: title, graphic, link, button, menu, and frame (if any).

10. Describe some of the ways that Web page designers use links. Describe external links, mailto links, and internal links.

Fill in the Best Answer

1. The _____ is a collection of documents that can be related by links.

2. HTML is called a markup language because authors insert special instructions called HTML _____ that specify how a document should appear when printed or displayed on a computer screen.

3. A(n) _____ is the client half of the client/server software that facilitates communication between a personal computer and Web server.

4. _____ is a protocol that works in conjunction with TCP/IP to get Web resources to your desktop.

5. A Web server usually listens for HTTP requests on _____ 80.

6. If you use a text _____ to create an HTML document, you must manually enter HTML tags.

7. A browser displays a "_____ Not Found" message when a Web server sends a status code to indicate that the requested resource does not exist.

8. A(n) _____ style sheet allows you to create an HTML document that contains style specifications for multiple Web pages.

9. A(n) _____ is a collection of coordinated graphics, colors, and fonts applied to individual pages or all pages in a Web site.

10. The _____ HTML tag is used to reference an image that will appear on a Web page.

11. A(n) _____ is an advertisement, typically embedded at the top of a Web page; a(n) _____ is an advertisement that appears in a separate window when you enter a Web site or connect to Web pages.

12. A(n) _____ link is used to send an e-mail message to an address specified by the Web page author.

13. A Web page that contains clickable hot spots is referred to as a(n) _____ map.

14. Many Web page authors and designers use _____ as a layout tool for positioning the elements of a Web page.

15. On a Web page, a(n) _____ scrolls independently of other parts of the page.

16. _____ is typically used to describe shopping for goods and services over the Internet.

17. Most shopping carts work because they use _____ to store information about your activities on a Web site.

18. A(n) _____ wallet stores and handles the information that a customer typically submits when finalizing an e-commerce purchase.

19. _____ e-commerce involves one business buying goods or services from another business, whereas _____ e-commerce aims to help businesses sell to governments.

20. In the context of the Web and e-commerce, _____ is technology that secretly gathers information and relays it to advertisers or other interested parties.

Practice Tests

When you use the Interactive CD, you can take Practice Tests that consist of 10 multiple-choice, true/false, and fill-in-the-blank questions. The questions are selected at random from a large test bank, so each time you take a test, you will receive a different set of questions. Your tests are scored immediately, and you can print study guides to determine which questions you answered incorrectly. If you are using a Tracking Disk, save your test scores.

INDEPENDENT CHALLENGE 1

Many people have their own home pages. A home page is a statement of who you are and what your interests may be. You can design your own home page. Depending on the tools you have available, you might be able to create a real page and publish it on the Web. If these tools are not available, you will still be able to complete the initial design work.

1. Write a brief description of the purpose of your home page and your expected audience. For example, you might plan to use your home page to showcase your résumé to prospective employers.

2. List the elements you plan to include on your home page. Briefly describe any graphics or media elements you want to include.

End of Unit Exercises

3. Create a document that contains the information you want to include on your home page.

4. Make a sketch of your home page, showing the colors you plan to use and the navigation elements you plan to include. Annotate this sketch to describe how these elements follow effective Web page design guidelines.

INDEPENDENT CHALLENGE 2

 Surfing the Web will take you to many interesting sites. As you visit each one, you will notice differences among Web pages. To some extent, good design is a matter of taste. When it comes to Web page design, there are usually many possible solutions that will provide a pleasing look and efficient navigational tools. On the other hand, some designs just do not seem to work because they make the text difficult to read or the site difficult to navigate.

1. Select a Web page or several pages that have many of the elements described in this unit, including hot spots, image maps, links, images, or other media.

2. Find the page by browsing on the Web; save and print the page or pages.

3. Using colored markers or pens, identify each of the elements and write a brief explanation of how each element enhances or detracts from the message of the page.

4. What tools do you think the Web page designer used to organize the information on the page? Was it done effectively? Identify the sections of content on the printouts.

5. Do you think styles were used in developing the page? Do you see common fonts and colors in the text portions? Identify these elements on the printout.

6. Next, find one Web page that you think could use improvement. Use colored pencils or markers to sketch your plan for improving the page. Annotate your sketch by pointing out the features you would change and explain why you think your makeover will be more effective than the original Web page.

INDEPENDENT CHALLENGE 3

 Shopping on the Web has benefits for consumers as well as merchants. You will take a quick shopping tour of the Web and compare a few sites to see how they differ. You do not have to make any purchases to complete this independent challenge.

1. Find three retailers on the Internet. If possible, find e-commerce retailers that also have "brick and mortar" stores, such as Bed, Bath, and Beyond; Barnes and Nobles Books; or Sears.

2. Besides the name of the Web site, what clues on the Web page help you identify the products or services being offered?

3. For each of the retailers, search for two items and place them in a shopping cart. Do not complete the purchase and do not enter any credit card or personal information.

4. Create a chart with three columns, one for each retailer. Complete the chart by answering the questions that follow:

   a. What procedures did you go through to find the merchandise?

   b. Was there a shopping cart or comparable way of gathering your purchases?

   c. What methods of payment did they offer you?

   d. Were there any warning dialog boxes that opened in your browser during the shopping trip?

   e. Did the retailer make use of cookies? Could you find them on your computer after you exited the retailer?

   f. Select one store that has a brick-and-mortar counterpart. Would you prefer to shop online or at the brick-and-mortar store? Write a brief summary supporting your response.

INDEPENDENT CHALLENGE 4

 The World Wide Web Consortium is required to maintain standards for working on the Web. New versions of browsers with new features are constantly being released. Companies develop plug-in and add-in programs that have to be compatible with browsers, and then the media have to be available on the Web sites to make downloading the additional software worthwhile for consumers. Keeping up with all this change can make any Web surfer dizzy. How can you keep up?

1. Go to the World Wide Web Consortium site at www.w3c.org. Find two recent news items that relate to updates in programming Web pages and write a brief summary of your findings. Be sure to include the sources.

2. Go to the Microsoft Web site at www.microsoft.com and find one recent news item about the latest release of the Internet Explorer Web browser. Write a brief summary of your findings. Be sure to include the sources.

3. Go to the Netscape Web site at www.netscape.com, click the Download link, and find one recent news item about the latest release of the Netscape Web browser. Write a brief summary of your findings. Be sure to include the sources.

4. Go to the Opera Web site at www.opera.com and find one recent news item about the latest release of the Opera Web browser. Write a brief summary of your findings. Be sure to include the sources.

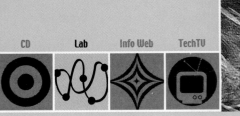

5. Go to the Firefox Web site at www.mozilla.org and find one recent news item about the latest release of the Firefox Web browser. Write a brief summary of your findings. Be sure to include the sources.

6. Write a summary of the features that are advertised for each of the four browsers. Which features are similar and which are different?

LAB: Working with Cookies

1. Start the interactive part of the lab. Insert your Tracking Disk if you want to save your QuickCheck results. Perform each of the lab steps as directed and answer all of the lab QuickCheck questions. When you exit the lab, your answers are automatically graded and your results are displayed.

2. Use Windows Explorer to look at the cookies stored on your computer. Indicate how many cookies are currently stored. Examine the contents of one cookie and indicate whether or not you think it poses a threat to your privacy.

3. Indicate the name and the version of the browser that you typically use. To find this information, open your browser and select the About option from the Help menu. Next, look at the cookie settings provided by your browser. Describe how you would adjust these settings to produce a level of privacy protection that is right for your needs.

4. Adjust your browser settings so that you are prompted whenever a Web server attempts to send a cookie to your computer. Go to several of your favorite Web sites and watch for third-party cookies. When you receive a message from a third-party Web site, record the name of the third-party site and the contents of the cookie that it is attempting to send. Finally, indicate whether or not you would typically accept such a cookie.

Student Edition Labs

Student Edition Labs

Reinforce the concepts you have learned in this unit through the **Creating Web Pages**, **E-Commerce**, and **Web Design Principles** Student Edition Labs, available online at the Illustrated Computer Concepts Web site.

SAM Labs

If you have a SAM user profile, you have access to additional content, features, and functionality. Log in to your SAM account and go to your assignments page to see what your instructor has assigned for this unit.

End of Unit Exercises

Visual Workshop

The Internet has opened government up to anyone with a computer, an Internet connection, and the willingness to spend some time searching. Web sites are available for politicians and citizens to discuss issues. Political action committees as well as environmental organizations all have Web sites promoting their agendas and providing information to citizens. You can research bills, send e-mails, participate in government, and even download government podcasts! See **Figure G-31**.

Figure G-31

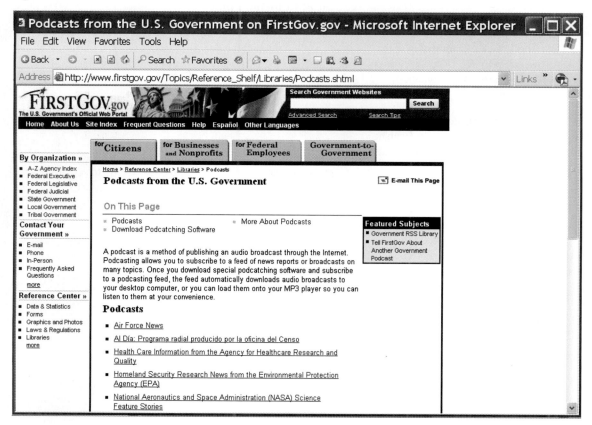

Select a current political event, personality, or issue that interests you. Your topic should incorporate the influence of technology. Create a question about your topic that you will answer based on research you will conduct on the Web.

1. Log onto the Internet, and then use the Web to research your topic and find an answer to your question. Use your favorite search engine to find relevant sites on the Web.

2. As you browse the Web, maintain a log describing the Web sites you visit. For each site, include its URL, the name of the organization that maintains the Web site, a brief description of the site's content, and your assessment of the reliability and validity of information on the site.

3. Write a short essay describing your findings. Your essay should include an answer to the question you originally posed. Include a summary paragraph on how the Internet and computers influenced the topic, and how the Internet facilitated your research.

4. If your computer has the capability, search for, download, and listen to a podcast on a topic of your choice. In a few short words, explain the steps that you followed to complete this task.

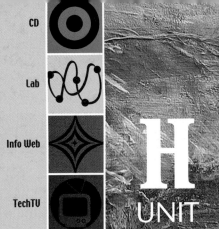

Overview

This unit explores digital media, taking a close look at bitmap graphics—the most popular format for photographs and for images placed in Web pages. You will learn about vector graphics, which are often used for clip art and provide the underlying technology for 3-D graphics and 3-D animations. You will explore desktop video technology. You will learn about digital sound, including the different music formats, the technology behind portable digital audio players, speech synthesis, and techniques for recording and distributing voice. The Tech Talk explores the topic of data compression; you will find out how it works and learn how to use a popular compression utility. You will also have an opportunity to look at computers in the context of the film industry. The Issue discusses digital rights management, specifically the legal and ethical implications of sharing all types of digital media, including graphics, animations, music, and videos, via the Internet.

Introducing digital graphics

Digital graphics are images that have been created as or converted to a digital format. There are many sources for digital graphics; for example, images converted by a scanner, photos from a digital camera or sent as an e-mail attachment, and most Web page graphics.

- A **bitmap graphic**, also called a raster graphic, or simply a bitmap, is composed of a grid of dots. Think of a grid superimposed on a picture. The graphic is mapped to a grid. The color of each dot is stored as a binary number in a data file. The grid divides the picture into cells, called pixels. Each **pixel** is assigned a color, which is stored as a binary number.

- You can create a bitmap graphic from scratch using the tools provided by graphics software—specifically paint software. Paint software provides tools for freehand sketching, filling in shapes, adding realistic shading, and creating effects.

- When you have an existing printed image, such as a photograph, you can use a **scanner** to convert the image into a bitmap graphic. A scanner divides an image into a fine grid of cells and assigns a digital value for the color of each cell—that is, it converts the visual information you see into digital information the computer can understand. These values are transferred to your computer's memory, where they are processed so the image can be displayed, printed, modified, sent via e-mail or saved as a bitmap graphic file to a storage medium. Scanners, such as the one pictured in **Figure H-1**, are relatively inexpensive and easy to use.

Figure H-1: A scanner

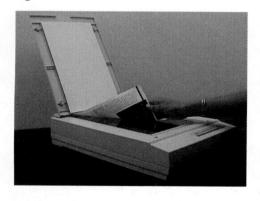

To scan an image:
1. Turn on the scanner and start your scanner software
2. Place the image face down on the scanner glass
3. Use the scanner software to initiate the scan
4. The scanned image is stored in RAM
5. Save the image on your computer's hard disk

- A scanner digitizes printed images, whereas a **digital camera** creates digitized images of real objects, converting the images into digital information that can be stored as a bitmap graphics file. Instead of taking a photo with a conventional camera, developing the film, and then digitizing it with a scanner, you use a digital camera, such as the one in **Figure H-2**, to take a photo in digital format. Digital cameras include features such as high resolution, optical digital zooms, and digital image stabilization to guarantee a good picture even if the camera shakes. User interface options include image management menus and options for saving various image formats. Most cameras store photos in JPEG or TIFF formats.

Figure H-2: A digital camera

Viewfinder

Shutter release button

Built-in flash

Menu button

Preview window

Lens

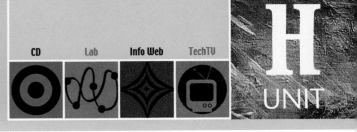

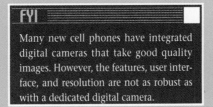

■ **Storing images:** Some digital cameras store images on a variety of magnetic and optical media. Other digital cameras store images on removable solid-state storage media, sometimes called memory cards. A camera will use only one type of media, so be sure you know which type your camera uses. Solid-state storage is a popular technology for digital cameras. Like RAM, it can be erased and reused. Unlike RAM, solid-state storage holds data without consuming power, so it does not lose data when the camera is turned off. **Figure H-3** illustrates several storage options for digital cameras, including memory cards and a miniature hard disk drive.

Figure H-3: Digital camera storage options

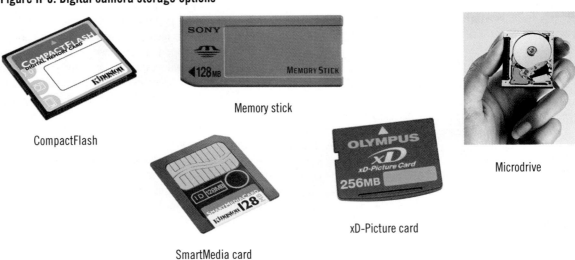

CompactFlash

Memory stick

SmartMedia card

xD-Picture card

Microdrive

■ **Retrieving images:** Digital cameras allow you to preview images while they are still in the camera and delete those that you do not want. The photos that you want to keep can be transferred directly to some printers, but typically you will transfer the photo data to your computer's hard disk. This transfer can be achieved in several ways, depending on your camera.

Media transfer. If your camera stores data on disks, CDs/DVDs, flash memory cards, or other storage media, you can simply remove the medium from your camera and insert it into the appropriate drive of your computer.

Direct cable transfer. If your computer and camera have USB or FireWire ports (also called IEEE-1394 ports), you can connect a cable between these two ports to transfer the photo data. You can also use a cable if your computer and camera have a serial port.

Infrared port. Some cameras can "beam" stored data to your computer's infrared port. Some camera models are Wi-Fi enabled. Infrared and Wi-Fi methods eliminate the need for a cable, but are much slower than using a USB, FireWire, or serial port.

Docking station. Some camera manufacturers offer a camera docking station that connects to a computer by cable. A camera can be placed in the docking station to transfer photos to the computer's hard disk.

Card reader. A **card reader** is a small device connected to your computer's USB or serial port and designed to read data contained in a solid-state memory card. A card reader acts in the same way as an external disk drive. To transfer the photo data from a memory card, you remove it from the camera and insert it into the card reader, as shown in **Figure H-4**.

E-mail. If you are using a camera phone to take pictures, cell phone photos can be transferred to a computer by e-mailing the photo to your e-mail account. The photo arrives as an attachment, which can be saved as a separate file.

Figure H-4: A card reader

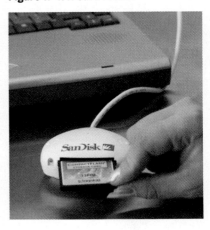

Regardless of the technology that you use, transferring photo data from your camera to your computer requires software, which may be supplied along with your camera, with your card reader, or by a stand-alone graphics software package, such as Adobe Photoshop. This software allows you to select a file format, specify a filename, and determine the location for each image file. After you store your digital photos on your computer's hard disk, you can modify them, send them as e-mail attachments, print them, post them on Web pages, or archive them onto a CD.

Modifying bitmap graphics

Because bitmap graphics are stored as bits that represent pixels, you can use software to modify or edit bitmap graphics. In order to modify bitmap graphics, you need an understanding of image resolution, density, and file formats.

- Using graphics software, you can enhance or change bitmap graphics with a variety of effects. For example, you can retouch or repair old photographs to eliminate creases, spots, and discoloration. See **Figure H-5**.

Figure H-5: Modifying a bitmap graphic

Before

After

- Bitmap graphics tend to require a lot of storage space. Each pixel in a bitmap graphic is stored as one or more bits. The more pixels in a bitmap graphic, the more bits are needed to store the image in a file. So while a large bitmap graphic file might provide the necessary data for a high-quality printout, these files take up space on your hard disk, can require lengthy e-mail transmission times, and make Web page downloads seem sluggish.

- **Resolution**, the dimensions of the grid that forms a bitmap graphic, is usually expressed as the number of horizontal and vertical pixels that it contains. For example, a graphic for a Web page might have a resolution of 150 x 100 pixels: 150 pixels across and 100 pixels up and down. Bitmap graphics are **resolution dependent**, which means that the quality of the image depends on its resolution. A high-resolution graphic contains more data and looks better than a low-resolution graphic. Why? Because each pixel contains data, so the high-resolution graphic contains more data that defines the image then the low-resolution graphic. With more data, it is possible to display and print high-quality images that are smoother and cleaner.

- In addition to resolution, the physical size of a bitmap graphic can affect the quality of the image. The concept of changing the physical size of a bitmap graphic—that is, stretching and shrinking it without changing its resolution (increasing or decreasing the number of pixels)—is important for understanding what happens when bitmap graphics are displayed on a monitor or printed on paper. When the physical size of an image is changed, the density of the image grid is also changed. The **density** of an image grid refers to the grid used for printing on paper or for displaying on a monitor. It can be expressed as dots per inch (dpi) for a printer or as pixels per inch (ppi) on a monitor. The denser the grid is (that is, the more dots or pixels per inch), the higher the quality of the image. The density of the grid depends both on the resolution of the image and its physical size. If the resolution stays the same and the image size is stretched to become larger, then the quality of the image deteriorates. As you stretch the surface, the grid maintains the same number of horizontal and vertical cells, but each cell becomes larger and the grid becomes less dense. See **Figure H-6**.

Figure H-6: The quality of an image is based on image size and resolution

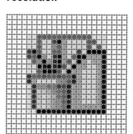

24 × 24 resolution

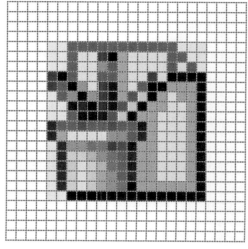

24 × 24 resolution

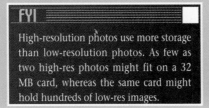

FYI

High-resolution photos use more storage than low-resolution photos. As few as two high-res photos might fit on a 32 MB card, whereas the same card might hold hundreds of low-res images.

CD　　Lab　　Info Web　　TechTU

■ One way to reduce the size of a bitmap graphic is to crop it. **Cropping** refers to the process of removing part of an image, just like cutting out a section of a photograph. Cropping decreases file size by reducing the number of pixels in a graphic. The visual presentation changes to reflect the cropped changes. For example, in **Figure H-7**, the cropped area is outside the red box.

Figure H-7: Cropping an image

■ You can increase the resolution of a bitmap graphic using graphics software; but when you do this, your computer must somehow add pixels because no additional picture data exists. Most graphics software uses a process called **pixel interpolation** to create new pixels by averaging the colors of nearby pixels to create the additional pixels. For some graphics, pixel interpolation results in an image that appears very similar to the original. However, images that contain strong curved or diagonal lines may develop an undesirable pixelated, or bitmap, appearance.

■ Most graphics software allows you to specify the size at which an image is printed or displayed on a monitor without changing the resolution of the bitmap graphic. You can specify a larger size for the printout, in which case the printer must create additional data to fill the print grid. This process can produce a fuzzy and blocky image if the printed image gets very large.

■ Sometimes the resolution and corresponding file size of a graphic might be too large for your needs. For example, a digital photo might have a high resolution and large file size that is unsuitable for a Web page or as an e-mail attachment. Not only would the photo take a long time to download, but if the resolution is high enough, it would also be larger than most screen resolutions. If you use graphics software to reduce the resolution, the computer eliminates pixels from the image, reducing the size of the image grid as well as the file size, compromising the image quality.

■ Bitmap graphics can be saved in a variety of graphics file formats. Most graphics software provides a choice of popular formats, such as **BMP**, **TIFF**, **JPEG**, **GIF**, and **PNG**. The file format you use depends on a variety of factors. See **Table H-1**.

Table H-1: Popular file formats for graphics

FORMAT	DESCRIPTION
BMP	Native bitmap graphic file format of the Microsoft Windows environment; supports True Color; used for graphical elements, such as buttons, as well as for a wide variety of graphics applications
TIFF	A highly flexible and platform-independent graphics file format that is supported by most photo editing software packages; supports True Color; used for high resolution scanned images and digital photos
JPEG	Joint Photographic Experts Group; a graphics format with built-in compression that stores True Color bitmap data efficiently in a small file; used for photographic or scanned images, such as for Web pages
GIF	Graphics Interchange Format; specifically designed to create images that can be displayed on multiple platforms, GIF graphics are limited to 256 colors; used for Web graphics; uses a built-in compression algorithm patented by Unisys
PNG	Graphics format used as an alternative to GIF for Web graphics; can display up to 48-bit True Color (trillions of colors); is a public domain format without any restrictions on its use

Working with color

Color depth refers to the number of colors available for use in an image. As the color depth increases, image quality improves and file size increases. You can adjust color depth in order to decrease the size of the file required for a graphic. This lesson looks at color depth and how it affects your bitmap graphics.

■ A **monochrome bitmap** graphic is displayed by manipulating the pattern of on and off pixels displayed on the screen. In a simple monochrome (one-color) device, each screen pixel is either on or off. To store the data for a monochrome bitmap, an "on" pixel is represented by a 1 bit. An "off" pixel is represented by a 0 bit. Each row of the bitmap grid is stored as a series of 0s and 1s, as shown in

Figure H-8. Monochrome bitmaps require very little storage space. Each pixel is set to display either a black dot or a white dot, and so requires only one bit for each pixel. Therefore, the number of bits required to represent a full-screen image is the same as the number of pixels on the screen.

Figure H-8: Monochrome bitmap graphic

1. The image can originate as a black-and-white silhouette, as a black-and-white photograph, or even as a color photo

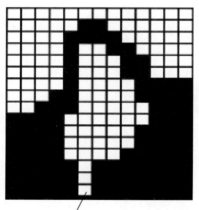

2. The computer divides the picture into a grid

3. If a cell is white, it is coded as a 1; if the cell is black, it is coded as a 0

■ Color monitors use a more complex storage scheme. Each screen pixel displays a color based on the intensity of red, green, and blue signals that it receives. Each red, green, and blue signal is assigned a value ranging from zero to 255, from absence of color to the highest intensity level for that color. A pixel appears white if the red, green, and blue signals are set to maximum intensity. If red, green, and blue signals are equal but at a lower intensity, the pixel displays a shade of gray. If the red signal is set to maximum intensity, but the blue and green signals are off, the pixel appears in brilliant red. A pixel appears purple if it receives red and blue signals, and so on.

These values (0 to 255 for red, blue, and green) produce a maximum of 16.7 million (256^3) colors. A graphic that uses this full range of colors is referred to as a **True Color bitmap** or a **24-bit bitmap** graphic. The data for each pixel in a True Color bitmap graphic requires three bytes of storage space: eight bits for red, eight bits for green, and eight bits for blue, for a total of 24 bits per pixel. True

Color bitmaps produce photographic-quality images, but they also produce very large files.

■ A **32-bit bitmap** graphic displays 16.7 million colors just like a 24-bit bitmap. The extra eight bits are used to define special effects, such as the amount of transparency, for a pixel. As a result of the extra byte of data for each pixel, 32-bit bitmap graphics files are even larger than 24-bit bitmap graphics files.

■ To reduce the size of a bitmap file, you can reduce its color depth by using graphics software to work with color palettes. A **color palette** (also called a color lookup table or color map) holds the selection of colors and allows you to select a group of colors to use for a bitmap graphic. If a palette contains only 256 colors, the data stored for each pixel is eight bits instead of 24 bits, which reduces the file to one-third the size required for a True Color bitmap graphic. A color palette is stored as a table within the file header; it contains the information used to translate the color data stored in the bitmap graphic.

■ Most graphics software offers a selection of ready-made palettes that you can select using the color palette or color picker tool. Ready-made palettes usually include a grayscale palette, a system palette, and a Web palette. A **grayscale palette** displays an image using shades of gray, which looks similar to a black-and-white photograph. Most grayscale palettes consist of 256 colors. **Figure H-9** illustrates a grayscale bitmap graphic and a grayscale palette.

Figure H-9: Grayscale bitmap graphic and grayscale palette

■ A **system palette** is the selection of colors used by the operating system for the graphics that represent desktop icons and controls. Windows, for example, uses a system palette that contains 20 permanent colors and 236 colors that can be changed, depending on the application.

■ A **Web palette** contains a standard set of colors used by Internet Web browsers. Because most browsers support this palette, it is typically regarded as a safe choice when preparing graphics for Internet distribution. **Figure H-10** shows the collection of colors used by system and Web palettes. Additional palettes may be provided by your graphics software.

Figure H-10: Other palettes

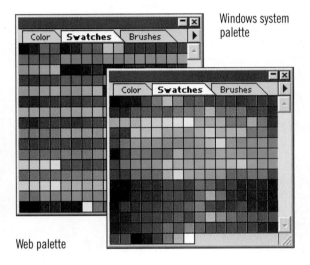

Windows system palette

Web palette

■ A particular 256-color palette sometimes does not contain the right selection of colors for an image. For example, the Windows system palette does not provide a wide enough selection of orange tones for a sunset photo. To make up for the lack of colors, your graphics software can dither the image. **Dithering** uses patterns composed of two or more colors to produce the illusion of additional colors and shading, relying on the human eye to blend colors and shapes. Most graphics software provides options that let you control the dithering.

Resolution and digital cameras

Digital camera manufacturers use the term megapixels (millions of pixels) to express the resolution of digital camera image; megapixel values indicate the total number of pixels in a graphic. For example, a 1.9 megapixel digital camera means the camera uses a resolution of 1,600 x 1,200 (1,600 multiplied by 1,200, which equals 1,920,000 pixels) to capture images. The megapixel rating of a camera is the highest resolution that the camera is capable of capturing. An 8.0 megapixel digital camera captures images at a higher resolution than a 3.1 megapixel digital camera. Generally, more pixels mean better quality because more data about the captured image can be stored. However, remember that more data means a larger file size. If you reduce the resolution used to capture a digital image, which some digital cameras allow you to do, then the resulting file size will be smaller. This way you can determine how many images you can store on the memory card. The higher the resolution is, the fewer images that can be stored. If you are looking to take a lot of pictures, reduce the resolution. Remember though that data is lost when you reduce the resolution because fewer pixels are used to store data, and as a result, the image quality is reduced.

Introducing vector graphics

A **vector graphic** consists of a set of instructions for creating a picture. Unlike a bitmap graphic file, which super-imposes a grid of pixels over an image and stores the color value for each pixel, a vector graphic file contains the instructions that the computer needs to create the shape, size, position, and color for each object in an image. This lesson explains the basics of two-dimensional vector graphics and how they differ from bitmap graphics.

- The parts of a vector graphic are created as separate objects, as seen in the Stonehenge image in **Figure H-11**.

- Vector graphics are suitable for most line art, logos, simple illustrations, and diagrams that might be displayed and printed at various sizes. When compared to bitmaps, vector graphics have several advantages and disadvantages. You should take the following distinctions into account when deciding which type of graphic to use for a specific project.

  - Vector graphics resize better than bitmap graphics. When you change the physical size of a vector graphic, the objects change proportionally and maintain their smooth edges. See **Figure H-12**.

Figure H-11: A vector graphic

A vector graphic is formed from lines and shapes, which can be colored or shaded; this image was created with a series of roughly rectangular objects for the stones and a circular object for the sun

Figure H-12: Resizing vector graphic image vs. resizing bitmap graphic image

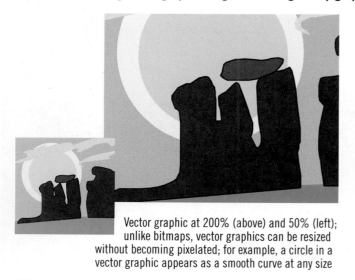

Vector graphic at 200% (above) and 50% (left); unlike bitmaps, vector graphics can be resized without becoming pixelated; for example, a circle in a vector graphic appears as a smooth curve at any size

Bitmap graphic at 200% (above) and 50% (right); images in a bitmap graphic might appear to have jagged edges after the graphic is enlarged

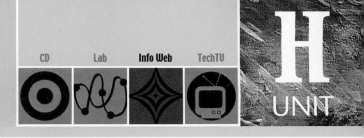
- Each instruction in a vector graphic requires storage space, so the more lines, shapes, and fill patterns in the graphic, the more storage space it requires. Even so, vector graphics usually require less storage space than bitmap graphics.

- It is easier to edit an object in a vector graphic than in a bitmap graphic. In some ways, a vector graphic is like a collage of objects. Each object can be layered over other objects but moved and edited independently. You can individually stretch, shrink, distort, color, move, or delete any object in a vector graphic. See **Figure H-13**.

- Vector graphics tend not to produce images that are as realistic as bitmap images. It is difficult to identify a vector graphic just by looking at an on-screen image. One clue that an image might be a vector graphic is a flat, cartoon-like quality. Think of clip art images, which are typically stored as vector graphics. The cartoon-like characteristic of vector images results from the use of objects filled with blocks of color. Because your options for shading and texturing vector graphics are limited, vector graphics tend to have a flat appearance. For a more definitive identification, however, you should check the filename extension. Vector graphics files have filename extensions such as .wmf, .dxt, .mgx, .eps, .pict, and .cgm.

Figure H-13: Vector graphics are layered

Vector graphic objects are layered, so it is easy to move and delete objects without disrupting the rest of the image

Deleting a shape from a bitmap image leaves a hole because the image is only one layer of pixels

Vector graphics on the Web

Web browsers were originally designed to support a limited number of bitmap graphics formats. Built-in browser support for vector graphics has been slow, but plug-ins and players are currently available for several of the most popular Web-based vector graphics formats. Vector graphics files require little storage space and can be transmitted swiftly from a Web server to your browser. A fairly complex graphic can be stored in a file that is under 30 KB. On Web pages, vector graphics appear with the same consistent quality on all computer screens, making it possible for browsers to adjust the size of an image instantaneously to fit correctly on a screen, regardless of its size or resolution. Any text contained in a vector image is stored as actual text, not just a series of colored dots. This text can be indexed by search engines so that it can be included in keyword searches, and the image can turn up in the list of search results.

A graphics format called **SVG**, or **Scalable Vector Graphics**, is designed specifically for the Web. Graphics in SVG format are automatically resized when displayed on different screens or when printed. SVG supports gradients, drop shadows, multiple levels of transparency, and other effects, along with transportability to other platforms like handheld computers and cellular phones. SVG graphics are typically used on the Web for maps, ads, organizational charts, and flowcharts. SVG graphics objects can include regular and irregular shapes, images, and text, and they can be animated.

Macromedia's Flash software, which requires a browser plug-in to be viewed, creates a popular vector graphics format called SWF, which is designed for Web use. **SWF graphics** use the .swf extensions. **Flash graphics**, which are SWF files, can be static or animated, and typically they require less storage space than SVG graphics. Flash animations created with SWF files have advantages over animated GIFs. GIF files are fairly large because they are bitmap images; most Flash animations are smaller because they are SWF files. As a result, they can be transferred from a Web server to a browser more rapidly than animated GIFs.

Creating vector graphics

To create vector graphics, you cannot use scanners or digital cameras. Instead, you must have special tools and software that work together to generate the instructions for the graphic. This lesson discusses the hardware and software you need to create and edit vector graphics and to create vector graphics from bitmap graphics.

■ Usually, vector graphics are created from scratch using vector graphics software, referred to as **drawing software**. Drawing software is sometimes packaged separately from the paint software used to produce bitmap graphics. In other cases, it is included with bitmap software as a graphics software suite. Vector graphics software provides an array of drawing tools that you can use to create objects, position them, and fill them with colors or patterns. For example, you can use the filled circle tool to draw a circle that is filled with a solid color. You can create an irregular shape by connecting points to outline the shape. **Figure H-14** illustrates how to use drawing tools to create a vector graphic.

Figure H-14: Drawing a vector graphic

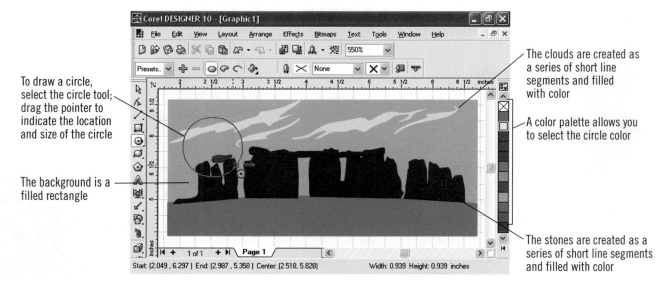

To draw a circle, select the circle tool; drag the pointer to indicate the location and size of the circle

The background is a filled rectangle

The clouds are created as a series of short line segments and filled with color

A color palette allows you to select the circle color

The stones are created as a series of short line segments and filled with color

■ Vector graphics software helps you edit individual objects easily within a graphic by changing their size, shape, position, or color. For example, the data for creating the circle is recorded as an instruction, such as CIRCLE 40 Y 200 150, which means create a circle with a 40-pixel radius, color it yellow, and place the center of the circle 200 pixels from the left of the screen and 150 pixels from the top of the screen. If you move the circle to the right, the instruction that the computer stores for the circle changes to something like CIRCLE 40 Y 500 150, which means the circle is now 500 pixels from the left of the screen instead of 200 pixels.

■ When filling in a shape with color, your vector graphics software might provide tools for creating a gradient. A **gradient** is a smooth blending of shades from one color to another or from light to dark. Gradients can be used to create shading and three-dimensional effects. See **Figure H-15**.

Figure H-15: Gradients can create shading and three-dimensional effects

The use of a gradient makes this shape appear to be a tube

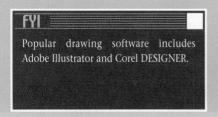
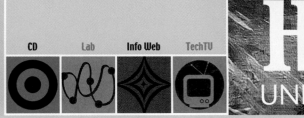
FYI

Popular drawing software includes Adobe Illustrator and Corel DESIGNER.

CD　　　Lab　　Info Web　　TechTV

■ Some vector graphics software provides tools that apply bitmapped textures to vector graphics objects, giving them a more realistic appearance. For example, you can create a vector drawing of a house and then apply a brick-like texture that is derived from a bitmap photograph of real bricks. These graphics that contain both bitmap and vector data are called **metafiles**.

■ Sometimes a special input device, called a digitizing tablet, is used to create vector graphics. A **digitizing tablet** provides a flat surface for a paper-based drawing, and a pen or puck is used to click the endpoints of each line on the drawing. The endpoints are converted into vectors and stored. Architects and engineers sometimes use a digitizing tablet, like the one in **Figure H-16**, to turn a paper-based line drawing into a vector graphic.

Figure H-16: A digitizing tablet

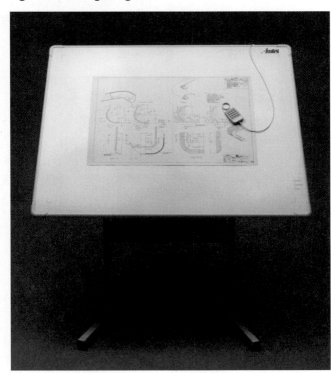

■ Converting a bitmap graphic into a vector graphic is more difficult than converting a vector graphic to a bitmap graphic. To change a bitmap graphic into a vector graphic, you must use special tracing software. **Tracing software** locates the edges of objects in a bitmap graphic and converts the resulting shapes into vector graphic objects. This software works best on simple images and line drawings, but it does not typically provide acceptable results when used on photos.

Using rasterization to create bitmap graphics from vector graphics

You can create a bitmap graphic from a vector graphic through a process called rasterization. **Rasterization** works by superimposing a grid over a vector graphic and determining the color for each pixel. This process is typically carried out by graphics software, which allows you to specify the output size for the final bitmap image.

It is important to output your rasterized images at the size you will ultimately need. If you rasterize a vector image at a small size and then try to enlarge the resulting bitmap image, you will likely get a poor-quality pixelated image. It is also important to know that once a vector graphic is converted to a bitmap, the resulting graphic no longer has the qualities of a vector graphic; you cannot edit the resulting bitmap graphic as you would the original vector graphic. For example, if you convert the Stonehenge vector graphic into a bitmap, you cannot grab the entire sun object and move it without leaving a "hole" where the original sun had been.

Exploring 3-D graphics

Now that you have covered the basics for two-dimensional graphics, this lesson expands what you learned to introduce static 3-D graphics and animated 3-D graphics. If you have played any computer games recently or watched a hit movie like *Shrek* or *Monsters, Inc.*, you have seen the product of computer-generated, 3-D, animated graphics. This lesson discusses 3-D graphics in more detail.

■ Like vector graphics, 3-D graphics are stored as a set of instructions. For a 3-D graphic, however, the instructions contain the locations and lengths of lines that form a wireframe for a three-dimensional object. The **wireframe** provides a framework for the 3-D graphic.

A 3-D wireframe can be covered with surface texture and color to create a graphic of a 3-D object. The process of covering a wireframe with surface color and texture is called **rendering**. The rendering process outputs a bitmap image. See **Figure H-17**.

Figure H-17: Creating a 3-D graphic

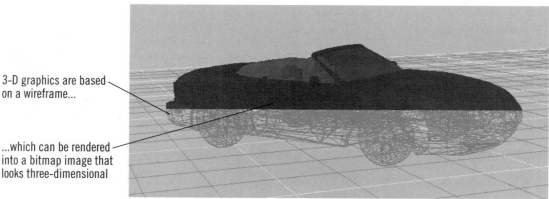

3-D graphics are based on a wireframe...

...which can be rendered into a bitmap image that looks three-dimensional

■ For added realism, the rendering process can take into account the way that light shines on surfaces and creates shadows. The technique for adding light and shadows to a 3-D image is called **ray tracing**. Ray tracing adds realism to 3-D graphics by adding highlights and shadows that are produced by a light source. Before an image is rendered, the artist selects a location for one or more light sources. The computer applies a complex mathematical algorithm to determine how the light source affects the color of each pixel in the final rendered image. This process can take hours for a complex image, even using today's most powerful personal computers. **Figure H-18** shows the image from the previous figure rendered with an additional light source using ray tracing.

Figure H-18: Ray tracing

Light source

Shadow

Highlight

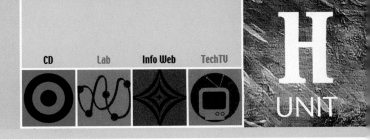
■ 3-D graphics can be animated to produce special effects for movies or create interactive animated characters and environments for 3-D computer games. Animated special effects are created by rendering a sequence of bitmaps in which one or more objects are moved, or otherwise changed, between each rendering. In traditional hand-drawn animation, a chief artist draws the key frames, and then a team of assistants creates each of the in-between frames, which include changes to the images in the key frame. It is common practice to create 24 frames for each second of animation. For 3-D computer animation, the computer creates the in-between frames by moving object(s) and rendering each necessary image. All of the frames are then combined into a single file, creating essentially a digital movie.

■ Graphic design companies like DreamWorks and Pixar Animation Studios use 3-D animation techniques to produce animated feature films, as well as special effects. The first full-length animated 3-D movie was *Toy Story*, released in 1995 by Walt Disney Studios and Pixar. Digitally animated films, such as *Finding Nemo*, the *Ice Age* series, and the *Shrek* series, illustrate the growing sophistication of 3-D animation. An important characteristic of special effects and animated films is that rendering can be accomplished during the production phase of the movie and incorporated into the final footage.

■ In contrast, 3-D computer game animation happens in real time. Each frame that makes the images seem to move must be rendered while you are playing the game—a process that requires an incredible amount of computer power. Consider a game displayed on a computer monitor at 1,024 x 768 resolution, so the screen contains 786,432 pixels. If the game is presented in 32-bit color, each frame of the animation requires 25,165,824 bits (multiply 786,432 by 32). Computer game designers have found that onscreen animation looks smoothest at 60 frames per second, which means that your computer must handle 1,509,949,440—that is, more than 1 billion—bits of information every second just to put the 3-D image onto the screen. In addition, the computer must process even more data to keep track of the movements of each player.

■ To create 3-D graphics, you need 3-D graphics software, such as AutoCAD or Caligari trueSpace. 3-D graphics software provides the tools that you need to draw a wireframe and view it from any angle. See **Figure H-19**. It provides rendering and ray tracing tools, along with an assortment of surface textures and colors that you can apply to individual objects. 3-D graphics software runs on most personal computers, though some architects and engineers prefer to use high-end workstations. A fast processor, lots of RAM, and a fast graphics card with its own video RAM all speed up the rendering process.

Figure H-19: 3-D graphics software

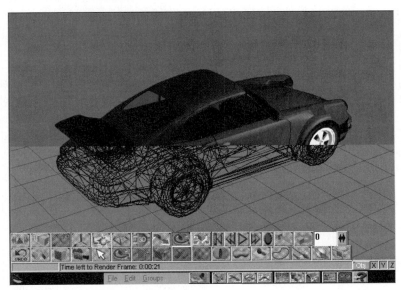

■ To handle all of this data, your computer's main processor gets help from a graphics processor located on your computer's graphics card. These graphics processors vary in their capabilities. For the fastest graphics capability, look for graphics cards identified as 3-D accelerators.

■ You can create 3-D animations on a desktop computer using commercially available software, but many of the best software packages are expensive and have a steep learning curve. These commercial products used by professionals produce higher quality but require powerful computer hardware. If you want to experiment with 3-D animations before making an expensive software investment, you might try one of the shareware programs.

Introducing digital video

A **video** is a series of frames, like those in **Figure H-20**, projected at a rate fast enough to fool the human eye into perceiving continuous motion. Each frame is essentially a still picture that can be stored as a bitmap graphic. You can use a consumer-quality camera and your personal computer to create videos that are suitable for a variety of personal and professional uses.

Figure H-20: A video is a series of frames

- **Digital video** is filmed sequences of images or footage of real objects. Digital video stores color and brightness data for each video frame. The process is similar to storing the data for a series of bitmap images in which the color for each pixel is represented by a binary number. Footage for digital videos can be obtained using a video camera, videotape, television, DVD, or even a **digital video recording (DVR) device** such as TiVo.

- **Desktop video** refers to videos that are constructed and displayed using a personal computer. Desktop video can be stored on a hard disk or distributed on CDs, DVDs, videotapes, memory cards, or the Web. Typically, the footage for a desktop video is captured by a video camera or converted into digital format from videotape. The basic process of creating desktop videos consists of the steps described in **Figure H-21**.

- Once the video footage is captured and transferred to your computer's memory, you must save the video footage to the hard drive. Although video playback requires no special hardware, it does require a software player that is designed to work with the file format in which the video is stored. Players for most video file formats are available for free as downloads from the Web. Most of today's personal computers are well-equipped for viewing videos; however, playback quality can vary depending on your computer's microprocessor, RAM capacity, and the capabilities of its graphics card. When viewing Web-based videos, the speed of your Internet connection also affects video quality.

- Your computer displays video frames as fast as they are received and processed. **Frame rate** refers to the number of frames shown per second; the higher the frame rate, the better the video image. Feature films are typically projected at a rate of 24 frames per second (fps). Most desktop videos have a frame rate of only 15 fps. On a slow computer or using a dial-up Internet connection, videos might appear in a very small window on the screen, images might appear choppy and pixelated, and the sound might get out of sync with the action.

- Digital video is stored in one of several different digital formats. Digital video encompasses several technologies and is classified by its format. Several file formats are popular for desktop videos including **AVI**, **QuickTime**, **MPEG**, **Real Media**, **WMV**, and **VOB**. **Table H-2** provides some basic information about each format.

- Digital video can also be classified according to the device on which it is played and viewed. As already mentioned, desktop video can be viewed using a personal computer. A player or plug-in is required, as determined by the video format.

Figure H-21: Steps to create a desktop video

1. Shoot the video footage, then transfer the footage to your computer's hard disk

2. Edit the video and soundtrack

3. Output the video in its final format

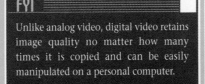
FYI

Unlike analog video, digital video retains image quality no matter how many times it is copied and can be easily manipulated on a personal computer.

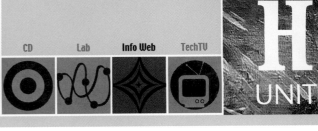
CD   Lab   Info Web   TechTV

H
UNIT

- **Web-based video** refers to digital video incorporated in Web pages and accessed with a browser; it might use one of several different formats. You need video player software to view Web-based video. The type of player you need depends on the format of the Web-based video.

- **DVD-video** refers to digital video used for commercial DVDs that contain feature-length films and that use a DVD format. DVD-videos can be played using a personal computer that has a DVD player. **PDA video** refers to digital video that uses a format designed to be viewed on a PDA or smartphone screen, as discussed next.

- Some PDAs and smartphones can be configured to play digital videos. See **Figure H-22**. The device requires video or multimedia player software, such as Pocket TV or Windows Media Player, and storage capacity for the video file—usually on a solid-state memory card. Videos specially optimized for handheld devices can be downloaded from Web sites to your computer, then transferred to handheld storage and played. Popular formats for handheld video include **MPEG** and **WMV**.

Figure H-22: A video plays on a smartphone

Table H-2: Popular desktop video file formats

FORMAT	EXTENSION	PLAYERS/ PLATFORM	DESCRIPTION
AVI (Audio Video Interleave)	.avi	Microsoft Media Player/PC	Sometimes called "Video for Windows," AVI is the most common format for desktop video on PCs
QuickTime Movie	.mov	QuickTime, Microsoft Media Player/PC, Mac, UNIX, Linux	Originally developed for the Mac platform, one of the most popular formats for desktop and streaming Web videos
MPEG (Moving Pictures Experts Group)	.mpg or .mpeg	Microsoft Media Player/PC, Mac, UNIX, Linux	MPEG is one of the most sophisticated digital video formats; used both for desktop videos and DVD movies, MPEG was formed in 1988 to establish an international standard for the coded representation of moving pictures and associated audio on digital storage media. Currently there are three MPEG standards: MPEG1, MPEG2, and MPEG4; used for desktop video, PDA video, HDTV, and streaming Web video
Real Media	.rm	RealPlayer, Microsoft Media Player/PC, Mac, UNIX, Linux	Produced by RealNetworks, a popular format for streaming Web videos
WMV (Windows Media Video)	.wmv	Microsoft Media Player/PC	Offers sophisticated compression options for high-quality images; used for desktop video, PDA video, and streaming video over the Web
VOB (Video Object)	.vob	Stand-alone DVD players, PC, Mac, Linux	Industry-standard format for stand-alone DVD players

Exploring video equipment

To create a desktop video, you need a video camera. To edit and modify video footage, you transfer the video footage from your video camera to your computer. This lesson explores cameras you can use to capture the video and the equipment that you need for transferring the video footage from your camera to your computer. It also reviews video capture software and video editing software and techniques.

- You can use either a digital or an analog video camera to shoot the footage for desktop video. A **digital video (dv) camera** stores footage as digital data, that is, as a series of bits. The video data is stored on a storage medium, such as a DVD, a flash memory card, or a tape. Digital videotape formats include miniDV, DVCPro, and DVCam. MiniDV is used by most consumer digital video cameras.

- You can also use an **analog video camera** to shoot the footage for your desktop video. As with digital video cameras, the footage is stored on a storage medium, usually tape; but instead of storing the video as digital data, an analog video camera stores the video as a continuous track of magnetic patterns. The three most popular analog video formats are Hi8, S-VHS, and VHS.

- In addition to video cameras, you might also be familiar with the small inexpensive videoconferencing cameras (often called a "Web camera" or a "Web cam") that attach directly to a computer. See **Figure H-23**. These cameras capture video data in digital format and are designed mainly for talking head applications, such as online video chats and videoconferences.

- Digital video cameras generally produce higher quality video than analog or videoconferencing cameras. Images produced using digital video cameras tend to be sharper and more colorful.

- In order to digitally edit, process, and store a desktop video, the video must be transferred from the camera to the computer. If an analog video camera was used, the video must be converted into digital format before it is stored on your computer's hard disk. This analog-to-digital conversion process is referred to as capturing a video. A **video capture device** converts the camera's analog signal into digital data. If your computer's graphics card does not include video capture capabilities, you can purchase a separate video capture device that connects to your computer's USB port or a video capture card that plugs into one of your computer's PCI slots. Most video capture devices support a variety of analog video sources, such as cameras and VCRs.

- A digital video camera captures video data in digital format, which can then be transferred directly to a computer for editing. The basic method for transferring video footage to a computer is to send the data over a cable that connects the video camera to a computer. Digital video data is usually transferred directly to the computer without conversion. Most digital cameras provide a **FireWire port** or **USB port** for this purpose. The computer needs a corresponding port to accept the cable from the camera. **Figure H-24** shows a personal computer with built-in FireWire port and USB port, respectively.

Figure H-23: Web cam

Figure H-24: FireWire and USB ports

FireWire ports

USB ports

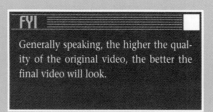

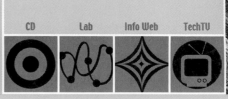

Figure H-25 shows one configuration that could be used to transfer video data from a digital camera to a notebook computer.

Figure H-25: Transferring video from a digital video camera to a computer

You can transfer video footage to a hard disk by connecting a cable between a video camera and a computer

■ Whether you are transferring footage from an analog camera or a digital camera, you must use **video capture software**, which allows you to start and stop the transfer and select the display size, frame rate, filename, and file format for your video footage. Once the footage is transferred and stored on a computer's hard disk or other storage medium, unwanted video footage can be cut from the file; the remaining video footage can be divided into separate clips and the clips can be rearranged. Videos are easier to edit if you divide them into several files, each containing a one- or two-minute video clip. Some video capture software automatically creates clips by detecting frame changes, such as when you turn your camera off, pause, or switch to a new scene. See **Figure H-26**.

Figure H-26: Transferring videos as short clips

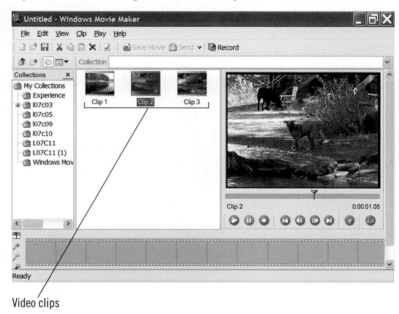

Video clips

Creating good desktop videos

When desktop videos are processed and stored, some of the image data is eliminated to reduce the video file to a manageable size. Simpler videos tend to maintain better quality as they are edited, processed, and stored. Camera movements, fast actions, patterned clothing, and moving backgrounds all contribute to the complexity of a video. The following techniques will help you produce video footage that maintains good quality as it is edited and processed:

- Use a tripod to maintain a steady image.
- Move the camera slowly if it is necessary to pan from side to side.
- Zoom in and out slowly.
- Direct your subjects to move slowly, when possible.
- Position your shot to eliminate as much background detail and movement.
- Ask the subjects of your video to wear solid-colored clothing, if possible.

Editing and processing desktop video

Before video cameras went digital, editing a video consisted of recording segments from one videotape onto another. This process, called **linear editing**, required at least two VCRs. Today's **nonlinear editing** simply requires a computer hard disk and video editing software, and it has the advantage of using a random-access device to edit and arrange footage. The disadvantage is that video footage requires a lot of available storage space, generally 1 GB of storage per 5 minutes of video.

■ Once the video footage is transferred to a computer and stored on the hard disk, it can be edited using **video editing software**. The completed video consists of video tracks containing video segments and transitions, plus audio tracks containing voices and music. The video tracks and the audio tracks can be arranged on a timeline. Most video editing software allows a video track to be overlayed with several audio tracks. See **Figure H-27**.

After the video tracks and the audio tracks are modified, the video editing software combines the data from all of the selected tracks into a single file. This file is stored on a computer's hard disk as a desktop video using a video file format, such as AVI or QuickTime.

Figure H-27: Video editing software

Use the video clips on the timeline to indicate the sequence for your video clips and transitions

Use the audio tracks to add sound clips

The video and sound clips that you import for the project appear in a list

A timeline stretches across the top of the video editing window and provides the structure for each second of your video

Preview your video to see how the video clips, transitions, and soundtrack all work together

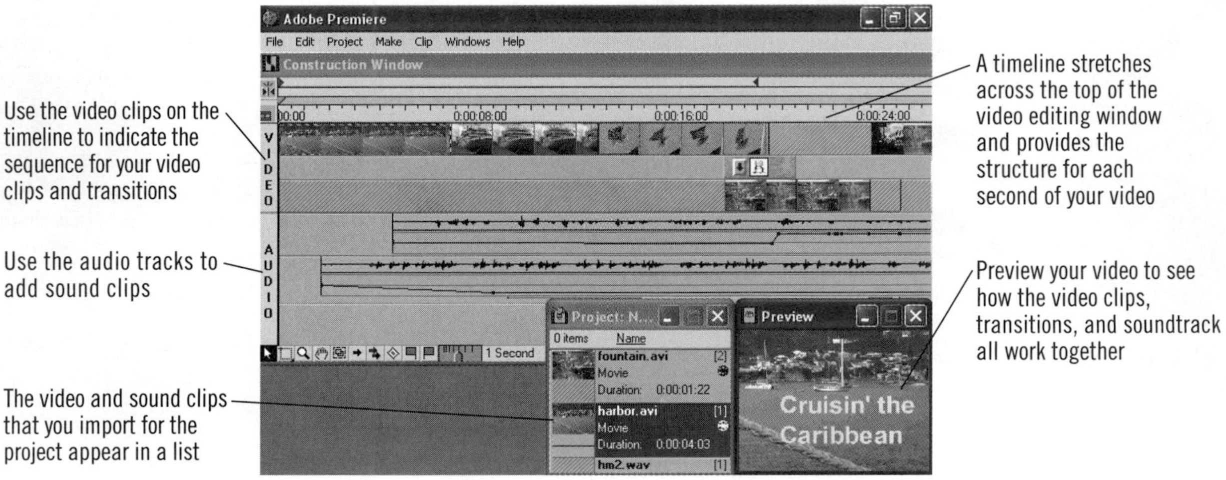

■ Because video footage contains large amounts of data, it is often necessary to reduce the number of bits used to represent the video data. The following steps can be taken to shrink videos to a more manageable size.

• Decrease the size of the video window. When creating desktop video, you can specify the size of the window in which your video appears. A smaller window contains fewer pixels than a full-screen window and requires fewer bits to represent the data, but some details become difficult to see in the smaller video window.

• Reduce the frame rate. The smooth motion that you expect from commercial films is achieved in a desktop video by displaying 24 fps. Reducing the frame rate to 15 fps—a typical rate for desktop video—cuts the file size almost in half. However, reducing the frame rate tends to increase the blurriness of a video, especially for fast-action sequences.

• Compress the video data. Several compression techniques were created specifically to reduce the size of video files. A **codec (compressor/decompressor)** is the software that compresses a file when a desktop video is created and decompresses the file when the video is played. Popular codecs include MPEG, Indeo, Cinepak, DivX, and Windows Media Video 9. Each of these codecs uses a unique compression algorithm and allows you to specify the level of compression that you desire. MPEG is both a file format and a codec, so files in MPEG format use the MPEG codec. Files in other formats, such as AVI and MOV, can also use the MPEG codec to compress file contents. The three videos associated with **Figure H-28** illustrate the differences in image quality and file size that result from using different compression techniques.

FYI

Most video editing software allows you to set the file format, frame rate, color depth, and compression levels as you are saving the video in its final form.

Figure H-28: Comparing compression and frame rates

To achieve the best compression for a particular video, experiment with different codecs, compression levels, and frame rates:

Compression ratio: 35:1
Frame rate: 3
File size: 35 KB

Compression ratio: 14:1
Frame rate: 10
File size: 76 KB

Compression ratio: 3:1
Frame rate: 15
File size: 353 KB

The codec used to compress a video must be used to decompress the video when it is played; videos should use one of the codecs included in popular video players, such as QuickTime or Windows Media Player; missing codecs account for a high proportion of desktop video glitches

■ A video for a Web page is stored on a Web server in a file. Usually a link for the video file appears on the Web page. When you click the link, the Web server transmits a copy of the video file to your computer. If you have the correct video player installed on your computer, the video appears on your computer screen. Sometimes your computer has to wait until it receives the entire video file before starting to play it. An alternative method, called **streaming video**, sends a small segment of the video to your computer and begins to play it while your computer continues to receive it. Streaming video is possible with MPEG4, MOV, WMV, RM, and Flash video formats.

Although it is possible to play streaming videos over a dial-up connection, it is not an optimal experience. High-speed Internet connections provide much more bandwidth for streaming video. Videos that are designed to be played over high-speed connections can have a larger video window and less compression, resulting in better quality. Until everyone has a high-speed connection, however, many Web sites provide one video file that is optimized for dial-up connections and a better-quality video file optimized for broadband connections.

Videos included on Web pages can be either external videos or internal videos. **External video** uses an HTML tag to display a link to a video file. When the link is clicked, the video file is downloaded, the video player is opened, and the video is displayed in a separate window. An **internal video**, or in-place video, uses the <embed> tag so, instead of opening a separate window for the video player, an internal video plays within the Web page. See **Figure H-29**.

Figure H-29: An external Web video vs. an internal, or in place, video

Internal Web video plays "in place"

An external Web video plays in a separate window

Introducing digital sound

Computers can record, store, and play sounds, such as narration, sound effects, and music. Swapping music files over the Internet is currently a popular use of digital sound, but digital sound also plays a key role in many other interesting applications. This lesson introduces digital sound concepts and technologies.

Figure H-30: Sampling a sound wave

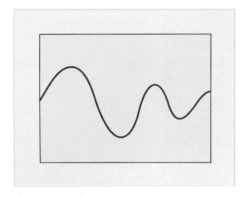

An analog sound wave is a smooth curve of continuous values

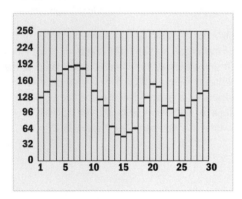

To digitize a sound wave, it is sliced into vertical segments, called samples; for purposes of illustration, this one-second sound wave was sliced into 30 samples

Sample	Sample Height (Decimal)	Sample Height (Binary)
1	130	10000010
2	140	10001100
3	160	10100000
4	175	10101111
5	185	10111001

The height of each sample is converted into a binary number and stored; the height of sample 3 is 160 (decimal), so it is stored as its binary equivalent—10100000

- **Waveform audio** is a digital representation of sound. Music, voice, and sound effects can all be recorded as waveforms. To record sound digitally, samples of the sound are collected at periodic intervals and stored as numeric data. **Figure H-30** shows how a computer digitally samples a sound wave.

- **Sampling rate** refers to the number of times per second that a sound is collected or measured during the recording process and is expressed in hertz (Hz). One thousand samples per second is 1,000 Hz or 1 KHz (kilohertz). Higher sampling rates increase the quality of the sound recording but require more storage space than lower sampling rates. The audio clips associated with **Figure H-31** illustrate how sampling rate affects sound quality.

Figure H-31: Comparing audio clips

Low sampling rate: File size = 66 KB

Medium sampling rate: File size = 124 KB

High sampling rate: File size = 235 KB

- Waveform audio can be stored in a variety of file formats. **Table H-3** presents some of the advantages and disadvantages of the most popular waveform audio file formats. Wave format files are supported by most Web browsers, so it is a popular audio file format. Web-based waveform audio is often delivered in streaming format over the Internet, so the sound plays as it is downloaded. Streaming audio avoids lengthy delays while the entire audio file is downloaded and provides the technology for real-time Internet radio broadcasts and voice chat sessions.

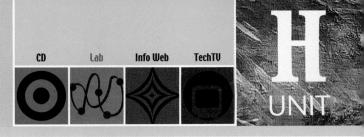
Table H-3: Popular waveform audio file formats

AUDIO FORMAT	EXTENSION	ADVANTAGES	DISADVANTAGES
Advanced Audio Compression (AAC)	.aac	Very good sound quality; compressed format, used on files available via the iTunes music download site	Files are copy protected and use is limited to approved devices
Audio Interchange File Format (AIFF)	.aif	Excellent sound quality; supported in browsers without a plug-in	Audio data is stored in raw, uncompressed format, so files are very large
MP3 (also called MPEG-1 Layer 3)	.mp3	Good sound quality even though the file is compressed; can be streamed over the Web	Requires a stand-alone player or browser plug-in
RealAudio	.ra, .rx	High degree of compression produces small files; data can be streamed over the Web	Sound quality is not up to the standards of other formats; requires a player or plug-in
Wave	.wav	Good sound quality; supported in browsers without a plug-in	Audio data is stored in raw, uncompressed format, so files are very large
Windows Media Audio (WMA)	.wma	Compressed format, very good sound quality; used on music download sites	Files can be copy protected; requires Windows Media Player 9 or above

■ An audio player, such as Microsoft Media Player, is required to play an audio file. These players tend to support several audio file formats. In the Windows environment, the Microsoft Media Player can be used to play **Wave**, **AIFF**, and **MP3** formats. Sound recording software, such as Microsoft's Sound Recorder software, is required to record sound.

■ Software called a CD ripper copies or "rips" tracks from an audio CD and stores them in Wave format. An **MP3 encoder** is used to convert the Wave file into MP3 format. MP3 files can be stored on a computer's hard disk, transferred to a CD, or relocated to a portable MP3 player.

■ A computer's **sound card** contains a variety of input and output jacks plus audio-processing circuitry. It contains the circuitry responsible for transforming the bits stored in an audio file into music, sound effects, and narration. A desktop computer's sound card usually is plugged into a PCI expansion slot inside the system unit. Sound card circuitry is sometimes built into the motherboard of notebook computers.

A sound card is typically equipped to accept input from a microphone and provide output to speakers or headphones. For processing waveform files, a sound card contains a special type of circuitry called a **digital signal processor** (see **Figure H-32**). The digital signal processor transforms digital bits into analog waves when a waveform audio file is being played, transforms analog waves into digital bits when a sound recording is being made, and handles compression and decompression, if necessary.

Figure H-32: How sound cards convert signals

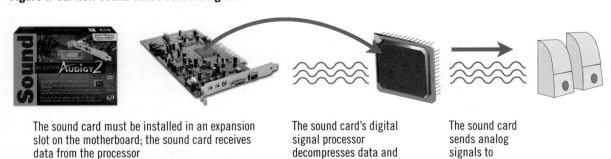

The sound card must be installed in an expansion slot on the motherboard; the sound card receives data from the processor

The sound card's digital signal processor decompresses data and converts it to analog signals

The sound card sends analog signals to speakers

Exploring synthesized sound

Waveform audio is a digital version of an analog sound signal. In contrast, **synthesized sound** is artificially created. This lesson explores synthesized sounds, which include MIDI music and synthesized speech.

■ **MIDI (Musical Instrument Digital Interface)** specifies a standard way to store music data for synthesizers, electronic MIDI instruments, and computers. MIDI is a music notation system that allows computers to communicate with music synthesizers. Waveform sound files contain digitized recordings of real sound passages, but MIDI files contain instructions for creating the pitch, volume, and duration of notes that sound like various musical instruments. MIDI files are much more compact than waveform audio files.

■ The computer encodes the music as a **MIDI sequence** and stores it as a file with a .mid, .cmf, or .rol filename extension. A MIDI sequence contains instructions specifying the pitch of a note, the point at which a note begins, the instrument that plays the note, the volume of the note, and the duration of the note.

■ Most computer sound cards are equipped to capture music data from a MIDI instrument as well as generate music from MIDI files. A MIDI-capable sound card contains a **wavetable** (sometimes called a patch set), which is a set of prerecorded musical instrument sounds. The sound card accesses these sounds and plays them as instructed by the MIDI file.

■ MIDI files are much more compact than waveform audio files. Depending on the exact piece of music, three minutes of MIDI music might require only 10 kilobytes of storage space, whereas the same piece of music stored in a high-quality, uncompressed waveform file might require 15 megabytes of storage space.

■ MIDI is not suitable for vocals, and it does not have the full resonance of waveform audio sound. Most musicians can easily identify MIDI recordings because they simply lack the tonal qualities of symphony-quality sound, as illustrated in the audio clips associated with **Figure H-33**.

Figure H-33: Music notation of one part of MIDI music associated with audio clip

■ MIDI is a good choice for adding background music to multimedia projects and Web pages. Using a procedure similar to that for waveform audio files, you can add a link to a MIDI file by inserting a tag within an HTML document. Most browsers include built-in support for MIDI music.

■ You can use MIDI software to compose your own tunes, or you can get permission to use MIDI files that you find on the Web. For composing your own MIDI music, you can input the notes from a MIDI instrument, such as an electronic keyboard, directly to your computer. The input is typically handled by music composition software, similar to that shown in **Figure H-34**. Music composition software provides tools for entering notes, specifying instruments, printing sheet music, and saving compositions. You can also use it to edit the notes and combine the parts for several instruments.

Figure H-34: Music composition software

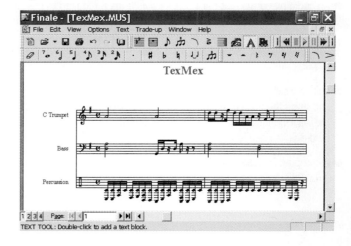

■ **Speech synthesis** is the process by which machines, such as computers, produce sound that resembles spoken words. **Speech recognition** (or voice recognition) refers to the ability of a machine to understand spoken words.

■ Speech synthesis is a key technology in wireless communication. For example, it is possible to have a speech synthesizer read your e-mail messages to you when you call for messages using your cell phone. A speech synthesizer can also read a computer screen aloud, which provides access to computers and the Internet for individuals with vision impairment. Most speech synthesizers string together basic sound units called **phonemes**. A basic speech synthesizer consists of **text-to-speech software**, which generates sounds that are played through your computer's standard sound card; other speech synthesizers are special-purpose hardware devices.

■ A speech recognition system typically collects words spoken into a microphone that is attached to the sound card. The sound card's digital signal processor transforms the analog sound of your voice into digital data, which is then processed by speech recognition software. **Speech recognition software** analyzes the sounds of your voice and breaks them down into phonemes. Next, the software analyzes the content of your speech and compares the groups of phonemes to the words in a digital dictionary that lists phoneme combinations along with their corresponding English (or French, Spanish, and so on) words. When a match is found, the software displays the correctly spelled word on the screen.

■ Speech recognition can be used to activate Windows controls instead of using a mouse. Most speech recognition software also works with your browser, allowing you to "voice surf" the Web. Windows XP includes speech recognition software that you can activate by using the Speech icon in the Control Panel. The first step in using XP's speech recognition feature is training the computer to recognize your speaking style—your accent, pronunciation, and idiomatic expressions—using the Voice Training Wizard. See **Figure H-35**. When training is complete, you can use the speech recognition feature to verbally issue commands in Windows and dictate text in applications, such as Microsoft Word and

Excel, which support the speech recognition feature. The Windows Voice Training Wizard displays short text passages; as you read each passage, the computer listens to the way you pronounce each word and stores it in your speech profile.

Figure H-35: The Windows Voice Training Wizard

What are portable audio players?

Portable audio players like those pictured in **Figure H-36** are pocket-sized, battery-powered devices that store digital music. You can transfer a series of digital music tracks, called a playlist, from your computer's hard disk to your portable audio player so you can listen to your personal collection of music anywhere.

Digital music is available from a wide variety of sources. The Web offers a wide selection of online music stores where you can buy songs or entire albums. You can sample free digital music before you buy it from performing artists who post sample tracks on Web sites. You can also digitize music from your CD collection by using CD ripper software that converts CD-audio music into computer-friendly waveform audio format.

The first generation of online music was distributed in MP3 format. Although MP3 remains a popular audio file format, newer standards offer better sound quality and compression. Apple uses the AAC format for music downloads at its iTunes Music Store. Microsoft uses its WMA format for music downloads at the Wal-Mart Music Downloads site and at MSN Music. Some portable audio players support a variety of digital music formats, whereas others support only one format. For example, Apple's iPod supports several digital music formats, including AAC, MP3, WAV, and AIFF. When purchasing a portable audio player, you should consider which music formats you are likely to use.

The trend in portable audio players is to include a screen, a high-capacity mini-hard disk, personal organizer software, games, and connections for an external microphone and memory card reader. Personal audio players now store a huge collection of digital music as well as document, photo, and video files. You can use it as a voice recorder and as a personal organizer for storing contacts and appointments.

Figure H-36

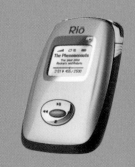

Tech Talk Data Compression

Digital media files can be quite large. They need lots of storage space, require lengthy transmission times, and easily become fragmented, which reduces the efficiency of your computer's hard disk drive. Reducing the size of a file would minimize these problems. **Data compression** is the general term used to describe the process of recoding data so that it requires fewer bytes of storage space; bytes are removed, which reduces the file size. Because data compression is reversible, bytes previously removed from a file can be restored. The process of reversing data compression is sometimes referred to as uncompressing, decompressing, extracting, or expanding a file.

The amount of shrinkage produced by data compression is referred to as the **compression ratio**. A compression ratio of 20:1, for example, means that a compressed file is 20 times smaller than the original file. Data compression is based on a **compression algorithm**—the steps that are required to shrink the data in a file and reconstitute the file to its original state. A compression algorithm is incorporated into a codec, which is used by a computer to compress and decompress file data. Some compression algorithms are generalized and work for any type of data, while others are designed to shrink text files; other algorithms are for graphics, sound, or video data.

Compression that reduces the file size without any data loss, known as **lossless compression**, provides the means to compress a file and then reconstitute all of the data into its original state. In contrast, **lossy compression** throws away some of the original data during the compression process. Lossy compression can be applied to graphics, videos, and sounds because, in theory, the human eye or ear will not miss the lost information. Most lossy compression techniques provide adjustable compression levels so that you can decide how much data you can afford to lose.

Although most of today's codecs contain sophisticated compression algorithms that are beyond the scope of this book, we can look at some examples of simple compression algorithms to get a general idea of how they work.

Dictionary-based compression replaces common sequences of characters with a single codeword, or symbol, that points either to a dictionary of the original characters or to the original occurrence of the word.

Statistical compression, such as the well-known Huffman algorithm, takes advantage of the frequency of characters to reduce file size. Characters that appear frequently are recoded as short bit patterns, while those that appear infrequently are assigned longer bit patterns.

Spatial compression takes advantage of redundant data within a file by looking for patterns of bytes and replacing them with a message that describes the pattern. **Run-length encoding (RLE)** is an example of a lossless, spatial compression technique that replaces a series of similarly colored pixels with a code that indicates the number of pixels and their colors. JPEG is a lossy version of run-length encoding that can be applied to images, such as photographs, that do not have large areas of solid color. A True Color photograph might not have any adjoining pixels of the same color. Applying run-length encoding to such a photo would not result in any compression whatsoever. JPEG "preprocesses" an image by tweaking the colors in adjoining pixels so that they are the same color whenever possible. Once this preprocessing is complete, run-length encoding techniques can be applied with more success.

Temporal compression is a technique that can be applied to video footage or sound clips to eliminate redundant or unnecessary data between video frames or audio samples. In the case of video, for example, if you are working with a video of a talking head, the background image is likely to contain lots of redundant information that does not change from one frame to the next. As the temporal compression algorithm begins to analyze the frames, the first frame becomes a **key frame** that contains all of the data. As the compression algorithm analyzes subsequent frames in the video, it stores only the data that is different from the data in the key frame.

Some file formats, such as PCX, GIF, and MP3, always compress data. Other file formats allow you to select not only whether or not you want to compress the file, but also the level of compression. The software that you use to save and open these files contains the codecs necessary to compress and decompress them. Codecs for JPEG, MPEG, AVI, DivX, and QuickTime files typically allow you to select compression levels before saving a graphic or video file. Some TIFF files are compressed, but others are not—it depends on the software used to store the file.

Most files that contain documents and databases are not stored in compressed format. BMP and Wave files are also stored as "raw," noncompressed bits. If you want to compress these files before sending them as e-mail attachments, for example, you can use file compression software. BMP and DOC file sizes might shrink by as much as 70 percent. Other noncompressed file formats, such as Wave, may compress by about 20 percent. File formats such as GIF, MP3, MPEG, and JPEG hardly shrink at all when you compress them because they are already stored in a compressed format.

To manually compress a file, such as a Word document or a Windows bitmap image, you can work with a **file compression utility**, to shrink one or more files into a single new file. You cannot use this compressed file until it has been decompressed. WinZip, a file compression utility, produces compressed files with .zip extensions. Compressing a file is called **zipping**; decompressing a file is called **unzipping**. **Figure H-37** shows files that were zipped using WinZip software.

Figure H-37: The WinZip window

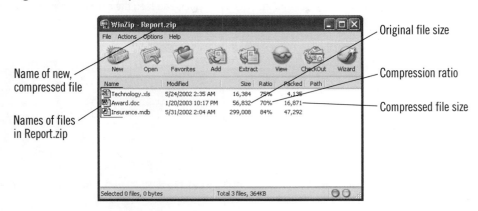

Name of new, compressed file

Names of files in Report.zip

Original file size

Compression ratio

Compressed file size

Windows XP includes a built-in compression feature that allows you to create compressed folders. Any files that you drag into a compressed folder are automatically compressed. Compressed folders provide fairly transparent compression. You do not have to do anything special to open a file from a compressed folder. Simply double-click the filename as usual and Windows automatically decompresses the file before displaying its contents. When you create a compressed folder, Windows automatically adds a .zip extension to the folder name. In this way, the folder is treated like a zipped file by other compression utilities, such as

PKZIP and WinZip. For example, if you want to e-mail several bitmap graphics, you can create a zipped folder to store the graphic files. First, you save them in BMP format. Next, create a compressed folder called Photos (see **Figure H-38**). Drag the bitmap graphics into the Photos folder. Attach the Photos folder to your e-mail message. The attachment will be named Photos.zip. The recipient of your e-mail can open the attachment using Windows or a file compression utility, such as PKZIP or WinZIP.

Figure H-38: Compressed folders

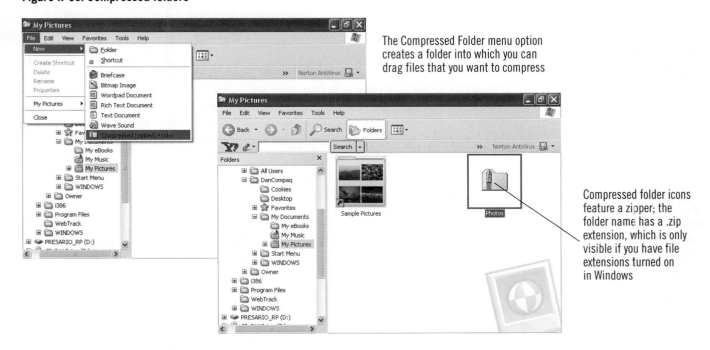

The Compressed Folder menu option creates a folder into which you can drag files that you want to compress

Compressed folder icons feature a zipper; the folder name has a .zip extension, which is only visible if you have file extensions turned on in Windows

Computers in Context Film

In 1895, eager Parisians crowded into a busy café to watch the first public presentation of an exciting new invention—the Cinematograph. The 10-minute film, mostly scenes of everyday life, was a smashing success and ushered in the motion picture era.

Early films were short, grainy, grayscale, and silent, but technology quickly improved. In the New York debut of *The Jazz Singer* (1927), Al Jolson spoke the first words in a feature film, "Wait a minute, wait a minute. You ain't heard nothin' yet!" The audience rose to its feet, applauding wildly. In 1935, RKO studios released *Becky Sharp*, the first feature-length movie filmed from beginning to end in Technicolor—a real milestone for the film industry. Even before "talkies" and Technicolor, filmmakers sought ways to escape the bounds of reality through special effects. As early as 1925, directors such as Willis O'Brien used stop-motion photography to animate dinosaurs, giant gorillas, and sword-wielding skeletons. Special-effects technologies—miniatures, blue screens, puppets, claymation, and composite shots—were used with varying degrees of skill over the next 50 years.

Films such as Stanley Kubrick's masterpiece, *2001: A Space Odyssey* (1968), and George Lucas's original *Star Wars* (1977) stretched these technologies to their limits, but audiences demanded even more spectacular, yet "realistic," effects. In 1982, Disney released *TRON*, a movie about a computer programmer who, at the whim of an evil Master Control Program, becomes trapped in the depths of a computer where programs are humanlike creatures. The movie included the first primitive attempts at computer-generated footage—30 minutes of computer-generated imagery (CGI) created by two Cray XMP supercomputers. CGI uses rendering techniques to create a 3-D scene from a 2-D image, a camera angle, and a light source. Sophisticated algorithms determine how textures, colors, and shadows appear in the rendered scene. Camera angles can be changed at will, and fantastic effects can be created by bending or stretching the image, manipulating light, creating textures, and adding movement to the scene.

> "Our ability to manufacture fraud now exceeds our ability to detect it."

Rendered scenes can be set in motion with computer animation techniques. Manual animation requires a painstaking process called "in-betweening," in which an artist draws a series of incrementally different images to produce the illusion of movement. See **Figure H-39**. Today, computers can easily generate in-between images and free up human animators for even more challenging work.

A captivating animation special effect called morphing was first seen on the big screen in James Cameron's *Abyss* (1989) and later used in *Terminator II* (1991) and other movies. Like in-betweening, morphing starts out with animators defining the morph's start and end points—for example, in *Terminator II*, the liquid metal face of the T-1000 robot and

actor Robert Patrick's face. The start and end points are rendered into digital images, and then the computer generates all the in-between

Figure H-39

images. Human animators tweak the images by inserting small discrepancies for a touch of less-than-perfect realism in the final image.

Although the process might sound simple, morphing complex objects realistically and believably takes a tremendous amount of time and computer power. The five-minute morphing sequence in *Terminator II* took special-effects company Industrial Light and Magic one year to create.

Memorable computer-generated scenes from 2002 blockbusters include the breathtaking aerial scenes in *Spiderman*, a furry blue monster named Sully careening downhill in *Monsters, Inc.*, and the endless army of Uruk-hai marching down the valley toward Helm's Deep in *The Two Towers*. Spiderman's acrobatic swing through Manhattan was generated with three professional rendering products: Maya, Houdini, and RenderMan. The Uruk-hai were created with MASSIVE, a custom program that gave each computer-generated warrior a unique sequence of actions. To individually animate each of Sully's 2,320,413 blue hairs, animators developed software called Fizt, a dynamic simulator.

Rendering, morphing, and other special-effects processing require sophisticated computer systems. Pixar Inc., the company that provided the technology behind *Toy Story*, *Finding Nemo*, *Monsters Inc.*, and many other feature-length animated films, uses a cluster of computers dubbed the "RenderFarm." Consisting of more than 100 Sun SPARCstation computers, the network can process 16 billion instructions per second. A movie such as *Toy Story* took more than 800,000 computer hours to produce using the RenderFarm. That might seem like a long time, but if Pixar animators had attempted to use a single-processor computer, it would have taken 43 years to finish the job!

Other CGI variations are being used for increasingly sophisticated effects. Special-effects guru John Gaeta developed bullet time and image-based rendering for *The Matrix* (1999), *The Matrix: Reloaded* (2003), and

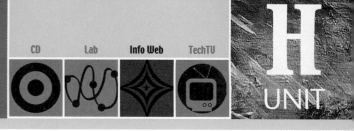
Hero (2002/2004). See **Figure H-40**. Bullet time produces reality-defying action sequences that slow time to a tantalizing crawl and then crank it back up to normal speed as the camera pivots rapidly around the scene. The effect requires a computer to meticulously trigger a circular array of more than 100 still cameras in sequence. Image-based rendering generates a digital image based on photos of objects, scenes, or people. The 2-D photos can be digitally manipulated to create 3-D objects, eliminating the need for conventional CGI's computationally intensive 3-D wireframes and ray tracing.

Films such as *Sky Captain and the World of Tomorrow* (2004) and *Sin City* (2005) took green-screen special effects to a new level. This technique allows actors and scale models to appear as though they are in a specific environment, a geographical location, or an imaginary situation. Filmed entirely indoors on a sound stage, these movies used a technique called compositing that layers two or more video clips over each other and merges them into one image. Actors were filmed against a green background screen. During post-production, video editing software removed the background and layered in scenery created with CGI or from real footage on location.

Sophisticated animation and rendering techniques now come close to producing realistic human figures. Animations were once clearly two-dimensional and far from lifelike, but CGI renderings are becoming more difficult to distinguish from real actors. What might happen in the future is the subject of *Simone* (2002), starring Al Pacino as a washed-up director who is given a hard disk containing code for a computer-generated movie star. Pacino uses her as the leading lady in a string of hits, all the while keeping her identity secret. According to reviewer Leigh Johnson, it becomes clear that Simone, a computer generated image, is more authentic than the people watching her. It is one of the film's main themes, expressed by Pacino's character: "Our ability to manufacture fraud now exceeds our ability to detect it."

The implications of computer-generated actors are just emerging. Not only do they blur the line between reality and fiction, but they also raise puzzling questions for actors and their agents, directors, and programmers. Is it possible to create CGI doubles for long-dead actors, such as Marilyn Monroe and James Dean? If so, who controls their use and profits from their work? Can aging actors sign contracts for use of their "young" CGI counterparts? Would it be legal and ethical for programmers to create and market virtual characters based on real actors or a compilation of the best traits of popular stars? As is often the case, new technologies present concerns along with their benefits—issues you might want to consider the next time you watch a movie.

Figure H-40

Issue Who Owns the Rights?

Suppose you purchase a music CD of your favorite recording group. Now you want to transfer the music to your computer, rip the best tracks, and transfer these songs to your portable audio player. As you attempt to copy the music files, you discover that the CD is copy protected and your computer CD drive will not copy the disc. Since you purchased the disc, shouldn't you be able to listen to the music on any device you choose?

The answer is "yes" and "no." Yes, copyright law gives you the right to make copies for your personal use and transfer works into a format that can be used on your equipment. However, the growing pervasiveness of digital rights management may curtail your ability to exercise these rights.

It is easy to copy digital material. Before the dawn of the digital age, copies produced by analog equipment, such as photocopiers and audio tape dubbing machines, often took a long time to create and were of considerably poorer quality than the originals. Copies of digital materials, however, are indistinguishable from the originals, and can be made quickly and easily. These factors have encouraged an alarming increase in software, music, and movie piracy.

"To date, all DRM systems have failed to meet the challenge of protecting the rights of the rights holder while also allowing the use of the rights of the purchaser. None have succeeded in preventing criminal copyright infringement by organized, unlicensed, commercial pirates."

Piracy made world headlines in a dispute about sharing music on Napster. In 1999, an 18-year-old student named Shawn Fanning developed a Web-based technology for sharing MP3 music files. This technology, dubbed "Napster" after Shawn's nickname, quickly became one of the hottest applications on the Internet. In less than a year, its base exceeded 25 million users. Many of these music lovers downloaded hundreds of songs without paying for any of them.

Almost immediately, Napster ran afoul of the Recording Industry Association of America (RIAA), a watchdog organization that represents record companies such as Columbia Records, Motown Records, and Epic Nashville. The RIAA compiled a list of 12,000 copyrighted songs that Napster technology made available as free downloads. The RIAA filed suit, accusing Napster of contributing to copyright infringement, which considerably reduced the revenues of record companies and artists. The ensuing court battle stirred up a cauldron of issues that relate to the use and abuse of digital media, including music, photos, and videos. However, even after shutting down Napster's free download network, music piracy continued unabated.

The RIAA then initiated a series of lawsuits targeting individuals who allegedly maintained large collections of pirated music.

The Napster experience hardened the resolve of digital stakeholders to stop illegal copying. The battle against piracy took shape as a concept called digital rights management (DRM), vigorously supported by Microsoft and backed by a host of industry leaders. Today, digital rights management encompasses a variety of technologies implemented by copyright holders, such as record companies and software publishers, which restrict the use of digital material. DRM systems address piracy by using a variety of technologies for manipulating data, media, devices, and transactions.

Software copy-protection techniques include reading data written to a restricted area on a CD or DVD that the drive cannot normally access, using hardware that must be plugged into the computer when the software is run, requiring a serial number during the installation process, and using Internet product activation that checks the validity of an installation. Most software copy-protection schemes have proved to be costly for publishers or inconvenient for consumers.

Cable television has a long history of signal scrambling and encryption to prevent piracy. Consumers seem to tolerate this form of DRM because once the signal arrives, it is descrambled and can be archived to a digital video recorder such as TiVo or videotape just as any broadcast television program.

Many consumers are not aware that they pay a surcharge for every blank audio tape, CD, or DVD they purchase. Collected revenues from this surcharge go to music publishers to compensate recording artists for the fact that many people duplicate works without authorization. Most of today's music download sites encrypt music files and embed codes that limit the number of times they can be copied and the devices on which they can be played. To do this, DRM systems, alternately referred to as digital rights management or digital restrictions management systems, are used. For example, Apple Computer's FairPlay DRM system is built into the QuickTime multimedia technology and used by iPod, iTunes, and the iTunes Music Store. Songs bought and downloaded from the iTunes Music Store are encoded with FairPlay. Windows Media DRM is a digital rights management service for the Windows Media platform. It is used on song files downloaded from Wal-Mart's Music Download site and Yahoo! Music Unlimited. RealNetworks secure RealAudio (.rax) format is used on song files that can be downloaded from the RealPlayer Music Store. These formats and DRM systems are not compatible with each other and require different players. As a result, music from several different download sites cannot be compiled into a single playlist. In addition to protecting music downloads, it is becoming more common for music CDs to use play-protection technology designed to make the CD unusable in devices, such as computer CD-R drives, that can also be conveniently used for duplicating CDs. Consumers who purchase these protected CDs find that they cannot be copied to a computer hard disk, then ripped to produce an MP3 file for a portable audio player.

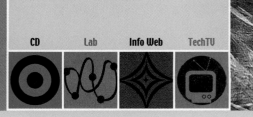

Some copy-protection techniques have generated outrage among users. One case in point was the discovery in late 2005 that Sony was using copy-protected CDs to surreptitiously install its rootkit DRM onto PCs. Rootkit software is a type of software used to make certain files and processes undetectable; it also provides a back door for hackers who could put malicious software on the computer. Simply playing the CD on a CD-ROM drive in a computer installed the software. This installed software was a hidden file; users did not know it was installed on their computers. In addition, this stealth software could not easily be detected. In fact, it took a savvy user to make the discovery and report it on a blog. The Sony rootkit DRM software also disabled existing DRM licenses and had the potential to wreak havoc on the unsuspecting user. Rootkit software is classified as a Trojan horse. Sony's initial response to provide a patch to antivirus software publishers to close the back door and insistence that the software was not harmful was met with further outrage. Due to a flood of bad publicity, Sony was forced to stop using the rootkit DRM technology.

Commercial movie DVDs use CSS (Content-Scrambling System) encryption to make DVDs playable only on authorized DVD players equipped with decryption key circuitry. Movies purchased in the United States and Canada cannot be played on devices manufactured for the European or Asian markets, so continent-jumping travelers and expatriates have to take along their DVD players or abandon their DVD collections. Despite DRM technologies and the inconveniences imposed on consumers, digital piracy remains rampant. According to an article about digital rights management posted on Wikipedia, "To date, all DRM systems have failed to meet the challenge of protecting the rights of the rights holder while also allowing the use of the rights of the purchaser. None have succeeded in preventing criminal copyright infringement by organized, unlicensed, commercial pirates." Current DRM technologies do not seem able to distinguish between pirates and legitimate consumers.

As a result, DRM technologies essentially pose restrictions on consumers that go beyond the intended limitations of copyright law. Circumventing DRM is possible and it would seem OK to do so for legitimate reasons, such as making a backup copy. However, the Digital Millennium Copyright Act makes it illegal to circumvent any technological measure that controls access to a work.

The current status of DRM seems to conflict with the original intent of copyright law to allow consumers to manipulate and copy works for their own use. Can technology eventually offer a solution that prevents piracy, but allows individuals to exercise their rights to fair use of copyrighted materials?

Interactive Questions

☐ Yes	☐ No	☐ Not sure	**1.** Have you had trouble using software, music CDs, or movie DVDs because of copy protection?
☐ Yes	☐ No	☐ Not sure	**2.** In your opinion, do sites like the iTunes Music Store provide consumers with enough flexibility for copying files and creating playlists?
☐ Yes	☐ No	☐ Not sure	**3.** Do you think digital rights management technologies are justified because of the high rate of piracy?

Expand the Ideas

1. Do you believe that it is not against the law to take music off the Web and create CDs, or to copy purchased music for personal use? Why or why not? Write a short paper supporting your position.

2. Research three current music-sharing networks. Are their policies stated on their Web sites? What restrictions, if any, do they impose on music taken from their sites? Find a site that charges for downloading music. Create a table to compile your findings. Write a brief summary comparing and contrasting the trends that you found.

3. Can you envision any way to create a system for digital rights management that not only protects the rights of the artists and publishers but is fair to consumers? Use the Internet to research the current state of DRM for music and video. Are new technologies being developed that work? Have any existing technologies generated controversy? Write a short paper discussing your ideas and findings. Be sure to include your sources.

End of Unit Exercises

Key Terms

24-bit bitmap

32-bit bitmap

Analog video camera

AIFF (Audio Interchange File Format)

AVI

Bitmap graphic

BMP

Card reader

Codec (compressor/ decompressor)

Color depth

Color palette

Compression algorithm

Compression ratio

Cropping

Data compression

Density

Desktop video

Dictionary-based compression

Digital camera

Digital graphics

Digital signal processor

Digital video

Digital video camera

Digital video recording (DVR)

device

Digitizing tablet

Dithering

Drawing software

DVD-video

External video

File compression utility

FireWire port

Flash graphic

Frame rate

GIF

Gradient

Grayscale palette

Internal video

JPEG

Key frame

Linear editing

Lossless compression

Lossy compression

Megapixels

Metafile

MIDI

MIDI sequence

Monochrome bitmap

MP3

MP3 encoder

MPEG

Nonlinear editing

PDA video

Phoneme

Pixel interpolation

PNG

QuickTime

Rasterization

Ray tracing

RealAudio

Real Media

Rendering

Resolution

Resolution dependent

Run-length encoding

Sampling rate

Scanner

Sound card

Spatial compression

Speech recognition

Speech recognition software

Speech synthesis

Statistical compression

Streaming video

SVG

SWF graphic

Synthesized sound

System palette

Temporal compression

Text-to-speech software

TIFF

Tracing software

True Color bitmap

Unzipping

USB port

Vector graphic

Video

Video capture device

Video capture software

Video editing software

VOB (Video Object)

Wave

Waveform audio

Wavetable

Web-based video

Web palette

Wireframe

WMA (Windows Media Audio)

WMV (Windows Media Video)

Zipping

Unit Review

1. Use your own words to define bold terms that appear throughout the unit. List 10 of the terms that are least familiar to you and write a sentence for each of them.

2. Make a list of the file extensions that were mentioned in this unit and group them according to digital media type: bitmap graphic, vector graphic, digital video, waveform audio, and MIDI. Circle any formats that are used on the Web.

3. Make a list of the software mentioned in this unit, indicating the type of task that it helps you accomplish.

4. Describe the devices that transfer photos from a digital camera to a computer. Explain the different procedures required to transfer analog or digital video from camera to computer.

5. Describe how resolution and color depth contribute to the file size of a graphic file.

6. Explain how a computer monitor displays color, and how a color palette can be used to reduce file size.

7. Explain how the concept of layering relates to your ability to modify a vector graphic.

8. Make a list of the advantages and disadvantages of bitmaps and vector graphics.

9. Explain how streaming audio and video work and contrast them to nonstreaming technology.

10. Explain sampling rate. Be sure to discuss how it affects sound quality and file size.

End of Unit Exercises

Fill in the Best Answer

1. A(n) _____ digitizes printed images, whereas a digital _____ digitizes images of real objects.

2. JPEG, _____ , and PNG are bitmap graphics formats and are supported by most browsers.

3. The dimensions of the grid that forms a bitmap graphic are referred to as its _____ .

4. Bitmap graphics are resolution _dependent_ , which means that the quality of an image relies on its resolution.

5. Color _Depth_ refers to the number of colors available for use in a bitmap graphic.

6. A color _pallette_ holds the selection of colors and allows you to select a group of colors to use for a bitmap graphic.

7. A(n) _____ graphic contains the instructions that a computer needs to create the shape, size, position, and color for each graphic.

8. Graphics that contain both bitmap and vector data are called _____ .

9. The process of applying color and texture to a 3-D graphic wireframe is called _____ .

10. Ray _____ is the process of adjusting the colors in a rendered image to coincide with the highlights and shadows that would be produced by a light source.

11. Several file formats are popular for desktop _____ including AVI, QuickTime, MPEG, Real Media, MMV, and VOB.

12. _____ editing moves footage from one videotape to another, whereas _____ editing uses a random-access device, such as a hard disk, to hold both the original footage and finished video.

13. The _____ of a video file can be reduced using three techniques: reducing the frame rate, decreasing the size of the video window, and compressing the video data.

14. A video capture device converts the camera's _____ signal into _____ data.

15. When you transfer footage from an analog or digital camera to your computer, you must use either a(n) _____ port or a(n) _____ port.

16. You use video _____ software to start and stop the transfer and select the display size, frame rate, filename, and file format for your video footage.

17. A(n) _____ is the software that compresses a file when a desktop video is created and decompresses the file when the video is played. Examples include MPEG, Indeo, Cinepak, DivX, and Windows Media Video 9.

18. The number of times per second that a sound wave is measured is referred to as the _sampling_ rate.

19. _Real_ audio is a digital version of an analog sound signal, _____ sound is artificially created.

20. Speech _recognition_ is the process by which machines, such as computers, produce sound that resembles spoken words.

Practice Tests

When you use the Interactive CD, you can take Practice Tests that consist of 10 multiple-choice, true/false, and fill-in-the-blank questions. The questions are selected at random from a large test bank, so each time you take a test, you will receive a different set of questions. Your tests are scored immediately, and you can print study guides to determine which questions you answered incorrectly. If you are using a Tracking Disk, save your test scores.

INDEPENDENT CHALLENGE 1

Do you own a digital image camera? Do you own a digital video camera? Do you know someone who does? If you look at the advertisements that come with the local papers, you will see that most consumer electronics retailers are selling both digital image and digital video cameras. How can you know which is best for you?

1. Research the latest offerings in digital image cameras. Find three leading manufacturers of digital image cameras. Research the latest offerings in digital video cameras. Do leading manufacturers make both video and still cameras?

2. List and compare the features and prices for both the video and image cameras that are being sold in your area.

3. For digital image cameras, what is the range of prices? How is price related to megapixels?

4. For both types of cameras, select three models, one in each price range (inexpensive, moderate, and expensive) that you might consider purchasing.

5. List any accessories that you would have to purchase with the camera.

6. Create a table comparing features and prices. Determine which is the best value. Write a summary of your findings and which camera you might purchase.

INDEPENDENT CHALLENGE 2

 The Web has a wide variety of music, video, and sound files available for download. You can sample new artists and, if you like what you hear, you can purchase the CD.

1. Log on to the Internet and search for music by your favorite artist.

2. Download and listen to the audio file. Was it the entire song? What was the format of the file? Write a brief summary of how you found the music, the source of the file, and what software you used to download and then listen to the music.

3. Locate, download, and view a video file from the Internet.

4. What was the content of the video? Was it an inline or external video? Did the video download all at once or did it stream? What was the format of the file? Write a brief summary of how you found the video and what software you used to download and then view the video.

End of Unit Exercises

INDEPENDENT CHALLENGE 3

The hardware used for digital media is evolving at a very rapid pace. Technology that was once the toolbox of professionals is now readily available for the consumer market. You can research and purchase printers, cameras, and a variety of input devices in local electronics shops.

1. Form a group with several of your classmates.

2. Use the local paper or Internet advertisements to research and then select a graphics-related digital device, such as a photo printer, scanner, digital camera, Web camera, digital video camera, video capture card, digitizing tablet, or accelerated 3-D graphics card. If one of the members of your group owns the device, ask them to bring it in.

3. Create materials for a tradeshow booth featuring your "product." Create a poster and marketing materials. You might include a product photo, list of specifications, and a short instruction manual. Be sure to research and include technical specifications as well as a list of applications.

4. If possible, create a 2- to 3-minute video commercial for the product. If you cannot film the commercial, create a storyboard for it.

5. If time permits, your instructor might ask your group to provide the rest of the class with your sales presentation or a demonstration for your device.

INDEPENDENT CHALLENGE 4

The Computers in Context section of this chapter focused on digital special effects technology used in recent films, such as *Lord of the Rings*, *Spiderman II,* and *The Matrix: Revolutions*. For this independent challenge, conduct your own research into the special effects that have appeared in your favorite movies.

1. Select two of your favorite films that incorporated computerized special effects.

2. Log on to the Internet, look for information about the specific movies using Web sites, such as the Internet movie database (www.imdb.com). Many movies also have dedicated Web sites, which you can find using a search engine.

3. Browse through the material presented in the Web sites.

4. Use your favorite search engine to research special effects software used in filmmaking.

5. Write a 2- to 4-page movie review that focuses on how the special effects contribute to the movie's overall quality. Try to incorporate information about how the special effects were developed, including the company that provided the effects and the type of equipment used. You can also consider comparing the special effects in your chosen movies with the effects in other movies. You might also incorporate some frames from the film as illustrations in your paper. Before doing so, however, make sure that you understand its copyright restrictions.

6. Follow your professor's instructions for formatting and submitting your movie review.

LAB: Working with Bitmap Graphics

1. Start the interactive part of the lab. Insert your Tracking Disk if you want to save your QuickCheck results. Perform each of the lab steps as directed and answer all of the lab QuickCheck questions. When you exit the lab, your answers are automatically graded and your results are displayed.

2. Use the Start button to access the Programs menu for the computer that you typically use. Make a list of the available bitmap graphics software.

3. Capture a photographic image from a digital camera, scanner, or Web page. Save it as "MyGraphic." Open the image using any available graphics software. Use this software to discover the properties of the graphic. Indicate the source of the graphic, then describe its file format, file size, resolution, and color depth.

4. Prepare this graphic file to send to a friend as an e-mail attachment that is less than 200 KB. Describe the steps that were required.

5. Suppose that you want to post this image on a Web page. Make the necessary adjustments to file size and bit depth. Describe the resulting graphic in terms of its resolution, bit depth, palette, and dithering.

LAB: Video Editing

1. Start the interactive part of the lab. Insert your Tracking Disk if you want to save your QuickCheck results. Perform each of the lab steps as directed and answer all of the lab QuickCheck questions. When you exit the lab, your answers are automatically graded and your results are displayed.

2. Use the Control Panel's Add/Remove Programs icon to view and make a list of the video players that are available on your computer.

3. Locate a video clip on the Web and indicate the URL of the Web page on which it can be found. Describe the video's properties, including file size and format.

4. Play the video that you located. Describe the visual and sound qualities of the video and discuss how they relate to your Internet connection speed. Also describe the length and content of the video, the use of transitions or special effects (if any), and the use of sound tracks. If you could edit this video yourself, what changes would you make to make it more effective?

Student Edition Labs

Student Edition Labs

Reinforce the concepts you have learned in this unit through the **Working with Graphics**, **Working with Audio**, and **Working with Video** Student Edition Labs, available online at the Illustrated Computer Concepts Web site.

SAM Labs

SAM

If you have a SAM user profile, you have access to additional content, features, and functionality. Log in to your SAM account and go to your assignments page to see what your instructor has assigned for this unit.

End of Unit Exercises

Visual Workshop

Digital photography and digital cameras have changed the way we view and manage images. Without having to incur the cost of film or the cost and time of developing images, you can enjoy the freedom of taking as many pictures as your digital camera memory card will permit. You can send and share pictures instantly with friends and family in your home or across the world. Online photo sites, such as www.kodakgallery.com, www.Shutterfly.com, and www.Snapfish.com, make it possible to instantly upload the images and then send e-mail notification to anyone you want. Viewing the photos online is free, and then you or whoever views your online photo album can order the prints.

Digital image manipulation is readily available at the consumer level with affordable software packages that put professional tools right on the desktop. Adobe Photoshop (see **Figure H-41**) and Corel PaintShop Pro are two of many commercial packages that are available. Picasa2 is a free download available from Google. Most photo editing software includes professional digital editing tools for your photos. Most digital cameras come with some kind of proprietary software to not only download and save files but also to erase lines and reduce red eye through airbrush and other tools.

Figure H-41

1. Log on to the Internet and search for information on digital photography. List three interesting facts that you find about camera and software manufacturers, new trends in digital photography, and image processing.

2. Use your favorite search engine to find three online photo sites. Create a comparison chart for the three sites. List and compare features such as services offered, pricing, and various options.

3. Review current digital image manipulation software packages. Make a comparison chart for at least three software packages. Write a summary paragraph indicating how the packages are alike, how they are different, and why a consumer might purchase one over the other.

Buyer's Guide Worksheets

Whether you are a first-time buyer or you are upgrading your computer system, when the time comes to make your computer buying decision, you might find yourself overwhelmed by the vast amount of information available. There are thousands of computer advertisements on the Web, on television, in magazines, and in newspapers that list detailed technical product specifications. To get the best deal on a computer that meets your needs, you need to understand what these technical specifications mean and how they will affect your computing power. You also need to establish a budget for your computer system. This Buyer's Guide will help you to organize your purchasing decisions.

Organize Your Findings: A Buyer's Guide Summary

You can refer to the table that follows to organize your research on purchasing a computer system.

CONSIDERATIONS	NOTES
Basic computer system	
Desktop or notebook?	
Platform: Macintosh or IBM-compatible PC?	
Case type: tower, desktop?	
Display device: type, size, and resolution	
Computer architecture	
Which processor?	
How much RAM?	
What type of video card?	
System and application software	
Operating system	
Software for basic applications	
Virus protection	
Spyware protection	
Networking considerations	
Wired or wireless	
Interface card	
Hub	
Router	
Internet service	
Wireless/DSL/Cable/Dial-up	
Internet Service Provider	
Web browser	
E-mail client	

Buyer's Guide Worksheets (continued)

CONSIDERATIONS	NOTES
Special considerations for notebook computers	
Display size and resolution	
External monitor	
PCMCIA slot	
Weight	
Power source/battery type	
Pointer type	
Carrying case	
USB ports	
FireWire ports	
Peripheral devices and storage	
Hard disk capacity	
CD-ROM/DVD	
Sound card/speakers	
Floppy disk drive	
USB ports	
FireWire ports	
Pointing device	
Printer	
Fax modem/modem	
Expansion cards	
Scanner	
Digital camera	
Web cam	
Backup system	
Surge protector/UPS	

Comparing Computers: A Buyer's Specification Worksheet

Before you make a decision, shop around to collect information on pricing, features, and support. You can find comparative pricing at Web-based price-quote sites. When you use a price-quote site, be aware that some of these sites search only those merchants that have paid to participate. Although you might be tempted to buy the computer with the lowest price and best features, do not forget to consider the warranty and the quality of the support you are likely to get from the vendor.

Use the worksheet that follows to organize the information you gather about pricing, features, and support. Complete the worksheet for each computer system you are considering, then compare the information.

Manufacturer: _____

Model: _____

Price: _____

Processor model: _____

Processor speed: _____

RAM capacity: _____

Hard disk drive capacity: _____

Hard disk drive type and speed: _____

Speaker description: _____

Graphics card slot type (desktop only): _____

Graphics card video RAM capacity: _____

Display type (LCD/CRT/Plasma): _____

Display screen size and dot pitch: _____

Type of pointing device: _____

Number/type of expansion ports: _____

Number/type of expansion slots: _____

CD/DVD access drive speed: _____

CD/DVD writer: _____

Number of USB/FireWire ports included: _____

Modem speed: _____

Sound card model: _____

Operating system version: _____

Bundled software: _____

Overall weight (notebook only): _____

Battery type/time (notebook only): _____

Questions to Ask about Service and Support

- What is the warranty period?
- What is the average length of time for service?
- Does the warranty cover parts and labor?
- Are the costs and procedures for fixing the computer acceptable?
- Does the vendor have a good reputation for service?
- Are technical support hours adequate?
- Are other users satisfied with this brand and model of computer?
- Is there a toll-free number for technical support?

- Can I contact technical support without waiting on hold for a long time?
- Is the vendor likely to stay in business?
- Are the computer parts and components standard?
- Are technical support people knowledgeable?

Refer to the online Buyer's Guide for up-to-date information about current pricing and offerings as you gather information before purchasing your computer system.
Go to www.course.com/illustrated/concepts6e

Visual Workshop

Magazines and newspapers often list computer specifications as part of the computer advertisements. Even when shopping online, you can often find a way to compare features of a computer by checking off components and seeing how two models compare to one another.

Computer ads include the type of processor, the amount and type of RAM, hard disk capacity, and peripheral devices that come with the computer. The ad shown in **Figure BG-1** lists the specifications for a typical desktop computer.

Figure BG-1

- Intel Pentium EE 840 64-bit dual core processor 3.2 GHz with Hyper-Threading
- 2 MB L2 cache
- 2 GB 533 MHz SDRAM (max. 4 GB)
- 160 GB SATA HD (7200 rpm)
- 48X CD-RW + 16X DVD+RW/+R with double-layer write capable
- 3.5" 1.44 MB floppy disk drive
- 19" LCD TV/monitor
- 256 MB NVidia AGP graphics card
- Sound Blaster PCI sound card
- Altec Lansing speakers
- U.S. Robotics 56 Kbps modem
- Mouse and keyboard
- External drive bays: 2 5.25" bays for disk, tape, or CD drives; 1 3.5" bay for a floppy drive
- Internal drive bays: 1 HDD bay
- 8 USB ports: 2 front, 6 back
- 2 serial, 1 parallel, and 1 video port
- 1 network port (RJ45 connector)
- 4 PCI slots and 1 AGP slot
- Windows Vista operating system
- Home/small business software bundle
- 3-year limited warranty

1. Based on the ad, answer the following questions:
   a. What processor is in this computer?
   b. How much memory is in the computer?
   c. What peripheral devices are included?
   d. What storage devices are included?
   e. Is this computer expandable? Why or why not?
   f. For what type of user would this computer be best suited?

2. Based on the ad, would you buy this computer? Why or why not?

3. Research a computer using current ads, either in print or on the Internet, what is the approximate price that you would pay for this computer?

Glossary

10BaseT network An Ethernet network that uses twisted-pair cables with a maximum length of 100 meters and supports data transmission rates of 10 Mbps.

100BaseT network An Ethernet network that uses 100BaseT cables and supports data transmission rates of 100 Mbps.

24-bit bitmap A True Color graphic that requires 24 bits for each pixel, used for photographic-quality images that can include any of 16.7 million colors.

32-bit bitmap A True Color graphic that requires 32 bits for each pixel, used for photographic-quality images that can include any of 16.7 million colors.

3-D graphic A type of digital graphics format that represents a three-dimensional image in a two- dimensional space.

3-D graphics software The software used to create three-dimensional wireframe objects and render them into images.

802.11b A popular wireless network standard that operates between 200 and 400 Kbps, with a range of up to 300 feet.

Access time The estimated time for a storage device to locate data on a disk, usually measured in milliseconds.

Accounting and finance software A category of software that helps you keep a record of monetary transactions and investments.

Accounting software See Accounting and Finance Software.

ActiveX control A compiled computer program that can be referenced from within an HTML document, downloaded, installed on your computer, and executed within the browser window to add interactive features to Web pages.

Ad-serving cookie A cookie distributed by marketing firms that is used to track activities at any site containing banner ads from that third party. Used to target ads to users, but privacy advocates are worried that shopper profiles can be compiled, sold, and used for unauthorized purposes.

AES (Advanced Encryption System) An encryption standard based on the Rijndael encryption algorithm that uses three key sizes of 128, 192, or 256 bits.

AGP (accelerated graphics port) An AGP is a type of interface, or slot, that provides a high-speed pathway for advanced graphics.

AIFF See Audio Interchange File Format.

ALU (arithmetic logic unit) The part of the CPU that performs arithmetic and logical operations on the numbers stored in its registers.

Always-on connection A permanent connection to the Internet, as opposed to a connection that is established and dropped as needed.

Analog device A device that operates on continuously varying data, such as a dimmer switch or a watch with a sweep second hand.

Analog video camera A device used to collect, store, and process video in an analog format on a magnetic tape.

Animated GIF A type of GIF image that displays a sequence of frames to create the appearance of continuous motion.

Antivirus software A computer program used to scan a computer's memory and disks to identify, isolate, and eliminate viruses.

Application software Computer programs that help you perform a specific task such as word processing. Also called application programs, applications, or programs.

Archive The process of moving infrequently used data from a primary storage device to a storage medium such as a CD-R.

ARCnet (Attached Resource Computer network) One of the oldest, simplest, and least expensive LAN technologies that permits twisted-pair, coax, and fiber-optic cables to be mixed on the same network to connect up to 255 workstations.

ASCII (American Standard Code for Information Interchange) A code that represents characters as a series of 1s and 0s. Most computers use ASCII code to represent text, making it possible to transfer data between computers.

ASF (Advanced Streaming Format) Microsoft's video format for streaming video on the Web.

Asynchronous protocol A data transmission method in which the sender and receiver are not synchronized by a clock signal, and which uses start and stop bits to control the beginning and ending of transmissions.

ATM (asynchronous transfer mode) A network technology that transmits all packets in a message over the same channel.

Glossary

Audio editing software A category of software that includes sound playback as well as recording capabilities. Menus provide additional digital editing features, such as speed control, volume adjustments, clipping, and mixing of sounds.

Audio encoding software Converts raw audio file into a format such as MP3. Sometimes called an audio format converter.

Audio Interchange File Format (AIFF) A popular cross-platform audio format developed by Apple; has the .aif file extension.

Authentication security feature A way to restrict access to computer systems; used to positively identify a person as an authorized user by verifying the person through one of three methods: something a person carries, something a person knows, or some unique physical characteristic.

Automated System Recovery disk Created by the Windows XP Backup utility, or any operating system as a method for recovering system or data lost in a disk crash.

AVI (Audio Video Interleave) A video file format developed by Microsoft that is the most common format for desktop video on the PC.

B2B (business-to-business) An e-commerce exchange of products, services, or information between businesses.

B2C (business-to-consumer) An e-commerce transaction involving products, services, or information between businesses and consumers.

B2G (business-to-government) An e-commerce transaction involving products, services, or information between businesses and governments.

Backdoor Software flaw that allows unauthorized access to victims' computers, providing a way for hackers to download and execute files on your computer, upload a list of other infected computers, and use your computer as a relay station for breaking into other computers.

Backup A duplicate copy of a file, disk, or tape. Also refers to a Windows utility that allows you to create and restore backups.

Backup software The software used to copy program and data files to a storage media for backup purposes; most provide options that make it easy to schedule periodic backups, define a set of files that you want to regularly back up, and automate the restoration process.

Bandwidth The data transmission capacity of a communications channel.

Banner ad An advertisement typically embedded at the top of a Web page.

Baud rate The transmission speed of a modem measured as the number of times per second that a signal in a communications channel varies; a 300-baud modem's signal changes state 300 times each second; however, each baud doesn't necessarily carry one bit, so a 300-baud modem might be able to transmit more than 300 bits per second.

Beep code A series of audible beeps used to announce diagnostic test results during the boot process.

Benchmark A test used to measure computer hardware or software performance.

Binary digits A series of 1s and 0s representing data.

Binary number system A method for representing numbers using only two digits, 0 and 1; contrast this system to the decimal system, which uses ten digits: 0, 1, 2, 3, 4, 5, 6, 7, 8, and 9.

Biometrics A method of personal identification based on some unique physical trait, such as a fingerprint or the pattern of blood vessels in the retina of the eye.

Bit A bit is the smallest unit of information handled by a computer. A bit can hold one of two values, either a 0 or a 1. Eight bits comprise a byte, which can represent a letter or number.

Bit depth The number of bits that determines the range of possible colors that can be assigned to each pixel. For example, an 8-bit color depth can create 256 colors. Also called color depth.

Bitmap graphic An image, such as a digital photo, that is stored as a gridwork of colored dots.

Bitmap image See Bitmap graphic.

Blended threat Threats that combine more than one type of malicious program such as Trojan-horse/virus combinations and worm/virus combinations.

Blog Derived from the phrase "WeB LOG," refers to a personal journal focusing on a single topic or covering a variety of issues posted on the Web for access by the general public.

Bluetooth A wireless technology used in conjunction with standard Ethernet networks that allows data transfer rates between 200 and 400 Kbps, up to a maximum range of 35 feet.

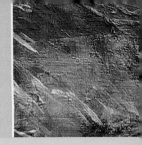

BMP The native bitmap graphic file format of the Microsoft Windows OS.

Body section A part of a Web page that begins with the <BODY> HTML tag and contains the text, graphics, and links.

Bookmark A link to a Web page; a list of saved URLS in a browser. Click the URL to return to the page. Also called Favorites.

Boot disc A DVD or CD that contains the essential instructions needed for the boot process.

Boot process The sequence of events that occurs within a computer system between the time the user starts the computer and the time it is ready to process commands.

Boot sector virus A computer virus that infects the sectors on a disk containing the data a computer uses during the boot process.

Bootstrap program A program stored in ROM that loads and initializes the operating system on a computer.

Bot Any software that can automate a task or autonomously execute a task when commanded to do. Also called an intelligent agent.

Botnet Many bot-infested computers linked together into a network to provide combined computing power of their zombie computers for many types of evil tasks.

Broadband A term used to refer to communications channels that have high bandwidth.

Broken link A non-functioning hyperlink on a Web page.

Browser A program that communicates with a Web server and displays Web pages.

Brute force method A method of breaking encryption code by trying all possible encryption keys, usually employing supercomputers.

Bus topology A network topology that uses a common backbone to connect all network devices. The backbone functions as a shared communication link, which carries network data, and stops at each end of the network with a "terminator."

Byte An 8-bit unit of information that represents a single character.

C2C (consumer-to-consumer) An e-commerce exchange of products, services, or information between consumers.

Cable Used to connect a peripheral device to a computer through a port.

Cable modem A communications device that can be used to connect a computer to the Internet via the cable TV infrastructure.

Cable modem service Internet access offered to a cable company's customers for an additional monthly charge. The connection usually requires two pieces of equipment: a network card and a cable modem.

Cache Special high-speed memory that gives the CPU rapid access to data that would otherwise be accessed from disk. Also called RAM cache or cache memory.

CAD software See Computer-aided design software.

Card reader A small device connected to your computer's USB or serial port to read the data that's contained in a flash memory card; acts just like an external disk drive.

Cascading style sheet (CSS) A template that can be set to control the layout and design of Web pages.

CD See CD-ROM disc.

CD-DA (compact disc digital audio) The format for commercial music CDs. Music is typically recorded on audio CDs by the manufacturer.

CD drive A storage device that uses laser technology to read data from a CD.

CD-R An acronym for compact disc-recordable. CD-R is a type of optical disk technology that allows the user to create CD-ROMs and audio CDs.

CD ripper software Pulls a track off an audio CD and stores it in raw digital format.

CD-ROM disc An optical storage media that can store up to 700 MB of data.

CD-RW An acronym for compact disc-rewritable. CD-RW is a type of optical disk technology that allows the user to write data onto a CD, then change that data.

CD-writer A general term for recordable CD technologies such as CD-R and CD-RW.

Cell (1) In spreadsheet terminology, the intersection of a column and a row. (2) In cellular communications, a limited geographical area surrounding a cellular phone tower.

Cell reference The column letter and row number that designates the location of a worksheet cell. For example, the cell reference C5 refers to a cell in column C, row 5.

Glossary

Cellular-ready modem A device that is packaged as a PC card that slips into the PCMCIA port of a notebook or tablet computer used to dial your ISP through a plan offered by your cellular phone provider.

Central processing unit See CPU.

Character data Letters, symbols, or numerals that will not be used in arithmetic operations (name, social security number, and so forth).

Chat group A discussion in which a group of people communicates online simultaneously.

Checksum A value calculated by combining all the bytes in a file that is used by virus detection programs to determine whether any bytes have been altered.

Ciphertext An encrypted message.

Circuit switching The method used by the telephone network to temporarily connect one telephone with another for the duration of a call.

CISC (complex instruction set computer) A general-purpose processor chip designed to handle a wider array of instructions than a RISC chip.

Clear GIF A 1x1 pixel graphic on a Web page that can be used to set cookies to third party Web sites. Unlike ad-serving cookies, you don't have to click a banner ad to receive a GIF activated cookie. Also called Web bug.

Click-through rate The number of times that site visitors click an ad on a Web site to connect to the advertiser's site. The hosting merchant is paid a small fee for each click through.

Client A computer or software that requests information from another computer or server.

Client/server network A network where processing is split between workstations (clients) and the server.

Client-side script Scripting statement, embedded in an HTML document, that is executed by a client's browser.

Clip art Graphics designed to be inserted into documents, Web pages, and worksheets, usually available in CD-ROM or Web-based collections.

Clock speed The pace for executing instructions as set by the processor clock specified in megahertz (MHz)—or gigahertz (GHz).

Cluster A group of sectors on a storage medium that, when accessed as a group, speeds up data access.

CMOS (complementary metal oxide semiconductor) memory A type of battery-powered integrated circuit that holds semi-permanent configuration data.

CMYK color A printing technology used by most ink jet printers that requires only cyan (blue), magenta (pink), yellow, and black inks to create a printout that appears to have thousands of colors.

Coaxial cable A type of cable with BNC connectors made of a center wire surrounded by a grounded shield of braided wire and used to connect nodes on a network. Also called coax cable.

Codec (COmpressor/DECompressor) Hardware or software routine that compresses and decompresses digital graphics, sound, and video files.

Color depth The number of bits that determines the range of possible colors that can be assigned to each pixel. For example, an 8-bit color depth can create 256 colors. Also called bit depth.

Color palette The selection of colors used in graphics software.

Commercial software Copyrighted computer applications sold to consumers for profit.

Communications channel Any pathway between the sender and receiver; channel may refer to a physical medium or a frequency.

Communications network A combination of hardware, software, and connecting links that transports data.

Communications protocol A set of rules for ensuring orderly and accurate transmission and reception of data.

Communications satellite Satellite used to send to and receive data from ground stations.

Compact Privacy Policy The HTTP header defined in a standard set of security tags that becomes part of the header for every cookie, that describes how cookie data is used by a Web site.

CompactFlash (CF) card A solid state storage device that is about the size of a matchbook and provides high storage capacities and access speeds; includes a built-in controller that reads and writes data within the solid state grid; are ideal for use on high-end digital cameras that require megabytes of storage for each photo.

Compiler Software that translates a program written in a high-level language into low-level instructions before the program is executed.

Compression algorithm The steps required to shrink data in a file and restore it to its original state.

Compression ratio A measurement of the amount of shrinkage when data is compressed.

Compression software A type of software, such as WinZip, that effectively reduces the size of files. See file compression utility.

Compression utility Software to reduce file size for quick transmission or efficient storage.

Computer A device that accepts input, processes data, stores data, and produces output.

Computer file A single collection of data stored on a storage medium.

Computer language A set of tools that allows a programmer to write instructions that a computer can execute.

Computer literacy A person's ability to use computer terms properly and computer programs proficiently.

Computer network A collection of computers and related devices, connected in a way that allows them to share data, hardware, and software.

Computer program A set of detailed, step-by-step instructions that tells a computer how to solve a problem or carry out a task.

Computer programmer A person who codes or writes computer programs.

Computer projection device An output device that produces a large display of the information shown on the computer screen.

Computer system The hardware, peripheral devices, and software working together to input data, process data, store data, and produce output.

Computer virus A program designed to attach itself to a file, reproduce, and spread from one file to another, destroying data, displaying an irritating message, or otherwise disrupting computer operations.

Computer-aided design (CAD) software A type of 3-D graphics software designed for architects and engineers who use computers to create blueprints and product specifications.

Computer-aided music software Helps musicians compose, edit, and print the notes for their compositions. For non-musicians, designed to generate unique musical compositions simply by selecting the musical style, instruments, key, and tempo.

Concurrent-user license Legal permission for an organization to use a certain number of copies of a software program at the same time.

Control unit The part of the ALU that directs and coordinates processing.

Controller A circuit board in a hard drive that positions the disk and read-write heads to locate data.

Cookie A message sent from a Web server to a browser and stored on a user's hard disk, usually containing information about the user.

Copyright A form of legal protection that grants certain exclusive rights to the author of a program or the owner of the copyright.

Copyright notice A line such as "Copyright 2007 ACME Co." that identifies a copyright holder.

CPU (central processing unit) The main processing unit in a computer, consisting of circuitry that executes instructions to process data.

Cropping The process of selecting and removing part of an image.

CRT (cathode ray tube) A display technology that uses a large vacuum tube similar to that used in television sets.

Cryptographic algorithm A specific procedure for encrypting and decrypting data.

Cryptographic key A specific word, number, or phrase that must be used to encrypt or decrypt data.

CSMA/CD (Carrier Sense Multiple Access with Collision Detection) A method of responding to an attempt by two devices to use a data channel simultaneously; used by Ethernet networks.

Cursor A symbol that marks the user's place on the screen and shows where typing will appear.

Cybercrime Crimes that use computers, such as transmitting trade secrets to competitors, reproducing copyrighted material, and distributing child pornography. Also crimes targeted at computers, such as denial-of-service attacks on servers, Web site vandalism, data theft, and destructive viruses.

Cyberterrorism Threatening computer systems using viruses and worms to destroy data and otherwise disrupt computer-based operations, including critical national infrastructures such as power grids and telecommunications systems.

Glossary

Cyclic redundancy check An error-checking protocol used by some LANs to ensure accurate delivery of data.

Cylinder A vertical stack of tracks that is the basic storage bin for a hard disk drive.

Data In the context of computing and data management, the symbols that a computer uses to represent facts and ideas.

Data bus An electronic pathway or circuit that connects the electronic components (such as the processor and RAM) on a computer's motherboard.

Data center A specialized facility designed to house and protect computer systems and data; typically includes special security features, such as fireproof construction, earthquake proof foundations, sprinkler systems, power generators, secure doors and windows, and anti-static floor coverings.

Data compression The process of condensing data so that it requires fewer bytes of storage space.

Data file A file containing words, numbers, or pictures that the user can view, edit, save, send, or print.

Data module A file linked to a program that provides data necessary for certain functions of the program.

Data representation The use of electrical signals, marks, or binary digits to represent character, numeric, visual, or audio data.

Data security Techniques that provide protection for data.

Data transfer rate The amount of data that a storage device can move from a storage medium to computer memory in one second.

Database A collection of information that may be stored in more than one file.

Database software The category of software designed for tasks associated with maintaining and accessing data stored in files in the form of a database. Sometimes called data management software.

Decryption The process of converting ciphertext into plaintext.

Defragmentation utility A software tool used to rearrange the files on a disk so that they are stored in contiguous clusters.

Demodulation The process of restoring a received signal to its original state. For example, when a modem changes an audio signal back to a digital pulse.

Denial of Service attack The result of hackers sending malicious software that is designed to overwhelm a network's processing capabilities, shutting it down.

Density A measure of an image, expressed as dots per inch (dpi) for a printer or scanner, or as pixels per inch (ppi) on a monitor. The denser the grid, the smaller the image will appear.

DES (Data Encryption Standard) An encryption method based on an algorithm developed by IBM and the U.S. National Security Agency that uses 56-bit symmetric key encryption.

Desktop computer Computer small enough to fit on a desk and built around a single processor chip.

Desktop operating system An operating system such as Windows ME or Mac OS X that is specifically designed for personal computers.

Desktop publishing software A category of software used to create high-quality output suitable for commercial printing. DTP software provides precise control over layout.

Desktop search tool Utilities that help you also find and access information stored in e-mails, Web pages, contact lists in addition to data and program files; are offered by third party vendors such as Google and Yahoo! and are also being included in operating system utilities.

Desktop video Video stored in digital format on a PC's hard disk or CD, videotapes, memory cards, or the Web.

Device driver The software that provides the computer with the means to control a peripheral device.

DHTML (dynamic HTML) A variation of the HTML format that allows elements of Web pages to be changed while they are being viewed.

Dial-up connection A connection that uses a phone line to establish a temporary Internet connection.

Dictionary-based compression A data compression scheme that uses a codeword to represent common sequences of characters.

Differential backup A copy of all the files that changed since the last full backup of a disk.

Digital Any system that works with discrete data, such as 0s and 1s, in contrast to analog.

Digital camera An input device that records an image in digital format.

Digital certificate A security method that identifies the author of an ActiveX control.

Digital device A device that works with discrete (distinct or separate) numbers or digits.

Digital electronics Circuitry that's designed to work with digital signals.

Digital Satellite Service (DSS) An Internet connection option that uses a geosynchronous or low-earth satellite to transmit television, voice, or computer data directly to and from a satellite dish, or base station, owned or leased by an individual.

Digital signal processor Circuitry that is used to process, record, and playback audio files.

Digital video Filmed sequences of images or footage of real objects, which is then stored in one of several different digital formats. Encompasses several technologies and is classified by its format including AVI, QuickTime, MPEG, RealMedia, MMV, and VOB.

Digital video camera A device used to collect, store, and process video in a digital format.

Digital video recording (DVR) device Used to record and store footage for digital videos.

Digitize The conversion of non-digital information or media to a digital format through the use of a scanner, sampler, or other input device.

Digitizing tablet A device that provides a flat surface for a paper-based drawing, and a "pen" used to create hand-drawn vector drawings.

DIMM (dual in-line memory module) A small circuit board that holds RAM chips. A DIMM has a 64-bit path to the memory chips.

DIP (dual in-line package) A chip configuration characterized by a rectangular body with numerous plugs along its edge.

Direct satellite service (DSS) A service that uses a geosynchronous or low earth orbit satellite to send television, voice, or computer data directly to satellite dishes owned by individuals.

Direct source input device An input device, such as a bar code reader, that collects data directly from a document or object; used to reduce the incidence of operator error.

Directory A list of files contained on a computer storage device.

Disaster Recovery Plan A step-by step plan that describes the methods used to secure data against disaster, and explains how an organization will recover lost data if and when a disaster occurs.

Disk density The closeness of the particles on a disk surface. As density increases, the particles are packed more tightly together and are usually smaller.

Display device The main output device for a computer; one of two key components of a display system—a monitor or a screen uses one of three technologies: CRT, LCD, and gas plasma.

Distribution media One or more disks or CDs that contain programs and data, which can be installed to a hard disk.

Dithering A means of reducing the size of a graphics file by reducing the number of colors. Dithering uses patterns composed of two or more colors to produce the illusion of additional colors and shading.

DMA (direct memory access) Technology allows a computer to transfer data directly from a drive into RAM, without intervention from the processor.

DOCSIS (Data Over Cable Services Interface Specification) A security technology used for filtering packets to certain ports.

Document production software Computer programs that assist the user in composing, editing, designing, and printing documents.

Document reader utility Computer program, such as Acrobat Reader, that transforms files into a portable format that can be created and read by any computer on which it is installed.

Domain name An identifying name by which host computers on the Internet are familiarly known; for example, cocacola.com. Also referred to as fully qualified domain name.

Domain name server Computers that host the domain name system database.

Domain name system A large database of unique IP addresses that correspond with domain names.

DOS (disk operating system) The operating system software shipped with the first IBM PCs and used on millions of computers until the introduction of Microsoft Windows.

Dot matrix printer A printer that creates characters and graphics by striking an inked ribbon with small wires called "pins," generating a fine pattern of dots.

Glossary

Dot pitch The diagonal distance between colored dots on a display screen. Measured in millimeters, dot pitch helps to determine the quality of an image displayed on a monitor.

Downloading The process of transferring a copy of a file from a remote computer to a local computer's disk drive.

Dpi (dots per inch) Printer resolution as measured by the number of dots it can print per linear inch.

Drawing software Provides tools to draw lines, shapes, and colors that can be assembled into diagrams, corporate logos, and schematics that tend to have a flat cartoon-like quality, but are very easy to modify and look good at just about any size.

Drive bay An area within a computer system unit that can accommodate an additional storage device.

Drive mapping In network terminology, assigning a drive letter to a network server disk drive.

DSL (Digital Subscriber Line) A high-speed Internet connection that uses existing telephone lines, requiring close proximity to a switching station.

DSL modem A device that sends to and receives digital data from computers over telephone lines.

DSLAM (DSL Access Multiplexor) Special equipment used to interpret, separate, and route digital data in telephone lines for DSL providers.

DSS See Digital Satellite Service.

DTD (Document Type Definition) file A type of file that defines how markup tags are interpreted by a browser.

DTP Software See Desktop publishing software.

Dual core processor An alternative to using more than one processor, a single chip containing the circuitry for two processors; is faster than a processor with a single core.

Duty cycle Determines how many pages a printer is able to print out; is usually measured in pages per month.

DVD (digital video disc or digital versatile disc) An optical storage medium similar in appearance and technology to a CD-ROM but with higher storage capacity.

DVD drive An optical storage device that reads data from CD-ROM and DVD disks.

DVD+R (digital versatile disc recordable) A DVD disk that stores data using recordable technology.

DVD+RW (digital versatile disc rewritable) A DVD disc that stores data using rewritable technology.

DVD-R (digital versatile disc recordable) A DVD disk that stores data using recordable technology.

DVD-ROM A DVD disk that contains data that has been permanently stamped on the disk surface.

DVD-RW (digital versatile disc rewritable) A DVD disc that stores data using rewritable technology.

DVD-Video (digital versatile disc video) The format digital video used for commercial DVDs that contain feature-length films and that use a DVD format.

DVD-writer A device that can be used to create and copy CDs and DVDs.

Dye sublimation printer An expensive, color-precise printer that heats ribbons containing color to produce consistent, photograph-quality images.

Dynamic IP address A temporarily assigned IP address usually provided by an ISP.

Ear training software The category of software that targets musicians and music students who want to learn to play by ear, develop tuning skills, recognize notes and keys, and develop other musical skills.

EBCDIC (Extended Binary-Coded Decimal Interchange Code) A method by which digital computers, usually mainframes, use 0s and 1s to represent character data.

E-commerce (electronic commerce) Business connected over the Internet, including online shopping, linking businesses to businesses (sometimes called e-business or B2B), online stock trading, and electronic auctions.

Educational software A category of software that helps you learn and practice new skills.

Electronic Serial Number (ESN) A unique number that is printed on the back of a cellular modem or other electronic devices used to activate service through a provider.

Electronic wallet Software that stores and processes customer information needed for an e-commerce transaction.

E-mail (electronic mail) A single electronic message or the entire

system of computers and software that handles electronic messages transmitted between computers over a communications network.

E-mail account A service that provides an e-mail address and mailbox.

E-mail address The unique address for each mailbox on the Internet, which typically consists of a user ID, an @ symbol, and the name of the computer that maintains the mailbox.

E-mail attachment A separate file that is transmitted along with an e-mail message.

E-mail client software A category of software that is installed on a client computer and has access to e-mail servers on a network. This software is used to compose, send, and read e-mail messages.

E-mail message A computer file containing a letter or memo that is transmitted electronically via a communications network.

E-mail server A computer that uses special software to store and send e-mail messages over the Internet.

E-mail system The collection of computers and software that works together to provide e-mail services.

Encryption The process of scrambling or hiding information so that it cannot be understood without the key necessary to change it back into its original form.

Ethernet A type of network on which network nodes are connected by coaxial cable or twisted-pair wire; the most popular network architecture, it typically transmits data at 10 or 100 megabits per second.

Ethernet card A type of network interface card (NIC), or network adapter, designed to support Ethernet protocols sending data to and from network devices such as workstations or printers over the network usually using cables.

EULA (end-user license agreement) License agreement that is displayed on the screen when you first install the software; accept the terms of the license by clicking a designated button.

Exa- Prefix for a quintillion.

Executable file A file, usually with an .exe extension, containing instructions that tell a computer how to perform a specific task.

Expansion bus The segment of the data bus that transports data between RAM and peripheral devices.

Expansion card A circuit board that is plugged into a slot on a PC motherboard to add extra functions, devices, or ports.

Expansion port A socket into which the user plugs a cable from a peripheral device, allowing data to pass between the computer and the peripheral device.

Expansion slot A socket or slot on a PC motherboard designed to hold a circuit board called an expansion card.

Extended ASCII Similar to ASCII but with 8-bit character representation instead of 7-bit, allowing for an additional 128 characters.

Extensible A term used when describing XML tags that define fields of data by explicitly identifying a particular kind of information; means individual users and groups of users can create their

own tags and even their own markup languages.

External link A hyperlink to a location outside the Web site.

External style sheet A template that contains formatting specifications for a group of Web pages.

External video A video on the Web that downloads and opens in a media player window when its link is clicked.

Extranet A network similar to a private internet that also allows outside users access.

Favorites A list of URLs for Web sites that you can create for your browser to store so that you can revisit those sites easily.

FDDI (Fiber Distributed Data Interconnect) A high-speed network that uses fiber-optic cables to link workstations.

Fiber-optic cable A bundle of thin tubes of glass used to transmit data as pulses of light.

Field The smallest meaningful unit of information contained in a data file.

File A named collection of data (such as a computer program, document, or graphic) that exists on a storage medium, such as a hard disk, solid state storage device, floppy disk, or CD-ROM.

File allocation table (FAT) A special file that is used by the operating system to store the physical location of all the files on a storage medium, such as a hard disk.

File compression utility A type of data compression software that shrinks one or more files into a single file that occupies less storage space than the separate files.

Glossary

File date Saved as part of the file information, the date on which a file was created or last modified; useful if you have created several versions of a file and want to make sure that you know which version is the most recent.

File format The method of organization used to encode and store data in a computer. Text formats include DOC and TXT. Graphics formats include BMP, TIFF, GIF, and PCX.

File header Saved as part of the file, information that can be read by the computer, but never appears on the screen.

File management To organize files and folder on storage media.

File management software A category of operating system software that helps the user organize and find files and folders on their hard drive or other storage media.

File management utility Software, such as Windows Explorer, Mac OS Finder, or Spotlight, that helps users locate, rename, move, copy, and delete files.

File size The physical size of a file on a storage medium, usually measured in kilobytes (KB).

File specification A combination of the drive letter, subdirectory, filename, and extension that identifies a file (for example, A:\word\filename.doc). Also called a path.

File system A system that is used by an operating system to keep files organized.

File virus A computer virus that infects executable files, such as programs with .exe filename extensions.

Filename A set of letters or numbers that identifies a file.

Filename extension A set of letters and/or numbers added to the end of a filename that helps to identify the file contents or file type.

Filenaming conventions A set of rules established by the operating system that must be followed to create a valid filename.

Finder On computers with Mac OS, the file management utility that helps you view a list of files, find files, move files from one place to another, make copies of files, delete files, and rename files.

FireWire port A port on a digital camera or computer used to transfer photo data. Also called IEEE-1394 port.

Fixed wireless Internet service Technology used to connect a computer to the Internet using wireless technology.

Flash animation A proprietary technology developed by Macromedia; it is one of the most popular animation formats and provides more flexibility than animated GIFs and can be used for more complex animations. You have to download the Flash client software which is free and required for viewing flash animation.

Flash graphics A popular vector graphics format developed by Macromedia that can be used for still images or animations.

Flash memory A type of memory module that can store data without power consumption. It can be reused, making it popular for digital camera memory.

Floppy disk A removable magnetic storage medium, typically 3.5" in size, with a capacity of 1.44 MB.

Floppy disk drive A storage device that writes data on, and reads data from, floppy disks.

Folder The subdirectory, or subdivision, of a directory that can contain files or other folders.

Font A typeface or style of lettering, such as Arial, Times New Roman, and Gothic.

Footer In a document, text that you specify to appear in the bottom margin of every page.

Format Refers to how all text, pictures, titles, and page numbers appear on the page.

Formatting tag HTML code that is used to change the appearance of text.

Fragmented file A file stored in scattered, noncontiguous clusters on a disk.

Frame rate Refers to the number of frames displayed per second in a video or film.

Freeware Copyrighted software that is given away by the author or owner.

Frequency The number of times that a wave oscillates (moves back and forth between two points) per second. Short wave lengths have high frequencies.

Full backup See Full system backup.

Full system backup A copy of all the files for a specified backup job. Also called full backup.

Fully justified The horizontal alignment of text in which the text terminates exactly at both margins of the document.

Function key   One of the keys numbered F1 through F12 located at the top of the computer keyboard that activates program specific commands.

Gateway   An electronic link that connects one computer system to another.

GIF (Graphics Interchange Format)   A bitmap graphics file format popularized by CompuServe for use on the Web.

Giga-   Prefix for a billion.

Gigabit (Gb)   Approximately one billion bits.

Gigabyte (GB)   One billion bytes, typically used to refer to RAM and hard disk capacity.

Gigahertz (GHz)   A measure of frequency equivalent to one billion cycles per second, usually used to measure speed.

Gradient   A smooth blending of shades of different colors from light to dark.

Graphical user interface (GUI)   A type of user interface that features on-screen objects, such as menus and icons, manipulated by a mouse. Abbreviation is pronounced "gooey."

Graphics   Any pictures, photographs, or images that can be manipulated or viewed on a computer.

Graphics card   A circuit board inserted into a computer to handle the display of text, graphics, animation, and videos. Also called a video card.

Graphics software   Computer programs for creating, editing, and manipulating images.

Graphics tablet   A device that accepts input from a pressure-sensitive stylus and converts strokes into images on the screen.

Grayscale palette   Digital images that are displayed in shades of gray, black, and white.

Groupware   Business software designed to help several people collaborate on a single project using network or Internet connections.

Hacker   Refers to anyone who writes malicious code, including viruses, worms, and Trojan horses, to use a computer to gain unauthorized access to data, steal information, or crash a computer system.

Handheld computer   A small, pocket-sized computer designed to run on its own power supply and provide users with basic applications.

Handshaking   A process where a protocol helps two network devices communicate.

Hard disk   See hard disk drive.

Hard disk drive   A computer storage device that contains a large-capacity hard disk sealed inside the drive case.

Hard disk platter   The component of a hard disk drive on which data is stored. It is a flat, rigid disk made of aluminum or glass and coated with a magnetic oxide.

Hard disk utility   Software used for backing up, securing, permanently deleting, and cleaning up files on hard disks.

Hardware   The electronic and mechanical devices in a computer system.

Head crash   A collision between the read-write head and the surface of the hard disk platter, resulting in damage to some of the data on the disk.

Head section   A part of a Web page that begins with the <HEAD> HTML tag and contains information about global properties of the document.

Header   Text that you specify to appear in the top margin of every page automatically.

Helper application   A program that understands how to work with a specific file format.

High-level language   A computer language that allows a programmer to write instructions using human-like language.

History list   A list that is created by your browser of the sites you visited so that you can display and track your sessions or revisit the site by clicking the URL in the list.

Home page   In a Web site, the document that is the starting, or entry, page. On an individual computer, the Web page that a browser displays each time it is started.

HomePLC   A network that uses a building's existing power line cables to connect nodes.

HomePNA   A network that uses a building's existing phone lines to connect nodes.

Horizontal market software   Any computer program that can be used by many different kinds of businesses (for example, an accounting program).

Glossary

Host computer A computer system that stores and processes data accessed by multiple terminals from remote locations. In Internet terminology, any computer connected to the Internet.

Hot spot A clickable image, photo, or diagram within an image map on a Web page.

Hotspot The range of network coverage in a public Wi-Fi network that provides open Internet access to the public. Any Wi-Fi equipped device that enters a hotspot can gain access to the network's services.

HTML (Hypertext Markup Language) A standardized format used to specify the format for Web page documents.

HTML document A plain text or ASCII document with embedded HTML tags that dictate formatting and are interpreted by a browser.

HTML form An HTML document containing blank boxes prompting users to enter information that can be sent to a Web server. Commonly used for e-commerce transactions.

HTML frame Part of a Web page that scrolls independently of other parts of the Web page.

HTML tag An instruction, such as ..., inserted into an HTML document to provide formatting and display information to a Web browser.

HTTP (Hypertext Transfer Protocol) The communications protocol used to transmit Web pages. HTTP:// is an identifier that appears at the beginning of most Web page URLs (for example, http://www.course.com).

HTTP status code A code used by Web servers to report the status of a browser's request.

Hub A network device that connects several nodes of a local area network.

Hyperlink Provides the fundamental tool for navigating Web pages. Click a text or graphic hyperlink to jump to a location in the same Web page, open a different Web page, or go to a different Web site. Also called link.

Hypertext A way of organizing an information database by linking information through the use of text and multimedia.

Hypertext link An underlined word or phrase that, when clicked, takes you to its designated URL; also called link.

Hyper-Threading Refers to a technology that enables processors to execute multiple instructions in parallel.

ICANN (Internet Corporation for Assigned Names and Numbers) A global organization that coordinates the management of the Internet's domain name system, IP addresses, and protocol parameters.

Image map An area on a Web page consisting of a single graphic image containing multiple hot spots.

IMAP (Internet Messaging Access Protocol) A protocol similar to POP that is used to retrieve e-mail messages from an e-mail server, but offers additional features, such as choosing which e-mails to download from the server.

Incremental backup A copy of the files that changed since the last backup.

Information The words, numbers, and graphics used as the basis for human actions and decisions.

Infrared light A wireless transmission technology that uses a frequency range just below the visible light spectrum to transport data signals for short distances with a clear line of sight. Its most practical uses seem to be transmission of data between a notebook computer and a printer, between a PDA and a desktop computer, and in remote controls to change television channels.

Infrared port Device that accepts infrared light containing photo data that was beamed by a camera to a computer. This method, though slow, eliminates the need for a cable.

Ink jet printer A non-impact printer that creates characters or graphics by spraying liquid ink onto paper or other media.

Input As a noun, "input" means the information that is conveyed to a computer. As a verb, "input" means to enter data into a computer.

Input device A device, such as a keyboard or mouse, that gathers input and transforms it into a series of electronic signals for the computer.

Insertion point Appears on the screen as a flashing vertical bar or flashing underline and indicates where the characters you type will appear on the screen. Change the location insertion point using the arrow keys or the mouse pointer. Also called cursor.

Install The process by which programs and data are copied to the hard disk of a computer system and otherwise prepared for access and use.

Installation agreement A version of the license agreement that appears on the computer screen when software is being installed and prompts the user to accept or decline.

Instant messaging (IM) A private chat in which users can communicate with each other by typing messages through the computer.

Instruction cycle The steps followed by a computer to process a single instruction; fetch, interpret, execute, then increment the instruction pointer.

Instruction set The collection of instructions that a CPU is designed to process.

Integrated circuit (IC) A thin slice of silicon crystal containing microscopic circuit elements, such as transistors, wires, capacitors, and resistors; also called chips and microchips.

Intelligent agent Any software that can automate a task or autonomously execute a task when commanded to do so. Also called a bot.

Internal link A hyperlink to a location within the same Web site.

Internal video A video on the Web that plays within a frame inside the Web page when its link is clicked.

Internet The worldwide communication infrastructure that links computer networks using TCP/IP protocol.

Internet backbone The major communications links that form the core of the Internet.

Internet Service Provider (ISP) A company that maintains Internet computers and telecommunications equipment in order to provide Internet access to businesses, organizations, and individuals.

Internet telephony A set of hardware and software that allows users to make phone-style calls over the Internet, usually without a long-distance charge. Also called Voice over IP (VoIP).

Interpage link A hyperlink that links to a different location on the same Web page.

Interpreter A program that converts high-level instructions in a computer program into machine language instructions, one instruction at a time.

Intranet A LAN that uses TCP/IP communications protocols, typically for communications services within a business or organization.

IP (Internet Protocol) One of the main protocols of TCP/IP that is responsible for addressing packets so they can be routed to their destination.

IP address A unique identifying number assigned to each computer connected to the Internet.

ISA (Industry Standard Architecture) A standard for moving data on the expansion bus. Can refer to a type of slot, a bus, or a peripheral device. An older technology, it is rapidly being replaced by PCI architecture.

ISDN (Integrated Services Digital Network) A telephone company service that transports data digitally over dial-up or dedicated lines.

ISDN terminal adapter A device that connects a computer to a telephone jack and translates the data into a signal that can travel over an ISDN connection.

ISP (Internet Service Provider) See Internet Service Provider.

Java A high-level programming language for Web-based projects.

Java applet Small Java applications that a browser downloads and runs on a computer to perform specialized tasks.

JavaScript Popular scripting language for Web-based applications.

Joystick A pointing input device used as an alternative to a mouse.

JPEG (Joint Photographic Experts Group) A file format that uses lossy compression to store bitmap images. JPEG files have a .jpg extension.

Kernel The core module of an operating system that typically manages memory, processes, tasks, and disks.

Key frame Frames at equal intervals in a digital video clip that contain all data for that frame. The rest of the frames in the video contain only the information that is different from the last key frame.

Keyboard An arrangement of letter, number, and special function keys that acts as the primary input device to the computer.

Keyboard shortcut The use of the [Alt] or the [Ctrl] key in combination with another key on the keyboard to execute a command, such as copy, paste, or cut.

Keylogger A type of program that records your keystrokes; notorious for stealing passwords.

Keyword A word or term used as the basis for a database or Web-page search.

Kilobit (Kbit or Kb) 1,024 bits.

Glossary

Kilobyte (KB) Approximately 1,000 bytes; exactly 1,024 bytes.

Label In a worksheet, any text that is used to describe data.

LAN (local area network) An interconnected group of computers and peripherals located within a relatively limited area, such as a building or campus.

Lands Non-pitted surface areas on a CD that represents digital data.

LAN-jacking A practice that occurs when hackers cruise around with a Wi-Fi-equipped notebook computer set up to search for Wi-Fi signals coming from home and corporate Wi-Fi networks so they can access and use unsecured Wi-Fi networks to hack into files and gain unauthorized access to larger, wired networks. Also called war driving.

Laptop computer See Notebook computer.

Laser light A focused beam of light that, with a clear line of sight, can transmit data over long distances.

Laser printer A printer that uses laser-based technology, similar to that used by photocopiers, to produce text and graphics.

Layout The physical position of each element on a page, in a spreadsheet, slide, or any report from a database.

LCD (liquid crystal display) A type of flat panel computer screen, typically found on notebook computers and available as a screen for desktop computers.

Linear editing A video editing technique that records segments of video from one tape to another.

Link Provides the fundamental tool for navigating Web pages. Click a text or graphic hyperlink to jump to a location in the same Web page, open a different Web page, or go to a different Web site. Also called hyperlink.

Link tag HTML code that is used to designate text as a hyperlink in a document.

Linux A server operating system that is a derivative of UNIX and available as freeware.

Listserv A public list of people who are interested in a particular topic; messages sent to the mailing list server are automatically distributed to everyone on the mailing list server.

Logical address A network address that is assigned to a network device when the physical address is in an incorrect format.

Logical storage model Any visual aid or metaphor that helps a computer user visualize a file system.

Logical topology Network topology that corresponds with the way messages flow across the network, not necessarily identical to the network's physical topology.

Lossless compression A compression technique that provides the means to restore all of the data in the original file.

Lossy compression Any data compression technique in which some of the data is sacrificed to obtain more compression.

Mac (Macintosh computer) A personal computer platform designed and manufactured by Apple Computer.

Mac OS The operating system software designed for use on Apple Macintosh and iMac computers.

Machine code Program instructions written in binary code that the computer can execute directly.

Machine language A low-level language written in binary code that the computer can execute directly.

Macro A small set of instructions that automates a task. Typically, a macro is created by performing the task once and recording the steps. Whenever the macro is played back, the steps are repeated.

Macro virus A computer virus that infects the macros that are attached to documents and spreadsheets.

Magnetic storage The recording of data onto disks or tape by magnetizing particles of an oxide-based surface coating.

Mailing list server Any computer and software that maintains a list of people who are interested in a topic and that facilitates message exchanges among all members of the list.

Mailto link A link on a Web page that automatically opens a pre-addressed e-mail form.

Main executable file A program that is used to start and run software, usually with an .exe file extension.

Mainframe computer A large, fast, and expensive computer generally used by businesses or government agencies to provide centralized storage processing and management for large amounts of data.

Malicious code Any program or set of program instructions that is designed to surreptitiously enter a computer and disrupt its normal operations. Malicious code, including viruses, worms, and Trojan horses, is created and unleashed by individuals referred to as "hackers" or "crackers."

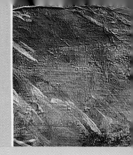

MAN (metropolitan area network) A public, high-speed network that can transmit voice and data within a range of 50 miles.

Markup language A language that provides text and graphics formatting through the use of tags. Examples include HTML, XML, and SGML.

Mass-mailing worm Worms often include an attachment that contains the worm and are difficult to track; spreads by sending itself to every address in the address book of an infected computer and caused havoc on personal computers, LANs, and Internet servers.

Master File Table (MFT) Special files used by the operating system of NTFS computers to keep track of the names and locations of files that reside on a storage medium, such as a hard disk.

Mathematical modeling software A category of software such as MathCAD and Mathematica, that provides tools for solving a wide range of math, science, and engineering problems.

Media tag HTML code that specifies how to display media elements in a document.

Megabit (Mb or Mbit) Approximately 1 million bits; exactly 1,048,576 bits.

Megabyte (MB) Approximately 1 million bytes; exactly 1,048,576 bytes.

Megahertz (MHz) A measure of frequency equivalent to 1 million cycles per second.

Megapixels A million pixels; used to express the resolution and quality of an image.

Memory The computer circuitry that holds data waiting to be processed.

Memory card reader A device that connects to a PC via a USB or Serial cable that reads data from a flash memory module.

Mesh topology A network topology that connects each network device to many other network devices. Data traveling on a mesh network can take any of several possible paths from its source to its destination.

Metafile Graphics file that contains both vector and bitmap data.

Microcomputer A category of computer that is built around a single processor chip.

Microprocessor An integrated circuit that contains the circuitry for processing data. It is a single-chip version of the central processing unit (CPU) found in all computers. Often called processor.

Microsoft Windows An operating system developed by Microsoft Corporation that provides a graphical interface. Versions include Windows 3.1, Windows 95, Windows 98, Windows ME, Windows 2000, Windows XP, Windows NT, and Windows Vista.

Microwave Electromagnetic wave with a frequency of at least 1 gigahertz.

MIDI (Musical Instrument Digital Interface) A standardized way in which sound and music are encoded and transmitted between devices that play music.

MIDI sequence Digitally encoded music stored on a computer. Usually a file with a .mid, .cmf, or .rol file extension.

MIDI sequencing software A category of software used for creating sound effects and for controlling keyboards and other digital instruments.

Millisecond (ms) A thousandth of a second.

MIME (Multipurpose Internet Mail Extension) A conversion process used for formatting non-ASCII messages so that they can be sent over the Internet.

Modem A device that sends and receives data to and from computers over telephone lines.

Modem card A device that provides a way to transmit data over phone lines or cable television lines.

Modifier key The [Ctrl], [Alt], or [Shift] key, used in conjunction with another key to expand the repertoire of available commands.

Modulation The process of changing the characteristics of a signal. For example, when a modem changes a digital pulse into an analog signal.

Monitor A display device that forms an image by converting electrical signals from the computer into points of colored light on the screen.

Monochrome bitmap Displayed by manipulating the pattern of off and on pixels on the screen. Each pixel is set to display either a black dot or a white dot. Monochrome bitmaps require very little storage space.

Motherboard The main circuit board in a computer that houses chips and other electronic components.

Mouse An input device that allows the user to manipulate objects on the screen by moving the mouse on the surface of a desk.

Glossary

MP3 A file format that provides highly compressed audio files with very little loss of sound quality.

MP3 encoder Software that compresses a WAV file into an MP3 file.

MP3 player Software that plays MP3 music files.

MPEG (Moving Pictures Expert Group) A highly compressed file format for digital videos. Files in this format have a .mpg extension.

MPEG-2 A special type of data coding for movie files that are much too large to fit on a disk unless they are compressed.

MTBF (mean time between failures) The reliability of computer components as calculated by observing test equipment in a laboratory, then dividing the number of failures by the total number of hours of observation. This statistic is an estimate based on laboratory tests of a few sample components.

Multifunction device A hardware device that works both as input and output devices to combine the functions of a printer, scanner, copier, fax, and answering machine.

MultiMedia card (MMC) Solid state storage that includes a built-in controller in a package about the size of a postage stamp that was initially used in mobile phones and pagers, but now also used in digital cameras and MP3 players.

Multi-partite virus A computer virus that is able to infect many types of targets by hiding itself in numerous locations on a computer.

Multiple-user license Legal permission for more than one person to use a particular software package.

Multitasking Provides processor and memory management services that allow two or more tasks, jobs, or programs to run simultaneously. Most of today's operating systems offer multitasking services.

Multitasking operating system An operating system that runs two or more programs at the same time.

Multithreading Allows multiple parts, or threads, of programs to run simultaneously.

Multiuser operating system An operating system that allows two or more users to run programs at the same time and use their own input/ output devices.

NAN (neighborhood area network) A public, high-speed network that can transmit voice and data within a limited geographical area, usually spread over several buildings.

Nanosecond A unit of time representing 1 billionth of a second.

Narrowband A term that refers to communications channels that have low bandwidth.

Native file format A file format that is unique to a program or group of programs and has a unique file extension.

Navigation keypad On a keyboard, the keypad with the Home, End, and arrow keys, which you can use to efficiently move the screen-based insertion point or cursor.

Netiquette Internet etiquette or a set of guidelines for posting messages and e-mails in a civil, concise way.

Network address translation (NAT) An Internet standard that allows a LAN to use one type of IP address for LAN data and another type of address for data to and from the Internet.

Network card An expansion board mounted inside a computer to allow access to a local area network.

Network device An electronic device that broadcasts network data, boosts signals, or routes data to its destination.

Network interface card (NIC) A small circuit board that sends data from and collects incoming data for a workstation over a network.

Network operating system Programs designed to control the flow of data, maintain security, and keep track of accounts on a network.

Network service provider (NSP) Company that maintains a series of nationwide Internet links.

Networked peripheral A device, such as a printer or scanner, directly connected to a network rather than to a workstation.

Newsgroup An online discussion group that centers around a specific topic.

Node Each device on a network, including workstations, servers, and printers; in a hierarchical database, a segment or record type.

Non-linear editing A digital video editing technique that requires a PC and video editing software.

Notation software A category of software used to help musicians compose, edit, and print musical scores.

Notebook computer Small, lightweight, portable computer that usually runs on batteries. Sometimes called a laptop computer.

Numeric data Numbers that represent quantities and can be used in arithmetic operations.

Numeric keypad Calculator-style input devices for numbers located towards the right side of a keyboard.

Object code The low-level instructions that result from compiling source code.

Object-oriented database A database model that organizes data into classes of objects that can be manipulated by programmer-defined methods.

Online Refers to being connected to the Internet.

Online shopping cart An e-commerce cookie that stores information about items selected and collected for purchase.

Op code (operation code) An assembly language command word that designates an operation, such as add (ADD), compare (CMP), or jump (JMP).

Open source software A category of software, such as Linux, that includes its uncompiled source code, which can be modified and distributed by programmers.

Operand The part of an instruction that specifies the data, or the address of the data, on which the operation is to be performed.

Operating system (OS) Software that controls the computer's use of its hardware resources, such as memory and disk storage space.

Operational tag HTML code used to specify the basic setup and database integration for Web pages.

Operator error The most common cause of lost and/or inaccurate data; mistakes made by a computer user such as entering the wrong data or deleting a needed file.

Optical storage A means of recording data as light and dark spots on a CD, DVD, or other optical media.

Output The results produced by a computer (for example, reports, graphs, and music).

Output device A device, such as a monitor or printer, that displays, prints, or transmits the results of processing from the computer memory.

P3P (Platform for Privacy Preferences Project) A specification that allows Web browsers to detect a Web site's privacy policies automatically.

Packet A small unit of data transmitted over a network or the Internet.

Packet sniffer A computer program that monitors data as it travels over networks to observe and open any packet traveling on the network. Also called a protocol analyzer.

Packet switching A technology used by data communications networks, such as the Internet, in which a message is divided into smaller units called "packets" for transmission.

Palm OS One of the operating systems used in handheld computers.

PAN (personal area network) A term used to refer to the interconnection of personal digital devices within a range of about 30 feet (10 meters) and without the use of wires or cables. For example, to wirelessly transmit data from a notebook computer to a PDA or portable printer.

Parallel port Commonly used to connect most printers to a computer; however some printers are designed to connect to a USB port or a serial port.

Parallel processing A technique by which two or more processors in a computer perform processing tasks simultaneously.

Password A special set of symbols used to restrict access to a computer or network.

Password protection Security feature used to identify authorized users and are a way to restrict access to a computer system.

Patch A section of program code that replaces part of the software currently installed to correct a security breach, to add functionality, or to enhance the exisitng program in some way.

Path A file's location in a file structure. See File specification.

Payload The virus instructions that are delivered by the virus; migh be as harmless as displaying an annoying message or as devastating as corrupting the data on your computer's hard disk.

Payroll software Horizontal market software used by business to maintain payroll records, collect data and make calculations in order to produce payroll checks and W2 forms.

PC A microcomputer that uses Windows software and contains an Intel-compatible processor.

PC card A credit card-sized circuit board used to connect a modem, memory, network card, or storage device to a notebook computer.

Glossary

PCI (Peripheral Component Interconnect) A method for transporting data on the expansion bus. Can refer to type of data bus, expansion slot, or transport method used by a peripheral device; newer versions include PCI-Express and PCI-X.

PCMCIA (Personal Computer Memory Card International Association) slot An external expansion slot typically found on notebook computers.

PDA (Personal Digital Assistant) A computer that is smaller and more portable than a notebook computer.

PDA video Refers to digital video that uses a format designed to be viewed on a PDA or cell phone screen.

Peer-to-peer network (P2P) The arrangement in which one workstation/ server shares resources with another workstation/server; each computer on such a network must act as both a file server and workstation.

Peripheral device A component or equipment, such as a printer or scanner, that expands a computer's input, output, or storage capabilities.

Personal computer A microcomputer designed for use by an individual user for applications such as Internet browsing, , graphics, email, and word processing.

Personal finance software A category of software designed to help manage individual finances.

Personal firewall software A category of software designed to analyze and control incoming and outgoing packets.

Person-to-person payment An e-commerce method of payment that bypasses credit cards and instead uses an automatic electronic payment service.

PGA (pin-grid array) A common chip design used for processors.

PGP (Pretty Good Privacy) A popular program used to encrypt and decrypt e-mail messages.

Phoneme Unit of sound that is a basic component of words; can be produced by speech synthesizers.

Photo editing software A category of software that provides tools and wizards that simplify common photo editing tasks.

Photo printer Uses inkjet technology to produce photographic quality images.

Physical address An address built into the circuitry of a network device at the time of its manufacture.

Physical storage model The way data is stored on a storage media.

Physical topology The actual layout of network devices, wires, and cables.

Ping (Packet Internet Groper) A command on a TCP/IP network that sends a test packet to a specified IP address and waits for a reply.

Pipelining A technology that allows a processor to begin executing an instruction before completing the previous instruction.

Pits Dark spots that are burned onto the surface of a CD to represent digital data.

Pixel (picture element) The smallest unit in a graphic image. Computer display devices use a matrix of pixels to display text and graphics.

Pixel interpolation A process used by graphics software to average the color of adjacent pixels in an image.

Plaintext An original, un-encrypted message.

Plasma screen technology Display device technology that is used in gas plasma screens to create an on-screen image by illuminating miniature colored fluorescent lights arrayed in a panel-like screen.

Platform A family or category of computers based on the same underlying software and hardware.

Plug and Play The ability of a computer to recognize and adjust the system configuration for a newly added device automatically.

Plug-in A software module that adds a specific feature to a system. For example, in the context of the Web, a plug-in adds a feature to the user's browser, such as the ability to play RealVideo files.

PNG (Portable Network Graphics) A type of graphics file format similar to, but newer than, GIF or JPEG.

Podcast Free downloadable Internet broadcast that includes newscasts, radio shows, and teleconferences; typically downloaded to a portable mp3 player. The term is derived from the popular portable audio player the Apple iPod and the word "broadcast."

Podcasting A way to deliver a podcast audio file through RSS feed technology.

Pointing device An input device, such as a mouse, that you use to manipulate an on-screen pointer and other screen-based graphical controls.

Pointing stick Pointing device typically used with notebook computers as an alternative to a mouse that looks like the tip of an eraser and is embedded in the keyboard of a notebook computer. Push up, down, or sideways to move the on-screen pointer. Also called TrackPoint.

Polymorphic virus Virus that can escape detection by antivirus software by changing its signature.

POP (Post Office Protocol) A protocol that is used to retrieve e-mail messages from an e-mail server.

POP server A computer that receives and stores e-mail data until retrieved by the e-mail account holder.

Popup ad An advertisement that appears in a separate window when you enter a Web site or connect to Web pages.

PostScript A printer language developed by Adobe Systems that uses a special set of commands to control page layout, fonts, and graphics.

POTS An acronym for plain old telephone service.

Power failure A complete loss of power to the computer system, usually caused by something over which you have no control.

Power spike An increase in power that lasts only a short time—less than one millionth of a second. Spikes can be caused by malfunctions in the local generating plant or the power distribution network, and they are potentially more damaging to your computer system and data than a power failure.

Power strip A device that provides additional outlets for power but provides no protection against power spikes, surges, or failures.

Power surge A fluctuation in power that lasts a little longer than a power spike—a few millionths of a second. Surges can be caused by malfunctions in the local generating plant or the power distribution network, and they are potentially more damaging to your computer system and data than a power failure.

Power-on self-test (POST) A diagnostic process that runs during startup to check components of the computer, such as the graphics card, RAM, keyboard, and disk drives.

Presentation software A category of software that provides tools to combine text, graphics, graphs, animation, and sound into a series of electronic slides that can be output on a projector, or as overhead transparencies, paper copies, or 35-millimeter slides.

Printer A peripheral device used to create hard copy output.

Printer Control Language (PCL) A standard language used to send page formatting instructions from a computer to a laser or ink jet printer.

Private IP address IP address that cannot be routed over the Internet.

Processing The manipulation of data using a systematic series of actions.

Processor An integrated circuit that contains the circuitry for processing data. It is a single-chip version of the central processing unit (CPU) found in all computers.

Processor clock A device on the motherboard of a computer responsible for setting the pace of executing instructions.

Program data file Supplied with a software package, contains any data that is necessary for a task, but that is not supplied by the user. For example, a dictionary file. Program data files have file-name extensions, such as .txt, .bmp, and .hlp.

Programming language Provides the tools that a programmer uses to create software. Also called computer language.

Project management software A category of software specifically designed as a tool for planning, scheduling, and tracking projects and their costs.

PROM (programmable read-only memory) Memory that can be created using a special machine through a process called burning.

Protocols Rules that ensure the orderly and accurate transmission and reception of data. Protocols start and end transmission, recognize errors, send data at the appropriate speed, and identify the correct senders and recipients.

Public domain A category of software that is available for use by the public without restriction, except that it cannot be copyrighted.

Public key encryption (PKE) An encryption method that uses a pair of keys—a public key (known to everyone) that encrypts the message, and a private key (known only to the recipient) that decrypts it.

Public Wi-Fi network A wireless LAN that provides open Internet access to the public.

Glossary

QuickTime A video and animation file format developed by Apple Computer that can also be run on PCs. QuickTime files have a .mov extension.

RAM (random access memory) A type of computer memory circuit that holds data, program instructions, and the operating system while the computer is on.

Random access The ability of a storage device (such as a disk drive) to go directly to a specific storage location without having to search sequentially from a beginning location.

Ransomware Malicious code that encrypts documents and other files, then demand payment for the decryption key.

Rasterization The process of superimposing a grid over a vector image and determining the color depth for each pixel.

Ray tracing A technique by which light and shadow are added to a 3-D image.

RDRAM (Rambus dynamic RAM) A fast (up to 600 MHz) type of memory used in newer personal computers.

Read-only (ROM) technology Data stamped on the CD or DVD surface when it was manufactured, such as commercial software, music, and movies.

Read-write head The mechanism in a disk drive that magnetizes particles on the storage disk surface to write data, or senses the bits that are present to read data.

RealAudio (.ra) An audio file format developed by Real Networks especially for streaming audio data over the Web.

RealMedia A video file format developed by Real Networks that is popular for streaming Web videos.

Record In the context of database management, a record is the set of fields of data that pertain to a single entity in a database.

Recordable technology (R) Uses a laser to change the color in a dye layer sandwiched beneath the clear plastic disc surface.

Recovery CD A CD that contains all the operating system files and application software files necessary to restore a computer to its original state.

Reference software A category of software that provides you with a collection of information and a way to access that information; spans a wide range of applications.

Refresh rate The speed at which the screen is repainted. The faster the refresh rate, the less the screen flickers. measured in cycles per second, or Hertz. Also referred to as vertical scan rate.

Register A "scratch pad" area of the ALU and control unit where data or instructions are moved so that they can be processed.

Rendering In graphics software, the process of creating a 3-D solid image by covering a wireframe drawing and applying computer-generated highlights and shadows.

Repeater A network device that receives and retransmits amplified signals so that they can retain the necessary strength to reach their destinations.

Reserved word Special words used as commands in some operating systems that may not be used in filenames.

Resolution The density of the grid used to display or print text and graphics; the greater the horizontal and vertical density, the higher the resolution.

Resolution dependent Graphics, such as bitmaps, for which the quality of the image is dependent on the number of pixels comprising the image.

Resource In the context of a computer system, refers to any component that is required to perform work such as the processor, RAM, storage space, and peripherals.

Restore The act of moving data from a backup storage medium to a hard disk in the event original data has been lost.

Retro virus Virus designed to corrupt antivirus software.

Revolutions per minute (rpm) A unit of measure that specifies how many times a platter spins each minute: used for the speed of a hard disk drive and to classify the access time for a hard disk.

Rewritable technology (RW) An optical storage technology for CDs and DVDs that uses phase change technology to alter a crystal structure on the disc surface to create patterns of light and dark spots.

RF signals (radio frequency signals) Data that is broadcast and received via radio waves with a transceiver.

RIMM (Rambus in-line memory module) A memory module using RDRAM.

Ring topology A network topology that connects all devices in a circle, with each device having exactly two neighbors, so that

data is transmitted from one device to another around the ring.

RISC (reduced instruction set computer) A processor chip designed for rapid and efficient processing of a small set of simple instructions.

Risk management The process of weighing threats to computer data against the amount of expendable data and the cost of protecting crucial data.

ROM (read-only memory) One or more integrated circuits that contain permanent instructions that the computer uses during the boot process.

ROM BIOS (basic input/output system) A small set of basic input/output system instructions stored in ROM that causes the computer system to load critical operating files when the user turns on the computer.

Root directory The main directory of a disk.

Router A device found at each intersection on the Internet backbone that examines the IP address of incoming data and forwards the data towards its destination. Also used by LANs.

RSA The most commonly used public key encryption algorithm used to encrypt the data in most digital certificates; the technology used for SSL connections. RSA is named for its inventors—Ron Rivest, Adi Shamir, and Leonard Adleman.

RSS (Rich Site Summary or Really Simple Syndication) A format for feeding or syndicating news or any content from Web sites to your computer.

RSS aggregator Downloaded software used to view the RSS feeds on your computer.

RSS feeds Software that provides subscribers with summaries that link to the full versions of the RSS content.

Run-length encoding A graphics file compression technique that looks for patterns of bytes and replaces them with messages that describe the patterns.

Safe Mode A menu option that appears when Windows is unable to complete the boot sequence. By entering Safe Mode, a user can gracefully shut down the computer then try to reboot it.

Sampling rate The number of times per second a sound is measured during the recording process; a higher sampling rate means higher-quality sound.

Scanner An input device that converts a printed page of text or images into a digital format.

Screen size On a display device, the measurement in inches from one corner of the screen diagonally across to the opposite corner.

Script Program that contains a list of commands that are automatically executed as needed.

Scripting error An error that occurs when a browser or server cannot execute a statement in a script.

SCSI (small computer system interface) An interface standard used for attaching peripheral devices, such as disk drives. Pronounced "scuzzy."

SDRAM (synchronous dynamic RAM) A type of RAM that synchronizes itself with the CPU, thus enabling it to run at much higher clock speeds than conventional RAM.

Search engine Program that uses keywords to find information on the Internet and return a list of relevant documents.

Search operator A word or symbol that has a specific function within a search, such as "AND" or "+".

SEC (single edge contact) cartridge A common, cassette-like chip design for processors.

Sector Subdivision of the tracks on a storage medium that provide a storage area for data.

Secure connection Technology that encrypts data transmitted between a computer and a Web site to protect the data during electronic transactions so that the data must be decrypted before it can be used. Technologies that create secure connections include SSL and S-HTTP.

SecureDigital (SD) card Solid state storage device popular for MP3 storage featuring fast data transfer rates and cryptographic security protection for copyrighted data and music.

Security utility Protects and secures the computer. Helps control nuisance ads, intrusion attempts, and spam; also provides file-encryption and antivirus software.

Self-closing tag Any single HTML tag that includes a closing "/" symbol, such as the <hr/> tag which produces a horizontal line on a Web page. The slash comes at the end of the tag, whereas in a closing tag such as </b>, the slash comes at the beginning.

Glossary

Semiconducting material Materials such as silicon and germanium that are used to make chips. The conductive properties create miniature electronic pathways and components, such as transistors. Also called semiconductors.

Sequential access A form of data storage, usually on computer tape, that requires a device to read or write data one record after another, starting at the beginning of the medium.

Serial processing Processing of data that completes one instruction before beginning another.

Server A computer or software on a network that supplies the network with data and storage.

Server farm A group of multiple Web servers used to handle large volumes of requests.

Server operating system Provides communications and routing services that allow computers to share data, programs, and peripheral devices by routing data and programs to each user's local computer, where the actual processing takes place.

Server-side script Scripting statements that are executed by a Web server in response to client data.

Server software The software used by servers to locate and distribute data requested by Internet users.

Service pack A software update, usually to an operating system.

SET (Secure Electronic Transaction) A system that ensures the security of financial transactions on the Web.

Setup program A program module supplied with a software package for the purpose of installing the software.

Shared resource On a network, hardware, software, and data made available for authorized network users to access.

Shareware Copyrighted software marketed under a license that allows users to use the software for a trial period and then send in a registration fee if they wish to continue to use it.

Shrink-wrap license A legal agreement printed on computer software packaging that goes into effect when the package is opened.

S-HTTP (Secure HTTP) A method of encrypting data transmitted between a computer and a Web server by encrypting individual packets of data as they are transmitted.

Single-user license A legal agreement that typically allows only one copy of the software to be in use at a time.

Single-user operating system A type of operating system that is designed for one user at a time with one set of input and output devices.

Site license A legal agreement that generally allows software to be used on any and all computers at a specific location, such as within a corporate office or on a university campus.

Skins utility Used to customize screen-based desktops with screensavers that display clever graphics when the machine is idle.

Slides The 'canvas' for the delivery of ideas in presentation software that combines text, graphics, graphs, animations, and sound; a series of electronic slides display on a monitor for a one-on-one presentation or on a computer projection device for group presentations.

Small business accounting software A category of software that is geared towards small businesses to help invoice customers, keep track of what they owe, store customer data, such as contact information and purchasing history. Inventory functions keep track of the products. Payroll capabilities automatically calculate wages and deduct federal, state, and local taxes.

SmartMedia card The least durable of the solid state storage media, was originally called "solid state floppy disk card" because it looks like a miniature floppy disk, it does not include a built-in controller, so it requires a SmartMedia reader to manage the read/write process.

SMTP (Simple Mail Transfer Protocol) server A computer used to send e-mail across a network or the Internet.

Socket A communication path between two remote programs.

Software The instructions that prepare a computer to do a task, indicate how to interact with a user, and specify how to process data.

Software license A legal contract that defines how a user may use a computer program.

Software suite A collection of application software sold as a single package.

Solid ink printer A printer that creates images on pages by melting sticks of crayon-like ink and then spraying the liquefied ink through the print head's tiny nozzles.

Solid state storage A variety of compact storage cards, pens, and

sticks that stores data in a non-volatile, erasable, low-power chip in a microscopic grid of cells.

Sound card A circuit board that gives the computer the ability to accept audio input from a microphone, play sound files stored on disks and CD-ROMs, and produce audio output through speakers or headphones.

Source code Computer instructions written in a high-level language.

Spam Unwanted electronic junk mail that arrives in your Inbox.

Spam filter Software that automatically routes advertisements and other junk mail to the Deleted Items folder maintained by your e-mail client; can be effective for blocking spam and other unwanted e-mails.

Spatial compression A data compression scheme that replaces patterns of bytes with code that describes the patterns.

Speakers Output devices that receive signals for the computer's sound card to play music, narration, or sound effects.

Speech recognition A category of software that analyzes voice sounds and converts them into phonemes.

Speech recognition software The process by which computers recognize voice patterns and words and convert them to digital data.

Speech synthesis The process by which computers produce sound that resembles spoken words.

Spotlight One of the file management utilities included with Mac OS; use to view a list of files, find files, move files from one place to another, make copies of

files, delete files, discover file properties, and rename files.

Spreadsheet A numerical model or representation of a real situation, presented in the form of a table.

Spreadsheet software A category of software for creating electronic worksheets that hold data in cells and perform calculations based on that data.

Spyware On the Web, any technology that secretly gathers information and relays it to advertisers or other interested parties.

SSL (secure sockets layer) A security protocol that uses encryption to establish a secure connection between a computer and a Web server.

Star topology A network topology that features a central connection point for all workstations and peripherals.

Stateless protocol A protocol that allows one request and response per session, such as HTTP.

Static IP address A permanently assigned and unique IP address, used by hosts or servers.

Statistical compression A data compression scheme that uses an algorithm that recodes frequently used data as short bit patterns.

Statistical software A category of software that helps you analyze large sets of data to discover relationships and patterns, summarize survey results, test scores, experiment results, or population data. Most statistical software includes graphing capability.

Stealth virus Virus that can escape detection from antivirus software by removing its own signature and hiding in memory.

Storage The area in a computer where data is retained on a permanent basis.

Storage capacity The amount of data that can be stored on a storage media.

Storage device A mechanical apparatus that records data to and retrieves data from a storage medium.

Storage medium The physical material used to store computer data, such as a floppy disk, a hard disk, USB Flash drive, or a CD-ROM.

Storage technology Defines the data storage systems used by computers to store data and program files. Each data storage system has two main components: a storage medium and a storage device.

Store-and-forward technology A technology used by communications networks in which an e-mail message is temporarily held in storage on a server until it is requested by a client computer.

Stored program A set of instructions that resides on a storage device, such as a hard drive, and can be loaded into memory and executed.

STP (shielded twisted pair) A type of cable consisting of two wires that are twisted together and encased in a protective layer to reduce signal noise.

Streaming video An Internet video technology that sends a small segment of a video file to a user's computer and begins to play it while the next segment is sent.

Strong encryption Encryption that is difficult to decrypt without the encryption key.

Glossary

Structured file A file that consists of a collection of records, each with the same set of fields.

Style A combination of attributes—colors, sizes, and fonts—that specify the way text is displayed.

Style sheet Acts as a template to control the layout and design of Web pages. Style sheets work in conjunction with HTML tags to make it easy to change the format of elements in a Web page globally and consistently. Also called cascading style sheet (CSS).

Subdirectory A directory found under the root directory.

Supercomputer The fastest and most expensive type of computer, capable of processing more than 1 trillion instructions per second.

SuperDisk A storage technology manufactured by Imation. Disks require special disk drives.

Support module A file that can be called by the main executable program to provide auxiliary instructions or routines.

Support program A file that can be called by the main executable program to provide auxiliary instructions or routines.

Surge strip A low-cost device used to protect computer systems from power spikes and surges. Also called surge protector or surge suppressor.

Surge suppressor See surge strip.

SVG (Scalable Vector Graphics) A graphics format designed specifically for Web display that automatically resizes when displayed on different screens.

SWF graphic A popular vector graphics format created with Macromedia's Flash software, which requires a browser plug-in to be viewed. SWF files use the .swf extensions. which are SWF files, can be static or animated, and typically they require less storage space than SVG graphics. See also Flash graphic.

Symbian OS An operating system based on open standards for mobile phones, PDA, and smartphones.

Symmetric key encryption An encryption key that is used for both encryption and decryption of messages.

Synchronous protocol Sender's signals and receiver's signals are synchronized by a signal called a clock; the transmitting computer sends data at a fixed clock rate, and the receiving computer expects the incoming data at the same fixed rate.

Synthesized sound Artificially created sound, usually found in MIDI music or synthesized speech.

System palette A selection of colors that are used by an operating system to display graphic elements.

System requirements Specifications for the operating system and hardware configuration necessary for a software product to work correctly. The criteria that must be met for a new computer system or software product to be a success.

System software Computer programs that help the computer carry out essential operating tasks.

System unit The case or box that contains the computer's power supply, storage devices, main circuit board, processor, and memory.

System utility Software that providse disk maintenance, such as tracking down and fixing disk errors, corrupted files. These utilities can also give your PC a performance-enhancing tune-up.

Table (database) An arrangement of data in a grid of rows and columns. In a relational database, a collection of record types with their data.

Table (layout) Grid-like structure that can hold text or pictures.

Tablet computer A portable computing device featuring a touch-sensitive screen that can be used as a writing or drawing pad.

Tape A sequential magnetic storage technology that consists of a tape for the storage medium and a tape drive for the storage device.

Tape backup A copy of data from a computer's hard disk, stored on magnetic tape and used to restore lost data.

Tape cartridge A removable magnetic tape module similar to a cassette tape.

Tax preparation software A specialized type of personal finance software designed to help you gather your annual income and expense data, identify deductions, and calculate your tax payment.

TCP (Transmission Control Protocol) One of the main protocols of TCP/IP that is responsible for establishing a data connection between two hosts and breaking data into packets.

TCP/IP (Transmission Control Protocol/Internet Protocol) A standard set of communication rules used by every computer that connects to the Internet.

Telnet A common way to remotely control another computer or server on a network or the Internet.

Temporal compression A data compression scheme that, when applied to video or audio data, eliminates unnecessary data between video frames or audio samples.

Tera- Prefix for a trillion.

Text editor A program similar to a word processor that is used to create plain, unformatted ASCII text.

Text-to-speech A category of software that generates speech based on written text, that is played back through a computer's sound card.

TFT (thin film transistor) An active matrix screen that updates rapidly and is essential for crisp display of animations and video.

Theme A collection of coordinated graphics, colors, and fonts applied to individual pages or all pages in a Web site. Themes are generally available as part of Web authoring software.

Thermal transfer printer An expensive, color-precise printer that uses wax containing color to produce numerous dots of color on plain paper.

Third-party utility Utility purchased from a third-party vendor.

Thumbnail A graphical link that expands in size when clicked.

TIFF (Tag Image File Format) A file format (.tif extension) for bitmap images that automatically compresses the file data.

Toggle key A key that switches back and forth between two modes, such as Caps Lock on or Caps Lock off.

Token Ring network A type of network on which the nodes are sequentially connected in the form of a ring; the second most popular network architecture.

Top-level domain The major domain categories into which groups of computers on the Internet are divided: com, edu, gov, int, mil, net, and org.

Touchpad An alternative input device often found on notebook computers.

Traceroute A network utility that records a packet's path, number of hops, and the time it takes for the packet to make each hop.

Tracing A category of software that locates the edges of objects in a bitmap graphic and converts the resulting shape into a vector graphic.

Trackball Pointing input device used as an alternative to a mouse.

TrackPoint An alternative input pointing device often found on notebook computers. Also called pointing stick.

Tracks A series of concentric or spiral storage areas created on a storage medium during the formatting process.

Transceiver A combined transmitter/receiver used to send and receive data in the form of radio frequencies.

Transponder A device on a telecommunications satellite that receives a signal on one frequency, amplifies the signal, and then retransmits the signal on a different frequency.

Tree topology A network topology that is a blend of star and bus networks to offer excellent flexibility for expansion.

Trigger event An event that activates a task often associated with a computer virus.

Trojan horse A computer program that appears to perform one function while actually doing something else, such as inserting a virus into a computer system, or stealing a password.

True Color bitmap A color image with a color depth of 24 bits or 32 bits. Each pixel in a True Color image can be displayed using any of 16.7 million different colors.

Twisted-pair cable A type of cable used to connect nodes on a network; has RJ-45 connectors on both ends and two separate strands of wire twisted together.

Typing keypad The basic keys on a computer keyboard that include the keys or buttons with letters and numbers as well as several keys with characters and special words to control computer-specific tasks.

UDMA (Ultra DMA) A faster version of DMA technology.

Unicode A 16-bit character representation code that can represent more than 65,000 characters.

Uninstall routine A program that removes software files, references, and Windows Registry entries from a computer's hard disk.

UNIX A multi-user, multitasking server operating system developed by AT&T's Bell Laboratories in 1969.

Unzipped Refers to files that have been uncompressed.

Unzipping Restoring files that have been compressed to their original size.

Glossary

Uplink port A connection port on a router to which additional hubs can be attached.

Uploading The process of sending a copy of a file from a local computer to a remote computer.

UPS (uninterruptible power supply) A device containing a battery that provides a continuous supply of power and other circuitry to prevent spikes and surges from reaching your computer. It represents the best protection against power problems because it is designed to provide enough power to keep your computer working through momentary power interruptions.

URL (Uniform Resource Locator) The address of a Web page.

USB (universal serial bus) port Popular ports for connecting peripheral devices including mice, scanners, printers, and joysticks that have USB connections.

USB flash drive A portable solid state storage device featuring a built-in connector that plugs directly into a computer's USB port. Also called USB drive.

Usenet A worldwide Internet bulletin board system of newsgroups that share common topics.

User ID A combination of letters and numbers that serves as a user's identification. Also referred to as user name.

User interface The software and hardware that enable people to interact with computers.

User rights Rules that limit the directories and files that each user can access; they can restrict the ability to erase, create, write, read, and find files.

User-executable file At least one of the files included in a software package designed to be launched, or started, by users. On PCs, these programs are stored in files that typically have .exe filename extensions. Also called executable file.

Username See User ID.

Utility A subcategory of system software designed to augment the operating system by providing ways for a computer user to control the allocation and use of hardware resources. Also called utilities.

UTP (unshielded twisted pair) A type of cable consisting of two unshielded wires twisted together. It is less expensive but has more signal noise than a shielded twisted pair.

Validation code Series of alphanumeric characters supplied by the software publisher that is required to complete the installation of software.

Value A number used in a calculation.

VBScript A popular scripting language that allows Web pages to become more interactive and incorporate activities that would otherwise require a computer program.

Vector graphic Image generated from descriptions that determine the position, length, and direction in which lines and shapes are drawn.

Vertical market software Computer programs designed to meet the needs of a specific market segment or industry, such as medical record-keeping software.

Video A recorded series of images that displays motion with sound.

Video capture A category of software used to control the capture process of digital and analog video data.

Video capture device A device that is used to convert analog video signals into digital data stored on a hard drive.

Video editing A category of software that provides tools for capturing and editing video from a camcorder.

Videogame console A computer specifically designed for playing games using a television screen and game controllers.

Viewable image size (vis) A measurement of the maximum image size that can be displayed on a monitor screen.

Viewing angle width Measurement of a monitor or display device that indicates how far to the side you can still clearly see the screen image.

Virtual memory A computer's use of hard disk storage to simulate RAM.

Virtual private network (VPN) A way to secure these remote connections so a remote user can connect to his or her ISP as usual. After the connection is established, a second connection to the remote LAN server creates an encrypted channel for data transmission. Windows XP and several stand-alone products provide VPN software.

Virus A set of program instructions that attaches itself to a file, reproduces itself, and spreads to other files. It can corrupt files, destroy data, display an irritating message, or otherwise disrupt computer operations. A virus generally infects files executed by your computer—files

with extensions such as .exe, .com, or .vbs. Also called computer virus.

Virus definition A file that stores the information that your antivirus software uses to identify and eradicate viruses, Trojan horses, and worms.

Virus hoax A message, usually e-mail, that makes claims about a virus problem that doesn't actually exist.

Virus signature The unique computer code contained in a virus that helps with its identification. Antivirus software searches for known virus signatures.

VOB (Video Object) Industry-standard format for stand-alone DVD players.

Voice band modem The type of modem that would typically be used to connect a computer to a telephone line. See Modem.

Voice over IP (VoIP) A technology that allows computer users with Internet access to send and receive both data and voice simultaneously.

Volatile Data that can exist only with a constant power supply.

Voltage spike Power-related problem caused by malfunctions in the local generating plant or the power distribution network, that can damage sensitive computer components. and they are potentially more damaging than a power failure. Also called a power spike.

WAN (wide area network) An interconnected group of computers and peripherals that covers a large geographical area, such as multiple branches of a corporation.

WAP (Wireless Access Protocol) A communications protocol that provides Internet access from hand-held devices, such as cell phones and PDAs. WAP-enabled devices contain a microbrowser that simplifies Web and e-mail access on a small, low-resolution screen.

War driving A practice that occurs when hackers cruise around with a Wi-Fi-equipped notebook computer set up to search for Wi-Fi signals coming from home and corporate Wi-Fi networks so they can access and use unsecured Wi-Fi networks to hack into files and gain unauthorized access to larger, wired networks. Also called LAN-jacking.

Wave (.wav) An audio file format created as Windows "native" sound format.

Waveform audio A digital representation of sound in which a sound wave is represented by a series of samples taken of the wave height.

Wavetable A set of pre-recorded musical instrument sounds in MIDI format.

Weak encryption Encryption that is relatively simple to decrypt without the encryption key.

Web (World Wide Web) An Internet service that links documents and information from computers distributed all over the world using the HTTP protocol.

Web authoring software Computer programs for designing and developing customized Web pages that can be published electronically on the Internet.

Web browser A software program that runs on your computer and helps you access Web pages. Also called a browser.

Web bug A 1x1 pixel graphic on a Web page that can be used to set cookies to third party Web sites. Unlike ad-serving cookies, you don't have to click a banner ad to receive a GIF activated cookie. Also called clear GIF.

Web cam An input device used to capture live video and transmit it over the Internet.

Web page A document on the World Wide Web that consists of a specially coded HTML file with associated text, audio, video, and graphics files. A Web page often contains links to other Web pages.

Web page header A subtitle that appears at the beginning of a Web page, also called "header."

Web page table A grid of cells that is used as a layout tool for elements such as text and graphics placement on a Web page.

Web palette A standard selection of colors that all Internet browsers can display.

Web resource Any data file that has a URL, such as an HTML document, a graphic, or a sound file.

Web server A computer that uses special software to transmit Web pages over the Internet.

Web site Location on the World Wide Web that contains information relating to specific topics.

Web-based e-mail An e-mail account that stores, sends, and receives e-mail on a Web site rather than a user's computer.

Web-based video Refers to digital video incorporated in Web pages, accessed with a browser, and might use one of several different formats.

Glossary

WEP (Wired Equivalent Privacy)
A securtity method that encrypts transmitted data so that the data is useless to intruders who may intercept and try to steal it by LAN Jacking or other methods.

Whistleblower Someone in an organization who decides to speak out against on-the-job activities that are contrary to the mission of the organization or threaten the public interest.

Whistleblowing The disclosure by an employee (or professional) of confidential information which relates to some danger, fraud or other illegal or unethical conduct connected with the workplace, be it of the employer or of fellow employees.

Wi-Fi (Wireless Fidelity) A set of wireless networking technologies defined by IEEE 802.11 standards. Wi-Fi networks operate at 2.4 or 5 GHz. In a typical office environment, Wi-Fi's range varies from 25 to 150 feet, although considerably more range is possible with additional equipment.

Wi-Fi card Required for transmission on a Wi-Fi network, required by every workstation and network peripheral; includes a transceiver (transmitter and receiver) and an antenna to transmit signals. Wi-Fi cards for notebook or tablet computers plug into a PCMCIA slot.

Wi-Fi hotspot The range of network coverage where any Wi-Fi equipped device that enters a hotspot can gain access to the network's services. Some Wi-Fi public networks offer free service; others require a subscription or one-time use fee.

Wi-Fi network A wireless network that transmits data as radio waves over predefined frequencies, much like cordless telephones.

WiMAX An Ethernet-compatible network technology that is essentially wide-area Wi-Fi, with a range of 30 miles and data transmission rates of 70 Mbps.

Windows Explorer A file management utility included with most Windows operating systems that helps users manage their files.

Windows Mobil OS A version of the Windows operating system designed for portable or mobile computers.

Windows operating system (OS) See Microsoft Windows.

Windows Registry A crucial data file maintained by the Windows operating system that contains the settings needed by a computer to correctly use any hardware and software that has been installed on the system. Also called the Registry.

Windows Startup Disk A disk that is created by the user to load the operating system and the CD-ROM drivers, allowing for system restoration.

Windows XP tablet edition A version of the Windows operating system designed for tablet computers.

Wired network A type of network in which the data travels over cables or wires from one device to another.

Wireframe A representation of a 3-D object using separate lines, which resemble wire, to create a model.

Wireless access point Provides a central point for data transmitted over a wireless network by broadcasting signals to any devices with compatible Wi-Fi cards.

Wireless network A type of network that uses radio or infrared signals (instead of cables) to transmit data from one network device to another.

WMV (Windows Media Video) Offers sophisticated compression options for high-quality images; used for desktop video, PDA video, and streaming video over the Web.

Word processing software Computer programs that assist the user in producing documents, such as reports, letters, papers, and manuscripts.

Word size The number of bits a CPU can manipulate at one time, which is dependent on the size of the registers in the CPU and the number of data lines in the bus.

Worksheet A computerized, or electronic, spreadsheet.

Workstation (1) A computer connected to a local area network. (2) A powerful desktop computer designed for specific tasks.

World Wide Web Consortium (W3C) An international consortium of companies involved with the Internet and developing open standards.

Worm A software program designed to enter a computer system, usually a network, through security "holes" and then replicate itself.

WWAN (wireless wide area network) A network over a large geographic area that uses cellular phone networks to offer data communications and Internet access for cell phones, PDAs, and portable computers.

XHTML The follow-up version to HTML 4, set of specifications for creating HTML documents that a browser can display as a Web page. XHTML, which includes all HTML 4 tags, is extensible, therefore it can be extended by adding customized tags.

XML (eXtensible Markup Language) A document format similar to HTML that allows the Web page developer to define customized tags generally for the purpose of creating more interactivity.

XML parser A tool in most browsers used for reading XML documents.

XSL (eXtensible Stylesheet Language) A technology that is similar to XML, used to create customized tags for displaying data in an XML document.

Zip disk Removable magnetic storage technology manufactured by Iomega available in 100 MB, 250 MB, and 750 MB versions.

Zipped Refers to files that have been compressed.

Zipping The process of compressing files.

Index

Index

cables
  CATV, 160–161
  coaxial, 146–147
  fiber-optic, 146–147, 151
  for peripheral devices, 57
  power, 25
  twisted-pair, 146, 151
caches, 108–109
CAD (computer-aided design) software, 81
CAI (computer-aided instruction), 166
CAL (computer-aided learning), 166
Calculator, 13
Calendar, 13
cameras, digital, 56, 243, 247, 256–257
capacitors, 111
card readers, 46, 243
CATV cable, 160–161
CBT (computer-based training), 166
Cc: copies, of e-mail, 23
CD discs. *See also* CD drive(s)
  CD-DA (compact disc digital audio), 44–45
  CD-R (compact disc recordable), 44–45
  CD-ROM (compact disc read-only memory), 44–45
  CD-RW (compact disc writable), 41, 44–45
  DRM and, 268–269
  storage capacity of, 41
CD drive(s). *See also* CD discs
  backups and, 192
  bays, 40
  classification of, as storage devices, 36–37
  described, 8–9, 44–45
  optical storage and, 38–39
CD rippers, 261, 263
cell(s)
  active, 79
  references, 78
cellular-ready modems, 163
censorship, 234–235
CGI (computer-generated imagery), 266–267
character data, 105
chat groups, 14
ciphertext, 230
circuit switching, 148, 158
CISC (complex instruction set computer), 109
click-through rates, 225

client/server networks, 141. *See also* servers
clip art, 79, 249. *See also* graphics
Clock, 13
clusters, 122
CMOS (complementary metal oxide semiconductor), 112, 113–114
CMSs (course management systems), 167
coaxial cable, 146–147
COBOL, 72
codec (compressor/decompressor), 258–259
colon (:), 114
color
  CMYK, 52
  depth (bit depth), 51
  gradients, 250–251
  monitors, 246
  palettes, 247
  printers and, 52
  vector graphics and, 250–251
  Web-safe, 247
  working with, 246–247
communications channels, 146–147
Compact Privacy Policy, 229
CompactFlash (CF) cards, 46
compatibility, with specific operating systems, 13
compilers, 72
compression
  described, 264–265
  digital video and, 258–259
  lossless, 264
  lossy, 264
  ratio, 264
  utilities, 86, 264–265
computer(s). *See also specific types*
  -aided music software, 82
  buyer's guide worksheet, 277–280
  categories of, 6–7
  described, 2–3
  literacy, 1
  recycling, 62–73
  systems, 2, 8–9
computer projection devices. *See* projection devices
computer programmers. *See* programmers
computer programs. *See* programs
computer software. *See* software
confidentiality, 200. *See also* privacy
Control Panel, 86, 164, 194

control unit, 108, 109, 125
controllers, 43
cookies, 225, 227, 229
Copy command, 21
copyrights, 88–89, 96, 198–199, 268–269
corrective procedures, 179
cps (characters per second), 53
CPUs (central processing units). *See also* processors
  boot process and, 24
  described, 4–5
  integrated circuits and, 106–107
  operating systems and, 75
cropping graphics, 245
CRT (cathode ray tube) monitors, 50–51
cryptographic
  algorithms, 230
  keys, 230
CSMA/CD (Carrier Sense Multiple Access for Collision Detection), 151
CSS (cascading style sheets), 220–221
CSS (Content-Scrambling System), 269
CTP (computer-to-plate) technology, 92
cybercrimes, 177, 196–197
cyberterrorism, 177
cylinders, 42

D

data. *See also* files
  bus, 55
  centers, 193
  described, 4–5
  exploring, 10–11
  information and, difference between, 10
  representation, 37, 104–105
  responsible use of, 85
  transfer rates, 40
databases, 78–79
DDS (digital data storage), 43
DE (distance education), 167
decimal number system, 105
decompression, 264–265
decryption, 230
Defense Department (United States), 60, 128
defragmentation utilities, 123
Deleted Items folder, 28

Index

described, 8–9
magnetic storage and, 38–39
miniature, 42
platters, 42
removable, 43
speed of, 43
storage capacity of, 41
technology, 42–43
utilities, 87
hardware. *See also* devices
described, 35–38
failures, 176
network, 144–145
security and, 176
HDSL (high-rate DSL), 159
HDTV, 45, 50
head section, 219
headers, 79
Help system, 86
helper applications, 212
HFS (Hierarchical File System), 122
high-level languages, 72
History lists, 20
home pages, 19–20. *See also* Web pages
HomePLC, 146
HomePNA, 146
honeypots, 197
horizontal market software, 84
host computers, 141
hot spots, 215
Hotmail, 23, 92
HTML (HyperText Markup Language)
browsers and, 21, 212–213
described, 19, 149, 208–209
e-mail and, 22
exploring, 210–211
filename extensions and, 11
forms, 223
frames, 223
tags, 20–21, 210–211, 220–222
viruses and, 183
Web page authoring and, 218–219
HTTP (HyperText Transfer Protocol), 18–19, 149, 208–209, 212, 216–217, 226
hubs, 145–146, 151, 164
Hyper-Threading, 109
hypertext, 208. *See also* HTML (HyperText Markup Language); links

I

IBM (International Business Machines), 13, 76, 106
ICANN (Internet Corporation for Assigned Names and Numbers), 156
ICF (Internet Connection Firewall), 194
icons, 12, 13, 76
ICs (integrated circuits), 106–107
identity card readers, 179
IEEE (Institute for Electrical and Electronics Engineers)
standards, 150, 152–153, 168
IM (instant messaging), 14
images. *See* graphics
IMAP (Internet Messaging Access Protocol), 23, 149
information
data and, difference between, 10
exploring, 10–11
infrared light, 146
ink jet printers, 52–53
input
described, 4–5
devices, 2, 48–49
instruction(s)
cycles, 124–125
sets, 108
integrated circuits. *See* ICs (integrated circuits)
intelligent agents. *See* bots
Intelliseek, 26
internal links, 214–215. *See also* links
Internet. *See also* Web
backbone, 14
basics, 13–14
connecting to, 16–17, 154–155, 158–163
described, 2
marketing and, 26–27
telephony, 14, 149
Internet Explorer browser (Microsoft), 212–213. *See also* browsers
interpage (anchor) links, 214–215. *See also* links
interpreters, 72–73
IP (Internet Protocol) addresses, 156–157, 197, 234
described, 14
security and, 161, 194, 195
iPAQ. *See* handheld computers

iPod, 15, 42
ISA (Industry Standard Architecture), 54
ISDN (Integrated Services Digital Network), 156, 159
ISPs (Internet Service Providers), 149, 189, 197, 234
described, 16, 17, 154
dial-up connections and, 158–159
e-mail and, 22, 28
equipment used by, 155
hosting services, 218
IP addresses and, 156
security and, 17, 161, 183, 194, 195
viruses and, 183
iTunes, 82, 263, 268

J

Java, 72, 220
Jaz disks, 41
journalism, 92–93
joysticks, 49
JPEG (Joint Photographic Experts Group) format, 221, 242, 245, 264

K

KDE (K Desktop Environment), 77
kernel, 75
keyboard(s)
cables, 57
boot process and, 24
described, 8–9
ports, 55
shortcuts, 48
types of, 48–49
keychain drives. *See* USB flash drives
keyloggers, 180
keywords, 19
kilobits, 105
kilobytes, 40, 105

L

LANs (local area networks)
cable connections and, 160
described, 2, 140
hubs and, 145
installing, 164–165
security and, 194–195

Index

Index

Index

U

validation codes, 91
VBScript (Microsoft), 220
vector graphics, 248–251. *See also* graphics
vertical bar (|), 115
vertical market software, 84
VGA cables, 57
video. *See also* digital video
capture devices, 256
capture software, 257
editing software, 82, 83, 258–259
external, 259
internal, 259
streaming, 259
videoconferencing cameras (Web cams), 256
videogame consoles, 7
viewable image size. *See* vis (viewable image size)
virtual memory, 112
viruses, 180–186
vis (viewable image size), 51
Visual Basic (Microsoft), 72
VOB (Video Object) format, 254–255
voiceband modems, 16, 158
VoIP (Voice over IP), 149, 154
volatility, of RAM, 36
voltage spikes, 176
voting, 128–129, 233
VPNs (virtual private networks), 195

W

W3C (World Wide Web Consortium), 210
WANs (wide area networks), 140
WAP (Wireless Access Protocol), 163
Wave format, 261, 263
waveform audio, 260
wavetables, 262
Web. *See also* browsers; Internet; Web pages; Web sites
-based e-mail, 23
-based video, 255

bugs (clear GIFs), 227
cams, 56
described, 18–19, 207–240
marketing and, 26–27
palettes, 247
resources, 216
servers, 18, 209, 216–217
technology, 208–209
Web browsers. *See* browsers
Web page(s). *See also* Web sites
authoring, 78, 218–219
copying items from, 21
creating, 220–221
described, 18, 210
headers, 219
testing/publishing, 222–223
Web sites, 15, 18. *See also* Web pages
backups and, 191, 192
described, 14
viruses and, 183
WebCT, 167
WEP (Wired Equivalent Privacy), 152
whistleblowers, 199–200
Wi-Fi (Wireless Fidelity) technology, 152–153, 167, 194, 196. *See also* wireless networks
cards, 152–153
described, 162–163
free, 168–169
hotspots, 162
Wikipedia, 269
WiMAX, 155, 162
Windows (Microsoft). *See also specific versions*
described, 76
file locations and, 116–117
file systems and, 114–117, 122
interface, 12–13
Registry, 58–59
Safe Mode, 25
utilities, 86
Windows Mobile (Microsoft), 12, 77
Windows Voice Training Wizard, 263
Windows XP (Microsoft)
file systems and, 122
filenames and, 114
Tablet Edition, 77

WinZip, 264–265
wired networks, 146, 150–151. *See also* networks
wireframes, 252–253
wireless access points, 153
wireless networks, 146, 152–154, 162–163, 196. *See also* Wi-Fi (Wireless Fidelity) technology
wiretapping, 197
WISP (wireless ISP), 162
WMA (Windows Media Audio) format, 261, 263
WMV (Windows Media Video) format, 254–255
Word (Microsoft), 11, 78–79, 115, 219
word size, 108
worksheets, 78, 79
workstations, 7, 141, 142, 150, 195
World Wide Web. *See* Web
World Trade Center attacks, 177
worms, 181, 185. *See also* viruses

X

xDSL, 159
XHTML (Extended HTML), 210, 211
XML (eXtensible Markup Language), 220
XSL (eXtensible Stylesheet Language), 220

Y

Yahoo!, 217, 235, 268
mail, 23, 92
search tools, 119

Z

Zip disks, 36–37, 41
ZIP files, 264–265